WASTE MANAGEMENT Guide

Laws, Issues & Solutions

WASTE MANAGEMENT
Guide
Laws, Issues & Solutions

◆

Deborah Hitchcock Jessup

BNA Special Correspondent

formerly Staff Editor,
Air & Water Pollution Control

The Bureau of National Affairs, Inc., Washington, D.C.

Copyright © 1992
All Rights Reserved

The Bureau of National Affairs, Inc.

Library of Congress Cataloging-in-Publication Data

Jessup, Deborah Hitchcock.
　Waste management guide laws, issues & solutions / Deborah Hitchcock Jessup. — 1991 ed.
　　p.　　cm.
　Includes bibliographical references and index.
　ISBN 0-87179-713-5
　1. Refuse and refuse disposal—Law and legislation—United States. I. Title.
KF3816.R4J47　1992
344.73'0462—dc20
[347.304462]

91-37809
CIP

Authorization to photocopy items for internal or personal use, or the internal or personal use of specific clients, is granted by BNA Books for libraries and other users registered with the Copyright Clearance Center (CCC) Transactional Reporting Service, provided that $0.50 per page is paid directly to CCC, 27 Congress St., Salem, MA 01970. 0-87179-713-5/92/$0+.50.

Published by BNA Books
1250 23rd St., NW, Washington, D.C. 20037-1165

Printed in the United States of America
International Standard Book Number: 0-87179-713-5

PREFACE

Waste management issues have become a national preoccupation. Recycling, little known and even less practiced as recently as five years ago, has become the norm in an ever increasing number of communities. Driven both by new regulations and consumer pressure, companies are finding ways to remove toxic chemicals from raw materials, change manufacturing processes, and alter purchasing practices to reduce waste and favor products that do not harm the environment. Meanwhile, the traditional methods of disposal are increasingly expensive as regulatory requirements proliferate and citizen opposition grows.

This book is a pragmatic guide through the morass of regulations and issues affecting solid waste management. It starts by stating the rules of the game—laws, regulations, and guidelines under the federal Resource Conservation and Recovery Act (RCRA), Pollution Prevention Act, Comprehensive Environmental Response, Compensation, and Liability Act (CERCLA), and Clean Air Act and trends in state regulation. It goes on to discuss industrial and municipal waste recycling policies and issues, pollution prevention and hazardous waste reduction requirements, incentives, and practices, disposal technologies, siting issues, and more. The book also examines some of the societal attitudes that create and exacerbate waste management problems: traditional purchasing and marketing behaviors that mitigate against efforts to reduce the formation of waste; varying and often confusing perceptions of risk; the friction generated when waste moves over state lines; and the growing sense of outrage and powerlessness on the part of citizens everywhere who worry about all assaults to "planet earth" but feel at a loss to effect any change.

The emphasis of this book is on the responsible management of waste. Therefore provisions of RCRA and the CERCLA concerning the remediation of poorly managed sites under Superfund are covered only peripherally. Similarly, emergency response requirements and the enforcement policies of the U.S. Environmental Protection Agency (EPA) and the state governments are considered for the most part to be beyond the scope of this book.

It suffices to say that the future costs of compensation and cleanup of past environmental blight can be overwhelming. EPA's current enforcement tactics also have become increasingly tough. The agency revised its enforcement policy in late 1989 to make daily penalties mandatory for firms in violation of RCRA more than 180 days. For shorter periods of violation, the penalties may be discretionary, presumed, or mandatory, depending on circumstances. A case will not have to be egregious to merit fines as high as $25,000 per violation per day, according to Bruce M. Diamond, EPA director of waste programs enforcement. The agency will pursue generators of hazardous wastes that are in violation of RCRA as well as the "vast number of companies that should be but never have become part of the RCRA world," Diamond said.

In preparing this guide, the author used the abundant information sources within BNA, which include the full text of state and federal regulations, the current reports of *Environment Reporter* and *Chemical Regulation Reporter,* and the regulatory summaries and newsletters of *Chemical Substances Control* and *Air and Water Pollution Control.* In addition, she consulted countless materials issued by EPA, other governmental offices and organizations, and associations, and conducted many telephone and on-site interviews with waste management practitioners from industry and government.

The guide should prove invaluable as a reference tool for anyone seeking a dispassionate view of waste management issues and as a desktop guide to waste management professionals.

A NOTE ON LAWS, REGULATIONS, AND GUIDELINES

Throughout this book, note is made of laws, regulations, guidelines, and proposed regulations and guidelines. In order to understand the importance of these developments, a word on how federal environmental programs are developed and implemented is appropriate here.

Laws: Enacted either by the U.S. Congress or state legislatures, laws generally direct and enable regulatory agencies to take certain actions. In recent years, the federal environmental laws have become lengthier and more detailed in order to simplify implementation and reduce exposure to litigation. The federal laws usually direct EPA to craft model programs, for which administration and enforcement eventually will be delegated to states. Therefore, state environmental laws are always at least as stringent as those enacted by Congress, but often go much farther, especially when citizen advocacy is strong and EPA is perceived as dragging its feet. A glance at BNA's *Guide to State Environmental Programs* (see Bibliography) shows the many ways in which state waste management laws differ from the federal norm.

Regulations: Even when deadlines are mandated by Congress, EPA's regulations tend to fall behind schedule. The pathway leading from idea to rule becomes longer and more tortuous as the issues become more complex. Commonly, EPA places notice in the regulatory calendar when it first begins work on a proposed new rule. For instance, in the October 29, 1990, calendar, the notice concerning the agency's intentions to develop a municipal ash management scheme contains no date even for proposal, much less for final implementation.

Once a rule is proposed, there must be a prescribed period for comment, normally 60 days or so. This period often is extended because the issues require a longer airing. Even after the period closes, the comments may be so extensive that EPA must spend months in evaluating them and making the necessary regulatory adjustments. For instance, the agency almost met the congressionally mandated target date of March 31, 1988, to propose new criteria for municipal solid waste landfills that receive household hazardous wastes or hazardous waste from small quantity generators. The proposed new criteria were aired in August 1988, only four months late; the established comment period ended in November 1988; but the final rule still was not forthcoming in February 1991.

Even after they become final, rules often are challenged in the courts. Such legal challenges add uncertainty but under law may not delay a rule's implementation.

A new requirement that originated under the Reagan administration also slows the regulatory process. The Office of Management and Budget (OMB), which is part of the executive branch, must review all significant EPA rules or proposed rules before they may be published in the *Federal Register.* By the end of 1990, the OMB review requirement was causing major delays because the office had fallen behind schedule.

Furthermore, should EPA and the OMB reach an impasse concerning the advisability of a proposed provision, a relatively new President's Council on Competitiveness first serves as a mediator and then may step in with its own decision, which then may be appealed only to the President. The council is chaired by Vice President Quayle.

In the first manifestation of its power, the council voted overwhelmingly to reject EPA's proposal to include a 25 percent recycling requirement in a new source performance standard of waste recovery incinerators (see Chapter 4). In what Allen Hershkowitz, senior scientist with the Natural Resources Defense Council, termed "the worst environmental decision ever made by the administration," the council ruled that the requirement's costs would exceed its benefits; in any event, the council determined, a recycling provision does not belong in an air pollution rule.

The council's active part in the rejection of the recycling proposal will prove to be the exception rather than the rule, according to Bush administration sources. However, the council staff is closely monitoring agency regulations as they pass through the OMB and is prepared to adjudicate further disputes as necessary, according to officials both within and outside government. President Bush established the council in the image of the President's Task Force on Regulatory Relief, which he chaired during the Reagan administration.

State Programs: When EPA adopts a final rule regarding waste management, the states step in. As is the case with environmental laws, they craft their regulations to conform with the federal model, again taking opportunities to strengthen requirements according to their respective political climates. An interesting manifestation of the relative alacrity of many states to adopt and go beyond federal policies is the speed with which many went forward with a 25 percent waste reduction requirement without even awaiting a final decision on the incinerator standard. It is not likely that states will rescind these more stringent laws because of the decision by the council.

Guidelines: Finally, federal environmental programs may be set forth in guidelines rather than rules. This is most likely to take place when a matter is best handled by states and/or when there is insufficient federal funding. Guidelines are more flexible than rules and are not as readily challenged in the courts. However, they also lack the force of regulation and therefore are more easily ignored. Much of the federal solid waste management program has been articulated in the form of guidelines, as described in Chapter 3.

States also issue guidelines, most typically when the regulating agency is pitted against a pro-business government or legislature. Such guidance is especially common with regard to programs that go beyond federal requirements and are perceived as politically unpopular, such as infectious waste management strictures or facility siting stipulations. When an agency's will is so expressed, confusion is inevitable. Firms looking for rules in codified form may remain unaware that a particular guidance document even exists. Moreover, uncodified guidance is hard, if not impossible, to enforce because in most cases it does not have any legal underpinnings.

ACKNOWLEDGMENTS

This book could not have been written without the help of many state and federal regulators, members of the business community, and others, who answered my countless questions and requests for information. Special thanks are due to Janeth A. Campbell, waste reduction program manager for Florida; A.W. (Gus) Cummings, Jr., site manager for Browning Ferris Industries; Harry M. Freeman, director of the Environmental Protection Agency's pollution prevention research program; H. Gordon Kenna, southern region community relations manager for Chemical Waste Management, Inc.; Linda W. Little, executive director of the North Carolina Governor's Waste Management Board; Cindy McBrearty of the Fairhope, Alabama, waste management advisory committee; Robert Mitchell, manager of procurement and industrial relations for Mobile (Alabama) Paperboard, Inc.; Kenneth E. Nelson, associate environmental consultant for Dow USA's Louisiana Division; Thomas Overcamp of Environmental Systems Engineering at Clemson University, South Carolina; and Gary M. Trahey, president of Rampart Industries Inc., in Detroit, Michigan.

Thanks also are due to many employees of The Bureau of National Affairs, Inc., in Washington, D.C., including Eileen Joseph, managing editor of the Environment Safety and Health Series; Peter J. Adams, editor (retired) of Chemical Substances Control (CSC); James C. Gibbons, editor of CSC; Regina Cline, editor of Air and Water Pollution Control; and Carole Macko, editor of Right To Know Planning Guide. Further appreciation is due to Harriet G. Berlin and James Fattibene of BNA Books. Finally, thanks go to the

Mobile, Alabama, law firm, Hand, Arendall, Bedsole, Greaves, and Johnston and their librarian Betty Byrd, for graciously offering me the use of their extensive library.

TABLE OF CONTENTS

Preface v
Acknowledgments xi

1. **Federal Laws: An Overview** 1
    Resource Conservation and Recovery Act (RCRA) 2
    CERCLA (The Superfund Law) 12
    Medical Waste Management 13
    The Pollution Prevention Act of 1990 16
    PCB Regulation under TOSCA 17
    Ocean Dumping Laws 18

2. **Rules for Hazardous Waste Management** 21
    Hazardous Waste Classification 22
    Generators and Their Obligations 34
    Standards for Treatment, Storage, and Disposal
        Facilities 37

3. **Nonhazardous Solid Waste: Guidelines and Rules** ... 49
    Federal Legislative Activity 51
    Guidelines for State Solid Waste Management Plans .. 53
    A Strategic Approach to Solid Waste Management ... 55

Solid Waste Facility Criteria 56
Council of State Governments Model Laws 58
Agenda For Action 60
Costs of Solid Waste Management 62
Risk Assessment 67

4. **State Waste Management Programs** 73
Solid Waste Management 74
Trends in State Hazardous Waste Planning 79
State Technical Assistance Initiatives 87
Pollution Prevention Laws 92

5. **Air Emissions from Waste Facilities** 95
Clean Air Act Rules 96
RCRA Rules Governing Air Pollution 100

6. **Pollution Prevention** 107
Pollution Prevention Vis-A-Vis Waste Minimization . 107
Institutional Aspects of Pollution Prevention 109
EPA's Initiatives 111
EPA's Pollution Prevention Strategy 112
EPA's Pollution Prevention Research Program 113
Pollution Prevention Act Analysis 119
State Activities 121
Industrial Activities 123
A How-To Guide To Waste Reduction From Dow
    Chemical U.S.A. 124
Regional And Private Pollution Prevention Assistance
    Sources 129

Table of Contents

7. RCRA Hazardous Waste Minimization 133
    EPA's Activities: An Overview 134
    Conducting a Waste Minimization Audit 140
    Model State Law 154

8. Industrial Waste Recycling 157
    Waste Classification Rules for Recycling 158
    Regulations For Recycling Activities 161
    Waste Exchanges 166

9. Municipal Solid Waste Recycling 171
    Source Reduction 173
    The Recycling Advisory Council 174
    Markets for Recycled Materials 175
    Municipal Recycled Products and Markets 183
    Other Recycling Activities and Issues 195
    Community Recycling Programs 197

10. Hazardous Waste Pretreatment Requirements 207
    Implementation of the Land Disposal Ban 208
    Treatment Standards 212
    Standards for Pretreatment Facilities 214
    Pretreatment Methods 218
    Pretreatment or Recycling 221

11. Disposal Facilities: Technical Standards, Issues, and Guidelines 223
    Solid Waste Combustors 223
    Hazardous Waste Incinerators 232
    Industrial Boilers and Furnaces 236
    Solid Waste Landfills 236

Hazardous Waste Landfills 239
Underground Injection Wells 247

12. Siting Waste Facilities: An Endless Pursuit 249
Citizen Activist Organizations 250
How Citizens View Risk 252
Rules of Risk Communication 254
Site Considerations 258
Site Studies 261
Public/Private Partnerships 263
Siting on an Indian Reservation 266
Reducing Liability Exposure 267

13. Hazardous Waste Facility Siting Case Studies 269
The Colorado Saga 271
Arizona's Stalled Hazardous Waste Facility 279
The Case of North Carolina 284

Appendix A: Directories 287

Appendix B: Hazardous Waste Tables 323

Appendix C: Pretreatment Standards 365

Index 417

Bibliography 441

Chapter 1

FEDERAL LAWS: AN OVERVIEW

All through the explosive industrial growth of the 19th and early 20th centuries, through two world wars, when weapons production paved the way to massive petrochemical and synthetic chemical expansion, waste accumulated in the United States, little noticed and even less regulated. Industries mingled their trash with municipal waste in crude landfills or stored it carelessly in abandoned warehouses or elsewhere within plant boundaries. There was no national policy. Trash was largely a local problem; too often, out of sight was out of mind.

The first federal waste management law, adopted in 1965, was weak and little noticed. Amendments and expansions over the next 10 years heightened national attention and created a fledgling disposal industry but the program remained fragmentary and noninvasive. Finally, in 1976, Congress passed the Resource Conservation and Recovery Act (RCRA), a much stronger law requiring pervasive regulation of hazardous waste and federal oversight of municipal and industrial solid waste as well.

Even after RCRA's passage, its implementation, as well as later amendments and ancillary laws, were more often than not reactive rather than visionary. It took crises to trigger not only the enactment of the laws described in this chapter but also their implementation by the Environmental Protection Agency (EPA) and the states. Together, the laws–and the regulations made under these laws–constitute a reasonably comprehensive scheme of waste management. The scheme came much too late, according to many critics. For its ultimate success, there must be continued dedication and strong leadership.

RCRA is the flagship law governing waste management and is described in detail here and in other chapters. Other important laws covered briefly include the Comprehensive Environmental Response, Compensation, and Liability Act of 1980 (CERCLA), the Superfund Amendments and Reauthorization Act of 1986 (SARA), the Pollution Prevention Act of 1990, the Medical Waste Tracking Act of 1988 (actually an amendment to RCRA), the Toxic Substances Control Act (TOSCA), and the Marine Protection, Research, and Sanctuaries Act (which concerns ocean dumping).

The Clean Air Act (CAA) and Clean Water Act (CWA) also should be noted here. Neither discusses waste per se, but each has a bearing on how waste is managed. Using the CAA's mandate to prevent air pollution, EPA has developed several regulations governing emissions from various hazardous waste disposal facilities, as described in Chapter 5. Similarly, the CWA is silent on the subject of waste but is important in the hazardous waste regulatory scheme because sludge, a waste often containing hazardous constituents, is exempt from RCRA coverage if treated in a facility permitted under the CWA. In fact, EPA reports that some 50 percent of all hazardous waste generated is exempted in this manner.

RESOURCE CONSERVATION AND RECOVERY ACT

The nation's first waste management law was the Solid Waste Disposal Act of 1965, which focused on open burning, considered at that time to be a fire hazard rather than a risk to public health. In 1970 the act was amended and renamed the Resource Recovery Act. New provisions called for the recycling of solid materials and a study of U.S. hazardous waste management practices. By that time concerns were raised that the garbage burden was getting out of hand, but public consciousness remained relatively untouched, according to William D. Ruckelshaus, a former EPA administrator.

The 1976 RCRA act gutted the language of these earlier laws and took on much of its present form: a comprehensive law aimed at controlling both solid and hazardous waste, applying to the latter a level of custodianship designed to end the creation of unauthorized hazardous waste sites. Revolutionary as it was, the act was merely another step in the leisurely progression toward development of a national waste management program.

EPA made little headway in writing regulations to implement the law until environmental disaster struck in August 1978. The discovery that long-forgotten chemicals were seeping through the ground and into the homes of residents in Love Canal, New York, galvanized national attention to the hitherto unremarked threat of buried hazardous waste. Literally thousands of abandoned waste sites were identified almost overnight.

Forced into action by court order, EPA issued the first two portions of the RCRA hazardous waste rules on May 5, 1980. As might be expected in the aftermath of the Love Canal debacle, the regulations covered only hazardous waste, leaving the development of solid waste guidance to take a more desultory course.

RCRA Hazardous Waste Provisions

The 1976 law provides what has become known as "cradle to grave" control of hazardous wastes from their generation to their ultimate disposal. This concept directly affects hazardous waste generators; transporters; and owners and operators of treatment, storage, and disposal facilities.

In 1984, Congress passed comprehensive amendments to the 1976 RCRA. These amendments are often called the Hazardous and Solid Waste Amendments, or HSWA. Signed into law November 6, 1984, the amendments are lengthier and more precise than the original law and include specific deadlines within which EPA must take regulatory action. For instance, HSWA called for generators to certify that they would have a waste minimization program in place by September 1, 1985. Even more pervasively, the amendments mandated that untreated hazardous waste be banned from land disposal except under very narrow conditions within 5½ years of the

November 6, 1984, effective date. These "hammers" or "triggers," as the mandated dates have come to be called, give EPA far less discretion over how to regulate hazardous waste than it had under the earlier law.

The 1984 amendments also forbid the burning of toxic substances in industrial and apartment furnaces and pull under the regulatory net the estimated 600,000 generators of small quantities of hazardous wastes and petroleum products. In addition, the amendments set in motion the regulation of underground storage tanks.

Pertinent aspects of RCRA's hazardous waste provisions, as amended in 1984, are summarized below. EPA's regulations carrying out these provisions are described in Chapter 2 primarily, but also in other chapters as pertinent.

Identification and Listing of Hazardous Waste

RCRA directs EPA to identify which wastes are hazardous and in what quantities, qualities, concentrations, and forms of disposal they become a threat to human health or the environment.

The 1984 amendments directed the agency to act concerning certain specific wastes within given time frames, as follows:

- Within 6 months of the effective date: list additional wastes containing chlorinated dioxins or chlorinated dibenzofurans

- Within 1 year of the effective date: where appropriate, list wastes containing halogenated dioxins and halogenated dibenzofurans

- Within 15 months of the effective date: determine whether or not to list chlorinated aliphatics, dioxin, dimethyl hydrazine, toluene diisocyanate (TDI), carbamates, bromacil, linuron, organobromines, solvents, refining wastes, chlorinated aromatics, dyes and pigments, inorganic chemical industry wastes, lithium batteries, coke byproducts, paint production wastes, and coal slurry pipeline effluent

- Within 28 months: list wastes that are hazardous because they contain carcinogenic, mutagenic, or teratogenic constituents at levels dangerous to human health

- Within 2 years: make a final determination as to whether to list or identify used automobile and truck crankcase oil and other used oil as hazardous wastes (see below)

EPA also was ordered to change its toxicity measurement procedure so as to make it a more accurate predictor of a waste's leaching potential.

Hazardous Waste Generators

The act requires EPA to issue standards that govern generators and transporters of hazardous wastes, to include recordkeeping, labeling, containerization, and quantity and disposition reporting requirements. The keystone of this provision is the manifest system, designed to document the movement of hazardous wastes from the generator's premises to an authorized off-site facility for treatment, storage, or disposal.

Every two years, generators must submit to EPA or to an authorized state office documented reports detailing the quantity and nature of wastes generated during each year, how the wastes were disposed of, and the strategies used to reduce the amount and toxicity of the wastes. These reductions must be documented. The generator also must certify that it has implemented a waste minimization plan.

Small-Quantity Generators

Recognizing that waste from small businesses often is very hazardous and most likely to be improperly disposed of, Congress in 1984 ended the small generator exemption that provided what it considered a gaping loophole in the 1976 RCRA. The amendments require firms generating 100 to 1,000 kilograms per month to carry out most of the labeling, reporting, and disposal obligations that apply to larger firms. The amendments further authorize EPA to regulate generators of even smaller quantities of waste if it deems that public health is at stake.

Hazardous Waste Transporters

Transporters of hazardous waste must exert tight control over the waste they transport, keep records of the point of departure and delivery, and notify EPA or state regulators of their hazardous waste activities. The waste must be taken to the approved disposal site specified by the generator on the manifest.

The act stipulates that EPA's regulations for transporters be consistent with the requirements of the Hazardous Materials Transportation Act and coordinated with Department of Transportation regulations.

Storage, Treatment, and Disposal Facilities

RCRA directs EPA to develop minimum standards for facilities that treat, store, and dispose of hazardous wastes. Owners and operators of such facilities are required to file for permits within 90 days of the time a waste they handle has been identified and listed as hazardous. The permit application must give specific information as to the composition, quantity, disposal rate, and location of the disposal site for each waste received.

Because the final permit application procedure is a lengthy process, the act and its amendments include provisions to allow existing facilities to continue operation under so-called interim status until final approval can be given. Facilities that were operating under interim permit status before the 1984 amendments would lose such status unless they had filed by specified dates complete permit applications together with certification that they were in compliance with groundwater monitoring and financial responsibility requirements. All facilities also must be covered by an emergency contingency plan.

The amendments also order EPA to issue or deny within specified time periods final permits to facility owners or operators that had completed their applications before the effective date of the amendments. The time limit for landfills and incinerators has already passed. For other facilities, the deadline is November 5, 1992. New facilities–except for polychlorinated biphenyls (PCBs) incinerators, which are regulated under the Toxic Substances Control Act–may not be constructed until a final RCRA permit has been issued.

Permits for all facilities must be renewed every 10 years. Landfill permits must be reviewed every 5 years, however, and provisions must be modified as necessary to ensure that the facility continues to comply with all applicable requirements.

Land Disposal Restrictions

Congress found in writing the 1984 amendments that "certain classes of land disposal are not capable of assuring long-term containment of certain hazardous wastes, and to avoid substantial risk to human health and the environment, reliance on land disposal should be minimized or eliminated, and land disposal, particularly landfill and surface impoundment, should be the least favored method for managing hazardous wastes."

Accordingly, the amendments restrict the types of waste that may be deposited in landfills, surface impoundments, waste piles, injection wells, land treatment facilities, salt dome formations, salt bed formations, or underground mines or caves. The land disposal ban first applied only to bulk liquid wastes; however, by November 1990 it was extended to disposal of all untreated hazardous waste except under certain defined conditions.

The statute allows EPA to determine that a particular land disposal practice, deposit in salt domes, for instance, is protective of human health and the environment. The agency also may extend a statutory deadline when current treatment capacity cannot meet demand or when a prescribed treatment method does not exist. Finally, facility owners and operators may submit petitions demonstrating that a nontreated waste will not migrate from the disposal unit for as long as its constituents remain hazardous. Wastes that were disposed of before the ban took effect need not be removed.

Minimum Technological Requirements

New and interim status landfills, under most circumstances, must be double-lined, with a leachate collection system above and between the liners. However, if the owner or operator can demonstrate that alternative design and operating practices, together with location characteristics, will prevent the migration of any hazardous constituents into the groundwater or surface water at least as effectively as the double-lined system, a variance may be granted. Moreover, existing surface impoundments and monofills containing only hazardous wastes from foundry furnace emissions control or metal casting molding sand are exempt from the double-lining requirement if they are equipped with a one-liner system that does not leak; they are located more than one-quarter mile from an underground drinking water source; and, in the case of foundry monofills, they do not contain constituents that would render the wastes hazardous for reasons other than specified characteristics identified using the Toxicity Characteristic Leaching Procedure (see Chapter 2). Other exemptions include impoundments that comply with relevant CWA permits and impoundments that contain treated wastewater undergoing aggressive biological treatment.

All such exempted facility owners or operators must demonstrate that they comply with groundwater monitoring requirements by supplying monitoring information and analysis along with evidence that the impoundment is not leaking. The evidence must be certified by a registered professional engineer with academic training and experience in groundwater hydrology.

All of the above exemptions apply only to facilities that made application by November 1986.

Fuels Produced from Wastes

Burning fuels produced from hazardous waste was a common practice until Congress placed restrictions on the practice through the 1984 amendments. The law allows EPA to exempt facilities that burn hazardous waste fuels in de minimis quantities, provided the wastes are burned at the site where they are generated in order to recover useful energy. The combustion device must have a combustion and removal efficiency sufficient to protect human health and the environment.

Recycled Oil Provisions

EPA was directed to issue regulations to protect the public against the risks associated with recycled oil within a year of the effective date of the RCRA and to make a final determination by November 1986 as to whether to identify used automobile and truck crankcase oil and other used oil as hazardous wastes.

In making these demands, Congress recognized that such oil should be recycled. The act states that EPA should ensure that its regulations do not discourage the recovery or recycling of used oil, consistent with protection of the environment and public health.

Used oil generators are to be made exempt from EPA regulation provided they arrange to have the oil transported to a permitted recycling facility or recycle the oil on their own permitted premises. The oil must not be mixed with other types of hazardous waste, and records must be kept.

RCRA Solid Waste Provisions

In contemplating the key RCRA provisions that address solid waste management, it is important to be aware that many of the programs prescribed were not implemented or have not been active since early in the 1980s. EPA's activities under the law, which regained impetus after 1988, are described in Chapter 3.

Comprehensive Plans

In setting forth the objectives of Subchapter IV (also known as Part D) of RCRA, Congress called for the formation of comprehensive plans so that waste management could become a regional matter amenable to long-range planning. The legislature stressed the cooperative role between federal, state, and local government and private industry in sound solid waste planning that would make maximum use of the waste to produce energy and other recoverable materials. (It is worth noting, in this regard, that the so-called energy crisis was in full swing at the time the objectives were written.)

The act directed EPA to develop guidelines for comprehensive waste management plans within 180 days of its passage. Within 18 months, the agency was to have encoded these guidelines, taking the following issues into consideration:

- The varying regional, geologic, hydrologic, climatic, and other circumstances under which different solid waste practices are required in order to protect surface water and groundwater

- Characteristics and conditions of collection, storage, processing, and disposal methods, taking into account location of the facilities and the nature of the solid waste

- Methods for closing or upgrading open dumps for the purpose of eliminating potential health hazards

- Population density, distribution, and projected growth

- Geographic, geologic, climatic, and hydrologic characteristics

- The type and location of transportation

- The profile of industries

- The constituents and generation rates of waste

- The political, economic, organizational, financial, and management problems affecting comprehensive solid waste management

- Appropriate types of resource recovery facilities and resource conservation systems

- Available new and additional markets for recovered material and energy and energy resources recovered from solid waste as well as methods for conserving such materials and energy

The act also enumerated what states must do to gain approval of their plans.

Landfill Criteria

Seeking an end to open dumping, Congress directed EPA to issue regulations containing criteria for determining which facilities should be classified as sanitary landfills and which should be termed open dumps. At a minimum, a facility could not be classified as a sanitary landfill unless the owner or operator could show that there would be no likelihood of adverse effects on health or the environment from disposal of garbage at such a facility.

The section also placed a ban on dumping solid or hazardous waste into landfills that do not meet the sanitary landfill criteria. In areas where other alternatives were lacking, the act provided for a timetable or schedule of compliance. The act further required that landfills receiving hazardous household waste or small generator waste be permitted.

Studies Required

RCRA also contains a substantial research, development, demonstration, and information subtitle (Subtitle V) that gives EPA broad authorization to conduct research on both solid waste and hazardous waste issues. The provisions call for special studies on such issues as glass, plastics, tires, waste composition, small-scale technology, and source separation. EPA also is directed to gather information on methods to reduce the amount of solid waste generated, the availability of markets for energy and materials recovered, methods and costs of collection and management practices, and research and development projects for solid waste management. A central reference library, full-scale demonstration facilities, and grants for resource recovery systems and other improved solid waste disposal facilities also were to be established.

Procurement Guidelines

After consultation with the General Services Office, the Commerce Department, and the Public Printer, EPA was to develop guidelines on procurement to encourage purchase of recycled materials. The agency was required to prepare guidelines for paper and three other product categories, including tires, by 1985. In addition, each procuring federal agency must establish a procurement program. To carry out this program, the Commerce Department was directed to do the following:

- Develop accurate specifications for recovered materials
- Stimulate and develop markets for recovered materials
- Evaluate and promote proved energy and material recovery technologies
- Establish a forum for the exchange of technical and economic data relating to resource recovery facilities

The programs developed by EPA and the Commerce Department to carry out these procurement requirements are described in Chapter 8.

CERCLA (THE SUPERFUND LAW)

CERCLA is a crisis-driven law, spawned in the aftermath of Love Canal. It has great influence over how firms respond to emergencies as well as how they dispose of waste. First and foremost, CERCLA establishes the mechanism for cleaning up hazardous waste sites once they have gotten out of hand and been abandoned. More specifically, the act was designed to:

- Provide a system for identifying and cleaning up chemical and hazardous substances releases. The identified sites are ranked on the National Priorities List.
- Establish a fund to pay for cleanup of environmental contamination where no responsible parties can be found, or where those responsible cannot or will not pay for cleanup. This includes inactive sites previously managed under RCRA.
- Enable the government to collect costs of cleaning up a release from responsible parties.

The main Superfund trust fund is financed through taxes paid by the petroleum and chemical industries on petroleum products, feed stock chemicals, and imported chemical derivatives. Further revenues accrue from a broad-based surtax collected from certain corporations, appropriations from the general fund, costs recovered from responsible parties, and interest earned on trust fund monies. As reauthorized on October 27, 1990, the Superfund will have available $5.1 billion through the end of the 103rd Congress in 1994.

In addition to its provisions affecting hazardous waste, CERCLA incorporates the spill-cleanup provisions of the Clean Water Act and establishes a trust fund for cleanup of petroleum underground storage tanks.

The CERCLA amendments of 1986, known as SARA, vastly strengthen the original Superfund statute; incorporate strict cleanup standards favoring permanent remedies at waste sites; give EPA more power in negotiating settlements; allow states and the public to get more involved in the decision-making process; and create, under a new Title III, an emergency planning and community right-to-know program.

According to Joel Hirschhorn, a project director specializing in hazardous waste and the Superfund with the Congressional Office of Technology Assessment, work under the Superfund law has only begun: "The federal government, states, and private industry have spent more than $10 billion on Superfund cleanups in the past decade; yet EPA can show no major Superfund site, no well-known Superfund site, that has been cleaned up."

MEDICAL WASTE MANAGEMENT

Medical waste disposal problems made the headlines in 1988, when the nation's seashores were sullied by what appeared to be dangerous medical paraphernalia–hypodermic needles, blood vials, and syringes. Such grisly sights suddenly appeared everywhere, from Martha's Vineyard to the Carolinas, and from the shores of Lake Erie to the Gulf of Mexico. With fear of acquired immune deficiency syndrome (AIDS) at a height, national attention was riveted and yet another crisis-driven law was born.

Congress did not respond to the furor with massive legislation, however. As hospital waste management costs soared and states worked overtime to produce their own flurry of infectious waste regulations, investigation revealed that much of the environmental harm was not the work of the medical establishment but of illegal operators, careless household waste management, and dumping at sea. Further study revealed that substantial information already was available to hospitals on how to manage waste. The Centers for Disease Control, the Joint Commission on Accreditation of Health Care Organizations, and the Occupational Safety and Health Administration all had developed recommendations, advisories, and guidelines that were in use by hospitals and large clinics everywhere. These materials and other medical waste management information are available in a BNA Special Report, *Infectious Waste: The Complete Resource Guide* (see Bibliography).

The Medical Waste Tracking Act therefore was crafted not so much to dictate a national policy as to prompt better management where necessary and to gather information for use in determining future action. The act called for a demonstration program for managing and tracking medical waste in New York, New Jersey, Connecticut, the Great Lakes states, and any other state that chose to be included.

The states promptly expressed their preference for managing their own medical waste. The law permitted the Great Lakes states to opt out of the demonstration if they preferred to run their own programs. All did. New York, New Jersey, and Connecticut also could opt out, but only if they could demonstrate to EPA that their own laws were just as stringent as the federal demonstration program. They did. No other state petitioned to be part of the federal program.

The act also required that four studies be completed by specified dates. The first three, to be prepared by EPA, were to provide information on a variety of medical waste issues. In order to form a basis for this information, the agency engaged the three eastern states designated above, along with Rhode Island and Puerto Rico, in a two-year demonstration tracking program. The idea was to learn whether a national program would be feasible. This demonstration did not begin until June 1989.

Because of this tardiness in establishing a demonstration program, the agency fell behind the mandated schedule for completing the three studies. The second report, due early in 1990, was released in December of that year. While containing far more information than the first interim report, the second still did not represent enough information for EPA to make recommendations to Congress. Among other findings, the report showed that hospitals generate the vast majority of regulated medical waste, some 77 percent. The remainder emanates from laboratories, physicians' offices, veterinary clinics, and other assorted small-quantity generators.

The fourth report required by the act was a health impacts report from the Agency for Toxic Substances and Disease Registry of the Department of Health and Human Services.

Medical Waste From Ships

According to Mary Greene of EPA's Office of Waste Management, dumping of medical and other wastes from ships at sea remains a big problem, despite great improvements in beach cleanup and medical waste oversight. Some of the wastes encountered in 1988 were discovered to have come from ships belonging to the U.S. Navy, Greene said. In disposing of its trash in the usual manner–dumping it into the ocean 25 miles away from land–the navy had discharged unused, outdated hospital materials along with the regular trash. As a result, pill bottles and other medical waste washed up on East Coast beaches.

In the wake of this discovery, the navy changed its waste management policy. According to Larry Koss, an environment, safety, and health program manager for the navy, all waste generated aboard ship is identified, sterilized, held, and disposed of in an environmentally sound way.

According to EPA's Greene, only a small amount of medical waste is generated by the navy. Other vessels also must be under better control, she claimed.

THE POLLUTION PREVENTION ACT OF 1990

During 1990, Congress was engrossed in enacting amendments to the Clean Air Act, which had not been substantially changed or reauthorized since 1977. Waste issues continued to be of concern, however, and the urgency to stem the generation and proliferation of hazardous waste was strong enough to engender passage in the Senate of a minor but worthwhile pollution prevention bill late in the session, as a rider to a major budget package. The House had passed a similar bill earlier in the year, and a combined measure was promptly signed into law.

The Pollution Prevention Act requires companies to report to EPA information about their waste-handling practices. It inaugurates a national policy of placing a priority on the reduction or elimination of hazardous wastes at their sources and the recycling or treating of the hazardous waste that is still generated. Disposal, according to the law, is the last resort.

The new information must be reported on the Toxic Release Inventory forms required under Section 313 of the Emergency Planning and Community Right-To-Know Act (also known as Title III of the Superfund Amendments and Reauthorization Act). Section 313 requires owners or operators of manufacturing facilities with more than 10 employees to report annually, by July 1, statistics on their toxic emissions to all environmental media during the previous year. This requirement applies if a facility produces, imports, processes, or otherwise uses any of more than 300 chemicals. Hence, the new pollution prevention requirement covers a large universe of firms that generate, treat, or dispose of hazardous waste.

The reports must include data on all aspects of a company's source reduction and recycling programs. Additionally, companies must estimate changes in hazardous waste amounts, explain production modifications, and detail what techniques they use to encourage employees and management to commit to pollution prevention. More specifically, the reports must include the following:

- Amount entering waste stream before recycling, treatment, or disposal and the percentage change from previous year

Federal Laws

- Amount recycled, percentage change from previous year, and the recycling process used
- Amount treated on-site and off-site and the percentage change from previous year
- Estimates of amounts that will be reported for the next two years
- Specific source reduction practices used by the facility
- Techniques used to identify source reduction opportunities
- Ratio of production in the reporting year to production in the preceding year
- Amount released because of accidents or other one-time events

Because Section 313 is the vehicle for this new reporting requirement, the waste reduction measures reported will be limited to toxic or hazardous waste, despite the more broad title of the act. It seems clear that multimedia source reduction of pollutants, from Congress's viewpoint, at least, continues to focus on hazardous constituents rather than on the broader spectrum of waste.

The law also directs EPA to establish an office to implement its provisions. In fact, the agency already had a strong pollution prevention (waste minimization) program, carried out by a research facility in Cincinnati and two offices in Washington, as described in Chapters 5 and 6. The Waste Minimization Branch of the Office of Solid Waste is responsible for coordinating the new data with other information gleaned under Section 313. The measure authorizes $8 million in matching grants for state programs. For analysis of how this act may influence hazardous waste generation and enforcement, see Chapter 5.

PCB REGULATION UNDER TOSCA

TOSCA, as a whole, is concerned with the introduction of chemicals as raw materials rather than the manner in which end products are disposed of. However, Section 6 of the act authorizes EPA to prohibit or limit the manufacture, processing, distribution in commerce, use, or *disposal* of a chemical posing an unreasonable risk to human health or the environment. All aspects of the regulation of PCBs, including disposal, are covered under this act rather than RCRA.

TOSCA Section 6 is an enabling rather than a mandatory provision. EPA therefore had discretion as to when and how to regulate PCBs as well as other chemicals covered by the act's provisions. As developed by the agency, the regulations apply to PCBs in concentrations of above 50 parts per million. Except under narrow circumstances spelled out in the rules, all PCBs and heavily contaminated encapsulated materials such as capacitors must be incinerated in units with 99.9999 percent destruction efficiency.

EPA's rules also prohibit the manufacture, processing, distribution, and most uses of the material regardless of concentration, unless such activities are performed in a totally enclosed manner, the PCBs are recycled, the PCBs are very low in concentration, or the activities are otherwise authorized. This prohibition, together with the tough disposal requirements, has provided considerable business for waste management facilities, as described briefly in Chapter 10. Details on PCB management can be found in BNA's *PCB Compliance Guide for Electrical Equipment* (see Bibliography).

Since 1987, EPA has begun to use TOSCA's authorities for additional programs, including the gathering of test information on chemicals that it is considering for regulation as hazardous under RCRA. Much of the activity under TOSCA comes about through negotiation and consent agreements.

OCEAN DUMPING LAWS

The Marine Protection, Research, and Sanctuaries Act of 1972, last amended in October 1986, and the Ocean Dumping Ban Act of 1988 govern the dumping of wastes into the sea. In the main, EPA is responsible for carrying out these provisions.

Permit Programs

Under the sanctuaries act, dumping of any material except fish waste into U.S. territory waters, or in lowlands within 12 miles of these waters, is prohibited unless authorized by permit. All permits except those covering dredging spoils, radioactive waste, and agents of biological, chemical, or radiological warfare are issued by EPA. Before issuing a permit, the agency must determine that the dumping will not harm the environment. The agency also may decide whether dumping should be allowed at all.

The act also contains prohibitions. Industrial waste may only be dumped in small amounts for research purposes or in emergencies. Low level radioactive waste may not be dumped at all unless a Radioactive Material Disposal Impact Assessment is completed and copies sent to the House Committee on Merchant Marine and Fisheries and the Senate Committee on Environment and Public Works. Permits to conduct even these activities must be approved by Congress. The act also declares a ban on ocean disposal of sewage sludge. However, this ban was not enforced until Congress enacted a second law, the Ocean Dumping Ban Act of 1988, which sets December 1, 1991, as an absolute deadline for ending this practice.

Dredging permits are issued by the U.S. Corps of Engineers with EPA oversight. A dredge spoil dumping permit must designate the amount and type of waste to be dumped and the location and duration of the permit. Permit fees and reporting requirements may be imposed. General permits may be issued, but all permits must be reviewed from time to time and the information made available to the public.

Chapter 2

RULES FOR HAZARDOUS WASTE MANAGEMENT

The latest Environmental Protection Agency (EPA) estimates show that the United States is producing more than 280 million metric tons of hazardous waste, 16 million metric tons more than in 1984. Thus, 14 years after passage of the landmark Resource Conservation and Recovery Act of 1976 (RCRA), hazardous waste generation continues unabated, fueled by a nation seemingly unable to resist cheap, convenient, throw-away synthetic products. As noted in Chapter 1, this enormous waste buildup began after World War II, as industries turned from weapons production to the creation of a whole new generation of consumer goods made of synthetic organic chemicals: plastics, solvents, detergents, pesticides. The chemical detritus returned to the environment and festered there, eventually creating the abandoned hazardous waste sites that cost our society billions of dollars each year.

According to a study by Brett R. Schroeder of Independent Project Analysis in Reston, Virginia, estimates on exactly what it will cost to clean up all U.S. Superfund sites range from $8 million to more than $500 billion.

In the struggle to clean these earlier disasters and to prevent new ones, one major event was the catalyst. The pollution at Love Canal was an environmental time bomb. When it went off, when citizens were forced to abandon their houses and President Carter called a national emergency, the regulatory program described in this chapter finally took hold.

EPA's regulations under RCRA now constitute a comprehensive hazardous waste management scheme, as described here and throughout this book. As the act prescribes, the regulations control all stages of the hazardous waste management cycle–"from cradle to grave"–whether the waste is managed on-site or at an off-site storage, treatment, or disposal facility. The regulatory program includes the following components:

- Rules and guidelines governing the classification of hazardous waste

- Standards for hazardous waste generators and transporters

- Performance, design, and operating requirements for treatment, storage, or disposal facilities

- A system for issuing permits to such facilities

- Procedures for notifying regulators of hazardous waste activities

- Guidelines for states to receive authorization to carry out their own hazardous waste management programs (discussed in Chapter 4)

The first five of these components are described below. The state authorization component is explained in Chapter 4.

HAZARDOUS WASTE CLASSIFICATION (40 CFR 261)

The sources of hazardous waste are legion. Best known are the large industries such as chemical plants, petroleum refineries, and automotive manufacturers. Other smaller sources, such as hospitals, research laboratories, print shops, dry cleaners, auto repair shops, and metallurgical operations, also generate hazardous waste. These diverse small sources have come under intensified regulatory scrutiny in recent years.

Rules for Hazardous Waste Management

RCRA defines a hazardous waste as a solid waste that may cause or significantly contribute to serious illness or death or that may pose a substantial threat to human health or the environment if managed improperly. The term *solid waste* encompasses liquids, semisolids, and compressed gases. In its regulations, EPA amplified the RCRA definition to include any solid waste that is not specifically excluded from regulation and that exhibits any one of the following attributes:

- Has one or more of the following characteristics of a hazardous waste: ignitability, corrosivity, reactivity, or toxicity (such waste is called characteristic waste)
- Is listed as a hazardous waste
- Is a mixture of solid waste and one or more of the listed hazardous wastes
- Is revealed to be hazardous through testing

From time to time EPA may add or delete substances from the list as well as alter its waste characterization criteria. The regulated community also may petition EPA to delist an RCRA hazardous waste. Firms may demonstrate that a particular waste from a facility should not be considered hazardous for any of the following reasons:

- It does not exhibit the characteristics or contain the constituents for which it was originally listed.
- It contains hazardous constituents but at relatively low concentrations.
- The waste's hazardous constituents are present in an immobile form.

Details on how to delist a waste can be found in BNA's *Chemical Substances Control* (see Bibliography).

As an example of how this delisting provision works, EPA announced on November 13, 1990, that it removed certain specific wastes from its list of hazardous wastes in response to generator petitions. The agency granted a petition by the Kawneer Co., Inc., of

Springdale, Arkansas, to exclude from hazardous waste control its F019 wastewater treatment sludge, which is produced in the chemical conversion coating of aluminum. The listed constituents of this waste are hexavalent chromium and complex cyanide. On the same date, the agency granted a similar petition from Perox, Inc., of Sharon, Pennsylvania, to exclude its iron oxide waste from hazardous waste control. This waste is a byproduct of the regeneration of spent pickle liquor, currently listed as K062, which contains hexavalent chromium and lead.

In each case the agency declared that the waste as described by the companies would not present a threat to human health or the environment. EPA stressed that the exclusion only covers the amount stated in the original petition and that if any changes are made in either plant's process, a new exclusion would be required.

When Is Hazardous Waste Regulated?

Waste that has any of the hazardous attributes is subject to regulation if it is:

- Disposed of; burned or incinerated; or accumulated, stored, or treated (but not recycled) before being disposed of or burned.

- Recycled as a means of disposal or accumulated, stored, or treated before recycling. "Recycling as a means of disposal" means placing waste on the land, as fertilizer, for instance, or using it to produce products placed on the land. Chapter 8 includes further discussion on the recycling activities covered by RCRA.

- Burned to recover energy or produce a fuel; reclaimed to recover or regenerate materials (this applies to certain wastes only).

- Accumulated speculatively before recycling.

- Inherently waste-like. This term covers wastes that contain toxic constituents (see Appendix) that are not ordinarily found in raw materials or products and that pose a substantial risk to human health and the environment. These wastes must be disposed of, burned, or incinerated rather than recycled because they are toxic.

Hazardous Waste Listing

EPA's hazardous waste lists are composed primarily of wastes that are process residues, emission control dusts, or wastewater treatment sludge. The following hazard codes indicate EPA's basis for listing waste: ignitable waste (I), corrosive waste (C), reactive waste (R), toxicity leaching characteristic waste (E), acute hazardous waste (H), and toxic waste (T).

EPA assigns a hazardous waste number to each listed hazardous waste. The number must be used in some notification, record-keeping, and reporting obligations. The list is broken down into three categories: nonspecific sources, specific sources, and discarded commercial chemical classes. The lists of chemicals from nonspecific and specific sources are found at p. 325 in the Appendix. Discarded commercial chemical products are listed beginning at p. 335. A list identifying what constituent(s) caused EPA to define a waste as toxicity leaching characteristic waste (E) or toxic waste (T) in the lists identified above appears beginning at p. 343. A further list of constituents, any one of which could render a waste hazardous, appears at p. 351.

POINTER➤ The hazardous waste lists are updated periodically. Readers therefore are advised to consult a BNA binder service such as *Chemical Substances Control* or *Chemical Regulations Reporter* to check on the status of a newly listed or delisted substance.

Identifying Hazardous Waste

The following shows how one can determine whether wastes exhibit any of the four hazardous waste characteristics: ignitability, corrosivity, reactivity, and toxicity. EPA has issued test methods for making these determinations but also invites labs to devise their own methods, according to Gail Hansen, an environmental scientist in the agency's Waste Characterization Office.

Determining Ignitability

This characteristic identifies a waste that may cause a fire during routine waste disposal and storage conditions. A waste is ignitable under the following conditions:

- It is a liquid other than an aqueous solution containing less than 24 percent alcohol by volume that has a flash point of 140°F (60°C) or less.

- It is not a liquid and is capable of causing a fire at standard temperature or pressure through friction, moisture absorption, or spontaneous chemical changes.

- It is a compressed gas classified as flammable by the Department of Transportation (DOT).

- It is an oxidizer according to DOT's rules.

Solid wastes that exhibit these characteristics have the EPA hazardous waste number D001.

Determining Corrosivity

The correct choice of how to determine corrosivity requires an understanding of the waste being tested. Any watery solid waste that does not contain oil or organics may be tested for pH level. It is corrosive if it has a pH of less than or equal to 2 or greater than or equal to 12.5. According to Hansen, waste containing organics should be tested using what EPA calls the coupon test. It is corrosive if it can corrode a steel coupon at a rate greater than 0.250 inches per year at a test temperature of 130°F (55°C). The agency is working on a corrosivity test for nonliquid solid waste, Hansen said, but has no timetable for its issuance.

A waste that exhibits corrosive characteristics has the EPA hazardous waste number D002.

Rules for Hazardous Waste Management

Determining Reactivity

A solid waste is reactive if it does any of the following:

- Readily undergoes violent change without detonating and is normally unstable

- Reacts violently with water

- Forms potentially explosive mixtures with water

- When mixed with water, generates sufficient toxic gases, vapors, or fumes to pose a danger to human health or the environment

- Contains cyanide or sulfide-bearing waste that, when exposed to pH conditions between 2 and 12.5, can generate sufficient toxic gases, vapors, or fumes to pose a danger to human health or the environment

- Can detonate or explosively decompose or react at standard temperature and pressure

- Is a forbidden explosive or a Class A or Class B explosive according to DOT's rules.

A reactive waste has the EPA hazardous waste number D003.

Determining Toxicity

A waste is a characteristic toxic waste if the Toxicity Characteristic Leaching Procedure (TCLP) shows that the extract from a representative sample has any of the contaminants listed in Table 1.

Table 1
Maximum Concentration of Contaminants for the Toxicity Characteristic

EPA Hazardous Waste Number	Contaminant	Maximum concentration (milligrams per liter)
D004	Arsenic	5.0
D005	Barium	100.0
D018	Benzine	0.5
D006	Cadmium	1.0
D019	Carbon Tetrachloride	0.5
D020	Chlordane	0.03
D021	Chlorobenzine	100.0
D022	Chloroform	6.0
D007	Chromium	5.0
D023	o-Cresol	* 200.0
D024	m-Cresol	* 200.0
D025	p-Cresol	* 200.0
D026	Cresol	* 200.0
D016	2,4-D	10.0
D027	1,4-Dichlorobenzene	7.5
D028	1,2-Dichloroethane	0.5
D029	1,1-Dichloroethylene	0.7
D030	2,4-Dinitrotoluene	# 0.13
D012	Endrin	0.02
D031	Heptachlor (and its hydroxide)	0.008
D032	Hexachlorobenzine	# 0.13
D033	Hexachlorobutadiene	0.5
D034	Hexachloroethane	3.0
D008	Lead	5.0
D013	Lindane	0.4
D009	Mercury	0.2
D014	Methoxychlor	10.0
D035	Methyl ethyl ketone	200.0
D036	Nitrobenzene	2.0
D037	Pentachlorophenol	100.0
D038	Pyridine	# 5.0
D010	Selenium	1.0
D011	Silver	5.0
D039	Tetrachloroethylene	0.7
D015	Toxaphene	0.5
D040	Trichloroethylene	0.5
D041	2,4,5-Trichlorophenol	400.0
D042	2,4,6-Trichlorophenol	2.0
D017	2,4,5-TP Silvex	1.0
D043	Vinyl chloride	0.2

* If o-, m-, and p-Cresol concentrations cannot be differentiated, the total cresol (D026) concentration is used. The regulatory level of total cresol is 200 mg/l.

Quantification limit is greater than the calculated regulatory level. The quantification limit therefore becomes the regulatory level.

Test Methods

The TCLP noted above determines the mobility of contaminants in solid and liquid wastes. An extract 20 times the weight of the solid phase of the waste must be filtered through a glass fiber filter and tested. If the extract reveals contaminants in concentrations above regulatory levels, the waste is hazardous. This procedure, adopted in September 1990, increased considerably the number of wastes and sludges subject to RCRA Part C disposal requirements.

There are two other methods for testing whether noncharacteristic solid waste is hazardous: *representative sampling methods* and *chemical analysis test methods*. Methods for conducting any of these tests are available from EPA's Solid Waste Information Office, 26 Martin Luther King Drive, Cincinnati, Ohio 45268.

Exemptions

In addition to the small generator exemptions that are described later in this chapter, there are several other exemptions available under prescribed circumstances. However, several of these exemptions are under review, as described below. The exempted substances are as follows:

- Waste pickle liquor sludge generated by lime stabilization of spent pickle liquor from the iron and steel industry (SIC Codes 331 and 332)

- Wastes from burning scrap metal, oil reclaimed from hazardous waste during normal petroleum management that will be further refined, coke and coal tar containing K087 decanter tank tar sludge, hazardous waste from iron and steel production processes, and hazardous waste fuel produced from oil-bearing hazardous wastes from petroleum management so long as resulting products are not hazardous

- Petroleum coke produced from hazardous wastes generated from the same facility, so long as the wastes are oil-containing refinery wastes and the coke displays hazardous characteristics

- Certain wastewaters/hazardous waste mixtures with small amounts of listed hazardous wastes that are discharged into a plant's wastewater treatment unit

- Certain solid wastes including empty containers or inner liners that have held any hazardous waste, provided EPA's definitions of empty are followed; discarded arsenic-treated wood product wastes that are deemed hazardous solely because they fail the TCLP toxicity test; pipeline wastes until they are removed or the pipeline has ceased to operate for more than 90 days; permitted wastewater treatment units; elementary neutralization units; typical tannery wastes; wastewater treatment sludges from titanium dioxide production; mining wastes from the extraction, beneficiation, and processing of ores and minerals, including coal, phosphate rock, and uranium ore (see below); other mining wastes under study by EPA (see below); cement kiln dust waste; accidental hazardous waste spills during immediate cleanup; agricultural wastes used as fertilizer; waste from fossil fuel combustion; wastes from oil, natural gas, or geothermal energy production; animal manures; household wastes and the facilities that receive these wastes; and petroleum-contaminated media and debris that fail the TCLP (hazardous waste codes D016 through D043 only)

- Reclaimed secondary materials, so long as they are returned to the original process through a closed system, not used as a fuel or combusted, and not stored for more than 12 months

- Nonsolid wastes including industrial wastewater discharges regulated under the Clean Water Act; special nuclear or byproduct material; nonextracted materials subject to in situ mining techniques; domestic sewage and mixtures of domestic sewage with other wastes passing through publicly owned treatment works; irrigation return flows; pulping liquors that are reclaimed and reused; and spent sulfuric acid used to produce virgin sulfuric acid, unless it is accumulated speculatively

- Samples from treatment studies, so long as prescribed conditions are met

On November 2, 1990, EPA ended a 10-year debate by discontinuing exemptions covering sludge from petroleum refineries. The rule, which took effect May 2, 1991, regulates sludges regardless of the type of device used to separate the wastes from the process waste waters and oily cooling waste waters, and regardless of where treatment takes place. The action means that between 156,000 and 300,000 metric tons of sludge now are regulated under tougher hazardous waste regulations than were in effect previously.

Pending Actions Concerning Exempted Waste

Certain currently exempted forms of hazardous or potentially hazardous waste are being reviewed as follows:

- **Ash from municipal waste combustors:** In light of expressed congressional intentions to regulate municipal waste combustor ash under Subtitle D of RCRA and as a result of its own findings, EPA has started work on a regulatory package. However, no deadlines for this activity have been set. Further information on how incinerator ash may be regulated is found in Chapter 4.

- **Used oil:** EPA made a decision in 1986 not to list recycled oil as a hazardous waste. However, the decision was remanded to EPA by the U.S. Court of Appeals for the D.C. Circuit in 1988. The agency currently is reexamining its position and looking at ways that it can list and then manage used oil in a way that will protect the environment while not discouraging the recycling of this valuable resource. The agency projects a final decision on this matter by August 1991. Under the current scheme, those who combust this oil must notify state regulators and must test to ensure that the oil does not contain more than 1,000 parts per million of halogen or specified levels of arsenic, cadmium, chromium, or lead and does not have a flash point above a specified limit.

- **Metallic ore processing:** EPA has completed development of a list of "high volume, low hazard" ore processing wastes for study under Section 8002(p) of RCRA and has also completed a study and an accompanying report to Congress, which was submitted and made available for comment August 7, 1990. On June 13, 1991, a final rule was promulgated identifying 20 wastes from the processing of ores and minerals. Eighteen of the wastes are regulated under RCRA Subtitle D and two wastes under a newly established program under the Toxic Substances Control Act.

- **Chlorotoluene production:** The 1984 RCRA amendments directed EPA to identify and list certain wastes from chlorotoluene production. The agency proposed this rulemaking in 1991, but has made no final decision as to how or when to regulate this substance.

- **Coke byproduct industrial waste:** A decision on these wastes was mandated for completion by 1986. However, not until late 1990 did the agency propose to list eight new waste codes from the coke byproducts industry. Final action is not expected before November 1991.
- **Certain de minimis waste constituents:** EPA has on its regulatory agenda the development of a proposed rule that would exempt from RCRA Subtitle C regulation "any currently listed wastes that are not hazardous because the hazardous constituents are present at levels lower than concentration levels" to be established. This combines two earlier rulemaking projects titled "Concentration-Based Relisting of Wastes from Chlorinated Aliphatics" and "Concentration-Based Relisting of Wastes from Explosives, Inorganic Chemicals, and Iron and Steel Industries."
- **Mining waste management:** EPA has determined that regulation of wastes from the extraction and beneficiation of ores and minerals under Subtitle C is not warranted. However, criteria will be developed for states to use in regulating disposal of these wastes under Title D.
- **Sewage sludge:** EPA is developing a regulation to control sludge disposal practices of more than 5,000 publicly owned sewage treatment plants. The regulation, due for issuance in late 1991, has run into trouble with the Office of Management and Budget, which asked EPA to show why it is calculating risk to protect sensitive individuals rather than simply calculating it to protect the general population. This rule is under the Clean Water Act and will be administered by the agency's water criteria and standards office.

Incompatible Wastes

Owners or operators of hazardous waste facilities must analyze wastes to determine whether they are incompatible. Potentially incompatible wastes can be mixed so as to preclude reaction, be neutralized, or be mixed to control hazardous substances that might be produced. In Table 2, the mixing of a Group A material with a Group B material may be incompatible and cause the reactions indicated.

Table 2
Lists of Incompatible Wastes

Group 1-A

Acetylene sludge
Alkaline caustic liquids
Alkaline cleaner
Alkaline corrosive liquids
Alkaline corrosive battery fluid
Caustic wastewater
Lime sludge and other corrosive alkalies
Lime wastewater
Lime and water
Spent caustic

Group 1-B

Acid sludge
Acid and water
Battery acid
Chemical cleaners
Electrolyte, acid
Etching acid liquid or solvent
Pickling liquor and other corrosive acids
Spent acid
Spent mixed acid
Spent sulfuric acid

Potential consequences: Heat generation; violent reaction.

Group 2-A

Aluminum
Beryllium
Calcium
Lithium
Magnesium
Potassium
Sodium
Zinc powder
Other reactive metals and metal hydrides

Group 2-B

Any waste in Group 1-A or 1-B

Potential consequences: Fire or explosion; generation of flammable hydrogen gas.

Group 3-A

Alcohols

Water

Group 3-B

Any concentrated waste in Groups 1-A or 1-B
Calcium
Lithium
Metal hydrides
Potassium
SO_2Cl_2, $SOCl_2$, PCl_4, CH_3SiCl_4
Other water-reactive waste

Potential consequences: Fire, explosion, or heat generation; generation of flammable or toxic gases.

Group 4-A

Alcohols
Aldehydes
Halogenated hydrocarbons
Nitrated hydrocarbons
Unsaturated hydrocarbons
Other reactive organic compounds and solvents

Group 4-B

Concentrated Group 1-A or 1-B wastes
Group 2-A wastes

Potential consequences: Fire, explosion, or violent reaction.

Group 5-A

Spent cyanide and sulfide solutions

Group 5-B

Group 1-B wastes

Potential consequences: Generation of toxic hydrogen cyanide or hydrogen sulfide gas.

Group 6-A

Chlorates
Chlorine
Chlorites
Chromic acid
Hypochlorites
Nitrates
Nitric acid, fuming
Perchlorates
Permanganates
Peroxides
Other strong oxidizers

Group 6-B

Acetic acid and other organic acids
Concentrated mineral acids
Group 2-A wastes
Group 4-A wastes
Other flammable and combustible wastes

Potential consequences: Fire, explosion, or violent reaction.

GENERATORS AND THEIR OBLIGATIONS
(40 CFR 262)

Large-quantity generators, for the purpose of regulation, produce or accumulate and dispose of over 1,000 kilograms (five 55-gallon drums or 2,200 pounds) of hazardous waste per month. Firms that generate more than 100 pounds but less than 1,000 pounds per month are known as small-quantity generators and must comply with most, but not all, of the requirements applicable to larger generators. Episodic generators must comply with rules applicable to their activities in any given month. Finally, generators of more than one kilogram of acutely hazardous wastes per month are subject to regulation.

The regulations are less stringent for generators that store, treat, and dispose of waste on-site than for those that ship waste off-site. "On-site" includes contiguous property if it is accessed by a crossroad or a restricted right of way. On-site generators do not have to use manifests or meet standards for containers, labels, marking, and placarding but must comply with the requirements for waste analysis; notification; the technical aspects of treatment, storage, and disposal; and obtaining permits.

Owners or operators of treatment, storage, and disposal facilities also are considered generators if they originate shipments of hazardous waste.

All regulated off-site generators must comply with the following requirements:

- Determine whether their wastes are hazardous.

- Obtain an EPA identification number.

- Offer their wastes only to transporters and facilities with EPA identification numbers.

- Comply with applicable DOT requirements for shipping wastes off-site.

- Use a multipart "round-trip" Uniform Hazardous Waste Manifest to accompany the waste to its final destination. If the generator does

Rules for Hazardous Waste Management

not receive back the manifest within 35 days, it must contact the designated disposal facility to determine what happened. If 45 days pass without return of the manifest, the generator must file an exception report with EPA. Small generators also must report unacknowledged shipments, but under less rigid provisions.

- Maintain copies of manifests or records of test results, waste analyses, or other waste determinations for at least three years.

- Except for small generators, submit reports to EPA every two years.

- Except for small generators, certify on the manifest that a waste minimization plan is in place and that the proposed method of treatment, storage, or disposal is the most practicable method available to minimize the present and future threat to human health and the environment.

POINTER➤ Small generators can avoid the manifest system entirely if they arrange to have their wastes reclaimed, the regenerated material is returned to its point of origin, and the vehicle used for transport belongs to the reclaimer of the waste.

Accumulation Restrictions

Large generators may store hazardous waste for 90 days in containers or tanks if they comply with EPA's standards, which include ongoing employee training, emergency preparedness and prevention, contingency planning, and air pollution control (see Chapter 4). If storage exceeds the 90-day period, the generator must comply with the rules for storage facilities unless EPA grants an extension.

However, generators may accumulate without a permit or interim status as much as 55 gallons of hazardous wastes or one quart of acutely hazardous wastes from the discarded commercial chemical products listed in the Appendix, if they are held in well-maintained, clearly marked containers stored near the point of generation.

The slightly lower regulatory burden imposed on small generators serves as their incentive to keep waste down. Such generators are subject to less restrictive rules on the amount they may accumulate. They may store up to 6,000 kilograms of wastes on-site in tanks or containers without a permit or interim status for 180 days, or 270 days if the wastes must be transported off-site over 200 miles for treatment or disposal. Generators that exceed these time or quantity requirements are bound by the interim status storage requirements.

Remaining Exempt from Regulation

Generators of less than 100 kilograms of hazardous waste per month must stay within the following prescribed limits if they are to avoid becoming subject to regulation (remain "conditionally exempt," in EPA's words):

- Produce no more than 100 kilograms of hazardous wastes, 1 kilogram of acute hazardous wastes, or 100 kilograms of residues, contaminated soil, or debris resulting from the cleanup of an acute hazardous waste spill in any given month.

- Accumulate no more than 1 kilogram of acute hazardous wastes or 100 kilograms of residues, contaminated soil, or debris resulting from the cleanup of an acute hazardous waste spill on land or water.

- Accumulate no more than 1,000 kilograms of hazardous wastes on-site at any time. Should the generator at any time stockpile wastes exceeding this amount, it becomes subject to the more rigid accumulation requirements that apply to generators of 100 to 1,000 kilograms per month.

EPA has proposed to add to this list of exemption stipulations a requirement that emissions into the air from small generator storage tanks be reduced (see Chapter 4).

Exempt small-quantity generators also can maintain their status by treating or disposing of hazardous wastes on-site or ensuring delivery to an authorized off-site storage, treatment, or disposal facility.

Determining Generator Status

The first key to determining generator status is to know the waste classification requirements described earlier in this chapter. The information here supplements that by showing how to quantify the waste.

The generator must count only regulated hazardous wastes in making quantity determinations. Only the accumulation, transportation, long-term storage, and management of residues or sludges resulting from the reclamation process are actually subject to regulation. Wastes are counted only once, when they are first accumulated. The waste is not counted again when it is removed from storage or when it is reclaimed and reused at the site. In other words, generators need not count treatment residues if the original hazardous waste was counted. EPA provides an example to help with the understanding of this provision, as follows:

Manufacturer A generates 120 kilograms of hazardous spent solvent in one month, which he distills without intervening storage. The regenerated solvent then is reused. Neither the spent solvent nor the regenerated solvent is counted because it was not accumulated, transported, stored, or disposed of as waste. Manufacturer A therefore is not a small quantity generator. However, if manufacturer B distills the spent solvent, stores it for any period at all, reuses the regenerated solvent until spent, and then distills it once again, the spent solvent would be counted because it was stored before reclamation, but it would only be counted once. The subsequent activities would not be counted. B is a small-quantity generator. If generator B stores its spent solvent for more than 180 days before reclamation, it also would need a storage permit.

Mixtures take on the characterization of their most hazardous portion and must be lumped together to ascertain quantity during a given month.

STANDARDS FOR TREATMENT, STORAGE, AND DISPOSAL FACILITIES

Any discussion of standards for TSD facilities is complicated by the fact that facilities constructed before the effective November 1984 date of the RCRA amendments are allowed to operate under so-called interim status until EPA issues final permits. Final permits have two parts: Part A, which consists of reasonably concise application forms, and Part B, which requires a voluminous narrative and is infinitely more complex for EPA to process. Interim status facilities all operate under the terms of Part A and must have filed complete Part B applications.

Existing Facilities Status Report

Except in California earthquake areas, all active hazardous waste incinerators now have final permits; landfills that plan to remain open also have final permits. The 11,000 landfills that are scheduled for closure because they cannot or will not meet the final permit standards are no longer active but remain under interim status permits until they are issued final postclosure permits that dictate how they will be kept safe in the future. Final permits for TSD facilities other than incinerators and landfills are in various stages of approval, with final decisions on their status due by November 1992.

New Facilities

Owners and operators of new facilities must submit both Part A and Part B at least 180 days before physical construction or operation may begin. This means that permits should be in hand before new TSDs or substantial modifications of existing facilities are made.

Unless scheduled for closure, facilities under interim status also may be expanded, provided minimum technological requirements are met. However, operators must notify EPA at least 60 days before receiving any hazardous waste into the expanded area and must apply for a final permit within six months of that notification.

Closed Facilities

As noted above, operators or owners closing a land-based facility also must apply for postclosure permits, even if the closure is necessary because an operating permit was denied. This requirement applies to any surface impoundment, landfill, land treatment unit, or waste pile that received wastes after July 26, 1982, or that certified closure after January 26, 1983. The permit may be waived if the owner

Rules for Hazardous Waste Management 39

or operator removes or decontaminates the waste in accordance with prescribed procedures. Postclosure permits require groundwater monitoring, unsaturated zone monitoring, corrective action, and postclosure care.

POINTER▶ Permits may be unit specific. EPA may issue a permit for one or more units at a plant, for instance a waste pile and an incinerator, without changing the status of other units at the same facility. Many large facilities currently are operating under a mixture of interim status and final permits.

Special Types of Permits

In addition to the general permit requirements noted above, EPA issues several special types of permits that have broad application, as follows:

- **Permit by rule:** This type of permit is granted to certain ocean disposal barges or vessels, injection wells, and public treatment works. Ocean vessels must have a permit for ocean dumping under the Marine Protection, Research, and Sanctuaries Act as well as comply with most RCRA requirements. Underground injection control (UIC) wells disposing of hazardous wastes must be in compliance not only with RCRA provisions but also with Clean Water Act conditions included in their permits. Publicly owned treatment works that treat hazardous wastes must have a National Pollutant Discharge Elimination System permit and must remain in compliance with RCRA manifest and record-keeping requirements.

- **Emergency permit:** This temporary, oral permit is issued if there is an imminent threat to human health and the environment. It allows for treatment, storage, or disposal for up to 90 days under carefully monitored conditions.

- **Incinerator permit:** To ensure that hazardous waste incinerators are in operational readiness, there must be a trial burn that cannot exceed 720 hours operating time and must demonstrate that the wastes are destroyed. EPA may extend the operating time once, for an additional 720 hours, but only if good cause is shown. Other permit requirements must be spelled out in Part B of the permit application.

- **Land treatment demonstration permit:** Owners or operators may demonstrate that a particular waste can be completely degraded, transformed, or immobilized in the treatment zone.

- **Interim permits for UIC wells:** EPA will issue a temporary permit for class I UIC wells containing hazardous wastes only in states lacking UIC programs.

- **Research, development, and demonstration permits:** These permits are available to hazardous waste treatment facilities that propose to use an innovative and experimental treatment technology or process for which permit standards have not been issued.

Standards for All Facilities (40 CFR 265)

Interim status and fully permitted facilities must be in compliance with a panoply of general rules covering notice, waste analysis, security, inspections, training, preparedness and prevention, contingency planning, manifest system procedures, groundwater monitoring, closure and postclosure plans, financial requirements for closure and postclosure, and liability coverage. There also are standards for each facility type, such as surface impoundments or waste piles; these are described in Chapters 9 and 10.

Most of the permit standards for hazardous waste operations are identical for interim status facilities and fully permitted facilities. Changed or additional requirements for permitted facilities are noted where appropriate.

Notification Requirements

Hazardous waste facility operators must notify the appropriate EPA regional office *four weeks* before the arrival of imported waste and must inform a new owner, prior to transfer, of all permit requirements. However, the failure of a former owner to tell a new owner of its responsibilities does not relieve the new owner of its obligations to comply with applicable requirements. Under the final permit rules, receivers of imported waste also must inform their customers of their permits and their waste handling capability. All permittees also must certify that a plan is in place to reduce the volume and toxicity of any hazardous wastes generated to a degree economically practicable. (The Pollution Prevention Act of 1990 builds on this requirement and requires firms to submit data concerning this plan, as described in Chapter 1.)

Waste Analysis

Owners or operators of TSD facilities must obtain a detailed chemical and physical analysis of a representative sample of a hazardous waste before they can receive it (see above on how to obtain information on testing). If the generator does not supply adequate information, the facility operator must obtain the data itself. Facility owners or operators must develop and follow waste analysis plans specifying which tests they will conduct and how often. EPA or an authorized state regulator must review these plans. Under the final permit rules, the waste analysis must contain all of the information needed to treat, store, or dispose of the waste in accordance to applicable rules and permit requirements.

Security and Inspections

Unless they pose no threat of injury or environmental assault, TSD facilities should be secured against intrusion by humans or livestock. In addition, plainly legible signs worded "Danger–Unauthorized Personnel Keep Out" should be posted at each entrance.

Owners or operators must make scheduled inspections of facilities, to include a look at monitoring equipment, safety and emergency equipment, security devices, and operating and structural equipment. Records of these results and of most other required hazardous waste management activities must be kept three years.

If an inspection reveals deterioration or malfunction, repair should be scheduled before any harm can be done. In the case of an imminent hazard, remedial action must take place right away.

Training

Within six months of employment, TSD facility employees must learn at least the following waste management procedures:

- Emergency response procedures, systems, and equipment

- Use, inspection, repair, and replacement of emergency monitoring equipment

- Key parameters for automatic waste feed cutoff systems

- Communications or alarm systems

- Response to fires, explosions, or groundwater contamination

- Operations shutdown

Facility owners and operators must maintain employee training records until a facility is closed. Records of terminated employees must be kept three years after the employee has left.

Handling Ignitable, Reactive, or Incompatible Waste

For safe management of a TSD site, ignitable and/or reactive waste must be protected from open flames, smoking, cutting and welding, hot surfaces, frictional heat, sparks, and spontaneous chemical reactions. "No Smoking" signs should be conspicuously placed. Precautions also must be taken to prevent undesirable reactions among reactive substances (see earlier charts). Under the final permit rules, facility owners or operators must document their compliance with the above provisions.

Emergency Plans

RCRA requires owners and operators to meet design and operation standards as follows:

- Equipment, including an internal alarm system; telephones or two-way radios; portable fire extinguishers; spill control and decontamination devices; and foam-producing equipment, automatic sprinklers, or water spray systems, must be accessible, tested regularly, and in good repair.

Rules for Hazardous Waste Management

- Aisle space must be adequate to allow free movement of personnel and emergency equipment.

- Contact must be maintained with appropriate local authorities. Police, fire departments, hospitals, and emergency teams must be familiar with plant layout and evacuation routes and the properties and hazards of the waste. Agreement must be made on jurisdictional and procedural issues with state emergency response teams, emergency response contractors, and equipment suppliers.

- Primary emergency authority must be designated to one police and one fire department.

- A contingency plan must be in place and include names of responsible employees, details of the arrangements described above, a list of the facility's emergency equipment, and an evacuation plan. The information may be incorporated into a facility's Spill Prevention Control and Countermeasures plan, which is required under Superfund.

- A designated emergency coordinator should be on call or on the premises and familiar with all aspects of the company's contingency plan and related operation. The coordinator must understand all of the emergency response provisions, not only under RCRA but also under the Comprehensive Environmental Response, Compensation, and Liability Act.

The final permit rules state that the contingency plan may be submitted to EPA with Part B of the permit application. New facility operators must supply EPA with the list of emergency coordinators and alternates at the time of certification, not when the application is completed. The contingency plan must be reviewed and amended whenever the facility permit is revised.

Manifests, Recordkeeping, and Reporting

As noted above, the manifest system is designed to keep track of waste from origin to disposal and beyond. The Uniform Hazardous Waste Manifest Form (8700-22 and 8700-22A) is most commonly used by generators who transport or hire others to transport hazardous waste for off-site treatment, storage, or disposal. Some authorized states provide their own manifests, however. Firms may reproduce the original forms if they so choose.

When the TSD facility receives a shipment of waste, the owner or operator must first make sure that the manifest information matches the shipment content and then sign, date, and return a copy of the manifest to the transporter. Within 30 days, a copy also must be sent to the generator. The facility owner must keep the form for three years. Bulk shipments by water or rail may be accompanied by shipping papers that contain all of the information on the manifest except the identification numbers and generators' certifications and signatures.

If a manifest discrepancy is noted, the TSD operator should attempt to resolve the problem with the transporter or the generator before also submitting to EPA a letter explaining the problem.

TSD owners and operators must keep voluminous records, including, among many other things, the type, quantity, and origin, as well as the method of treatment, storage, or disposal, of each hazardous waste received. It would be safe to say that every significant activity carried out at the facility should be recorded.

By March 1 of each even-numbered year, TSD firms also must submit biennial reports (Form 8700-13B) to the appropriate EPA regional office. The form includes instructions for its use. Many states have their own manifest reporting requirements as well, frequently at shorter intervals than specified by EPA.

Finally, TSD firms must notify EPA (or an authorized state) within 15 days of receiving wastes that arrive without a manifest. Form 8700-13B, designated as an "Unmanifested Waste Report," should be used for this purpose.

Groundwater Monitoring

Owners and operators of landfills, surface impoundments, and land treatment facilities are subject to groundwater monitoring programs unless they can show that there is a low potential for migration of hazardous wastes from the facility's uppermost aquifer to surface water or water supply wells. The programs must include an approved monitoring system, a sampling and analysis plan, and a certified groundwater quality assessment plan.

Details on monitoring plans may be found in BNA's *Chemical Substances Control* binder or in the EPA publications "Procedures Manual for Groundwater Monitoring at Solid Waste Disposal Facilities," EPA 530/SW-611, August 1977, and "Methods for Chemical Analysis of Water and Wastes," EPA-600/4-79-020, March 1979.

Closure and Postclosure

In order to prevent a new round of abandoned hazardous waste disposal sites from becoming environmental disasters, the RCRA rules require hazardous waste facility owners and operators to comply with closure and postclosure rules. The rules require the preparation of closure and postclosure plans, notification and participation of the public, decontamination and dismantling of equipment, monitoring, and maintenance. In addition to these general requirements, the closure rules include specific provisions for landfills, land treatment facilities, surface impoundments, miscellaneous units, incinerators, tanks, and treatment facilities.

The owner or operator remains responsible for the closed area, including tanks for storage or treatment of waste, for 30 years and must guarantee the costs of closure and postclosure care. After estimating what these costs will be, the responsible party may choose any one of five guarantee options: a trust fund, a surety bond, a letter of credit, an insurance policy, or a financial test. Except for the financial test, which is an all-or-nothing proposition, the options may be combined at a given facility.

The final permit rules include additional closure requirements, centered primarily on the proper closure of waste piles and surface impoundments.

Liability Coverage

EPA requires hazardous waste management facilities to be covered against liability to third parties for bodily injury or property damage from facility operation, as follows:

TSD facility operators must demonstrate, on a firm-wide basis, full liability coverage for sudden accidental occurrences such as fires or explosions. The coverage must be at least $1 million per occurrence, with an annual limit of at least $2 million.

Surface impoundments, landfill, land treatment facilities, and miscellaneous disposal units must be covered for damage over time, such as leakage into groundwater. EPA requires coverage of $3 million per occurrence with an annual limit of $6 million.

Financial responsibility may be demonstrated through the same mechanisms described above for closed facility guarantees. Because these guarantees sometimes were unavailable, EPA, in September 1988, expanded the options to allow firms that are not a direct corporate parent to purchase insurance for an owner or operator provided a substantial business relationship exists.

Under the final permit rules, facilities using the surety bond option for closure and postclosure financial assurance may use either financial guarantee bonds or performance bonds. Interim status facilities, on the other hand, may use only the guarantee bond. In addition, new facilities must submit all necessary documents–whatever the financial arrangement–to the regional office at least 60 days before the first shipment of hazardous waste is received at the facility.

Details on these financial provisions are in BNA's *Chemical Substances Control* binder.

Siting Requirements

The final permit rules prohibit the location of new hazardous waste management facilities within 200 feet (61 meters) of a Holocene fault, defined as a fault that has moved in the recent geologic past. Such faults have occurred or are expected to occur in numerous jurisdictions in Alaska, Arizona, Colorado, Hawaii, Idaho,

Montana, New Mexico, Utah, Washington, and Wyoming and in all of California and Nevada.

Facilities in a 100-year floodplain should be designed to prevent washout of hazardous waste from the active portion of the facility. Facility operators may obtain exemptions from this design requirement if they have procedures in effect to remove the waste to another authorized facility before flood waters rise. Surface impoundments, landfills, land treatment units, waste piles, or miscellaneous units also may be exempt from flood-proof design requirements if a demonstration shows that no adverse effects would result during washout, taking into account the waste's chemical and physical properties, concentrations, and impact on surface wastes and water sediments. This seemingly lax exemption would most likely be applied to a waste characterized as hazardous only because it is ignitable.

Chapter 3

NONHAZARDOUS SOLID WASTE: GUIDELINES AND RULES

Without significant changes in the American way of life, municipal solid waste generation will continue to escalate over the next decade to reach a staggering 216 million tons, or 4.4 pounds per person per day, by the year 2000, according to a 1990 Environmental Protection Agency (EPA) municipal solid waste characterization study (see Bibliography). Using its own computer model, Congress's Office of Technological Assessment (OTA) projects a slightly lower figure of 193 million tons.

Whether the lower or the higher of these amounts is reached, U.S. waste generation far exceeds the per capita amount generated by any other nation and may well exceed the nation's ability to create disposal capacity. Landfill space has almost disappeared in some areas, and alternative disposal methods become increasingly difficult to site because of the "not in my backyard" (NIMBY) syndrome, according to EPA's "Agenda for Action" (see below). Everyone remembers the forlorn "garbage barge" of 1987 that chugged from port to port looking in vain for a jurisdiction or even a foreign country that would accept its waste. In 1989 similar "ash barges" became symbols of America's inability to manage its own trash.

Because hazardous waste is so thoroughly regulated, one might wonder why there is no similar national plan to manage municipal and industrial solid waste. The short answer is that solid waste has not created a Love Canal, at least so far. Traditionally, municipal solid waste, known as garbage to almost everybody, has been a matter for local management or mismanagement, as the case may be. Congress acknowledged that there were solid waste management problems in crafting the Resource Conservation and Recovery Act of 1976 (RCRA), when it directed states to establish criteria for sanitary landfills as opposed to "open dumps." Such dumps dotted the nation's countryside and were only then recognized not only as eyesores but as health threats as well.

Congress was not willing at that time to wrest municipal waste management from municipalities, however. Instead, it constructed RCRA's solid waste provisions to give EPA discretion in the issuance of guidelines, and states and municipalities even more discretion in how to follow through. The result was that much planning took place in some states and very little in others. EPA's municipal solid waste management activity could best be summed up by saying that considerable guidance was generated in the late 1970s, very little during the early and mid-1980s, and far more since 1988. Even in this latest round of guidance and regulatory activity, EPA leaves most responsibility for implementation up to the states.

The agency has adopted national regulations to control air emissions from new municipal combustion facilities (discussed in Chapter 5) and to regulate gas emissions from landfills (also noted in Chapter 5), and has proposed to regulate municipal solid waste landfills that receive hazardous waste from households and small-quantity generators (discussed in Chapter 11). As in the case of the guidelines, states will be responsible for the administration and enforcement of these nationally applicable rules. The difference is that regulations are federally enforceable, whereas guidelines are not.

Once it accumulates the necessary data, the agency also plans a regulation to control activities at industrial solid waste disposal facilities.

FEDERAL LEGISLATIVE ACTIVITY

As of late 1990, neither Congress nor EPA was convinced that a strong federal regulatory framework is appropriate or even desirable for solid waste management. When Congress debates the Subtitle D amendments in 1991 and beyond, attitudes will depend heavily on whether there are any more incidents like the garbage barge, according to Lillian T. Bagus, acting section chief for implementation in EPA's Division of Municipal and Solid Waste.

Bills introduced during the 1990 Congress ran the gamut from requiring full-scale RCRA-type permits to stipulating only that states demonstrate capacity to manage and dispose of their own garbage. Three bills (HR 3735, 3736, and 3737) to reauthorize RCRA were introduced in the House by Rep. Thomas A. Luken (D-Ohio), who was anxious to see such legislation completed before his retirement at the end of the session. The bills, which concerned solid waste recycling, a solid waste export ban, and a virgin materials use tax, respectively, were passed by the House Energy and Commerce Subcommittee on Transportation and Hazardous Materials but were not considered by the full House. According to a congressional aide, the bills or their 1991 replacements might rival the Clean Air Act in debate and controversy. Luken's retirement at the end of the 101st Congress left some doubt as to how swiftly RCRA Part D legislation would be considered in the 102nd.

However, the ascendancy of Rep. Al Swift (D-Wash.) to the chairmanship points to hard work in this area in 1991. According to congressional sources, the arguments may break down regionally rather than along party lines. States with excess capacity champion laws to restrict the transport of other states' solid waste across their borders in the same manner as several have sought to restrict interstate transport of hazardous waste. While some sources believe Congress will start work in 1991, many contend that full reauthorization of Part D will take two to four years because of several controversial issues such as redefining solid waste, setting national waste management goals, tightening the rules on municipal hazardous waste disposal, and deciding whether such common substances as used motor oil should be regulated as hazardous.

On the Senate side, it remained unclear in early 1991 whether the Environment and Public Works Committee would take up reauthorization of the Clean Water Act before tackling RCRA. According to a staffer, solid waste management debate will first focus on two bills that originated in the 101st Congress. Introduced by Sen. Max S. Baucus (D-Mont.) and Sen. John H. Chafee (R-R.I.), the bills would establish national recycling goals, block disposal of cadmium and lead in landfills, and set preferences for waste disposal.

Individual members of the House wasted little time introducing solid waste bills for consideration. The following bills were introduced the first day of the new Congress:

- HR 231, introduced by Rep. Olympia J. Snowe (R-Maine), which would establish national goals for the reduction and recycling of municipal solid waste. (A glance at Chapter 11 shows that this law should have ready acceptance, as the vast majority of the states already have set goals, increasingly mandatory.)

- HR 230, reintroduced by Snowe, which would mandate that plastic containers be marked with symbols to aid in recycling efforts.

- Several measures to change procurement practices to encourage recycling.

- HR 171, introduced by Rep. Jim Olin (D-Va.), which would give states the authority to limit the amount of out-of-state garbage they receive and would require states to adopt 20-year solid waste management plans.

Pending RCRA changes, many aspects of solid waste management remain dictated by guidelines rather than rules, and remain entirely in state and local hands. Certain procurement guidelines and other activities EPA has undertaken to encourage recycling are described in Chapter 8. Described here are EPA's Guidelines for State Solid Management Plans and Solid Waste Facility Criteria, followed by a description of how Mercer County, New Jersey, went about the planning process; a Council of State Governments model waste management plan; Agenda for Action, a report by the Municipal Solid Waste Task Force, which was directed to fashion a strategy for improving U.S. municipal solid waste management; and certain cost and risk findings reached by the OTA in a 1988 municipal waste study, "Facing America's Trash, What Next for Municipal Solid Waste?" (see Bibliography).

GUIDELINES FOR STATE SOLID WASTE MANAGEMENT PLANS (40 CFR 256)

In response to the 1976 RCRA mandate that it develop guidelines to assist states in developing and carrying out solid waste management plans, EPA issued guidelines in 1979. Initially, states were offered financial assistance in preparing conforming plans. However, they were invited rather than required to submit these plans and, when funds were cut in 1981, many gave up, according to Michael P. Flynn of EPA's Office of Solid Waste. Only 25 states have federally approved Part 256 plans. The others have partially completed plans that vary in scope and levels of sophistication. EPA continues to process these plans for approval.

Scope of Waste Management Plans

An approved plan must specify methods for achieving environmentally sound management and disposal of both solid and hazardous wastes; the responsibilities of state, local, and regional authorities; the proposed allocation of federal funds; and means for coordinating regional planning and implementation.

In addition, the plan should

- Prohibit the formation of new open dumps and stipulate that existing dumps be upgraded or closed. (The difference between an open dump and a sanitary landfill is set forth in another criteria document, 40 CFR 57, described below.)

- Provide that solid waste, including nonhazardous solid waste from other states, be used for resource recovery or disposed of in sanitary landfills or in some other environmentally sound manner.

- Include a schedule and procedure for continual review and assessment of the program, which should encompass hazardous wastes;

residential, commercial, and institutional solid waste; water and wastewater treatment sludge; pollution control residue; industrial, mining, and agricultural wastes; and septic tank pumpings.

- Develop design and operational standards and a permit system to ensure that new landfills or upgraded existing dumps protect health and the environment.

- Establish inspection and monitoring systems to ensure that landfills are not producing leachate in quantities and concentrations that would contaminate groundwater.

- Include measures to protect people and the environment from the adverse effects of inactive facilities. Such measures may include actions by facility owners and operators, notification of the public, and notification of agencies responsible for public health and safety.

The guidelines stipulate that plans be effective for at least five years after submittal and that they be reviewed by the state every three years. EPA was also supposed to review the plans and make recommendations for improvement. In practice, the agency has neither reviewed the plans nor required the states to do so, according to Flynn.

POINTER▶ Because these are guidelines only, EPA does not have enforcement authority to ban open dumps or to carry out any of the other provisions shown here. For plans to be successful, states must have strong enforcement powers.

Assessing Capacity and Need

The guidelines direct states to encourage resource recovery and conservation in all aspects of capacity planning. Where storage, recovery, treatment, or disposal facilities are found lacking, states should establish a responsible hierarchy for new facility construction. To avoid duplication, the plan should be developed in conjunction with other program offices such as air quality, water quality, water supply, wastewater treatment, pesticides, ocean protection, toxic substances control, noise control, and radiation control. Most notably, cooperation must occur between waste and water quality agencies.

A STRATEGIC APPROACH TO SOLID WASTE MANAGEMENT

A paper presented at the American Society of Mechanical Engineers' (ASME) 14th National Waste Processing Conference & Exhibition in May 1990 advised communities on how to structure an integrated solid waste management program. Coauthored by Whitney A. Sanders II and Donald J. Birnesser of STV/Sanders & Thomas, Inc., Pottstown, Pennsylvania, the paper described the development of a long-term strategy to handle solid waste in Mercer County, New Jersey.

The planning process entailed weighing and sorting solid waste, collecting data, and reviewing past municipal records, the authors said. In order to perform these functions, the community needed to inoculate workers; provide rakes, dust respirators, gloves, and identification tags; hold orientation meetings with refuse haulers; and inspect haulers' trucks, among other things.

The weighing program, which was conducted over two-week periods in all seasons, used platform scales at both a landfill and a transfer station. Procedures were established to monitor all vehicles entering the landfill; drivers were interviewed for information such as garbage collection routes, capacity and weight of the truck, and weight of the men on board the truck, according to the paper. In addition, the waste was categorized into six types: residential, commercial, bulky, vegetative, animal and food processing, and dry industrial.

Once weighed, the waste was sorted to determine its overall composition. This process required several workers equipped with heavy gloves, respirators, shovels, rakes, and hand-held magnets to place 16 segregated waste types into 32-gallon containers mounted on casters. Once a container was filled, it was weighed and sampled for moisture and energy content.

These data were compared to existing data going back several years for use in determining how much waste could be recycled or reduced and how large an incinerator the community needed. The outcome of this analysis was the county's decision to install, by 1993, a resource recovery facility capable of processing 975 tons of solid waste per day. The facility will be a "key component" of the county's waste reduction, recycling, and energy recovery program, the authors said.

The paper, *Use of Solid Waste Quantification and Characterization Program to Implement an Integrated System in Mercer County, New Jersey,* is available by calling John Varrasi of ASME at (212) 705-7740.

SOLID WASTE FACILITY CRITERIA (40 CFR 257)

EPA established minimum national performance criteria covering all types of land disposal facilities, including landfills, surface impoundments, land application units, and waste piles. In developing conforming regulations, states are directed to designate all facilities that meet the criteria as sanitary landfills. Those that fail on even one count should be designated open dumps. This provision underlies EPA's reluctance to force states to inventory open dumps, according to Flynn. Interpreted literally, it equates a landfill with only a minor discrepancy to a facility plagued with environmental problems.

Certain wastes and facilities are exempt from these guidelines, including agricultural waste (since identified as a significant cause of water pollution), overburdens from mining operations that are to be returned to the site, land application of domestic sewage, the location and operation of septic tanks (but not the disposal of pumpings), solid or dissolved materials in irrigation return flows, industrial discharges that are point sources subject to permits under Section 402 of the Clean Water Act, special nuclear or byproduct material as defined by the Atomic Energy Act, hazardous waste disposal facilities subject to Subtitle C of RCRA, and disposal of solid waste by underground well injection under the Safe Drinking Water Act.

Classification Criteria

To be classified as a sanitary landfill, a facility must meet the following criteria:

Nonhazardous Solid Waste: Guidelines & Rules

- *Floodplains, surface water, and groundwater:* Facilities in floodplains must not restrict the flow of base floods, reduce the temporary water storage capacity of the floodplain, or result in washout of solid waste; dredge and fill material may not be discharged into surface water in violation of the National Pollutant Discharge Elimination System of the Clean Water Act; and no facility may contaminate an underground drinking water source beyond the plant boundary.

- *Air:* No open burning of residential, commercial, institutional, or industrial solid waste may take place. Certain periodic burning activities are exempt.

- *Farmland:* No solid waste facility border may lie within one meter (three feet) of land used for crop. If polychlorinated biphenyls are contained in the waste, special requirements apply.

- *Endangered species:* Facilities may not cause or contribute to the taking of any endangered or threatened species of plants, fish, or wildlife or their habitat.

- *Disease:* All facility operators must take steps to eliminate the population of rodents, mosquitoes, and flies by periodic application of cover material or other techniques. At sewage and septic waste disposal facilities, special processes must be used to reduce pathogens prior to incorporating the waste into the soil.

- *Safety:* The concentration of explosive gases generated by the facility or practice may not exceed 25 percent of the lower explosive limit (LEL) for the gases in facility structures. The concentration may not exceed the LEL for the gases at the property line. In addition, operators must reduce potential hazards from fire, employ methods to protect birds, and restrict uncontrolled public access.

National Sludge Management Program

Rules that became effective June 1, 1989, mandate a long-term permitting program to introduce technical standards for sewage sludge use. The rules also set forth various aspects of EPA's authority to take interim steps to protect public health from possible adverse effects of toxics in sewage.

In stating the rules' intent, EPA indicated that sewage sludge should be viewed as a resource rather than as a disposal problem. The rules therefore encourage beneficial reuse projects such as agricultural land application, but under careful management. Approved state programs must include the following:

- A description of the scope, structure, coverage, and processes of the state's sludge disposal plan, including the name of the lead agency

- Overviews of its permitting, administrative, and judicial review procedures

- An organizational chart showing the structure of the responsible agency

- An estimate of funding and its sources

COUNCIL OF STATE GOVERNMENTS MODEL LAWS

A useful document authored by the Council of State Governments is a model law for states to use when writing solid waste management and resource recovery incentive plans. Many of the aspects of this model would apply to any state environmental rule making. Key provisions are as follows:

- *Finding of necessity and declaration of purpose:* Typically, states point out the environmental damage caused by inefficient solid waste management and declare their intention to regulate procedures for storage, collection, and transportation of these wastes.

- *Powers and duties:* Duties and responsibilities should be assigned to ensure proper planning of the program.

- *Municipal responsibilities:* Municipalities may develop their own programs so long as they conform with state objectives; contiguous municipalities may want to enter into regional plans.

- *Permits:* States should develop a permit program to cover all solid waste management facilities, including recovery and recycling operations. Terms usually should be established for fees and permit renewal.

- *Inspection, notice, and hearings:* The law should include strong provisions to authorize inspection. The law may provide that any notice or order arising from an inspection be delivered in person or by certified mail. Hearing and appeals processes should be in place to prosecute these orders.

- *Penalties:* A schedule of fines and injunctive measures should be established to address violations of prohibited activities. Emergency powers to seize a violating facility may be granted to the director of the department charged with enforcement of the state's solid waste plan.

- *Solid waste transport:* States should not interpret their guidelines as permission to limit the flow of solid waste across municipal or state boundaries.

- *Incentive programs:* To encourage resource recovery, tax incentives are recommended. Suggested incentives include deductions for taxpayer expenditures for purchases of recovered resources, excluding home scrap. Furthermore, taxpayer deductions may be offered for the amortization of recovery or recycling facilities.

- *Advisory council:* It might be expedient to establish a Governor's Advisory Council on Solid Waste Management and Recycling to study the effects of existing public policies on recovery and recycling. The council might also recommend special studies and projects.

- *Impact statements:* Legislatures may direct municipalities to examine all ramifications of their solid waste management policies and report all actions that may significantly affect the state's ability to recover and recycle resources. An example of such conflict is that between resource recovery through combustion and resource recovery through recycling, because many recyclable materials also are good heat sources. For example, Arlington County, Virginia, collected newspapers for recycling until it went into partnership with neighboring Alexandria to incinerate waste, at which point the recycling program stopped. Under the 25 percent reduction requirement now undertaken by most states, including Virginia, the county undoubtedly must rethink its earlier decision.

AGENDA FOR ACTION

EPA's "The Solid Waste Dilemma: An Agenda for Action" was completed in February 1989 and has been in the process of update since that time. The goals and recommendations of the report are the result of the efforts of its Municipal Solid Waste Task Force, which gathered data on municipal waste and problems regarding its management, solicited input from many individuals and groups, and held public meetings. While quite lengthy, the report is repetitive and tends to emphasize the problems rather than identify solutions. Therefore, only the key aspects of the report's recommendations are discussed here.

Integrated Waste Management

The report recommends using "integrated waste management" systems to solve municipal waste generation and management problems at local, regional, and national levels. In this holistic approach, waste management systems are designed so that some or all of four options—source reduction, recycling, combustion, and landfills—are used to complement each other in a comprehensive plan. These options are not considered equally desirable, however. Instead, they are hierarchical, with source reduction (including reuse) considered the most desirable. As opposed to recycling, source reduction means an actual decrease in the volume and toxicity of raw materials and/or an increase of the useful life of products in order to reduce the volume and toxicity of waste. Recycling (including composting) is the next preferred waste management option, provided care is taken to avoid the transfer of risks from one medium to another. Finally, landfills and combustors must be part of any realistic plan but should be designed and managed to lower environmental and health risks substantially.

The original report supports EPA's stated goal of managing 25 percent of the nation's municipal solid waste through source reduction and recycling by 1992. A draft update released in August 1990 and scheduled for final action in 1991 speaks of a 10 percent waste reduction and a 40 percent national recycling goal to be reached by 1996. Critics of these projections asked the agency for more

Nonhazardous Solid Waste: Guidelines & Rules   61

documentation on successful state and industrial solid waste management plans. According to Bagus of EPA, such documentation would be included in the final report.

The original agenda also recognizes that this strategy leaves 75 percent of the waste in need of some other form of responsible management. Moreover, the report says, a similar hierarchy was recommended in an EPA position statement written in 1976 and has been incorporated in numerous state plans. Nevertheless, communities have been "overwhelmed by the burgeoning amounts of waste that must be removed from the curb every day," and most often have turned to the easiest option, landfill. As of the time the report was written, 80 percent of solid waste was land filled, 10 percent recycled, and 10 percent burned, sometimes for energy recovery.

As is shown later in this book, the scenario described in the agenda already is out of date. Most states now have waste management plans with muscle, strong waste reduction goals of 25 percent or more, and burgeoning recycling programs, including curbside pickup in community after community.

Progress in Agenda for Action Objectives

The report identifies six objectives, all of which call for EPA action as well as enthusiastic state response. The objectives, with some note of EPA's support so far, are as follows:

- Increase the waste planning and management information available to states, local communities, waste handlers, citizens, and industry and increase data collection for research and development. As part of this objective, EPA developed a manual on waste facility siting (discussed in Chapter 12) and has begun work on many other manuals. The agency notes that states and private associations also have a role to play in this process.

- Increase effective planning by waste handlers, local communities, and states. This is happening without much federal prodding. As waste handlers realize that communities are sincere in their recycling plans, they perceive an opportunity for profit. Many, if not most, municipal recycling plans rely on the services of major waste handlers.

- Increase source reduction activities by the manufacturing industry, government, and citizens (see Chapters 5 and 6).

- Increase recycling by government and by individual and corporate citizens. EPA has taken giant steps in this area, having set new procurement guidelines for federal agencies and businesses to use in purchasing recycled projects and established an information office to advise on supply and markets (see Chapter 8).

- Reduce risks from municipal solid waste combustion in order to protect human health and the environment. New source performance standards have been issued for municipal waste combustors and accompanying guidelines have been established for the updating of existing facilities (see Chapter 4).

- Reduce risks from landfills in order to protect human health and the environment. The agency's activities in this area are described elsewhere in this chapter and in Chapter 4.

National and Regional Recycling Councils

The report recommends that a national recycling council and regional councils be established to advise on all aspects of recycling and on U.S. as well as foreign markets. The national council has been formed (see Chapter 8). However, regional councils have not materialized and are not planned, according to Edgar Miller, a spokesperson for the Recycling Advisory Council.

COSTS OF SOLID WASTE MANAGEMENT

According to OTA, solid waste costs still represent a relatively small portion of most municipal budgets and an even smaller portion of the average family's budget. In a survey of 41 cities, the office found municipal solid waste budgets ranging from 0.1 percent to 19.2 percent and averaging 5 percent of total budget costs. On the basis of these data, annual per person expenditures on solid waste management range from $6 to $130 and average about $60. Thus, the average family spends less than 1 percent of its income on this item.

It is not surprising, therefore, that this budget item has received little attention in the past, the OTA report observes. Only about half of the survey respondents charged fees directly related to trash disposal costs, while the rest paid the garbage bill out of general revenues, bond funds, grants, or some combination of these, thereby obscuring waste costs within the budget.

Significantly, only 8 of the 19 respondents with curbside recycling programs had cost information on the program; only 11 percent even knew how much material was being recovered. Better information is essential to the kind of integrated management system envisioned by the Agenda for Action described above.

Computer Model

In order to supply better cost data on all of the municipal solid waste management options, OTA contracted with Energy Systems Research Group, Inc. (now Tellus, Inc.), to develop a computer model. The program calculates the costs under a variety of different demographic and economic situations but does not determine the most desirable system configuration. Therefore, OTA has not used the model to furnish comparisons of the costs of different management methods. Instead, it uses the model to show the effects of changing key parameters on system costs. All costs are reported in 1988 dollars unless otherwise stated. The model's base case assumptions are as follows:

- A municipality with a population of 500,000.

- Seventy-five percent of the population lives in single-family housing.

- Residential waste generation is 2.4 pounds per person.

- Commercial waste generation is 1.2 pounds per person.

- Commercial collection is paid for by commercial generators.

- All facilities are designed to accommodate commercial waste.

The landfill is state of the art, with leachate and methane collection systems, liner systems, and monitoring wells. Land costs are relatively low at $1,500 per acre, and transport distance from collection point to the landfill averages 15 miles. The cost includes closure and postclosure expenses.

The incinerator uses advanced pollution control methods, including a wet scrubber and baghouse, and generates electricity, which is sold at a rate of $.06 per kilowatt hour. Ash is disposed of in a monofill with a double composite liner system and a leachate collection system. The incinerator produces ash equal to 23 percent by weight of the waste burned. Residential wastes not sent to the incinerator include major appliances, tree stumps, and tires, which are sent to the landfill.

Results from the model indicate that a variety of factors can have quite an impact on the overall costs of solid waste management. For instance, if existing landfill costs are relatively low, system costs increase when additional management alternatives are added. Under the model's assumptions, waste-to-energy incineration increases costs by a larger percentage than do recycling programs. When landfill costs are extremely high, on the other hand, the addition of alternative management methods such as recycling and composting can reduce overall costs.

The model highlights the importance of paying close attention to every cost element of the municipal solid waste management system, according to OTA. The more complex the system, the more important it is to monitor each cost component carefully.

Landfills: The Most Prevalent Option

Thirteen of OTA's survey respondents depended exclusively on landfills for garbage disposal. These respondents also had relatively low disposal costs, ranging from $6 to $44. Landfill operating costs ranged from less than $3 to about $40 per ton. The most expensive costs were attributed to a landfill with very modern technology. The landfill is equipped with a triple liner system, leachate collection systems, and monitoring wells.

Using the model, OTA learned that in a landfill-only scenario for the hypothetical city described above, the total cost of collection and disposal would be $58 per ton, $18 of which is accounted for by landfill disposal costs. By contrast, if the municipality landfill had no pollution-control features, the disposal costs would have decreased by $10. Addition of a transfer station and a 50-mile transport distance to a regional landfill would boost costs by $20, however. Hence, the model showed that transportation and management costs could easily be a greater burden than incorporation of pollution controls into a facility's design.

Collection costs also make a difference in calculating landfill per-ton costs. According to the model, the costs of collection per ton decrease with increases in density and with the amount of waste picked up at each stop.

Incineration

A look at incinerator cost data derived from the survey, the model, and information in the 1986-1987 *Resource Recovery Yearbook* (see Bibliography) sheds some doubt on the desirability of rushing into this method of garbage disposal, especially if landfill space is available and environmental problems are resolved.

Among the survey respondents, 12 communities incinerated between 6 percent and 90 percent of their waste. Detailed information on 10 of these sites showed that per capita waste management costs ranged from $21 to $82 and averaged $46. Total waste management costs per ton were available on only four facilities and ranged from $77 to $230 per ton. The share of these costs attributed to incinerators ranged from 17 percent to 55 percent. Operating costs at six facilities ranged from $18 to $50 per ton, while capital costs were from $3 million for a 72 tons-per-day (TPD) modular unit to $80 million for a 1,200 TPD mass burn incinerator. Tipping fees varied among the communities but averaged about $31 per ton. However, two communities said these rates would increase because of disappointing yields from sale of power.

Of the six communities that reported on such revenues, only the two newest incinerators generated electricity, whereas the others sold steam. Revenues from the sale of this energy averaged about $10 per ton of waste incinerated per day.

The amount of ash generated from these facilities ranged from 11 percent to 31 percent by weight of waste burned, and averaged 20 percent. Ash disposal costs at three incinerators varied widely, from $4.50 to $49.00 per ton.

OTA found that the costs reported in its survey were comparable to other published data. The 1986-1987 *Resource Recovery Yearbook* reported adjusted capital costs (in 1986 dollars) of advanced-planned and existing incinerators ranging from $250,000 to $429 million and averaging $58 million. Capital costs of small modular plants were reported as below $10 million; average operating and maintenance costs were $22 per ton, within the range of the survey results.

Exercises with the model lead to two noteworthy conclusions:

- The economics of resource recovery facilities are highly sensitive to changes in revenues from selling electricity. Using the base case described above, the model showed that a reduction in revenues by half would increase costs of a hypothetical incinerator from $45 to $61 per ton of waste burned.

- Significant economies of scale do not exist for waste-to-energy facilities. The capital and operating cost per ton is relatively constant over a range of capacities. However, *running a plant below its operating capacity increases costs substantially*, because the fixed costs represent a large proportion of the total.

Recycling

The OTA survey revealed how difficult it is to gain consistent information on recycling costs and revenues as related to individual materials. One problem is that many communities contract the work out and do not receive details of transactions once the materials are picked up. The data that were reported showed a wild range in revenues, especially for aluminum. The range was from $12 per ton for aluminum mixed with glass (paid by an intermediate processor) to $1,075 per ton for separated aluminum collected at curbside, to $1,300 per ton for aluminum sold by a drop-off center, to a projected $1,340 per ton for commingled aluminum processed at an intermediate processing facility. Similarly, flint glass revenues from drop-off programs varied from $20 to $60 per ton.

OTA used the model to derive costs and revenues under several variables. In all instances, the greatest influences on costs include the time required for a fully loaded vehicle to unload and return to the collection route, the number of pickups the vehicle can make during a given time period, the overall participation rate, and the revenue from sales. Variables studied included curbside collection of separated and commingled materials, the effect of beverage container deposits on the profitability of residential recycling, the economics of marketing yard waste as compost, and the economics of recycling and composting in a community with high landfill costs. Details of these findings are shown in the *Resource Recovery Yearbook*.

Tellus maintains the copyright on this model and is marketing a license to use the software package for $20,000 (1990 dollars). According to Tellus's John Schall, the system is the most sophisticated model for states to use in developing comprehensive solid waste management plans. Using the training materials provided, states and communities can weigh the effects of various waste management options with a high degree of precision. The company conducts workshops and designs customized default data systems for its clients. Delaware, Illinois, Maine, Michigan, New York, New York City, and Ventura County, California, have purchased licenses to use the Tellus system. The company can be reached as follows:

> Tellus Inc.
> 89 Broad St.
> Boston, MA 02110
> (617) 426-5844

RISK ASSESSMENT

Risk assessment has been an important aspect of environmental regulatory development during the Reagan/Bush era. An inexact science that is only as accurate as the data fed into EPA's and other models, risk assessment is always controversial, with good reason. As discussed below, the available information on emissions from various facilities often is sparse. Moreover, agreement on the effects of exposure to many of the pollutants is far from complete. Finally, pollutants enter through various pathways, with different attendant risks that are not well understood.

Comparative Risks

In a discussion of the comparative risks of solid waste management facilities, OTA emphasizes the difficulty of making such assessments. Some risks are present any time waste is generated or handled, the research office claims. Some risks are created when the organic portion of waste, for instance yard wastes, paper, and plastics, is processed, burned, or decomposed. Others stem from the metals and organic chemicals contained in products discarded in hazardous household waste, including solvents, paints, batteries, and cleansers. According to OTA, industrial waste also contributes metals and organic chemicals, and after these substances are discarded they pose risks in any management activity, land filling, incineration, or recycling.

OTA concedes that there are common sense aspects of risk assessment. Plainly, well controlled waste-to-energy facilities pose much lower risks than outdated, uncontrolled combustors. Similarly, when materials are recycled, often many times, they reduce risks during production and during disposal.

It may be worth noting that the EPA and OTA analyses view risks purely from a health-related viewpoint. However, the manager carrying out risk-related decisions also might want to examine how various waste management options reduce the risk of liability. For instance, the health-related risk of incineration may be greater than the risk entailed in biological treatment and ultimate land disposal at a distant site. However, the financial risk of moving the waste to a transfer station, then to the treatment facility, and finally to a disposal site might well be higher, especially if more than one company handles the waste. Keeping in mind that RCRA imposes on generators a cradle-to-grave responsibility for hazardous waste, generators may prefer to incinerate waste on-site rather than risk what may happen to it elsewhere.

Risks from Landfills

As described in Chapter 10, the proposed regulation affecting municipal solid waste landfills calls on states and/or communities to decide what risks they are willing to accept from neighboring facilities.

To determine these risks, EPA uses a model to predict the release, transport, fate, and impacts of eight pollutants, including vinyl chloride, tetrachloroethane, and methylene chloride, found in landfill leachate. The variables accounted for in the model are the distance to the nearest down-gradient well, infiltration rate, landfill size, and aquifer characteristics. The model estimates that 5.5 percent of existing municipal solid waste landfills pose a lifetime cancer risk of one person out of every 10,000 to 100,000 people, while 11.6 percent pose lifetime risks of one person out of every 100,000 to 10 million people. As discussed below, the water-related risks even from older landfills are lower than those posed by air emissions from incinerators.

This model has been criticized as either underestimating risks or overestimating them, depending on the critic. EPA refined its model on the basis of these comments. According to OTA, however, estimating risks at landfills is frustrated by lack of groundwater monitoring data. Only 25 percent of all municipal solid waste landfill operators monitored groundwater in 1986.

This lack of data is alarming, according to OTA, because down-gradient drinking water wells exist within one mile of some *46 percent* of all such landfills. Even though the data are sparse, 100 potentially harmful substances have been identified in landfill leachate, according to an EPA report to Congress *(Solid Waste Disposal in the United States, Vol. 11,* EPA/530-SW-88-011B). EPA identified 135 out of a sampling of 163 landfills that constitute a threat to human health or the environment because of their potential for groundwater contamination, according to the report. The agency also made the startling finding that there are 184 municipal solid waste landfills on the National Priorities List under Superfund, most of which have caused groundwater contamination.

Incinerator Risks

Well-designed, modern waste-to-energy facilities are far less risky than older combustors, experts agree. Moreover, most new facilities emit even smaller amounts of an array of air pollutants than allowed by their permits. EPA has determined that the ideal control combination is a scrubber/filter system because it appears to remove particles (with attached pollutants) more efficiently than an electrostatic precipitator (ESP) combination. The agency concedes, however, that large three- or four-field ESPs work very well. Because large incinerators are small power plants, many operators think electrically and therefore favor ESPs.

In a series of waste combustion studies, EPA reached the following conclusions concerning risks of individual pollutants from incinerators:

- *Dioxins and furans*: The risks from airborne dioxins and furans are one or two magnitudes greater than the risks of cadmium, the second most worrisome pollutant. EPA's most shocking finding concerns emissions from older incinerators, which often are located in cities with large populations. EPA estimated that anywhere from 2 to 40 additional cancers per year occur in populations exposed to emissions of dioxins and furans from all existing incinerators. At the time these studies were completed in 1987, the estimated individual lifetime cancer risk from all incinerators was one in 1,000 to 10,000 people, a level considered unacceptable by almost any yardstick. As seems always to be the case with risk assessments, these estimates have been faulted as being both too high and too low. Most notably, EPA's own Science Advisory Board took issue, noting that the estimates are based too heavily on older, poorly controlled units. While agreeing that newer incinerators are less risky, OTA charges that the older facilities continue to pose high risks; moreover, questions remain as to whether low emissions from newer facilities can be sustained over long periods of time.

- *Metals:* The carcinogenic metals emitted from incinerators include antimony, arsenic, beryllium, cadmium, chromium, and nickel. Mercury and lead emissions cause other well-known health problems of equal concern. Few studies examine the total risks of these pollutants through all passageways. Focusing on inhalation, EPA es-

Nonhazardous Solid Waste: Guidelines & Rules 71

timated that arsenic, beryllium, cadmium, and chromium emissions might cause up to 0.5 additional cancers each year from existing facilities and 0.4 additional cancers from those proposed as of 1987. These projections might be a little out of date. A record number of new facilities went on line in 1990 and only a slightly lower number were slated for 1991. As suggested above, the most important risk-related issue regarding new incinerators is whether they allow older units to be shut down.

- *Acid gases:* EPA also examined the potential of hydrochloric acid gases to corrode metals. Emissions from poorly controlled existing incinerators do pose problems; however, proposed mass burn and refuse-derived fuel units would be equipped to reduce these emissions by about 90 percent, the agency found.

Technical information on how to control these risks from incinerators is found in Chapters 5 and 11.

Chapter 4

STATE WASTE MANAGEMENT PROGRAMS

While an understanding of federal regulations, guidelines, and advisory material is essential to responsible waste management, one's perspective would be incomplete without a grasp of individual states' programs. In the matter of solid waste particularly, states traditionally have had a great deal of autonomy. Even as the federal government exerts a stronger presence in this area, states and communities have important roles to play because they must carry out programs that are increasingly complex and technical.

Similarly, the states all manage their own programs governing infectious waste, business or so-called "special waste," and, to one extent or another, hazardous waste. In the case of hazardous waste, state rules must be at least as stringent as those issued by the federal Environmental Protection Agency (EPA), as described later in this chapter. Most states go beyond this minimum and add provisions covering matters of particular concern. Typical changes concern definitions of waste or of small-quantity generators and the frequency of reporting. Other states, struggling with inadequate budgets for environmental matters, leave at least some responsibility for these rules with EPA.

This chapter includes a discussion of trends in state waste management. More detailed information on state programs is found in BNA's *Guide to State Environmental Programs, Second Edition* (see Bibliography) and in BNA's *Environment Reporter.*

SOLID WASTE MANAGEMENT

As noted above, in the 1970s and early 1980s the states were given considerable flexibility in how they would craft solid waste management plans. Because federal funding was severely limited and EPA's attention was riveted to hazardous waste, state plans were neglected. Those states that perceived the necessity developed very comprehensive plans; those with fewer problems developed none. With EPA's proposals for more stringent technical requirements at landfills and for a 25 percent reduction of waste sent to a new incinerator, states have burst forth with new plans, dedicated especially to an increase in recycling and a reexamination of all aspects of waste management. Several states also adopted moratoriums on landfill development. Details on this trend follow.

New State Solid Waste Management Plans

State comprehensive recycling laws proliferated in 1990 and public acceptance of such laws increased, according to two special reports released in mid-1990 by the National Solid Wastes Management Association (NSWMA), as well as information from other sources.

In the report *Recycling in the States*, NSWMA revealed that 65 recycling laws were enacted in at least 27 states during the first five months of 1990. Thirty states and the District of Columbia were found by NSWMA to have comprehensive laws that require detailed statewide recycling plans and/or separation of recyclables as well as contain one or more other provisions to stimulate waste reduction. Notably, even those states with ample land and affordable tipping fees have entered into the spirit of waste reduction with strong recycling programs.

Market development efforts also are being made to support the flurry of recycling mandates, according to the report. Several states revised their government procurement programs to require purchase of recycled materials, extend tax credits to businesses that manufacture products from secondary materials, or require industries to use such materials. In keeping with the new federal emphasis on pollution prevention, there were also laws reducing the toxicity of packaging; managing problem wastes such as batteries, tires, and used oil; and developing waste reduction and recycling programs at businesses.

As a means of institutionalizing recycling statewide, comprehensive laws commonly include a recycling goal, grants to help communities establish programs, education protocols, and market development incentives. The following summaries of 1990 comprehensive recycling laws show these trends:

- *Arizona*: A new law, passed at the end of its 1990 legislative session, depends on market development as a means to stimulate recycling. Most notably, the law requires recycled content in newsprint; because the two largest newspapers in the state, the *Arizona Republic* and the *Arizona Gazette*, already use recycled newsprint for 40 percent of their paper, this provision passed easily. The law does not require recycling or specify a recycling goal. Instead, it establishes a recycling fund, supported by a 25-cent-per-ton tipping fee surcharge at landfills across the state. That money will fund grants to municipal recycling programs, research and development, and public education.

- *Georgia:* Typical of many state laws, the Georgia Comprehensive Solid Waste Management Act aims to reduce municipal solid waste disposal by 25 percent of 1992 per capita waste amounts by July 1, 1996. The law also calls for a new state waste management plan for counties to use in modeling their own plans. After July 1992 counties may not transport waste into other counties or receive state money for new solid waste facilities unless they are at work on a recycling plan. The law also provides for plastic bottle coding, state procurement of recycled goods, and battery recycling.

- *Indiana:* This state law aims to reduce the amount of waste incinerated or placed in a landfill by 35 percent by January 1, 1996, and 50 percent by that date in 2001. Both state and local waste management plans must include provisions for recycling and restrictions on the disposal of recyclables. The law also creates a fund to assist businesses that either convert recyclable material into useful products or help create recycling markets.

- *New Mexico:* This state's law, new in 1990, mandates detailed planning for improved waste management and sets goals for reduction of waste disposal of 25 percent by July 1, 1995, and 50 percent by July 1, 2000. The state regulatory board must adopt regulations to establish source reduction and recycling programs to meet these goals. The law authorizes municipalities to tax businesses to help finance waste management programs.

- *Oklahoma:* The law mandates preparation of a detailed waste management plan, to include waste reduction goals, by July 1, 1993. The State Department of Health must offer technical assistance for recycling, create a secondary materials market database, conduct public education programs, and carry out studies. A small annual generator fee will help fund the program.

- *Oregon:* An environmental leader in many respects, Oregon has had a statewide recycling plan since 1983 and in 1990 reported a 22 percent to 25 percent recycling rate, the highest in the United States. The state also has a comprehensive plan to regulate the disposal of used tires that includes a waste tire recycling account to help reimburse businesses for using waste tires and to fund cleanup of existing tire piles. To reduce the use of toxic materials and the generation of hazardous waste by business, the state has one of very few state-level mandatory waste reduction requirements. The act covers large users of toxic chemicals that are required to report under the Superfund Amendments and Reauthorization Act's (SARA) Title III as well as hazardous waste generators.

  However, an initiative designed to develop markets for recycled materials failed at the polls November 6, 1990. The measure would have required that packaging of products sold in Oregon meet one of three standards—that there be a recycling market for the material, that the packaging be made of at least 50 percent recycled material, or that the package be reusable at least five times.

- *Washington:* Washington State's Hazardous Waste Reduction Act has a goal of reducing hazardous waste generation by 50 percent by 1995. The department is developing rules to implement the act. Generators must have reduction plans to include goals for reducing the use of hazardous substances and cutting the amount of wastes generated. Fee structures must be included in the rules to pay for the program.

- *Wisconsin:* Revisions to the state's 1983 recycling law mandate separation of recyclables from the waste stream. Aluminum cans, cardboard, polystyrene foam packaging, glass containers, magazines, newspaper, office paper, plastic containers, steel, bimetal containers, and waste tires are banned from landfills and, except for tires, from incinerators, unless communities are certified as having an effective recycling program. To qualify for such certification, communities must have source separation and collection programs or a central facility to process commingled recyclables from residences, commercial buildings, and businesses.

Kentucky's Stringent Rules

Kentucky's new solid waste rules demonstrate the degree to which some states have been willing to go beyond federal requirements in managing solid waste activities within their borders. The state's incinerator laws, for instance, require that 40 percent of the volume of wastes received at new facilities be recycled. This provision can be relaxed only if there is no market for the material or the material is potentially hazardous, such as waste from hospitals. According to John Nichols, deputy director of the Kentucky Cabinet for Natural Resources and Environmental Protection, this strict law is not intended to stifle construction of incinerators entirely but does send a clear signal that other forms of waste management are preferred. Nichols also stated that the federal EPA's failure to include a 25 percent recycling provision in its new regulations for such facilities will not change Kentucky's determination to promote recycling to the highest degree possible.

The new rule also sets very stringent air emissions limits for both new and existing incinerators, bars the burning of yard wastes or vehicle and household batteries in municipal incinerators, and removes an exemption that once applied to small incinerators used primarily at hospitals.

The state also has adopted new regulations for solid waste landfills that require that all units be equipped by 1992 with a 12-inch clay liner and by 1995 with a double synthetic liner, with clay between the synthetic membranes and a leachate collection system. The owners of nearly half of the state's 75 landfills have warned that they will be forced to shut down or severely limit their operations under the regulations. Nichols maintains that the rules are necessary, "both from a geologic view and a groundwater protection view." The state was not willing to wait for EPA to issue nationally applicable landfill rules (see Chapter 10).

Recycling Provisions Aimed at Business

Recycling often is touted as a way individuals can help lessen environmental burdens. However, state laws are beginning to aim at business as well, the NSWMA report notes. Maine, New Jersey, Pennsylvania, Rhode Island, Washington, and the District of Columbia require businesses to separate materials such as paper, glass, metals, and plastic from the general waste stream.

Many businesses already recycle to save money, according to the report. More than half of the 23 million tons of material recycled in 1988 was composed of corrugated boxes, office paper, and lead-acid batteries recovered from businesses. NSWMA recommends that communities, in developing their recycling plans, include in their planning numbers those materials that businesses already recycle, adding that municipalities also must help find new markets for those materials.

Interstate Movement of Solid Waste

On February 4, 1991, a committee of the National Governors' Association (NGA) requested, before the Environment and Senate Public Works Subcommittee on Environmental Protection, that states have autonomy in managing interstate transportation of solid wastes. Echoing the arguments concerning interstate transport of hazardous waste (see below), the NGA's Energy and Environment Committee said the Resource Conservation and Recovery Act (RCRA) should be amended to provide a limited waiver of the Commerce Clause of the U.S. Constitution to allow states to impose fees on out-of-state wastes. Governors of the western states, primarily, feel they have received more than their share of solid waste imports and would like some relief. Senator Max Baucus (D-Mont.), subcommittee chairman, said his committee was aware of their concerns and seeks some sort of "hierarchical solution," whereby the states would maintain control over their programs, including the right to ban importation from out of state.

At the same committee hearing, the governors chided EPA for delaying issuance of the landfill rules, noting that the uncertainty contributes to the waste export problem. For instance, according to New Jersey Governor Jim Florio, "the whole process is chaos," without federal standards upon which states can make rational decisions. As a result, he claimed, New Jersey has become a net exporter of solid waste.

TRENDS IN STATE HAZARDOUS WASTE PLANNING

A major task for the states since 1984 has been to amend their hazardous waste regulations to bring them in line with the amendments made to RCRA in that year. Because this process is time-consuming, many states still are operating under partially approved programs, whereby they administer the pre-1984 requirements while leaving the administration of at least some of the post-1984 amendments to EPA regional offices. Thus, it is important for firms to know the status of the regulatory scheme of each state in which they do business.

EPA's Rules for State Authorization (40 CFR 271)

After passage of the original RCRA in 1976, states were afforded the opportunity to seek authorization in two ways, as follows:

- Apply for interim authorization, which would indicate that their hazardous waste permitting program was in substantial accord with the federal rules. Once the interim program was approved, they could apply for final authorization.

- Apply for final authorization without undergoing all phases of the interim program.

As noted above, the 1984 amendments made substantial changes in the federal RCRA program, necessitating another round of submissions from the states. Again, they may achieve interim status, so long as they apply for final status by January 1, 1993. Such status allows states to develop in-place programs while holding federal intrusion to a minimum. Another attraction to interim authorization is that the procedures are shorter than those for final authorization. The application need not be complicated; although an attorney general's statement is required, little explanation is necessary so long as the state's legal authority is clear. Moreover, no public hearing is necessary before interim status applications may be filed.

Despite these attractions of interim status, EPA encourages states to apply for final status expeditiously. In fact, they may apply directly for final status if they so choose.

EPA's requirement that state laws be fully equivalent to and consistent with federal laws does not prevent states from adopting more stringent provisions of their own, as noted below. However, under the following conditions a state program is inconsistent, and therefore unacceptable:

- It prevents the free transport of hazardous waste into or out of the state. In other words, EPA would not approve aspects of states' rules that ban imports of hazardous waste.

- The program is not fully protective of human health and the environment. In other words, the permit programs and other environmentally protective aspects of the programs must be at least as stringent as EPA's.

- The state manifest system fails to meet federal requirements.

In deciding whether to approve a state program revision, EPA may either enter into the standard rule-making procedure, which entails proposal, a comment period, response to comments, and final issuance, or make an immediate final ruling. In either case, pertinent announcements are made in the *Federal Register.* The agency normally uses the longer procedure when authorizing major changes or numerous revisions or when disapproving a state provision, reserving the shorter method to situations where little controversy is likely to arise.

Variations in State Laws

As noted above, states also adapt their laws to suit special priorities. The most universal difference is in the frequency of the reporting requirement. Whereas the federal law mandates that reports be submitted every two years, most states require that reports be submitted annually or even semiannually. States claim they need this material to develop more responsible waste reduction programs, among other things.

Another important difference among states is how they structure their fees. For instance, most states are increasing their generator fees to encourage recycling and waste reduction. While these fees generally are highest in states with shortages of capacity, waste importing states also have begun to raise fees, mostly to demonstrate that they are not to be other states' waste bins. Alabama, site of the enormous Emelle treatment, storage, and disposal facility, has taken highly visible steps to notify the nation that it will no longer make it easy for out-of-state firms to dump within its borders. In April 1990 the state raised its previously low fees to $40 per ton for hazardous waste generated inside the state and $112 per ton for waste shipped in from outside. The state also adopted other controversial requirements, including a stipulation that hazardous waste may not be deposited in a landfill unless its content is approved 60 days prior to shipment. These and other Alabama laws have been challenged on constitutional grounds. Meanwhile, the higher fees have reduced the amount of waste shipped to Alabama.

In July 1990, Louisiana also boosted costs by increasing the rate of tax on hazardous waste disposal as well as imposing a new transportation tax. Companies that transport waste off-site for disposal in Louisiana now must pay a transportation tax levied at $25 per gross weight ton. The hazardous waste tax increased from $12 to $30 per dry weight ton for on-site disposal and from $27 to $100 for extremely hazardous waste. Outsiders must pay these rates or their own state's rates, whichever are higher.

Taking another route toward lowering its hazardous waste burden, South Carolina, on June 13, 1990, limited imports of hazardous waste from 135 tons in 1990 to 110 tons by July 1, 1991. The state has one of only two comprehensive facilities in the Southeast.

South Carolina took this step because the North Carolina Council of State rejected a site that had been proposed for a regional hazardous waste incinerator (see Chapter 13). The rejection meant that the state could not meet the January 1, 1991, deadline for initiating a permit to construct a hazardous waste facility, as required by the Southeast hazardous waste compact made as part of the regional capacity assurance plan (CAP) noted below.

However, on January 11, 1991, the U.S. District Court for South Carolina struck this provision down, along with other provisions banning or limiting waste from other states. Federal District Judge Matthew J. Perry held that such provisions violate the Commerce Clause of the U.S. Constitution and are counter to the public interest, which "is best served when unconstitutional laws are enjoined" *(Hazardous Waste Treatment Council v. South Carolina*, DC SC, No. 3:90-1402-0, 1/11/91). Two weeks earlier a federal judge threw out a similar Indiana law, also on constitutional grounds. Alabama's bans, which apply not only to North Carolina but also to many other states without approved CAPs (see below), also have been found to be unconstitutional.

Richard Fortuna, executive director of the Hazardous Waste Treatment Council, lauded the South Carolina court's ruling, noting that the decision "ensures that those seeking proper treatment of hazardous waste, wherever they are located, have access to well-operated commercial treatment and disposal facilities in South Carolina."

Importing States: A Mutual Stand

In a show of mutual support, environmental regulatory officials from 13 waste importing states agreed, on September 12, 1990, to form an association to promote responsible waste management. The move came at a meeting sponsored by the Alabama Department of Environmental Management (ADEM) and the South Carolina Department of Health and Environmental Control. The states involved, in addition to Alabama and South Carolina, are California, Illinois, Indiana, Louisiana, Michigan, Nevada, New York, Ohio, Oklahoma, Texas, and Utah. The group meets regularly to discuss matters of mutual interest but does not have an executive director or offices. The ADEM acts as the principal coordinator. The association's goals are as follows:

- Promote development of a responsible national waste management strategy to protect public health and the environment while equitably sharing the burden for waste management

- Influence congressional action in the upcoming reauthorization of federal Superfund and hazardous waste legislation to include a more equitable system for responsible management of hazardous waste

- Explore development of CAPS to include only states demonstrating responsible waste management

- Evaluate legal options of states to require EPA to enforce CAP requirements effectively

- Share legal and technical resources and information

- Develop effective waste minimization programs

In promoting the association, Alabama Governor Guy Hunt (R) said the group believes EPA is approving CAPs for states that have not demonstrated a willingness to be part of the solution. Moreover, as noted above, restraints of the Commerce Clause are preventing states from taking initiatives to promote better compliance.

Hazardous Waste Movement

According to an NSWMA study released on February 1, 1991, even the net-importing states export some portion of their hazardous waste burden. In fact, the study found that all states send out some hazardous waste. In addition, all except Alaska and Montana receive waste from elsewhere. "An extensive network of interdependence has developed among states," according to Allen Moore, president of NSWMA, adding that interruption of this flow through bans or similar measures "would have serious environmental and economic consequences."

Using 1987 figures, the study found that Ohio imported the most waste for management—480,671 tons. Indiana, Louisiana, and Illinois were the next three largest importers. Pennsylvania also imported large quantities, some 241,806 tons, but exported even more, about 334,600 tons, to other jurisdictions. Texas and Georgia were the top two hazardous waste generating states in 1987, according to the report; they managed within their borders nearly the same amount of waste, but not necessarily the same waste, that they generated.

The report (see Bibliography) is based on data submitted for state CAPs. Copies are available for $35 from NSWMA, listed under the heading Associations in Appendix A.

Capacity Assurance Plans

The efforts on the part of importing states to make other states accountable for their own hazardous waste are supported by the Superfund Amendments and Reauthorization Act of 1986 (SARA). Under this act, states are required to show that they have the capacity through 2009 to store, treat, and dispose of hazardous waste. States that lack facilities within their borders may meet the requirement by entering into regional agreements with others, but only if the agreements are valid representations of combined capacity. SARA provides that states without an adequate plan be deprived of federal Superfund cleanup funds.

The states were slow in formulating these plans. Moreover, EPA has been accused by certain importing states of accepting inadequate plans. In fact, an internal memorandum circulated by the agency on October 17, 1989, set forth provisions whereby state plans could be approved provisionally, in effect allowing them more time to achieve a convincing demonstration of capacity as required by the law. Representing Alabama's position in this matter, Governor Guy Hunt has said on more than one occasion that EPA must enforce the capacity assurance provisions by, among other things, removing variances from treatment, insisting on waste minimization, and enforcing its own Superfund rules.

Notably, virtually all of the states have linked with others in their respective regions to form cooperative plans. Some of these alliances were expedient at best, according to Karen Lumino, CAP coordinator for EPA's Region V in Chicago. The allegiances "should not be viewed as etched in stone," she added, noting that in 1993 all of the existing plans will undergo a thorough review as to their adequacy. Even before that time, events may disturb seemingly viable compacts, she explained. A landfill counted on as one state's contribution could conceivably close as the result of a compliance action, she said. Or, as already has happened in North Carolina, an envisioned new site may not materialize. In such cases, new alliances may form, Lumino said.

In a paper describing North Carolina's problems, Linda W. Little, executive director of that state's Waste Management Board, said the CAP requirement exacerbated the already festering battle between "have states" (those with excess capacity) and "have not states," which traditionally exported hazardous wastes to the "haves."

"Until Congress, EPA, and/or the courts resolve the meaning of 'capacity assurance,' 'sanctions,' and 'regional agreement,' the civil war will rage on," Little said, "and neither states, generators, nor waste management companies will be able to plan with any certainty how and where hazardous waste will be managed."

The following is a region-by-region showing of how the states have fared as of early 1991 in this mandated and, some might argue, ill-conceived aspect of long-range planning.

- *Regions I, II, and III:* All of the states in these three regions except New York participate in the Northeastern States Consortium, which has worked out a joint CAP. However, each state's plan also must be approved. Most, including New York, have conditionally approved plans that require further demonstration of certain elements. The most uniform shortfall is in future landfill and incineration capacity planning and in metals recovery capacity, according to James Reidy, CAP coordinator for Region II.

- *Region IV:* Alabama, North Carolina (out of favor, as described above), South Carolina, and Kentucky, which has a joint plan with Tennessee, have a cooperative plan. Florida, Georgia, and Mississippi lack plans or capacity. Florida has made strong efforts to site a facility but has been stymied by citizen opposition.

- *Region V:* All of the states in this region—Illinois, Indiana, Michigan, Minnesota, Ohio, and Wisconsin—participate in a joint plan. As is true just about everywhere, they operate under conditionally approved plans. The discrepancies are relatively minor, however. Indiana, Michigan, and Ohio need to assemble more data on exempt waste; all of the states except Ohio must provide information on mixed low-level waste; and all most continue to monitor capacity shortfall as a regional matter.

- *Region VI:* All of the states in this region, which includes Arkansas, Louisiana, Missouri, New Mexico, Oklahoma, and Texas, have pooled their resources to have a cooperative CAP. Taking all facilities into account, the region has an excess of capacity, according to Patricia Brechlin, CAP coordinator. Moreover, all of the states except Texas and Arkansas have fully approved plans, Brechlin said. These two states must provide more details concerning exempt treatment facilities and the disposal of mixed waste. The viability of this plan also may be affected by an emergency rule adopted February 6, 1991, by the Texas Water Commission, which suspended the processing of all new or pending permit applications for the treatment, storage, or disposal of either hazardous or nonhazardous solid waste. The action was at the request of Governor Ann Richards.

- *Region VII:* Nebraska, Iowa, and Kansas all have conditionally approved plans, in each case showing capacity shortfalls over the long term, according to Carl Blongren, CAP review team leader for the region. Missouri has not submitted an approvable plan and argues that the requirement is unconstitutional under the Commerce Clause, Blongren said.

- *Regions VIII, IX, and X:* The 13 states in these three regions have banded together in the Western Governors' Regional Agreement to demonstrate collective capacity to meet EPA's planning obligations. Their decision was predicated on the fact that in 1987 over 95 percent of the hazardous waste generated in the West stayed there, according to Rebecca Smith, information management specialist and CAP coordinator for Region IX. Each state must have its plan approved separately; as is the case elsewhere, all have either fully approved or conditionally approved plans except for Arizona, which has asked EPA to hold judgment on its plan until issues surrounding the permitting of a large hazardous waste treatment, storage, in the state have been resolved (see Chapter 13).

STATE TECHNICAL ASSISTANCE INITIATIVES

Most state environmental departments offer some amount of technical assistance to firms generating solid or hazardous waste. An increasing number of states go farther than just offering compliance advice. Almost all of the states also have contrived, either within the primary regulatory agency or, more typically, through some sort of partnership with associations and/or universities, to offer a wide range of technical assistance and research and development support, focusing usually on pollution prevention or recycling. Often projects carried out by these entities are supported at least in part by EPA through programs described in Chapter 6.

The following information, taken mostly from EPA's *Pollution Prevention Training Opportunities* manual (see Bibliography), is a brief summary of each state's program(s). A directory of state pollution prevention contacts is included in Appendix A.

- *Alabama:* The state's Waste Reduction and Technology Transfer Program (WRATT) is a joint effort of the Alabama Department of Environmental Management, Shoals, Inc. (a nonprofit business development group), and the Tennessee Valley Authority (TVA). As do several other states, Alabama uses retired engineers and executives to form teams that visit companies free of charge. According to Roy Nicholson of TVA, the waste reduction ideas supplied by the assessment teams typically save small businesses $4,000 to $5,000 and large corporations as much as $100,000 per year. The WRATT training team has helped Iowa, Kentucky, Mississippi, and South Carolina develop similar programs. The Alabama Business Council and the Alabama Department of Environmental Management also offer pollution prevention workshops through the Auburn

University Extension Service. The University of Alabama conducts workshops and continuing education programs.

- *Alaska:* The Alaska Department of Environmental Conservation conducts waste reduction workshops, on-site audits in rural communities, and industry-specific workshops. The Alaska Health Project conducts numerous seminars for business groups, trade associations, and local government committees.

- *Arkansas*: The state Department of Pollution Control and Ecology's small-quantity generator program conducts waste minimization seminars for small companies.

- *California:* The state Department of Health Services provides training for its permit writers and compliance inspectors on pollution prevention alternatives. Continuing education also is available through several branches of the University of California.

- *Connecticut:* The Connecticut Department of Environmental Protection and the state Hazardous Waste Management Service cosponsor annual hazardous waste management and minimization training conferences. Waterbury State Technical College also offers such courses.

- *Florida:* The Department of Environmental Regulation used retired engineers to assist in a survey of industries to learn their waste reduction efforts and to track results. The department offers assistance in the preparation of waste reduction assessments and in turn asks for industry support. The new waste reduction assistance program is nonregulatory, according to program manager Janeth A. Campbell. The program includes, among other things, technical assistance, research and demonstration, incentives for pollution prevention, and awards for excellence in pollution prevention. Small businesses such as automobile repair and transportation services, dry cleaning, and boat building and repair are targeted by this service.

- *Georgia:* This state's Environmental Protection Division trains its inspectors in pollution prevention. The Georgia Tech Research Institute conducts workshops on the subject.

- *Idaho:* Idaho and U.S. EPA Region X conducted several workshops in 1989 and 1990 to educate industry about pollution prevention options. The Hazardous Materials Bureau also holds in-house awareness programs.

- *Illinois:* The Illinois Hazardous Waste Research and Information Center conducts workshops for trade groups as well as helps firms coordinate internal and company-wide pollution prevention plans.

- *Indiana:* This state's Department of Environmental Management's Office of Technical Assistance conducts industry-specific workshops and refers firms to qualified consultants.

- *Kansas:* In cooperation with the state Department of Health and Environment, the University of Kansas offers hazardous waste regulatory training conferences that include discussions on waste minimization, regulatory compliance, and technology transfer. The university also offers a hazardous waste engineering seminar that focuses on pollution prevention.

- *Kentucky:* KENTUCKY PARTNERS, operated out of the University of Louisville, makes information about a wide range of waste management and waste reduction techniques available to all generators. The state Waste Management Division has obtained more than $600,000 in two grants from EPA to supply free waste reduction audits to state industries on a priority need basis. This program also is coordinated by the KENTUCKY PARTNERS staff.

- *Massachusetts:* The Massachusetts Department of Environmental Management includes waste reduction workshops in its public outreach program. It also is the site of the Blackstone Project, described in Chapter VI, which is a project designed to test the best approach to promoting toxics use reduction.

- *Michigan:* The Office of Waste Reduction Services provides pollution prevention audit training for public employees and private companies.

- *Minnesota:* The Minnesota Pollution Control Agency conducts workshops. A technical assistance program operated out of the University of Minnesota also conducts workshops on pollution prevention opportunities.

- *Mississippi:* The Department of Environmental Quality and Mississippi State University's Department of Chemical Engineering and

Department of Home Economics have teamed up to provide technology transfer and technical assistance to Mississippi industries, businesses, municipalities, and residents. By mid-1990, technical assistance projects had been initiated with 16 companies. The state started a companion program to reduce the generation of solid waste. This program includes a computerized waste exchange covering materials such as plastic and rubber, solvents, and oils.

- *Montana:* Upon request, the Solid and Hazardous Waste Bureau will instruct facilities on how to conduct their own waste audits.

- *New Jersey:* The Hazardous Waste Advisement Program provides pollution prevention audit training for its inspectors. The state also contracted with the New Jersey Institute of Technology to conduct an assessment of reduction and recycling opportunities for hazardous waste (ARROW). Furthermore, the Hazardous Waste Division has launched numerous publications on waste management.

- *New York:* The state Department of Environmental Conservation is sponsoring, between 1989 and 1992, a series of 20 workshops for small-quantity generators and medium- and large-quantity generators separately. These are general workshops that include information on pollution prevention.

- *North Carolina:* This state's Pollution Prevention Pays program was the first in the nation and has served as a model for other states, according to state environmental officials. The program provides advice and shared funding to industry and local governments to promote the prevention, reduction, or recycling of wastes before they become pollutants. Many of its programs are managed in conjunction with North Carolina State University and the EPA Research Center for Waste Minimization and Management, also at the university. In 1986 alone, some 55 state industries realized an annualized savings of almost $14 million through waste reduction, program records show.

- *Ohio:* The Ohio Technology Transfer Organization conducts waste reduction sessions on industry-specific waste minimization ideas. It focuses on small- and medium-sized businesses.

- *Oregon:* The state's toxics use and hazardous waste reduction program (HWRP) is one of very few statewide mandatory waste reduction schemes. Created under law (H.B. 3515), the program aims to achieve in-plant changes that reduce, avoid, or eliminate the use of materials that generate toxic pollution or hazardous waste. Firms must develop toxics use and hazardous waste reduction plans as mandated in the law. The program also sponsors workshops on subjects such as developing waste reduction plans and how to conduct audits. HWRP has collaborated with the state university to encourage the inclusion of waste reduction technologies in its engineering curriculum.

- *Pennsylvania:* The state's Waste Minimization Award program, begun in 1987, recognizes outstanding efforts to reduce waste. To support this program, the Waste Management Bureau has hired staff to aid industry and offers financial help to similar efforts by university experts. The state also notes that U.S. EPA Region III trains state enforcement and permitting personnel on pollution prevention auditing.

- *Rhode Island:* This state's commercial recycling regulations require all businesses to separate recyclable materials from their waste. The state's hazardous waste reduction program provides technical assistance for businesses that use hazardous materials in production processes that generate hazardous waste.

- *Tennessee:* The University of Tennessee Center for Industrial Services and TVA offer a waste reduction assessment training program that includes a waste audit course, a comprehensive training manual (see Bibliography), and interactive video training modules. Targets include industry, U.S. EPA, and other regulatory personnel.

- *Texas:* The Texas Water Commission has an expressed goal of reducing hazardous waste generation in half by 1995. Among tactics that might be used are a waiver of the sales tax on waste prevention equipment and tax credits and other financial incentives for waste reduction. Texas Tech University has incorporated pollution prevention concepts into existing engineering courses.

- *Vermont:* The Hazardous Waste Division has taken several steps to encourage responsible waste management, among others the publication of a newsletter on hazardous waste reduction.

- *Washington:* The state's waste reduction and recycling programs are supported by two companion tax provisions, the Washington Hazardous Substances Tax Act and the Washington Model Toxics

Control Act. The state also has teamed with EPA Region X to produce workshops on pollution prevention options. The 1990 series focused on electroplaters, metal finishers, print shops, dry cleaners, and auto service and repair shops.

- *West Virginia:* The state's Waste Management Division operates a small-quantity generator's assistance program to advise and educate these generators.

- *Wisconsin:* The University of Wisconsin in Madison offers intensive, short courses on waste minimization, environmental audits and compliance, and many other topics concerning waste management. The university's extensions also offer workshops. The state Department of Natural Resources uses a cross-media approach toward permitting and has a strong bias toward waste reduction. To aid in the facility siting process, the state furnishes grants for community representatives to hire their own technical consultants. These consultants aid in communication about risks.

- *Wyoming:* The Department of Environmental Quality conducts a course called "Hazardous Help" that specifically aims at vehicle maintenance facilities. The state has used much of its waste management budget in recent years to develop a more comprehensive overall program.

POLLUTION PREVENTION LAWS

According to a report compiled by the National Environmental Law Center, the Center for Policy Alternatives, and the U.S. Public Interest Research Group (PIRG), 17 pollution prevention laws have been passed by states within the past two years. Among these, the report finds Massachusetts to have the most effective law, known as the Massachusetts Toxics Use Reduction Act. Carolyn Hartmann, an environmental attorney with U.S. PIRG, said the Massachusetts law requires large users of toxic chemicals to report in detail to the state on the amount of toxic chemicals they consume. The reportable chemicals are those listed under the Emergency Planning and Community Right-to-Know Act. The law also requires companies to develop plans for reducing their dependence on toxic chemicals and authorizes the state to give technical help in developing these plans (see below). The law sets a statewide goal of reducing by 50 percent the generation of toxic wastes by 1997, Hartmann said.

The other states with top-ranked laws include Oregon, Indiana, and Washington. Similar laws in California, Georgia, and Tennessee were given low ratings because they are too narrowly focused.

The report, *An Ounce of Toxic Pollution Prevention: Rating States' Toxics Use Reduction Laws,* may be purchased for $15 per copy from:
> U.S. Public Interest Research Group
> 215 Pennsylvania Ave., SE
> Washington, DC 20003
> (202) 546-9707

Chapter 5

AIR EMISSIONS FROM WASTE FACILITIES

With the Congress's and the Environmental Protection Agency's (EPA) heightened interest in examining the effect of pollution on all aspects of the environment, it may not be surprising to discover that many waste treatment, storage, and disposal facilities (TSDF) are subject to air pollution regulations under both the Clean Air Act (CAA) and the Resource Conservation and Recovery Act (RCRA). Some of these rules, for instance the RCRA provisions covering hazardous waste incinerators, have been in effect long enough for firms and state regulators to become accustomed to them. Other emerging rules governing organic compounds emissions from TSDFs are catching many regulators and firms off guard because they affect individually a multiplicity of sources that, until recently, were considered too minor an environmental menace to attract attention beyond plant boundaries.

This chapter describes these and other rules and proposed rules related to air emissions caused by waste management. Regardless of their legal underpinnings, the rules are as likely to be enforced by air regulatory personnel as by waste management staff.

CLEAN AIR ACT RULES

While the CAA is silent on the subject of waste per se, several regulations under that act include provisions dealing directly with waste management.

Municipal Waste Combustors (Subpart Ea 40 CFR 60)

The new source performance standard for municipal waste combustors, issued January 11, 1991, governs emissions from all such units constructed, reconstructed, or modified after December 20, 1989, the date on which the standard was proposed. Among the more controversial provisions of this proposal was a requirement that the waste stream prior to combustion be reduced by 25 percent by weight. However, this provision was dealt a death blow on December 19, 1990, when the President's Council on Competitiveness (see Preface) unanimously determined that the provision's benefits were not justified by the costs.

The crux of the council's decision was that a rigid recycling requirement does not belong in an air regulation. In fact, public comment ran nine to one against this method of encouraging recycling, according to administration sources. EPA was assured by the administration, however, that a recycling provision as part of a reauthorized RCRA would not be opposed, agency spokesperson David Cohen said, adding that an appeal to the president was not likely.

To control air emissions from combustors, the standard requires a combination of good waste management practices and technological reduction methods. More specifically, large incinerators must be equipped with spray dryers (dry scrubbers) followed by fabric filters (also known as baghouses) to reduce organics and control metals, particulate matter, and acid gas.

Nitrous oxide (NOx) emissions must be controlled using selective noncatalytic reduction, an add-on method of control entailing the injection of ammonia, urea, and/or other chemicals that reduce emissions by as much as 45 percent. Reduction using catalysts is an even more effective means of lowering NOx, but at higher costs. So far, this technology is used only in Japan, where some reduction of efficiency has been noted if the catalysts are "poisoned" by either metals or acid gas (technologies for controlling incinerator emissions are described in greater detail in Chapter 10).

Smaller incinerators (those that combust less than 250 tons per day) are expected to control organics by dry sorbent injection followed by an electrostatic precipitator or fabric filter to achieve additional control of organics as well as metals, particulates, and acid gas. These standards are numerical, however, and may be achieved through use of other technology or methods of combustion management, provided the method used is equally effective.

Existing Incinerator Guidelines

In conjunction with the new source performance standard for municipal incinerators, EPA proposed guidelines for states to follow in developing regulations for combustors burning more than 250 tons per day that were constructed before December 20, 1989. The states must adopt these guidelines within nine months after the standard is made final. However, EPA does not expect their full implementation until 1994, at which time some 100 existing incinerators will be either retrofitted or shut down.

The guidelines describe good combustion practices and how to control three classes of pollutants: organics (including dioxins and furans), metals, and gases. Combustors are divided into small, large, and regional categories for this purpose. The numerical standards governing each of these pollutant categories differ for each incinerator type (described in detail in BNA's *Air Pollution Control*). All such combustors must adhere to an emissions opacity standard of 10 percent (barely visible) and must be operated by trained personnel.

EPA expects the cost of this regulatory/guideline package to reach $170 million per year for new facilities and $302 million per year for existing facilities. In exchange, the agency expects that more than 200,000 tons of pollutants per year will be eliminated by 1994. Carol Kocheisen, counsel with the National League of Cities, said most local governments were happy with the new rules, noting that municipalities now can rest assured that their investments in incinerators will not jeopardize their citizens' health and welfare.

POINTER➤ As noted in Chapter 2, EPA has determined a need to develop a management scheme for handling and disposing of municipal waste combustor ash. The scheme would be developed under Subtitle D of RCRA and would entail the development of management standards for the treatment, transportation, storage, and recycling or reuse of municipal waste combustion ash.

Asbestos Waste Control (40 CFR 61, Subpart M)

The national emission standard for hazardous air pollutants (NESHAPS) for asbestos is an early example of cross-media regulation. Recognizing that air emissions do not end when asbestos is removed from a building site, the rule includes stringent provisions for the safe long-term disposal of asbestos waste.

Unless controlled by another effective means, emissions from asbestos waste material during collection, processing, packaging, incineration, transportation, disposal, or milling operations must be wetted so as to be invisible. Asbestos waste removed from control devices may be mixed with water to form a slurry.

All wet asbestos tailings must be sealed into leak-proof, clearly labeled containers before being transported to an appropriate site. As an alternative, the asbestos may be processed into nonfriable pellets before disposal.

Active or inactive asbestos waste disposal sites must be fenced and posted, as is the case for other hazardous waste land disposal facilities. Moreover, emissions from the facility must be invisible at all times. This may be accomplished through wetting, encapsulation, or petroleum-based dust suppression.

Benzene Waste Operations (40 CFR 61, Subpart FF)

The NESHAPS for benzene waste operations, effective for new facilities March 7, 1990, and for existing facilities March 7, 1992, created a stir because it requires what may be very expensive controls for some affected operations, especially in the coke industry. Because the rules cover wastewater containing benzene, adherence may be difficult if not impossible, according to some industry spokespersons.

These air pollution control rules apply to chemical plants; petroleum refineries; coke byproduct recovery plants; and treatment, storage, and disposal facilities that receive their waste. Briefly summarized, the rules require that tanks containing benzene waste, surface impoundments, containers, individual drain systems, and oil-water separators be equipped with covers and/or closed vent systems or their equivalent.

The rules apply to facilities at which the total annual benzene waste is more than 10 megagrams per year. The emissions must be removed or destroyed by a treatment process or wastewater treatment system that would reduce benzene levels to 10 parts per million by weight. The process must also remove 99 percent or more, on a mass basis, of the benzene from the waste stream. Before treatment, separate standards entailing covers and/or closed-vent systems must be met by all of the facilities named above.

Exempt from the rules are process off-gases, waste that is contained in a segregated stormwater sewer system, and in-process recycle streams such as intermediate and product distillation reflux streams. Details on this NESHAPS also are found in BNA's *Air Pollution Control* binder.

Uranium Mining (40 CFR 61, Subpart T)

Prior to December 15, 1989, the effective date of the NESHAPS governing radon emissions from uranium mines and mill tailings, spent uranium piles were licensed under Title II of the Uranium Mill Tailings Control Act of 1978, which made no mention of air emissions. Hence, some piles remained uncovered and emitted radon for decades, according to EPA. Even though some remedial action has been taken at some of the sites, the agency found, some piles would have remained uncovered for many more years without a limiting standard.

Included in the NESHAPS are a standard for mill tailings piles limiting air emissions of Radon-222 to 20 picocuries per square meter per second and a requirement that all waste piles be covered. The pile must meet this standard within two years of the time it ceases to be operational.

RCRA RULES GOVERNING AIR POLLUTION

EPA has developed several air pollution control rules under RCRA, most notably those governing emissions from hazardous waste incinerators and, more recently, TSDFs. As well, the agency used RCRA authority in the early 1970s to establish national guidelines for solid waste incinerators (described in Chapter 10) that focus on siting and health and safety issues with only a mention of air emissions, stating merely that such facilities must be in compliance with all applicable standards. The first national criteria for hazardous waste landfills also were nebulous, as described below.

Hazardous Waste Incinerators (40 CFR 264)

EPA has developed interim status and final permit rules for hazardous waste incinerators. Because virtually all such incinerators now are operating under final permits, only these provisions are noted here.

Operators of these facilities must draw up waste analysis plans demonstrating that the incinerator is capable of destroying specified waste feeds. They may burn only wastes specified in their permits and only under approved operating conditions, except during trial burns or under approved exemptions. EPA automatically exempts wastes from these rules if they contain no hazardous constituents and are hazardous only because they are ignitable, corrosive, or both. Some reactive wastes also are exempt.

Performance Standards

Hazardous waste incinerators must meet three technical performance standards to control air pollution, as follows:

- A destruction and removal efficiency (DRE) of 99.99 percent for each waste feed principal organic hazardous constituent (POHC), as identified on the permit. The DRE is determined for each constituent by dividing 100 percent of the difference between the POHC in the waste stream (Win) and the same waste in the exhaust (Wout) by Win.

$$\frac{(Win-Wout)}{Win}$$

- If the incinerator burns specified dioxins and furans, combustion efficiency must be 99.9999 percent for each designated POHC.

- Hydrogen chloride (HCL) emissions may not exceed the larger of either 1.8 kilograms per hour or 1 percent of the HCL in the stack gas before it enters any pollution control equipment. This applies only to hazardous waste incinerators that produce uncontrolled emissions of more than 1.8 kilograms per hour (four pounds per hour).

- Particulate matter emissions may not exceed 180 milligrams per dry standard cubic meter (0.08 grains per dry standard cubic foot), corrected for oxygen in accordance with prescribed formulas.

There also are numerous facility-specific conditions governing the operation of these incinerators. Among other things, the conditions require that steps be taken to eliminate fugitive (nonvented) air emissions and to ensure that no burning takes place except under design conditions. At a minimum, combustion temperature, waste feed rate, and gas velocity must be continuously monitored. To ensure complete combustion, carbon monoxide emissions also must be monitored.

The incinerator and associated equipment must be inspected daily for leaks, spills, fugitive emissions, and signs of tampering. The alarm system and emergency waste system must be inspected at least weekly unless such activity would restrict or upset operations, in which case this inspection may take place monthly.

POINTER▶ On April 27, 1990, EPA proposed to amend the incinerator standards to impose additional controls on emissions of metals and residual organic compounds. According to the October 1990 regulatory calendar, the rules should be final in mid-1991.

A further discussion of hazardous waste incinerators is included in Chapter 10.

Air Emissions from Landfills

The RCRA regulations governing hazardous waste landfills are overwhelmingly concerned with migration of poisons into the water supply. The rules give short shrift to air emissions control beyond specifying that if wind dispersal is likely, the landfill should be covered or otherwise managed so the hazardous waste is not carried into the air.

Solid waste landfills have received greater federal attention, however, primarily because open burning and spontaneous combustion have been problems at these facilities. Moreover, such landfills emit organic compounds that are precursors of ozone and may emit trace cancer-causing substances.

The current criteria governing these landfills, found in Part 257 of RCRA, prohibit the open burning of solid wastes with the exception that infrequent burning of agricultural or silvicultural waste, land-clearing debris, diseased trees, and debris resulting from emergency cleanups may occur. A proposed revision of Part 257 would create a new Part 258 to impose more stringent criteria on municipal solid waste landfills.

Studies of emissions from both municipal and industrial solid waste landfills are leading to further initiatives to control air emissions, as follows:

- In order to ascertain how great an air pollution problem exists at industrial landfills, EPA intends to solicit emissions data from industries. The agency also has signaled its intention to propose special rules for industrial landfills.

- The agency has announced its intention to propose a new source performance standard requiring that gas from new municipal landfills be captured. The agency also plans to issue guidelines for states to use in developing gaseous emissions standards for existing landfills.

POINTER▶ Gases emanating from landfills consist of about 50 percent methane, 50 percent carbon dioxide, and trace constituents of volatile organic compounds (VOC) and other toxic pollutants, including vinyl chloride, benzene, trichloroethylene, and methylene chloride. Gas emissions already must meet a safety standard that the methane concentration may not exceed 25 percent of the lower explosive limit within the facility or the lower explosive limit at the property boundary. An increasing number of large landfill operators are venting these gases for use as an energy source, thereby turning an emissions control requirement into an economic opportunity.

Air Emissions from Miscellaneous Waste Management Facilities

This broadly applicable package of final and proposed rules is an example of what comes from curing one environmental problem only to cause another, according to Kent C. Hustvedt, petroleum section chief for EPA's Office of Planning and Standards, who is responsible for their development. The September 1990 restriction on land disposal of all untreated hazardous waste has given rise to a spate of new waste treatment and recycling facilities, Hustvedt said at an EPA-sponsored workshop held in October 1990 in Atlanta. Without control, such facilities emit into the air a mixture of toxic organic pollutants that create a clear threat to human health, he asserted, estimating that they are responsible for some 12 percent of the organic compounds emitted by stationary facilities.

The rules are a three-phase affair, of which the first phase, covering total organics emissions from process vents and equipment leaks, was promulgated June 21, 1990. The other two phases are as follows:

- Total organics from tanks, surface impoundments, containers, and miscellaneous units, proposed July 22, 1991

- Individual constituent standards, as needed, to supplement the first two phases of regulation, still in the "early work group stage," which means *very* early, according to Hustvedt

The Phase I and Phase II rules are described here.

Process Vents (40 CFR Parts 264 and 265 AA)

The process vent standards limit organic air emissions at hazardous waste treatment, storage, and disposal facilities requiring a permit under Subtitle C of RCRA. They apply to process vents associated with distillation, fractionation, thin-film evaporation, solvent extraction, and air and steam stripping pretreatment facilities that manage hazardous wastes with 10 parts per million by weight or greater total organic concentration.

The rules require that emissions from these facilities be reduced to below 1.4 kilograms per hour (3 pounds per hour) and 2.8 megagrams per year (3.1 tons per year), or that they be controlled by 95 percent effective control equipment. The rules do not require use of any specific types of equipment or add-on control devices. However, condensers, carbon absorbers, incinerators, and flares have been demonstrated as available technologies for this purpose. The rules also require that control device operating parameters be continuously monitored.

Equipment Leak Standards (40 CFR 264, 265 BB)

This standard, modeled after CAA standards for benzene equipment leaks, synthetic organic chemical manufacturing facilities, petroleum refineries, and coke oven byproduct plants, covers leaks from pumps, valves, compressors, sampling connection systems, open-ended valves or lines, pressure-relief devices, flanges and other connectors, and closed-vent systems and control devices in hazardous VOC service. The affected equipment is found in destruction or recycling/recovery processes such as incineration, distillation, solvent extraction, steam stripping, and tank storage.

Just as is the case in the CAA standards noted above, the leak requirements apply only if the waste stream has a 10 percent or greater organic content. The control methods include equipment changes such as dual seals and closed tops and work practices to ensure that leaks greater than 10,000 parts per million are detected and repaired.

TSDF Controls: Phase II (40 CFR 264 and 265 CC)

The Phase II proposed regulations, which would control total VOC emissions from TSDF tanks, surface impoundments, containers, and certain miscellaneous units, in addition to making changes in the Phase I rules, will affect facilities at almost any plant that stores, treats, or disposes of any amount of hazardous organic waste. The rules apply to storage tanks, surface impoundments, waste containers, and miscellaneous units identified on a case-by-case basis. The standards are as follows:

- Storage tanks must be covered, with emissions vented to a control device. As an alternative, an external floating roof or a fixed roof with an internal floating roof, or work practices, may be substituted. Work practices may be employed to keep organic vapor pressure below certain limits or to manage waste in a "quiescent manner."

- If not managed in a quiescent manner, surface impoundments must be covered, with emissions vented to a control device. This requirement will lead to the drainage and closure of many surface impoundments, according to EPA and industry spokespersons.

- Containers must be covered, and designed for submerged fill. During certain waste treatment processes such as waste fixation, the containers should be enclosed with emissions vented to a control device.

- Miscellaneous units should be controlled according to requirements for those facilities that most resemble them.

POINTER▶ The Phase II proposal also includes two broad amendments to the Phase I rules. Most important, an amendment would require companies exempted from RCRA permitting requirements through the 90-day storage exemption (see Chapter 2) to adhere to relevant air emissions control requirements, including the use of covers (already required) and some monitoring tasks. The second amendment would require that VOC emissions from off-site regeneration, reactivation, or disposal of spent carbon be controlled.

When final, all three phases of the air regulations for waste management facilities would apply equally for interim status or finally permitted facilities.

Chapter 6

POLLUTION PREVENTION

"The vast majority of the advice that companies get from the pollution control sector is oriented toward treatment technologies rather than prevention," Environmental Protection Agency (EPA) Deputy Administrator F. Henry Habicht II said at the first International Conference on Pollution Prevention held in Washington, D.C., in mid-1990, adding that this attitude must change.

EPA has been trying since mid-1989 to complete an administration bill that would define what is meant by pollution prevention and establish a national prevention policy. However, no such bill was considered by Congress during 1990, though an abbreviated act was passed to elicit more data upon which to base further legislation (see Chapter 1 and below). Despite this failure to complete a comprehensive legislative package, an integrated approach toward pollution prevention is a priority of EPA, according to Habicht. Every piece of regulation that crosses EPA Administrator William K. Reilly's desk is being analyzed for pollution prevention opportunities, he said.

POLLUTION PREVENTION VIS-A-VIS WASTE MINIMIZATION

A definition of pollution prevention has proved elusive both for the federal government and for the states. Much to the chagrin of environmental groups, an early version of EPA's proposed legislation included incineration as a means of prevention. This controversial provision later was removed, but concerns linger that the meaning of prevention and its relationship with specific industrial processes is not clear. At a May 1990 meeting of the Association of State and Interstate Water Pollution Control Administrators, regional EPA officials were unable to agree on a definition. Attendees were left wondering whether prevention means reducing pollution or eliminating it. Moreover, Joel Hirschhorn, former senior associate with the Office of Technology Assessment, accused EPA of "screwing up the definition of waste reduction and pollution prevention" and "widening the definition of prevention and reduction so that any form of waste management or pollution control could be interpreted as prevention."

The confusion widens over EPA's seeming failure to abandon the term "waste minimization," which it used before allegedly turning to the more generalized expression "pollution prevention" and creating a new office under that name. According to Manik Roy, acting chief of the agency's Waste Minimization Branch, the confusion exists within EPA itself. The branch, which is within the Office of Solid Waste, was formed under the Resource Conservation and Recovery Act (RCRA) 1984 amendments, Roy explained, and continues to operate under the old name despite its basic agreement with the concept that pollution prevention should be multidisciplinary. For example, a proposed rule dated October 5, 1990, that came out of Roy's office announced that it "places the highest priority on waste minimization," more specifically as it applies to hazardous waste. At the same time, the Office of Pollution Prevention released and/or authorized materials stating that the old terminology was no longer in use (see below).

Congress added to the confusion by naming its new information-gathering legislation the Pollution Prevention Act of 1990 (PPA), even though the functions set forth in the act are to be carried out under the toxic releases information requirements of the Superfund Amendments and Reauthorization Act of 1986 (SARA), which is concerned only with hazardous and/or toxic emissions, regardless of the media into which they are released. Thus, while concerned with several media, the reporting provisions would have virtually no effect on nonhazardous solid waste management. According to Roy, these provisions are administered by the Office of Toxic Substances.

Patently, any distinction between hazardous waste minimization and pollution prevention so far is a matter of organization rather than substance. This book attempts to make such a distinction. Materials issued or discussed as pollution prevention, including the misleadingly named PPA, are covered in this chapter. Activities confined to hazardous waste minimization are described in Chapter 7.

- Telephones:

Waste Minimization Branch, Office of Solid Waste: (703) 308-8402

Office of Pollution Prevention: (703) 821-4800

Office of Toxic Substances: (202) 382-3810

INSTITUTIONAL ASPECTS OF POLLUTION PREVENTION

Underlying most institutional barriers to pollution prevention programs is lack of trust. Traditional command and control regulation assumes that firms will pollute unless rigorous enforcement programs are in place to prevent them from doing so. Thus, traditional programs are source and media specific; include strict numerical standards, reporting, and monitoring requirements; and entail periodic inspections designed to find infractions rather than opportunities for improvement.

In order for effective pollution prevention programs to take hold, industrial representatives argue, there must be a departure from this adversarial form of regulation. Time-consuming, source-specific permitting programs do not encourage firms to go beyond regulatory limits, Thomas Zosal of 3M Corp. said at a 1990 Association of State and Interstate Water Pollution Control Administrators conference.

In response to these concerns, EPA and Amoco Corp. are conducting a yearlong pilot project that promotes source reduction and recycling in exchange for multimedia permitting. Such permitting is preferred by industry as well as many governmental policymakers because it combines emissions into air, water, and land from an entire facility, thus achieving a better view of the total environmental impact.

EPA also has shown a willingness to incorporate pollution prevention programs into consent decrees and to reduce fines when firms establish such programs. For example, the agency's Office of Toxics Litigation agreed to:

- Reduce fines against Sherex Polymers, Inc., by $42,000 when the company proposed a pollution prevention project

- Shave $10,000 off a penalty proposed against Seekonk Lace, Inc., when the company agreed to modify a production process to eliminate the use of acetone

- Reduce from $25,000 to $11,250 the penalties against Frontier Oil when the company agreed to a sulfur oxides source reduction project

- Include in a settlement decree with Gunderson, Inc., a requirement that the company purchase and install eight or more air-assisted airless electrostatic guns to reduce paint waste and volatile organic compounds emissions

The manner in which federal and state rules work against pollution prevention is well illustrated by the metal finishing industry, however, whose level of regulation is second only to the nuclear power industry, according to industry spokespersons. For example, the RCRA land ban rule requires that the metal hydroxide sludge produced when metals are plated be stabilized before disposal. This is done by adding lime and putting the waste into concrete. Metal finishing companies complain that this process increases the amount of original waste and costs too much. For example, for every pound of cadmium waste, three pounds of solid waste are produced when the metal is encapsulated. With the enactment of the land ban rule, the cost of disposing a drum of waste went from $30 to $800, representatives claimed.

RCRA liability and permitting requirements also mitigate against efforts to develop innovative waste reduction policies, according to Gary M. Trahey, president of Rampart Industries, Inc., in Detroit, Michigan. Trahey said that in order to convert equipment into a less polluting operational mode, he needed assurance for a mere three days that he would not be held liable should an unintended emissions upset occur while equipment was off line. Neither Michigan state regulators nor EPA would offer such assurance, he said. Trahey's problems and his waste minimization solution are described in greater detail in Chapter 7.

EPA's INITIATIVES

EPA is serious in its intention to move toward a multimedia, prevention-oriented regulatory program despite the definitional and institutional barriers described above. Examples of this enlightened attitude include the air emissions control rules for RCRA waste management facilities described in Chapter 5 as well as the agency's failed attempt to include a recycling mandate in its Clean Air Act rules for municipal combustors, also described in Chapter 5. As noted above, further federal initiatives dealing with hazardous waste minimization are described in the next chapter. With regard to pollution prevention specifically, the agency has developed a multifaceted pollution research program and a more narrowly focused pollution prevention strategy, both of which are described below. As noted previously, the agency also has responsibility for administering the new Pollution Prevention Act described in Chapter 1. An analysis of how the agency will carry out this mandate is included here.

The EPA regional offices also promote pollution prevention ideas in their member states. The activities vary according to regional priorities and address such diverse problems as stratospheric ozone depletion, overuse of agricultural chemicals, lack of markets for postconsumer waste paper, air toxics, ground-level ozone pollution, and discharges of publicly owned treatment works. Plainly, the regional offices perceive pollution prevention as a multimedia exercise, not necessarily concentrated on waste reduction per se. A list of regional pollution prevention contacts is included in the EPA directory at Appendix A.

In addition to discussing EPA's activities, this chapter briefly describes state and industrial initiatives in pollution prevention and includes a longer "how to" guide identifying pollution prevention opportunities, as researched by Kenneth E. Nelson, an executive of Dow Chemical U.S.A.

EPA'S POLLUTION PREVENTION STRATEGY

EPA unveiled a new pollution prevention strategy in early 1991 that lists 17 chemicals targeted for reduction by 33 percent by the end of 1992 and at least 50 percent by year's end 1995. All of the chemicals are included on the agency's Toxic Release Inventory required under the reporting provisions of the Superfund amendments. Therefore, each year's reductions can be measured.

According to the pollution prevention office, several hundred companies were contacted to participate in this program, which is intended to be largely voluntary. The strategy favors flexible, cost-effective regulatory approaches that involve incentives where practical. For example, the strategy calls for flexible use of the Toxic Substance Control Act to create direct or indirect market-based incentives to reduce releases into all media. Another strategy is to group chemicals into clusters, such as the one appearing below, to foster improved cross-media evaluation and reduction.

Aware of institutional barriers within EPA, the strategy spells out several short-term measures to reduce these barriers, such as creating two new special assistants for pollution prevention, developing incentives and training to improve staff acceptance of the multimedia program, and incorporating pollution prevention into agency four-year planning.

The 17 pollutants identified as targets combine a high level of risk and ample opportunities for reduction, according to EPA. The list was drawn from recommendations submitted by program offices, taking into account such criteria as health and ecological risk, the likelihood of exposure, technical or economic incentives, and limitations of treatment.

Noting that opportunities exist in virtually all sectors of the economy, EPA indicated that it will focus first on the manufacturing sector. The agency will work with the departments of Agriculture, Energy, and Transportation to develop strategies for preventing pollution from agricultural practices and energy and transportation use. Finally, the agency has begun a separate program to bring pollution prevention ideas to the municipal sector.

The following is a list of the target chemicals and the pounds (in millions) that were released in 1988:

Benzene	33.1
Cadmium	2.0
Carbon tetrachloride	5.0
Chloroform	26.9
Chromium	56.9
Cyanide	13.8
Dichloromethane	153.4
Lead	58.7
Mercury	0.3
Methyl ethyl ketone	159.1
Methyl isobutyl ketone	43.7
Nickel	19.4
Tetrachloroethylene	37.5
Toluene	344.6
1,1,1-Trichloroethane	190.5
Trichloroethylene	55.4
Xylene	201.6

EPA'S POLLUTION PREVENTION RESEARCH PROGRAM

EPA's Pollution Prevention Research program, which lends technical support both to the Waste Minimization Branch and the

Pollution Prevention Office, is run out of the agency's Risk Reduction Engineering Research Laboratory (RREL) in Cincinnati, Ohio.

>   Pollution Prevention Research Branch
>   Risk Reduction Engineering Laboratory
>   26 W. Martin Luther King Dr.
>   Cincinnati, OH 45268
>   (513) 569-7529

In keeping with EPA's attempt to adopt an integrated approach to pollution prevention, this office changed its name to Pollution Prevention Branch in early 1990. Its old name was the Waste Minimization Research Program. In keeping with the agency's new emphasis on integrated environmental management, the newly formed research branch supports research on all pollutants in all media as well as energy reduction (which ultimately is a means of reducing waste). The fiscal year 1990 budget for the program was $5.4 million, of which the bulk is managed by the Cincinnati facility, with some $2 million allocated to other EPA offices and laboratories.

The agency has defined six fundamental goals for the program, as follows:

- Stimulate the development and use of products that result in reduced pollution. For this purpose, products include not only manufactured items but also chemicals used in manufacturing processes and service industries; packaging for parts, commodities, and manufactured items; fluids and gases used as solvents, carriers, refrigerants, coatings, and lubricants; and additional items of commerce.

- Stimulate the development and use of technologies and processes that result in broad-scale pollution reduction.

- Expand the reusability and recyclability of wastes and products — and the demand for recycled materials.

- Identify and promote the implementation of effective nontechnical approaches to pollution prevention. This research area encompasses socioeconomic and institutional factors that may motivate efforts toward pollution prevention.

- Establish a research program that will anticipate and respond to future environmental problems and pollution prevention opportunities.

- Conduct a vigorous technology transfer and technical assistance program.

Program Components

The pollution prevention research program has six areas that correspond to the six goals listed above. Each is briefly described here.

Products Research Program

This program attempts to identify the pollutants generated in the course of manufacturing products and to evaluate the manner in which products may become pollutants in the course of their life spans. Essentially all products are potential pollutants, according to program director Harry M. Freeman. Efforts therefore must be made to ensure the following:

- Unnecessary releases and disposal of toxic or otherwise hazardous products are eliminated.

- Products are not used or discarded unnecessarily or in inappropriate ways.

- Product designs that result in the release or disposal of hazardous or toxic materials are eliminated whenever possible.

- Toxic or otherwise harmful components are eliminated from product formulations whenever possible.

- Product designs that generate pollution are discouraged in favor of less polluting designs.

Process Research Program

An important component of process research is the Waste Reduction Innovative Technology Evaluations (WRITE) program, which supports projects to develop, demonstrate, and evaluate improved, lower waste generating local regulatory programs. This three-year effort provides $100,000 per year to cooperating organizations to support its goals. In 1989 WRITE agreements were developed with New Jersey, Minnesota, California, Illinois, Connecticut, and Washington. In 1990 a similar agreement was developed with Erie County, New York.

As an example of this program's function, Freeman described activities in Illinois, where the Hazardous Waste Research and Information Center in the town of Savoy is working with several industries to find less polluting process changes. Six projects have been selected for study: substitution of water-based inks for solvent-based inks in flexographic printing, evaluation of the use of soybean oil inks in offset printing, use of zinc hydroxide in place of zinc cyanide for zinc electroplating, substitution of citrus cleaners for chlorinated solvents in metal fabricating and printing, and recovery of metals and zircon sand in foundries.

The process research program also supports projects that demonstrate the use of an EPA manual for conducting waste minimization assessments. This manual, the *Waste Minimization Opportunity Assessment Manual*, is described in Chapter 7. Demonstration projects currently are under way in New Jersey and California.

Other program activities include waste reduction evaluations at federal sites and an assortment of smaller projects exploring technical and institutional barriers to waste reduction. Among these efforts is a study to quantify waste reduction measures by both industry sectors and across industry lines (this problem will be discussed further later in this chapter).

Recycling and Reuse Research

Relying heavily on the results of the products and processes research programs, this program will focus on community and industrial recycling and reuse opportunities and on markets for recycled materials. Two examples of this program's activities are as follows:

- An investigation by the U.S. Department of Agriculture's Forest Products Laboratory as to whether newsprint can be reclaimed by means of a dry fiberizing process. This is part of a larger project at the laboratory (partly funded by the American Newsprint Publishing Association) that will explore dry and semidry paper-making processes. For the dry fiberizing portion of the program, three methods for disintegrating newsprint – hammermilling, ballmilling, and single disk refining – are under examination.

- Laboratory and pilot-scale work to develop commercially viable thermo-formable composite products using recycled high-density polyethylene, wood flour, recycled wood fiber, and reclaimed polyester fiber. This project will build on existing research to develop a variety of composite products, the most promising of which will be piloted.

Socioeconomic and Institutional Research

According to Freeman, investigations in these areas are necessary because waste generation and waste management decisions are driven by nontechnical forces such as legal mandates, attitudes, habits, incentives, and benefits, all of which may be altered when there is sufficient impetus for change. All of EPA's efforts in this area are in the planning stages.

Anticipatory Research

Three major areas of long-term research considered essential but not yet under way by the research laboratory include the following:

- Anticipating and responding to emerging environmental issues

- Evaluating emerging technologies and advancing those that are superior

- Evaluating the effectiveness of EPA's pollution prevention research in meeting changing needs

Technology Transfer and Technical Assistance

To encourage technology transfer and furnish technical assistance, the research laboratory has entered into a cooperative agreement with the University City Science Center in Philadelphia. Through this project, waste minimization assessment centers have been established at the University of Tennessee (Knoxville) and at the University of Louisville. Faculty and student teams from these centers offer waste minimization assessments at no cost to small businesses without their own resources for such a program. During the project's first year, 12 assessments were completed over a broad spectrum of facilities including printed circuit board manufacturers, a railroad car and equipment refurbisher, a paint and coatings producer, a plastic bag printer, and an aluminum can manufacturer. An annual savings of $1.28 million would accrue from implementation of all of the waste reduction options presented to these firms, Freeman said.

Pollution Prevention Information Clearinghouse

This clearinghouse is operated by EPA's Office of Pollution Prevention, located in Washington, D.C, at the telephone number cited above. It was created in 1988 to ensure that pollution prevention concepts are incorporated into the agency's decision making and planning. The clearinghouse consists of a reference library, the information hotline noted above, an electronic bulletin board, and outreach activities. Indexed bibliographies and abstracts of reports, publications, and case studies on pollution prevention are available, either on line or in hard copy. The Pollution Prevention Information Exchange System (PPIES) is accessible through a personal computer and modem. The number is (703) 506-1025.

An example of the useful publications produced by this office is a manual, *Pollution Prevention Training Opportunities,* updated annually. The manual lists national and state training courses and fact sheets, includes a calendar of pollution prevention events, abstracts pollution prevention instruction manuals (see Bibliography), and lists pollution prevention videos and other pollution prevention resources. Information on states' activities, as described in this manual and other sources, are summarized in Chapter 14.

The office also publishes a newsletter, *Pollution Prevention News.* To receive the publication, a request to be added to the office's mailing list must be made by writing:

Pollution Prevention News
U.S. EPA
401 M St., SW (PM-219)
Washington, DC 20460

American Institute for Pollution Prevention

The institute is an EPA/University of Cincinnati joint effort to increase communication between EPA and those most in the position to reduce pollution generation. This new channel is important, Freeman said, because the agency's traditional dealings have been with people concerned with the treatment and disposal of waste rather than those concerned with the processes that generate the pollution in the first place.

A directory of the Pollution Prevention Research Program offices is included in Appendix A.

POLLUTION PREVENTION ACT ANALYSIS

As described in Chapter 1, PPA requires industry to report pollution prevention efforts on the same forms they use to report chemical releases under the Emergency Planning and Community Right-To-Know Act, better known as Title III of SARA. Under this provision all manufacturers with more than 10 employees must report annually, by July 1, statistics on toxic emissions to all environmental media during the previous year. These same firms now are brought under the PPA reporting net.

Previously, manufacturers could report their waste reduction achievements on their toxic release reports but were not required to do so. Few responded, and in 1989 fewer than 10 percent of the forms submitted under Section 313 contained any voluntary information on waste minimization or recycling activities. This low reporting influenced Congress's decision to require mandatory reporting as of January 1, 1991, according to an EPA official.

Under the Title III reporting schedule, the new information must be submitted on reports for 1991, due by July 1, 1992. EPA will propose regulations to implement this provision in time for that deadline, according to Sam Sasnett, Toxic Release Inventory management staff director in EPA's Office of Toxic Substances.

The task will not be simple, he added. The agency's Office of Toxic Substances anticipates adding 53 data fields to the reporting form (Form R), boosting the count to 113. Because pollution prevention information must be available to the public in the same manner as other data collected under Title III, the agency will have to make significant changes in all aspects of toxic release inventory data management, Sasnett said.

Implications of the Law

Few anticipate that this act is all Congress will have to say on the subject of pollution prevention. As noted in Chapter 1, in 1990 Congress was engrossed in the long-overdue reauthorization of the Clean Air Act; it is anticipated that in 1991 greater attention will be given to the reauthorization of RCRA, focusing on the solid waste management provisions. Pollution prevention can be expected to come up in this debate.

Environmental groups such as the National Wildlife Federation found the 1990 PPA inadequate, stating they would have preferred legislation imposing more specific and tougher controls on industry. Spokesperson Gerald Poje said, on November 20, 1990, that the federation would have liked Congress to adopt source reduction requirements as national policy. Other environmental groups indicated they would use the data to foster corporate accountability. They plan to check company reports to determine whether past promises to cut hazardous emissions were kept.

Some citizen groups have charged that many reported decreases in emissions were based solely on changes in estimation methods, delisted chemicals, changes in production levels, or increases in off-site transfers rather than on substantive reductions. Under the new law, companies will have to reveal the details of their waste reduction efforts.

As noted above, EPA has started building pollution prevention measures into settlement decrees. This trend will continue, according to Michael Walker, associate counsel in EPA's Office of Toxic Litigation. He cautioned, however, that innovative settlements must not be construed as "letting a company off the hook." Companies still must pay penalties, he said, though they may not be as stiff. Furthermore, agency officials must ensure that the proposed pollution prevention measure actually is in place. Decrees must include a provision for periodic inspection and for further litigation if the company does not honor its pledge. This represents a further strain on EPA's resources, Walker added.

Noting that the number of citizen suits has risen since companies started submitting toxic release data, Walker said the addition of pollution prevention information should add fuel to the fire. Companies that continue to disregard Title III reporting requirements are asking for trouble, he said.

STATE ACTIVITIES

As the example below shows, most states are several years ahead of EPA in their efforts to develop waste prevention programs. At least 35 have programs or legislation dealing with waste reduction. A growing number, including Louisiana, Massachusetts, and Oregon, have adopted rules requiring firms to develop effective waste reduction programs. In Louisiana, this requirement came as a direct result of information submitted under SARA. Several use retired engineers and scientists to work with companies in auditing their operations. Others have formed partnerships with EPA or university research laboratories to carry out waste reduction initiatives, some of which are described later in this chapter. However, enthusiastic as they may be, the states lack sufficient funding to manage the waste reduction programs by themselves and compete actively for a share of EPA's limited funds.

More information on state training and technical support for pollution prevention and related programs is found in Chapter 4.

Multimedia Inspection

One state-managed project that should lend considerable support to the multimedia pollution prevention approach is the Blackstone Project, which was carried out in early 1990 by two Massachusetts state agencies, the Department of Environmental Protection (DEP) and the Department of Environmental Management. The project targeted 26 metal-intensive manufacturing facilities located in the service area of the Upper Blackstone, the sewage treatment plant of greater Worcester. The project staff formed three-member teams that inspected each facility's compliance with air, water, hazardous waste, and Title III requirements and identified source reduction opportunities. In a report released following this activity, the team said the inspections were more efficient than single-media inspections and were better able to identify source reduction opportunities and violations.

More specifically, the project found 16 violations and five other problems that probably would not have been found during standard inspections, according to DEP's Manik Roy (Roy moved to his new post at EPA in late 1990) and Lee Dillard. Moreover, they identified specific source reduction opportunities at 16 of the 26 facilities. The technique received good marks from 21 of the facilities visited, where owners or operators indicated that they would support the DEP's adopting a multimedia approach to all inspections.

Copies of the 140-page report, "The FY90 Report on the Blackstone Project," are available for $8.60 from:

Commonwealth of Massachusetts State Bookstore
Room 116, State House
Boston, MA 02133

INDUSTRIAL ACTIVITIES

With more money available and more sophisticated research departments, large companies increasingly are setting ambitious aims in waste reduction. Monsanto Company's Pledge No. 7 is a commitment to search for technologies that will reduce or eliminate waste, with top priority being given to not generating waste in the first place. Other pledges define a vision of corporate environmentalism that goes beyond compliance with regulatory standards to promote active stewardship of environmental resources.

According to Nicholas Reding, executive vice president of Monsanto, such a shift in corporate culture is far from simple. Corporate environmentalism and voluntary initiatives cost money. To managers' charges that such costs are inappropriate in a competitive market, Reding replies that in the long run such efforts will lead to greater efficiency, far lower disposal costs, and better community relations. In 1988, the company announced a goal to reduce its toxic air emissions by 90 percent by the end of 1992. In early 1990, Monsanto's chemical company reassigned 50 research staff to work strictly on waste elimination, elevating the status of such research within the company's structure, Reding said.

Similarly, in 1984 General Dynamics set a corporate-wide goal of zero emissions. The initial aim was to eliminate manifested waste from each General Dynamics facility. Since then, the company has recorded a reduction of over 160 million pounds of hazardous waste, while sales have increased from $7.3 billion to $9.5 billion. The company produces defense systems and owns businesses in construction, aviation, and coal mining.

At General Dynamic's Fort Worth Division, a 70 percent reduction in hazardous waste generation was achieved between 1985 and 1990, according to company sources. An example of a successfully implemented project is the use of new sorbent materials. Hydrocarbon and oil residues, drips, leaks, and spills encountered during machining and metal working operations are controlled using organic materials that have a much higher sorptive capacity. Housekeeping is improved and labor reduced, while residual wastes can be incorporated as industrial furnace fuels. Cost savings are projected to run $140,000 annually.

A HOW-TO GUIDE TO WASTE REDUCTION FROM DOW CHEMICAL U.S.A.

Large companies often are leaders in pollution prevention because they have the financial resources and research capability necessary to set programs in motion. Dow Chemical U.S.A. has had such programs at individual plants for many years. In 1987 the company formalized its waste reduction scheme and dubbed it WRAP, an acronym for "Waste Reduction Always Pays." As well as projecting the top management support so necessary to successful waste reduction programs, the WRAP process recognizes outstanding waste reduction achievements at Dow's various sites through an award program.

Dow's Louisiana division has been an enthusiastic participant in this program. In fact, it had started its own waste reduction program several years earlier, according to Kenneth E. Nelson, associate energy consultant for the division. The Louisiana program began in 1981 with an energy savings contest and was expanded in 1983 to include all waste. Using ideas derived through these contests, as well as his 28 years of experience working for Dow in a variety of engineering capacities, Nelson compiled a waste reduction how-to article that is must reading for any company looking for ways to reduce process waste as well as waste of money.

The ideas are summarized here. For a copy of the article, "Use These Ideas to Cut Waste," readers may contact Nelson at

> Dow Chemical U.S.A.
> Louisiana Division
> P.O. Box 150
> Plaquemine, LA 70765-0150

Defining Waste

Nelson includes in his waste discussion streams or materials that are vented to the air, discharged to the water, sent to landfill or an incinerator, sent to a flare, or sent to a biological treatment facility. While observing that emissions and discharges may be reduced by using more efficient control equipment, Nelson limits his discussion to waste reduction at the source and recycling. He emphasizes that these ideas are not exhaustive. They are meant to stimulate "discussion and brainstorming."

Raw Materials

The first place to look for waste reduction opportunities is in raw material specification and use, Nelson suggests, touching on the following:

- Reduce the percentage of impurities in feedstock. Feed quality may be improved through discussion with the supplier, reexamining in-plant processes, or installing purification equipment.

- Use off-specification material (which otherwise might be discarded) if the undesirable quality of the material is not important to the process.

- Improve the quality of products to prevent waste at customer plants.

- Use inhibitors to prevent unwanted side reactions or polymer formation.

- Change shipping containers to include only recyclable materials.

- Reexamine the need for each raw material. The need for algae inhibitors in a cross-flow cooling tower, for example, was cut in half by shielding the area from sunlight.

Reactors

The reactor is the heart of many processes and can be a primary source of waste products, Nelson says. The quality of mixing in a reactor is crucial and too often ill-conceived, he adds. He lists a number of ways to reduce waste from reactors, the first three of which are concerned with the quality of mixing. His ideas are as follows:

- Improve physical mixing in the reactor by methods such as repositioning baffles or upgrading the motor.

- Improve the distribution of feeds.

- Streamline the manner in which reactants are introduced. The idea here is to get closer to ideal reactant concentrations before the feed enters the reactor, thereby avoiding secondary reactions that form unwanted byproducts, Nelson explains.

- Improve the catalyst to lengthen life and effectiveness.

- Provide a separate reactor for recycle streams.

- Examine heating and/or cooling techniques to avoid hot-spots or overheated feed streams.

- Consider a different design; many innovative hybrid designs are possible.

- Improve control, perhaps through installation of a computer; batch operations must be stabilized through adequate monitoring controls.

Heat Exchangers

Noting that faulty heat exchangers can damage heat-sensitive materials, Nelson lists several suggestions, most of which would reduce tube-wall temperatures. In order to cool things off, managers might consider reducing steam pressure, reducing the temperature of "superheated" steam, installing a thermocompressor capable of combining high- and low-pressure steams to produce a steam of intermediate pressure, or using staged heating. To reduce maintenance costs, save energy, or recover materials, Nelson has several other suggestions, as follows:

- Use on-line cleaning devices such as recirculated sponge balls or reversing brushes.

- Install scraped-wall exchangers that can recover saleable products from viscous streams. A typical application is to recover monomer from polymer tars.

- Monitor exchanger fouling to learn which operating conditions contribute to the problem and then use this information to recommend changes.

- Switch to noncorroding tubes.

Pumps and Distillation Columns

Pumps normally do not create waste if designed and operated properly. Nelson advises the use of seal-less pumps. Waste from pump seal flushing and purging should be recycled to the process whenever possible.

According to Nelson, distillation columns can produce waste in three ways:

- By allowing impurities to remain in a product; the solution is better separation, perhaps beyond normal product specifications.

- By forming waste within the column itself, usually because of excessive heat; the solution is lower column temperatures.

- By inadequate condensing, which results in vented or flared product; the solution is to improve condensing through a number of mechanisms explained in the article.

Furnaces

Noting that furnace technology is constantly evolving, Nelson suggests that energy may be saved by replacing the coil with one of more modern design, replacing the furnace with an intermediate heat exchanger, or eliminating the need for a furnace by using "superheat" from plant processes.

Piping

In a large chemical plant or refinery, piping presents several waste saving opportunities, Nelson states. In looking for these, managers should examine each waste stream separately to find wastes that might be diverted to a recovery facility. Temperatures should be monitored and appropriate steps taken to avoid damage to heat-sensitive materials and to eliminate the need to send hot material to storage. As is the case for pumps and distillation columns, leaks should be checked and eliminated and major vents and flare systems monitored. Whenever possible, vented materials should be recovered and used. In many cases, a small condenser or vent compressor may be all that is needed, he says.

Improving Overall Operations

Nelson reiterates the importance of installing modern computer monitors or their equivalent to improve on-line control; achieve efficient daily operation; automate start ups, shutdowns, and product changes in order to reduce waste; and program the plant to handle unexpected upsets and trips.

Summing up a list of other miscellaneous steps that could be taken to reduce or reuse waste, Nelson says waste reduction is a "never-ending activity." In a continuously changing regulatory climate, he continues, managers should never lose sight of one truism: "The way you reduce waste is by installing projects that reduce waste." Such projects need not reduce profits, he claims, adding that nearly every idea discussed here showed a return on investment greater than 30 percent. Most paid for themselves in less than a year. Finding these money-saving projects helps support other waste reduction projects with little or no payback, he concludes.

As a fitting reward for the Louisiana division's leadership in pollution prevention, the plant in Plaquemine won a Dow outstanding achievement award in 1990. The company's achievement, described in EPA's *Pollution Prevention News*, is the installation of a barge vent recovery system that captures vapors released when liquid hydrocarbon products are loaded into low-pressure barges. The hydrocarbons are separated from nitrogen vapors and returned to the production process for reuse. The vapor recovery unit operates at a recovery rate greater than 90 percent, translating into more than 100,000 pounds of annual hydrocarbon emissions that no longer go into the atmosphere. The installation also reduces human exposure to the vapors, according to EPA.

REGIONAL AND PRIVATE POLLUTION PREVENTION ASSISTANCE SOURCES

In addition to the federal agencies that generate information on pollution prevention and waste minimization, there are a growing number of interstate and even private information sources such as the following:

- *The Northeast Multimedia Pollution Prevention Program (NEMPP):* This program was established in 1989 to help environmental officials in New England, New Jersey, and New York bring about source reduction programs. The project has three components: an information clearinghouse, a program of training sessions, and research on source reduction strategies for the major toxic metals in incinerator emissions and ash.

    Terri Goldberg, Program Manager
    Northeast Multimedia Pollution Prevention
    Northeast Waste Management Officials' Association
    85 Merrimac St.
    Boston, MA 02114
    (617) 367-8558

- *Waste Reduction Resource Center for the Southeast:* This center was established in 1988 to foster multimedia waste reduction support for the eight Region IV states: Alabama, Florida, Georgia, Kentucky, Mississippi, North Carolina, South Carolina, and Tennessee. The center furnishes technical waste reduction information from federal government agencies, all 50 states, and numerous private sources. It serves as an information clearinghouse and assigns trained engineers to respond to questions regarding specific waste reduction problems.

Gary Hunt
Waste Reduction Center for the Southeast
512 North Salisbury St.
P.O. Box 27687
Raleigh, NC 27611-7687
(919) 733-7015

- *The American Institute of Chemical Engineers* (AIChE): The institute operates a Center for Waste Reduction Technologies, which is a focal point for research, education, and information dissemination on innovative waste reduction technologies. The center's key features reflect its overall philosophy, which is to engage industrial support toward finding technological solutions adapted to a competitive marketplace.

The center's research efforts are carried out by university-based consortia and single investigators. Companies may fund research directed toward their specific needs or the needs of their industry sector. Companies also are asked to test new and emerging waste reduction technologies. The center promotes educational programs to ensure that environmentally compatible design becomes a permanent feature of industrial practice.

Center for Waste Reduction Technologies
American Institute of Chemical Engineers
345 E. 47th St.
New York, NY 10017
(212) 705-7407

There also exists a free, privately operated bulletin board dedicated to source reduction and recycling topics. The service includes a message center, bulletins, and informational files. Known as the RecycleNet Bulletin Board, the service operates at 300, 1200, or 2400 baud.

Fred McCamic, S-204
5420 Repecho Dr.
San Diego, CA 92124
(619) 576-1996

Finally, numerous books and manuals have been and are continuing to be written on this subject. Consult the Bibliography for a partial list of these sources. Most states also provide resource materials and training for industries within their borders. For more information on these services, see Chapter 4 and the Appendix.

Chapter 7

RCRA HAZARDOUS WASTE MINIMIZATION

Even without new federal regulations or incentive programs, companies that generate hazardous waste have good economic reasons to change processes whenever possible. With the ban against depositing untreated hazardous wastes in landfills now fully in effect, wastes may need to go through more custody changes than formerly, thus increasing both expenditures and the risk of mishap. The costs of pretreatment also will increase as more stringent air pollution rules go into effect (see Chapter 4). The requirements of preparing and updating contingency plans under Title III of the Superfund Amendments and Reauthorization Act of 1986 (SARA) are time-consuming and labor-intensive. Moreover, the burden of reporting routine chemical releases and sharing with neighboring communities the details of plant operations has caused many companies to reduce chemical use voluntarily.

Congress, the Environmental Protection Agency (EPA), and the states continue to help this decision process along. Bills introduced in 1990 generally included provisions to reduce hazardous waste generation at the source. As noted earlier in this book, the one waste-related bill to reach the president's desk during that session was the Pollution Prevention Act of 1990, a data-gathering measure described in Chapters 1 and 6. More such legislation is almost certain to emerge before the end of 1991. The new act builds on the existing

Resource Conservation and Recovery Act (RCRA) requirement that hazardous waste generators and the owners or operators of waste treatment, storage, and disposal (TSD) facilities certify on their biennial manifests that they "have a program in place to reduce the volume and toxicity of waste generated to the extent that is economically practical." EPA also has issued numerous guidance documents and issue papers, but no final regulations, to stimulate ideas concerning the reduction of hazardous chemical use. Finally, the states are credited with being well ahead of the federal government in designing their own hazardous waste minimization programs.

In the previous chapter, policies and activities related to broad-scale pollution prevention were discussed. This chapter centers on "hazardous waste minimization" specifically and includes an overview of EPA's activities, including its ideas for future regulations; a case study of a small company's frustrations in designing an effective waste reduction scheme; a detailed summary of EPA's manual on how to conduct hazardous waste minimization audits; and a discussion of the Council of State Governments' model hazardous waste reduction rule.

EPA'S ACTIVITIES: AN OVERVIEW

On October 5, 1990, EPA's Office of Solid Waste issued a notice of proposed regulations on hazardous waste minimization that, in fact, contained no actual regulatory language. Instead, the notice traced the agency's earlier activities with regard to waste reduction and asked for comments on what further incentives or regulatory changes are needed.

1986 Report to Congress

As early as 1976, EPA published an environmental auditing policy that recognized the limits of pipe-end equipment to meet environmental goals. However, it was not until 1986 that the agency issued any information directly related to hazardous waste minimization, according to the notice. In response to a requirement of the Hazardous and Solid Waste Amendments of 1984 (HSWA), EPA prepared a report to Congress discussing its findings concerning methods to reduce hazardous waste generation. In that report, the agency said that it had very little information on companies' waste reduction efforts or on the potential for further reductions. EPA therefore told Congress in 1986 that it must delay until 1990 conclusions about the need for additional waste minimization regulations. Only then would the land disposal restrictions be in full effect so that a better measurement of progress could be made. In the interim the agency pledged to develop a technical assistance program, measure and report progress to Congress and the public, and assess longer term options, including regulatory and other incentives for waste minimization, according to the notice.

1989 Guidance

EPA next proposed, in the June 12, 1989, *Federal Register,* guidance to the regulated community on the elements of a waste minimization program, the notice continues. The guidance cites activities included in the definition of waste minimization and describes several basic waste minimization program elements the agency believes are essential. The information in the guidance is taken from the agency's waste minimization manual, which is summarized later in this chapter.

Data Gathering

In the October 5 notice EPA observes that both federal and state agencies have difficulty assessing and comparing waste generation and waste minimization efforts among facilities and production processes from different manufacturing sectors, and often among facilities within the same sector. The agencies have used the RCRA biennial reports and several specialized surveys to measure these efforts. However, a major weakness in all of these efforts is the attempt to calculate reduction as a ratio of the total volume of waste that goes to treatment to the units of production. This mass balance approach is blind to process-specific waste minimization changes, EPA claims, and therefore is not always accurate. Details of this problem are discussed in the manual.

Long-Term Options to Speed Progress in Waste Minimization

The remainder of the October 5 notice discusses the many issues surrounding further development of waste minimization efforts, some of which also were brought up by participants of the pollution prevention workshop noted in the previous chapter and below. The agency sought comment on several issues by December 1990. The questions and some of EPA's concerns are included here because the issues presented are likely to be debated for some time.

Should the solid waste definition be changed to promote additional source reduction and recycling? EPA has received many comments that the explanation of the circumstances under which recycled waste is regulated is anything but clear (see Chapter 8). In response, EPA explains that it tries to make a distinction between recycling that is production-oriented, and arguably out of RCRA's jurisdiction, and recycling that comprises waste management and therefore requires inclusion.

Should EPA consider marketable waste generation trading rights or other long-term economic incentives to reduce waste generation? In posing this question, EPA is taking a page from the air pollution control book. Under air rules, firms (or facilities) in polluted cities that reduce their emissions of specified pollutants to below required levels may have marketable pollution rights to sell to other firms or facilities with excessive emissions. As applied to hazardous waste, the concept might take the form of transferable rights to generate waste. If a firm reduces waste by more than the amount of its "rights" for a given year, it may sell the excess rights to a firm with higher needs. For this program to work, the available pool of rights must be reduced through time. EPA has a number of questions concerning this idea: Should all hazardous waste be included? What are appropriate reduction restrictions? Would these rights follow the waste as part of the manifest? Should certain hard-to-treat wastes constitute a separate and more restricted class? Would such a scheme create a new incentive for cross-media transfer of pollution? How would the program be implemented? Is privatization of such a program a good idea?

Should EPA consider waste characterization, assessment, and listing incentives? By these incentives, the agency means methods to encourage firms to reduce generation of a specific waste before it is listed. As the scheme works now, EPA says, firms claim that once they become subject to a new RCRA regulation, the statutory deadlines for compliance are too short to put waste minimization technologies in place. One way to add time would be to require collection and dissemination of source reduction and recycling information as part of the data-collection and analysis portion of the listing process, EPA suggests. This would give generators an "up-front opportunity" to reduce waste before the listing is adopted. Another idea might be to allow generators that become subject either to a new listing requirement or the toxicity characteristic rule to enter an agreement to install the necessary source reduction and recycling technologies.

How can EPA modify current performance standards for best demonstrated available treatment technologies to include waste minimization techniques? In a discussion of this question, EPA concedes that the standards for treating and disposing of certain heavy metals are especially problematical because they reduce neither the toxicity nor the volume of the hazardous constituents, instead depending on stabilization methods such as encapsulation. Information is available on source reduction technologies available to the electroplating industry, for instance, that have been tried by some industries but by no means all. Using electroplating wastewater treatment sludge (F006) as an example, EPA indicates that waste minimization standards might be appropriate for well-defined, relatively narrow generator categories. The case study below concerns how the president of one electroplating company faced inconsistent and changing regulations that acted as an impediment rather than an aid to experimentation with advanced forms of waste reduction equipment.

Should EPA consider waste minimization incentives in the RCRA TSD permit process? The notice presents two possible approaches to accomplishing this goal: requiring permittees to submit a waste minimization plan either as a condition for issuing the permit or as supplemental information that must be submitted within a prescribed period of time; or taking a broader approach, looking not only at hazardous waste reduction but also at efforts to reduce pollution of other media.

Should waste minimization requirements be included in hazardous waste treatment capacity assurance plans (CAPs) under SARA? Inclusion of waste minimization provisions in CAPs makes especially good sense now, because the land disposal restrictions have created a shortfall in treatment capacity in some regions of the country, according to the notice. The guidance manual for preparing these plans recommends the formation of a waste minimization program but does not require it. Several states have legislated such provisions as an integral part of their plans, the notice observes. However, states that are net importers of waste, such as Alabama, have criticized EPA for allowing states to substitute waste minimization goals (which may be unachievable) for firm commitments to increase treatment and disposal capacity.

Should compliance monitoring and enforcement play a greater role in promoting waste minimization? As noted in the previous chapter, EPA considers the inclusion of waste minimization requirements in enforcement settlement decrees a fruitful way of forcing firms to do what they may not have done otherwise.

Should EPA consider long-term incentives for minimizing the generation of hazardous wastes by RCRA-exempt treatment facilities? More than half of the hazardous wastes generated annually are exempt from the RCRA requirements because they are treated in units controlled under the Clean Water Act, EPA observes in the notice. Considering the "magnitude of this universe," it might be appropriate to focus waste minimization regulations on waste volume and toxicity, regardless of what sort of units are used for management of the wastes.

CASE STUDY: RAMPART INDUSTRIES

Speaking before the International Conference on Pollution Prevention held in Washington, D.C., in June 1990, Gary M. Trahey, president of Rampart Industries, Inc., described the woes of a relatively small business that has tried hard to develop waste reduction technologies in a regulatory environment that includes "lack of engineering support from the manufacturer of equipment, ever-changing regulatory laws, local publicly owned treatment works limit standards," and lack of capital to update and expand quickly outdated treatment systems. Despite these hurdles, Rampart ultimately did design a system that became a model for other metal finishers throughout the United States. "The high risk project" proved successful "but left the company unsteady for two years, eliminated seven jobs and three process systems, and caused a sales decline of nearly 20 percent," Trahey said.

Under regulatory pressure, Rampart, a medium-sized electroplating firm in Detroit, Michigan, began in 1979 to modify its waste management program, Trahey said. The company secured local engineering support, designed a precipitation system, and sought financing through a federal Job Development Authority/Small Business Administration bond funding program. After wasting a year of time and money in securing the loan, the offer was canceled by the government. "They called it Reaganomics," Trahey said.

Suffering from a recession and this absence of federal funding, the company was under "relentless pressure of the local control authority," he continued. The company carried out an environmental assessment study indicating that it could segregate its waste streams in a manner that would leave cadmium and cyanide as the only critical control problems.

This finding led the company, with support from industry associations and EPA, to try a reactor developed by HSA Reactors of Ontario, Canada, that proved capable of recovering single metals and oxidizing cyanide. Following the demonstration, Rampart spent 30 months developing and modifying the system to fit its needs. Test results showed that the reactor could remove 98 percent of the cadmium and cyanide in the waste stream of an automatic rack plating machine and a manual four-station barrel plating line.

This was not enough, however. The system still fell short of complying consistently with the categorical standards for electroplating waste streams. The company already had invested $150,000 in a recovery system "that worked, but not quite well enough," Trahey said. After additional discussion with local, state, and federal regulators, Rampart invested another $100,000 in a second recovery system to batch-treat the remaining metal in the rinses and residual metal from cleaning and pickling. The unit proved a total failure, Trahey said, noting that the problems sprung from toxic fumes, line-operator error, unanticipated mixed metal contamination during electrolytic recovery, and "no engineering support from the equipment manufacturer."

Again dialogue took place, primarily with the City of Detroit Industrial Control Division (IWC), which agreed to allow the company time to come up with a workable system within its budgetary limitations, Trahey said. Rampart and the IWC worked out a joint agreement to explore a new form of ion exchange, marketed by Douglas America, Inc., of Minneapolis, Minnesota. This system did work, Trahey said. Its success was due partly to the city's willingness to grant time to plan, purchase, install, operate, and assess the new system. The project was supported by the Michigan Association of Metal Finishers and demonstrated at a convention in Detroit of the National Association of Metal Finishers. Platers from all over the country had an opportunity to see the effectiveness of the ion-exchange system, Trahey said.

New ideas continue to emerge that could further perfect recovery and recycling techniques, according to Trahey. Unfortunately, he added, Rampart's money has run out. "If money were available in the form of grants, investment tax credits, or even a controlled short-term freeze on regulatory compliance, we could see an increase in waste reduction participation by industry," he claimed. He noted particularly the "tremendous responsibility being placed on the publicly owned treatment works in setting local limits," which "could very well generate unachievable levels that will virtually shut down waste reduction technology being developed today."

CONDUCTING A WASTE MINIMIZATION AUDIT

The key that opens most effective waste reduction opportunities is an audit. Such an activity may be broad enough to encompass an entire corporation, with top management at the helm, or as narrow as a particular shop with a pesky control problem. To help in the audit development process, EPA has developed the *Waste Minimization*

RCRA Hazardous Waste Minimization 141

Opportunity Assessment Manual, a July 1988 hands-on practical document that deals specifically with hazardous waste.

The manual (EPA/625/7-88/003) provides practical information on how to design and implement waste minimization plans under RCRA as well as carry out audits for other reasons. Because of its usefulness, the manual is summarized in some detail in this chapter. The manual also includes worksheets and other materials that would be useful to any firm undertaking a waste minimization plan. It should be consulted in full text before work on a plan actually starts. Copies are available free of charge from EPA's Pollution Prevention Research Laboratory (see Bibliography) or from the Office of Pollution Prevention. The same EPA laboratory also has produced a series of industry-specific waste minimization manuals (see Bibliography).

In view of the confusion and criticism over how the agency defines source reduction described in the previous chapter, it is worth noting that the manual defines the term *waste minimization* to include source reduction *and* recycling of wastes for the original purpose or some other purpose, such as materials recovery or *energy production*. Minimization includes any activity that reduces the total volume, quantity, or toxicity of hazardous waste. According to the manual, source reduction, when feasible, is preferable to recycling.

Starting the Program

To be successful, a waste minimization program must have top management support, explicit program scope and objectives, accurate waste accounting, accurate cost accounting, and an enveloping waste minimization philosophy, the manual states. Such support might best be expressed in a formal policy statement or management directive.

Companies then are advised to form a task force whose first mandate is to set goals that are consistent with management policy. If possible, the goals should be quantifiable. Often, they are expressed in terms of percentage reduction or ultimate objective—for instance, zero discharge by 1995. The manual makes the important point that effective goals must be acceptable to those who work to achieve them.

Assessment Phase

Once these planning and organizational activities are complete, waste minimization opportunities must be assessed. Tasks included in this phase include collection of process and facility data; setting of assessment targets; selection of people for assessment teams; review of data and site inspection; and generation, screening, and selection of options.

Development of Data

In order to develop sound waste reduction options, the task force must have a detailed understanding of the plant's wastes and operations. Such information may be derived from design information such as process flow diagrams, material and heat balances, operating manuals and process descriptions, and equipment specifications; environmental records; environmental audit reports; permits and/or permit applications; raw material/production information; cost information; and any other information available, including company environmental policy statements, standard procedures, and organizational charts.

After describing several pitfalls of material balances, the manual notes that they often are needed to comply with the release reporting requirements of SARA. In response to this need, the EPA's Office of Toxic Substances has prepared a guidance manual entitled *Estimating Releases and Waste Treatment Efficiencies for the Toxic Chemicals Inventory Form* (EPA 560/4-88-02).

Setting Priorities for Assessment

Small businesses, large companies with only a few waste generating operations, and businesses with many similar operations should assess the entire facility, EPA advises. Moreover, broad-scale operational imperatives such as soliciting of employee suggestions, awareness-building programs, better inventory and maintenance procedures, and internal cost accounting changes should be adopted throughout any company. However, EPA concedes that budgetary concerns normally dictate that waste streams be tackled in some sort of order of preference, starting with immediate compliance requirements and avoided costs.

Selecting Waste Assessment Teams

While the waste management program task force is concerned with the whole plant, the assessment teams should be experts in the process under study. The manual includes four process-specific examples of how such teams might be chosen. Inclusion of outsiders could enrich an assessment team. Possibilities are trade association representatives, consultants, or experts from a different facility of the same company.

Many companies have instituted so-called quality circles to improve product quality and production efficiency, the manual notes. In a quality circle, workers meet with supervisors to propose and evaluate improvements. Such activities make good sense, as they generate ideas and commitment from those most directly responsible for a program's success.

In an example of the effectiveness of quality circles, the manual cites a large consumer product company in California that created circles made up of employees in plant areas that generated hazardous wastes. The company reduced waste generation by 75 percent by instituting improved maintenance procedures suggested by the quality circle teams. Since the team members were also line supervisors and operators, they made sure the procedures were followed.

Site Inspection

Even when the assembled background information seems complete, a site inspection by the assessment team is essential, especially for those members not directly familiar with the process. The assessment team should track the process from the point where raw materials enter to the point where the products and wastes leave the area, identifying the suspected sources of excess waste. Trouble spots could include the production process, maintenance operations, storage areas, and the plant's waste treatment area itself.

The site inspection often becomes the basis for preliminary conclusions concerning waste generation. Full confirmation of these conclusions may require additional data collection, analysis, and additional site visits.

Generating and Screening Options

Following the collection of data and site inspections, the process of selecting and screening waste reduction options begins. According to the manual, this process should occur in an environment that encourages creativity and independent thinking by the assessment team members. Brainstorming sessions are one effective way of unleashing good ideas. Most management or organizational behavior textbooks describe group decision techniques, the manual notes.

All waste reduction options generated at team meetings should be screened so as to eliminate marginal, impractical, or inferior options without further examination. In screening options, team members should consider the following:

- What is the main benefit of the option — economic, compliance, liability reduction, safety, or a combination of these?
- Is there technology to develop the option?
- Is the idea cost-effective?
- Can the option be implemented in a reasonable amount of time without undue production interruption?
- Has the option been tried successfully elsewhere?
- What other benefits will occur?

Opportunities for source reduction through good operating practices should be top priorities in any waste minimization plan because they are the best bargains, the manual observes. Such opportunities include management and personnel practices; efforts to reduce loss of input materials through mishandling, expired shelf life, or improper storage conditions; leak and spill prevention; waste segregation, especially in areas where hazardous waste disposal costs are high; cost accounting practices to allocate waste treatment and disposal costs directly to the departments or groups that generate waste; and production scheduling to reduce the frequency of equipment cleaning and any other activity that generates additional waste with each repetition.

Waste reductions also may be made through technology changes in the production process; in equipment, layout, or piping; in use of automation; or in operating conditions, such as flow rates, temperatures, pressures, or residence times. For example, the manual tells how a manufacturer of fabricated metal products cleaned nickel and titanium wire in an alkaline chemical bath prior to using the wire in its product. Through experimentation, the company developed a mechanical abrasive system whereby the wire was passed through silk and carbide pads. After about a year of trial and error, the company eliminated the need for chemical cleaning.

Source reduction also can be accomplished through changes in input material. For instance, according to the manual, an electronic manufacturing facility of a large diversified corporation originally cleaned printed circuit boards with solvents. The company discovered an aqueous-based system that not only eliminated a hazardous waste but also cleaned six times more effectively under the same operating conditions.

The final method of source reduction is product change, either through substitution, conservation, or changes in product composition. The manual notes that many paint manufacturers have already switched from solvent-based to water-based materials. In addition to eliminating toxic and flammable waste, this switch reduces emissions of volatile organic compounds into the air.

Recycling and Reclamation

While emphasizing that source reduction is a superior method of eliminating waste to recycling or reclamation, the manual supports both practices as means to reduce still further the final waste stream. Two novel ideas from the manual are given here.

As an example of recycling, the manual cites a newspaper advertising printer in California that purchased a machine to produce black newspaper ink from various waste inks. The recycling unit blends the different colors of waste ink together with fresh black ink and black toner to create a new black ink. The price of the unit was realized in 18 months based only on the savings in fresh black ink purchases. The payback improved to 9 months when the costs for disposing of ink as a hazardous waste were included.

Reclamation is the recovery of a valuable material from a hazardous waste. Reclamation differs from use and reuse techniques in that the recovered material is sold. For example, a photo processing company uses an electrolytic deposition cell to recover silver out of the rinse water from film processing equipment. The silver then is sold to a small recycler. Removal of the silver allows the rinse water to be discharged to the sewer without pretreatment. The deposition cell paid for itself in less than two years with the value of silver recovered.

The company also sells used film to the same recycler, which burns the material and extracts additional silver from the ash, rendering the ash nonhazardous.

Feasibility Analysis

Some waste minimization methods unearthed through the early steps of the assessment process may be simple enough to implement without further feasibility analysis. If a large expenditure or a major change in operation is anticipated, however, a feasibility analysis should be completed. The analysis should include technical and economic evaluations and a final report.

Technical Evaluation

The manual suggests visits to existing installations when an equipment purchase is contemplated. Such a visit is important to substantiate vendors' claims. Often it is possible to obtain scale-up data using a rental test unit for bench-scale or pilot-scale experiments. Some vendors even install equipment on a trial basis, with acceptance and payment after a prescribed time. The technical evaluation must consider facility constraints and unique product requirements. Typical technical evaluation criteria are whether the system is safe for workers, whether product quality will suffer, whether space is available, effects on production flow, labor requirements, need for additional utilities, how long production must be stopped to install the equipment, whether special expertise is needed to operate the equipment, vendor reliability, and other environmental effects.

Economic Evaluation

The economic evaluation of a waste reduction project is carried out using standard measures of profitability, such as payback period, return on investment, and net present value.

Capital cost items associated with a large plant upgrading project include not only the fixed capital costs for designing, purchasing, and installing equipment, but also costs for working capital, permitting, training, start-up, and financing charges. Table 1 shows costs that should be considered for a large waste minimization project:

Table 1

Capital Investment for a Typical Large WM Project

Direct Capital Costs
    Site Development
        Demolition and Alteration work
        Site clearing and grading
        Walkways, roads, and fencing
    Process Equipment
        All equipment listed on flow sheets
        Spare parts
        Taxes, freight, insurance, and duties
    Materials
        Piping and ducting
        Insulation and painting
        Electrical
        Instrumentation and controls
        Buildings and structures
    Connections to Existing Utilities and Services (water, HVAC, power, steam, refrigeration, fuels, plant air and inert gas, lighting, and fire control)
    New Utility and Service Facilities (same items as above)
    Other Non-process Equipment
    Construction/Installation
        Construction/Installation labor salaries and burden
        Supervision, accounting, timekeeping, purchasing, safety, and expediting

Temporary facilities
　　　Construction tools and equipment
　　　Taxes and insurance
　　　Building permits, field tests, licenses
　Indirect Capital Costs
　　　In-house engineering, procurement, and other home office costs
　　　Outside engineering, design, and consulting services
　　　Permitting costs
　　　Contractors' fees
　　　Start-up costs
　　　Training costs
　　　Contingency
　　　Interest accrued during construction
　　　　TOTAL FIXED CAPITAL COSTS

　Working Capital
　　　Raw materials inventory
　　　Finished product inventory
　　　Materials and supplies
　　　　TOTAL WORKING CAPITAL

　TOTAL CAPITAL INVESTMENT

Source: Adapted from Perry, *Chemical Engineer's Handbook* (1985); and Peters and Timmerhaus, *Plant Design and Economics for Chemical Engineers* (1980).

The underlying economic goal of any waste minimization project is to reduce or eliminate waste disposal costs and to reduce input material costs. However, a variety of other operating costs and savings also should be considered in order to determine the incremental costs (or savings) of a proposed project. Table 2 shows incremental operating costs and savings and incremental revenues typically associated with waste minimization projects:

Table 2
Operating Costs and Savings Associated with WM Projects

Reduced waste management costs.

This includes reductions in costs for:
Off-site treatment, storage, and disposal fees
State fees and taxes on hazardous waste generators
Transportation costs
On-site treatment, storage, and handling costs
Permitting, reporting, and recordkeeping costs

Input material cost savings.

An option that reduces waste usually decreases the demand for input materials.

Insurance and liability savings.

A WM option may be significant enough to reduce a company's insurance payments. It may also lower a company's potential liability associated with remedial clean-up of TSDFs and workplace safety. (The magnitude of liability savings is difficult to determine.)

Changes in costs associated with quality.

A WM option may have a positive or negative effect on product quality. This could result in higher (or lower) costs for rework, scrap, or quality control functions.

Changes in utilities costs.

Utilities costs may increase or decrease. This includes steam, electricity, process and cooling water, plant air, refrigeration, or inert gas.

Changes in operating and maintenance labor, burden, and benefits.

An option may either increase or decrease labor requirements. This may be reflected in changes in overtime hours or in changes in the number of employees. When direct labor costs change, then the burden and benefit costs will also change. In large projects, supervision costs will also change.

Changes in operating and maintenance supplies.

An option may increase or decrease the use of O&M supplies.

Changes in overhead costs.

Large WM projects may affect a facility's overhead costs.

Changes in revenues from increased (or decreased) production.

An option may result in an increase in the productivity of a unit. This will result in a change in revenues. (Note that operating costs may also change accordingly.)

Increased revenues from byproducts.

A WM option may produce a byproduct that can be sold to a recycler or sold to another company as a raw material. This will increase the company's revenues.

Reducing or avoiding present and future operating costs associated with waste treatment, storage, and disposal are increasingly major elements in cost and savings calculations. As waste disposal costs soar and regulators require more in the way of treatment, such costs may be the dominant force behind any waste minimization project. Table 3 presents typical external costs in 1988 for off-site waste treatment and disposal. In addition to these costs (which continue to escalate), there are significant internal costs, including the labor to store and ship out wastes, liability insurance costs, and on-site treatment costs.

Table 3
Typical Costs of Off-Site Industrial Waste Management*

Disposal	
Drummed hazardous waste**	
Solids	$75 to $110 per drum
Liquids	$65 to $120 per drum
Bulk waste	
Solids	$120 per cubic yard
Liquids	$0.60 to $2.30 per gallon
Lab packs	$110 per drum
Analysis (at disposal site)	$200 to $300
Transportation	$65 to $85 per hour @ 45 miles per hour (round trip)

* Does not include internal costs, such as taxes and fees, and labor for manifest preparation, storage, handling, and recordkeeping.

** Based on 55 gallon drums. These prices are for larger quantities of drummed wastes. Disposal of a small number of drums can be up to four times higher per drum.

A project's profitability is measured using the estimated net cash flows (cash incomes minus cash outlays) for each year of the project's life. For projects with significant capital costs, a detailed profitability analysis is necessary, using the standard profitability measures: payback period, internal rate of return, and net present value.

Payback periods usually are measured in years, though particularly attractive projects may yield payback measured in months. Periods in the range of three to four years are considered acceptable for low-risk investments. This method of profitability analysis is recommended for quick assessments.

For large projects, the payback analysis should be followed by analyses of internal rate of return and net present value, both of which are discounted cash flow techniques for determining profitability. These methods recognize the time value of money by discounting the projected future net cash flows to the present. Most of the popular spreadsheet programs for personal computers can calculate these methods for a series of cash flows. For investments with a low level of risk, an after-tax internal rate of return of 12 percent to 15 percent is typically acceptable, according to the manual.

POINTER➤ According to the manual, calculations concerning the economic merit of a waste expenditure cannot always be made according to the accepted principles shown above. Liability risks and regulatory mandates are not always amenable to standard profitability calculations. Even when risks can be identified, prediction of an actual disaster is difficult. One way of valuing risk reduction is to ease the financial performance requirements of the project; for example, the acceptable payback may be lengthened or the required internal rate lowered. Because perceptions of risk are subjective and impossible to quantify, top-level management may need some persuading that risk reduction is worth more than can be expressed on a printout sheet.

Environmental regulations also throw traditional economic assessment awry. A company operating in violation of environmental regulations could face fines, lawsuits, and criminal penalties for the company's managers. Ultimately, the facility could be shut down.

Final Report

Once all of the above aspects of waste minimization assessment have been accomplished, the final report is needed to sell the idea to management and to the company at large. A good final report may be vital in obtaining funding for the project, the manual states. In presenting the feasibility analysis, it may be useful to evaluate the project under best case and worst case conditions. Sensitivity analyses that indicate the effect of key variables on profitability also are useful.

The report should include not only cost and performance expectations but also information on how the project will be done.

Promoting Waste Minimization

The champions of a waste minimization project are not finished when their report is handed in. Because such projects are not always adopted on their technical merits alone, the assessment team must be prepared to sell its project to a management that has other priorities in mind. The sponsors also must be flexible enough to recognize and appreciate different perspectives. For instance, an organization may be operating under a budget that is directed toward expansion rather than the reduction of current costs. In such circumstances, the team's best option may be to aim for the project's inclusion during the next budgeting period, the manual states.

Even when a project is perceived as valuable, a company may still have financing constraints. A thorough look at available federal, regional, and state funding provisions for innovative pollution reduction projects can be invaluable.

In companies with an ongoing waste minimization program, project sponsors surely have much smoother sailing. When waste minimization is an integral part of the company's operations, budgeting worries should not be so great. In such companies, waste minimization assessments concern all projects, existing and new. The earlier the assessment is performed, the less likely it is that the project will entail expenses later on, the manual asserts. EPA suggests that the waste minimization program task force be privy to all new development projects, from the planning stage forward.

Demonstration and Follow-Up

Follow-up evaluation of a waste reduction project can be trickier, perhaps, than in the case of other process or equipment changes. Such projects are evaluated primarily in terms of reduced waste management and raw materials costs. The easiest—but not necessarily the most accurate—method of measuring waste reduction is by recording the quantities of waste generated before and after the project has been put in place. The difference, divided by the original waste generation rate, represents the percentage reduction in waste quantity. However, this method ignores factors such as production rate. Therefore, a ratio of waste generation rate to production rate may work better, the manual notes, provided a distinction is made between production-related wastes and maintenance and cleanup-related wastes, which may occur only at long intervals.

In other words, care must be taken when expressing the extent of waste reduction. Such calculations must be made only after the means by which wastes are generated are well understood.

To rid oneself of these problems entirely, the manual suggests that a firm using chemicals that are not reactive could measure waste minimization progress during specific operations by using the ratio of input material quantity to material throughput or production rate.

Points to Keep in Mind

A manual developed in 1988 by the Alaska Health Project for small businesses makes many of the same points shown above. The state document also advises the audit team to be sensitive to the following issues:

- Conduct the audit during normal business hours so that the audit team can actually observe processes in operation and talk with the employees about what they are doing.

- Avoid alienating employees who are not directly involved with the audit, as they also have a role in implementing the program and may have good ideas as well.

- Follow the life cycle of your raw materials from their point of entry into the business to the point that they become a waste product (this procedure was used by Kenneth E. Wilson of Dow Chemical U.S.A.'s Plaquemine, Louisiana, plant, as described in the previous chapter).

- Establish a time line for the audit and stick to it.

- Record your observations on forms similar to those in the project manual (see Appendix E).

- Wear protective equipment to prevent exposure or injury. At a minimum, standard safety procedures should be followed, such as the use of safety boots, glasses, hard hats, and disposable work clothes.

- Establish the audit format prior to walking through the business.

- Review information collected during the earlier phases of the audit to help you during the walkthrough.

- Work as a group when conducting the walkthrough. By doing so, the team members can assist each other with record keeping and can improve observations.

The Alaska document, *Profiting from Waste Reduction in Your Small Business*, is available through the Pollution Prevention hotline, or from the Alaska Department of Conservation (see Bibliography).

MODEL STATE LAW

Having determined in mid-1989 that the federal government had not provided adequate leadership in promoting hazardous waste reduction, the Council of State Governments developed a model rule for states to use in developing their own programs. The components of such a regulation are summarized here. The full text of the regulation (see Bibliography) can be obtained from the council.

Components of State Hazardous Waste Reduction Legislation

In developing this legislation, the council found no existing state bills that addressed all of the possible legislative actions. The staff of the council's Center for the Environment and Natural Resources therefore compiled recommendations from numerous other organizations, and sifted out certain elements of existing and proposed state statutes.

General Items

The council recommends that states adopt a waste control hierarchy with a high-level person in charge. This person should have an industrial rather than a regulatory background. States should set a goal for hazardous waste reduction: 50 percent in five years, for example. Finally, states should encourage industry to use full-cost accounting for environmental controls back to the waste generating process.

Financial Issues

States are advised to structure fees for treatment and disposal to encourage waste reduction. Taxes on hazardous waste should be graduated to encourage source reduction or preferred treatment/disposal techniques. For instance, Kentucky assesses half as much for wastes treated on-site as for wastes treated elsewhere. States should also provide tax incentives to encourage treatment equipment purchases, authorize loans or loan guarantees where necessary, and exempt recycled waste products from sales taxes. They should not provide government subsidies, however.

Regulatory Overview

States should consider the following regulatory initiatives:

- Require proof of waste audits for in-state and out-of-state industries before they may dispose of waste in the state. (South Carolina already does this.)

- Develop source reduction plans that phase out certain other waste disposal techniques in favor of source reduction.

- Exempt source reduction improvements from particular permit reviews.

- Ban certain kinds of waste disposal.

- Restrict any disposal technique that is low-cost and inappropriate (such as incineration when recycling is available).

- Do not prescribe industry-specific reduction technologies. (This recommendation conflicts with EPA's findings, described above, that waste minimization requirements work best when they are industry specific.)

- Require waste reduction audits and plans and collect chemical-specific, plant-level mass balance data.

Other Program Components

Further components of a strong program might include technical assistance through state agencies such as the environmental department, commerce department, and independent organizations such as universities; encouragement of waste exchange programs such as those in effect in New York and Texas; research and development of waste reduction technologies; and the rewarding of good performance with "governor's awards" and similar public relations gestures.

Chapter 8

INDUSTRIAL WASTE RECYCLING

The Environmental Protection Agency (EPA) ranks recycling of spent materials directly below source reduction as a desirable means to reduce waste. Both the Waste Minimization Branch of the Office of Solid Waste and the Office of Pollution Prevention include in their rules, training materials, and other documents examples of recycling as well as incentives and policy discussion related to this practice. See Chapters 5 and 6 for discussion of these activities.

This chapter covers the Resource Conservation and Recovery Act (RCRA) hazardous waste recycling regulations, which first define recycling and then explain the conditions under which the activity is exempt from RCRA permitting requirements and the conditions under which it is not. Also included here is information on waste exchanges, which would seem to be indispensable if companies are to locate markets for the increased amount of material that they will want to recycle as they come to grips with waste reduction planning.

Detractors of EPA's recycling rules claim that they are vague and difficult to interpret. However, the agency tried to help by including some specific examples, as shown below. Both in the construction and the enforcement of these rules, EPA must continually balance its desire to encourage recycling with the need to protect the environment.

According to Michael Petruska of the regulatory development branch of EPA's Office of Solid Waste, the importance of the exemption is that it excuses firms from the expensive and often complex task of completing the RCRA permitting process. Petruska's thoughts on the distinction between recycling and pretreatment are described in Chapter 9.

The exemption should never be construed as a method of avoiding other aspects of RCRA rules such as the standards for preventing leaks and corrosion, however. Should an exemption lead to careless hazardous materials management, the more dire consequences of creating a need for corrective action could ensue. In point of fact, past abuses of the recycling systems have led to the inclusion of numerous recycling facilities on the list of Superfund sites.

WASTE CLASSIFICATION RULES FOR RECYCLING (40 CFR 261)

The waste classification rules explain in some detail which activities constitute recycling and which materials are hazardous even when recycled. In interpreting the rules, one must keep in mind the importance of determining whether the activity is oriented toward production. It also is important to understand the difference between reusing and reclaiming materials. As noted below, reclamation is more likely to be subject to RCRA regulation than is use or reuse.

According to EPA's definition, *recycle* is a broad term that includes "to use, reuse, or reclaim." A material is used or reused, in turn, if the following apply:

- The waste is employed as an ingredient (including its use as an intermediate) to make a product. However, a material does not satisfy this condition if its distinct components are recovered as separate end products (as when metals are recovered from metal containing secondary materials).

- The waste is used in a particular function as an effective substitute for a commercial product.

Industrial Waste Recycling

- A material is reclaimed if it is processed to recover a useful product or if it is regenerated. Examples include the recovery of lead values from spent batteries and the regeneration of spent solvents.

Regulated Recycling Activities

Under many conditions, recycled hazardous waste is not exempt from the RCRA provisions. The recycling activities subject to regulation are those that resemble disposal more than they do production, as follows:

- Using the waste in a manner constituting disposal, such as placing it on the land as fertilizer, for instance, or using it to produce materials that are placed on the land unless the materials have been reformulated as commercial fertilizer

- Burning the waste to recover energy or to produce a fuel, except for commercial products normally marketed as fuels

- Reclaiming the waste to recover or regenerate materials (certain wastes only, as specified later in this chapter)

- Accumulating the waste speculatively before recycling unless 75 percent of the waste is recycled during any one-year period

To determine whether a recycled material is hazardous, however, one must know what the material is and how it is being recycled, according to EPA. In other words, decisions often are made on a case-by-case basis.

Hazardous Materials

EPA reasons that the following secondary materials should not be exempt from RCRA coverage when recycled unless under the narrow conditions described below. Of particular importance is the fact that these materials may be recycled in closed-loop systems. As qualified, the prohibited materials include the following:

- Spent materials that are unfit for further use without being regenerated, reclaimed, or reprocessed. Spent solvents, spent activated carbon, spent catalysts, and spent acids are examples.

- Sludges defined as air and wastewater treatment residues, or other residues from pollution control operations, but only if they are listed hazardous wastes.

- Byproducts or nonprimary products that are generated incidentally and that are not intended for any end use. Byproducts cover a broad range of materials that are neither spent materials nor sludges. Again, this prohibition applies only to byproducts that are hazardous.

- Commercial chemical products such as nonspecification variants and spill and container residues (as listed). EPA explains that these wastes are not ordinarily hazardous when recycled and therefore will be regulated only when used in a manner constituting disposal or when burned for energy recovery, assuming they are not pesticides or commercial fuels.

- Scrap metal such as bits and pieces of metal that are discarded after commercial use – scrap automobile, radiator, and other postconsumer scrap and obsolete scrap, such as metal fines. These wastes, while included in EPA's list of prohibited activities, are exempt from RCRA rules until such time as the agency lists them as hazardous. So far, EPA has not signaled any intention to impose RCRA hazardous waste regulations on this large and important recycling industry.

- Inherently waste-like materials. These wastes contain toxic constituents not ordinarily found in raw materials or products exempt in small concentrations. They pose a substantial risk to human health and the environment and are not normally recycled because they are toxic. Examples include wastes F020 through F023, F026, and F028.

Nonhazardous Materials

Despite the number of materials EPA considers hazardous even when recycled, the agency concedes that not all substances are hazardous under such conditions. For example, an unlisted byproduct that is reclaimed is not defined as a hazardous waste unless it is placed on the land directly or used to make a product that is put on the land for beneficial use, burned as a fuel or used to make a fuel, or accumulated speculatively.

In addition, the agency does not consider the following activities to involve waste management, as they are like ordinary production operations and the secondary materials are functioning as raw materials:

- Materials used or reused as ingredients or feedstocks in an industrial process to make a product, provided the materials are not reclaimed

- Materials used or reused directly as effective substitutes for commercial products

- Materials returned to the original process from which they are generated, without first being reclaimed, as long as they are returned as a substitute for raw material feedstock and the process uses raw materials as principal feedstocks (in other words, a closed-loop process)

REGULATIONS FOR RECYCLING ACTIVITIES (40 CFR 266)

The RCRA regulations for recycling activities presuppose that many activities normally associated with recycling truly are exempt. The rules basically cover materials used in a manner constituting disposal or burned for energy recovery. The agency also regulates materials from which precious metals are reclaimed and spent lead acid batteries that are being reclaimed.

"A Manner Constituting Disposal" Defined

Hazardous wastes may not simply be placed on the land as fertilizer in order to be exempt from regulation. Whether used alone or mixed with another substance, they are not exempt unless the hazardous material has undergone a chemical reaction in the production process that makes it physically inseparable from other substances. Commercial fertilizers used for the benefit of the public are exempt under this provision. Even in this case, the hazardous wastes are subject to regulation prior to their incorporation into the fertilizer. Only the final product is exempt from regulation.

EPA illustrates how this provision applies. Generator G produces a hazardous sludge that can be used as a fertilizer ingredient. G stores the waste in a pile for 30 days and then ships it by truck to a fertilizer manufacturer (F). The manufacturer stores the waste in a pile, later blends it with other materials, and sells the resulting product as a commercial fertilizer. In this scenario, G must meet applicable generator standards and obtain a storage permit—waste piles are not exempt under the 90-day accumulation exemption. The hauler must comply with transport rules, and F must obtain a storage permit. Only the fertilizer product is exempt.

If owners or operators of hazardous waste management facilities sell materials to manufacturers of fertilizers or like products, they are subject to the same RCRA requirements as the generators described above.

Hazardous Waste Burned for Energy Recovery

Firms that burn blended hazardous waste fuel in boilers or industrial furnaces not already regulated under RCRA must meet certain requirements under this rule. Used oil burning for energy recovery is covered under different provisions, described below. Waste from small-quantity generators and exempt wastes described in Chapter 2 are not covered by these provisions.

The rules apply to anyone who burns, blends, or markets the fuel but do not apply to haulers of blended fuel or generators whose waste is passed through a middleman (for instance, a hazardous waste management facility) before being blended and burned.

Firms either must market fuels to qualified users, as described below, or obtain an EPA identification number to market it elsewhere. The qualified burners include the following:

- Industrial boilers located on-site and used to recover substances into new products by mechanical or chemical processes.

- Utility boilers used to produce electric power, steam, heated air, cooled air, or other gases or fluids for sale.

- Industrial furnaces or enclosed devices that are integral components of manufacturing processes and use a controlled flame device to accomplish recovery. Such burners may be cement kilns, coke ovens, or refining furnaces, except that no hazardous waste fuel may be burned in a cement kiln located within a municipality with a population greater than 500,000 unless the kiln complies with regulations applied to hazardous waste incinerators.

Boilers qualifying under this rule must be enclosed manufactured using controlled flame combustion that continuously maintains a 60 percent energy recovery efficiency and uses at least 75 percent of the recovered energy, calculated annually.

POINTER EPA announced, on December 31, 1990, that new final regulations would include more stringent air pollution control, recordkeeping, and notification requirements than those described here. See Chapter 10 for details on these rules.

Requirements for Marketers and Generators

Marketers and generators of blended hazardous fuel must notify EPA of their activities, whether or not they are required to have an identification number as noted above. They also must meet all applicable requirements for storage and generation of waste. EPA provides the following example to facilitate understanding of these provisions:

Generator G is a hazardous waste fuel marketer because it markets directly to a burner. Assuming that G is a large-quantity generator, it must comply with the requirements for marketers, including the manifest and storage requirements, and must notify as a hazardous waste fuel marketer. Prior to sending the first shipment, G also must obtain a certification from the burner (B) that it has notified EPA of its waste-as-fuel activities and that it will burn the fuel only in qualified units.

B is a hazardous waste fuel burner and an RCRA storage facility. Assuming it already is engaging in hazardous waste management activities as a facility, B must comply with applicable storage requirements and with the notification and certification requirements noted above. B will have one identification number for storage and burning.

POINTER▶ The above exemption from broad RCRA coverage for boilers and industrial furnaces would end under regulations proposed May 6, 1987, and again on October 26, 1989, and scheduled for final action in 1991. The proposed rules establish standards for controlling emissions of organic compounds, metals, and hydrogen chloride from boilers and industrial furnaces that burn hazardous waste for any purpose, including energy recovery, material recovery, or destruction.

Used Oil for Energy Recovery

Used oil that exhibits a hazardous waste characteristic but does not have so-called off-specification characteristics may be burned, hauled, marketed, and burned without undue regulatory oversight. Normally, the marketer of such oil must meet analysis and recordkeeping requirements. Either the marketer or the burner must notify EPA of its activities. Marketers that burn their own oil, or blenders that treat off-specification oil to meet the specifications, also must perform analysis and recordkeeping tasks.

Oil is off-specification if it exceeds any of the following levels:

- *Arsenic:* 5 parts per million (ppm)
- *Cadmium:* 2 ppm
- *Chromium:* 10 ppm
- *Lead:* 100 ppm
- *Total halogens:* 4,000 ppm

If the flash point is below 100°F, the oil also is off-specification. Used oil with a flash point below 200°F is subject to Department of Transportation regulations as well.

As in the case of hazardous waste blended fuel, EPA provides an example of how the RCRA rules apply to dealers in used oil.

P is a used oil processor who receives this product from a variety of sources and blends the oils to make fuels. The used oil is not mixed with hazardous waste, in which case it would be subject to the rules described above. The blended fuel is off-specification for lead. P sends this fuel to R, a retail fuel dealer. R blends the fuel further so that it meets the lead specification and then sells the fuel to industrial and other users.

As marketer, P may send (with an invoice) his off-specification oil only to a person (for example, R) who has certified to P that he has notified EPA of his waste-as-fuel activities and has obtained an identification number. R also is a marketer because he receives off-specification used oil fuel. Since R markets the used oil as specification fuel, which is exempt from invoice, notification, and other requirements, he must merely document with analysis or other information that the fuel now meets the specifications. R also must keep records of the shipment and the person to whom the fuel was sent.

As noted in Chapter 2, EPA's decision not to list used oil as a hazardous waste was remanded by the U.S. Court of Appeals for the District of Columbia Circuit on October 7, 1988. EPA is collecting additional information on just how toxic such oil may be. The agency projects issuing a new proposal for management of this material in 1991.

Precious Metal Recovery

Firms that generate, transport, or store reclaimable materials for precious metal recovery must comply with notification requirements of the appropriate manifest standards. EPA defines precious metals as significant amounts of gold, silver, platinum, pladium, irridium, osmium, rhodium, or ruthenium. Firms that store these materials must keep records to show that they are not accumulating them speculatively.

An illegal practice that has grown more prevalent with higher copper and other metal prices is burning to recover metal from materials such as insulated wire and transformer parts. The practice may seem profitable but can be lethal to the environment. Emissions that can occur from burning metal include lead, polychlorinated biphenyls, dioxins, and other metals, depending on what is burned.

In Kentucky, where the practice has been under particular scrutiny, the practice is illegal under air pollution regulations, solid waste disposal rules, and (if any of the above-listed metals are involved) the hazardous waste rules.

Spent Lead-Acid Batteries

Firms that store spent batteries before reclaiming them must comply with the notification requirements and all applicable provisions for permitted facilities, except for the waste analysis requirements and the rules dealing with the manifest and manifest discrepancies. Firms that generate, transport, or store spent batteries without reclaiming them are exempt from regulation.

WASTE EXCHANGES

Following the old adage that one man's meat is another man's poison, EPA has encouraged since 1976 the creation of waste exchanges on the premise that the useless byproducts generated by one company may prove useful to another.

Waste exchanges are of two types: the information clearinghouse and the materials exchange. Whereas an information exchange usually is a nonprofit organization sponsored by a chamber of commerce, an industry association, a state agency, or a combination thereof, a materials exchange traditionally is a profit-making venture.

Information clearinghouses are more numerous and are what usually come to mind during discussions of the subject. They publish updated waste listings by type. The generator offering a given waste is listed by code number. The potential user specifies its needs and the code number of the generator offering that waste. The clearinghouse, in turn, gives the generator the name of the potential user. At this point the information exchange bows out, leaving the next move up to the generator that listed the waste.

The materials exchange actually acts as a broker between the waste generator and the purchaser. It buys the waste from one company and sells it to another for profit. After negotiations are completed giving the exchange full title to the waste, it may choose

Industrial Waste Recycling   167

to treat the waste and resell it to another company to use as feedstock. Materials exchanges actually handle waste, and are therefore covered by RCRA provisions, including a share of liability.

Waste exchanges may be state specific or regional. The regional exchanges are the Canadian Waste Materials Exchange and six U.S. regional exchanges, in New York, Illinois, Michigan, North Carolina, Florida, and the state of Washington. Additional waste exchanges have been and are likely to continue to be formed in response to the new emphasis on waste reduction. New programs have been started in Kentucky and Mississippi, for example. A directory of regional, state, and Canadian waste exchanges is included in Appendix A.

National Classification System

Waste exchanges have agreed on a national classification system for waste, divided into the following 11 categories that encompass virtually all hazardous and nonhazardous waste:

- Acids
- Alkalis
- Other inorganic chemicals
- Solvents
- Other organics
- Oils and waxes
- Plastics and rubber
- Textiles and leather
- Wood and paper
- Metal and metal sludges
- Miscellaneous

Determining Markets

According to a report by the Southern Waste Information Exchange, Canadian and regional U.S. materials exchanges listed as available in 1988 some 8 million metric tons of material included in 1,929 listings. These listings generated approximately 9,000 responses. The exchanges mailed 300,000 catalogs, an increase of 59 percent since 1984. During the same time frame, listings and inquiries more than doubled as well. Waste exchange operators estimate that 10 percent to 30 percent of the available listings actually are exchanged.

Such estimates are made more difficult because of the information exchanges' arms-length method of doing business. They bow out before negotiations lead to a final contract. This actually is what many businesses prefer, according to Bob Smee, director of the Pacific Materials Exchange. Companies often view contracts to purchase waste materials as being just as confidential as information regarding raw materials purchases. The competition for some wastes is keen, Smee said.

Waste Exchange Constraints

The amounts listed on waste exchanges, much less the amounts actually exchanged, are "infinitesimal compared to the amount of wastes that are being produced," according to Jeffrey Dauphin, director of the Great Lakes/Midwest Waste Exchange. The actual amount of waste exchanged through the six large regional operations constitutes only between a tenth and a quarter of 1 percent of the waste produced in America, he said.

According to various representatives of the industry, several constraints limit greater use of the exchanges, as follows:

- Fear of potential liability is strong among hazardous waste generators. Large companies typically want to manage their own waste or to maintain relations with a trusted treatment, storage, and disposal facility. To ease these fears, businesses can use the same safeguards in an exchange relationship as those that apply to a standard waste disposal relationship. They can inspect the recycling facility, conduct spot checks, and otherwise ensure safe handling.

- The economics have traditionally been too weak to promote waste exchange, especially when transportation costs are high. Waste material often is voluminous, with very little intrinsic value. As treatment and disposal costs rise, however, the attractiveness of exchanges grows. Moreover, if firms can send unaltered waste to a recycling facility, they can have it reclassified to a nonhazardous category, thus reducing manifest costs and avoiding the generator taxes under the federal Superfund as well as many state laws.

- Permitting new recycling facilities is a "Catch-22" situation. New facilities are needed, especially to handle plating wastes, or acid wastes or solvents, but new facilities are slow to materialize because of what some consider an arduous permitting process. However, many of the liability fears noted above were prompted by past abuses of the recycling system. Streamlining the permitting procedure may bring the facilities on line more promptly but may also increase fears of liability.

- Time and staffing constraints plague both the generators and the exchanges. It is not uncommon for a waste exchange plan to take 18 months of study, often leading to changes in a waste's constituents to suit the needs of the recycler. Exchanges must convince companies that the effort is worth the time. At the same time, the exchanges are understaffed and cannot devote enough time to marketing.

Waste exchanges need to encompass wide areas in order to achieve successful results. Efforts are under way to convince all exchanges to publish their listings on a nationwide database. Concerns also have been raised by the large regional exchanges that states and even municipal areas may jump into the action, taking away business from them. Dauphin remarks that such exchanges "could create useless overlaps in service, which would cause interference and confusion for the more established exchanges and clients."

Future Opportunities

Waste exchange operators see great promise in the future, especially with regard to the recycling of nonhazardous waste. They believe that the greatest growth will be in the marketing of recyclables from the municipal waste stream and are heartened by the interest of large companies in purchasing recycled materials, Dauphin said.

Waste exchanges also are looking abroad to increase markets. The Pacific Rim countries present an especially attractive market, according to Smee, because "Asian people do not waste." The countries in this region that have or soon will have exchanges include

Australia, Indonesia, Japan, Korea, New Zealand, the Philippines, and Taiwan.

There are growing opportunities in many other countries as well, from Europe to the Bahamas. However, there are international laws regarding the transport of waste, especially hazardous waste, that are increasingly stringent. These, of course, increase costs.

The waste exchange industry has grown considerably since its beginnings in 1976, all agree. With the new emphasis on recycling and other forms of waste reduction, including the new requirements that companies design detailed waste reduction plans, the future of effective waste exchanges seems assured.

Chapter 9

MUNICIPAL SOLID WASTE RECYCLING

The Environmental Protection Agency (EPA) predicts that more than half of U.S. municipal solid waste will be recycled by the year 2000, according to Assistant Administrator for the Office of Solid Waste Don Clay. However, Clay is less optimistic about what can be accomplished by 1992, stating that he doubts the nation as a whole will reach EPA's expressed goal of a 25 percent reduction by that time. Advancing the procurement of recycled products by all levels of government is seen by the agency as a primary task in strengthening the markets for recycled products, Clay added (see below).

Public acceptance of recycling as a realistic answer to the U.S. solid waste problem is at an all-time high. In its most recent opinion research survey, conducted by telephone to 1,250 randomly selected adults and 500 "opinion leaders," the National Solid Wastes Management Association (NSWMA) found that 60 percent of the respondents consider a combination of recycling, incineration, and land filling necessary to solve the United States' waste management problems.

Recycling gained popularity in this poll, NSWMA found, noting that 92 percent of the general public and 94 percent of opinion leaders believe that a major commitment to recycling will substantially reduce the nation's solid waste. According to the 1990 general public survey, 74 percent believe that we can recycle more than 25 percent of our waste. Fully 25 percent of those surveyed believe that 41 percent to 50 percent of the waste stream can be recycled, while another 24 percent aim even higher, stating that 51 percent to 75 percent recycling goals are achievable.

However, there remain institutional barriers to extensive recycling of some materials. For instance, the Food and Drug Administration's (FDA) exclusion of recycled plastics from uses entailing direct contact with food has been a major barrier to further recycling by Rubbermaid Commercial Products, Inc., according to spokesman Charles J. Lancelot. However, in a major breakthrough, the administration, on January 15, 1991, gave Coca-Cola Co. and Hoechst Celanese Corp. (a recycler) permission to proceed with their plan to bottle Coke products in recycled plastic containers. In approving the application, FDA emphasized that the plastic in these bottles would be regenerated rather than merely recycled. An application by Pepsi-Cola, which has teamed with the Goodyear Tire and Rubber Co. in a recycling scheme using a slightly different regenerating process, was still pending at that time. FDA consumer safety officer Kenneth Falci said it plans to view each process separately. FDA also has issued favorable opinions on other recycled packaging used for food, including egg cartons and plastic grocery bags.

While supporting recycling as a principle, public policymakers are not always as enthusiastic about broad-scale recycling initiatives as are citizens and environmental groups. In the debate preceding the removal of the 25 percent recycling provision from the new source performance standard for municipal waste combustors, eight out of nine public comments were opposed to the measure. For example, Corey Stein, a regional vice president for the Public Risk Management Association, said most taxpayers do not realize the significant up-front costs associated with source separation. In addition to equipment costs, Stein cited potential liabilities of employees' excess exposure to bacteria and hazardous materials in trash.

In its opposition to the measure, the National Association of Counties indicated, among other things, how committed state and local environmental agencies are to media-specific regulation rather than the integrated approach recommended by EPA. Barbara Paley, associate director of the group, said inclusion of a recycling provision in an air pollution control regulation "would have a perverse impact on recycling, because it would have...put local air administrators in charge of solid waste."

SOURCE REDUCTION

The focus of this chapter is on recycling rather than source reduction. However, no amount of recycling will relieve the intense burden on landfills and incinerators unless the amount of solid waste also can be reduced at the source. Packaging must change; products must be made to last; sweeping categories of labor-saving, waste generating consumer goods that cannot easily be recycled—such as disposable diapers, prepackaged meals, and throwaway razors—must be rejected, an unlikely event when two-income families need more spare time, not less.

The objective of source waste reduction frequently conflicts with other marketing or societal objectives that are difficult for consumers to change. When grocery stores package fruits and vegetables to extend shelf life or ease checkout, or when manufacturers increase and toughen packaging to prevent tampering, make their products more visible, or crowd other products off the shelves, most busy consumers have neither the will nor the clout to effect change.

Manufacturers are beginning to help. The decision of McDonald's, Inc., to stop using styrofoam in the packaging of many of its products is a strong example of this kind of leadership. As another example, Procter and Gamble now markets a replacement box of concentrated fabric softener that can be placed in an existing plastic jug and mixed with water to make an equal but cheaper product.

However, most manufacturers balk at changing the packaging that they see as a way to boost sales. As an example, the makers of compact disks could package their products without the long box that immediately is removed and discarded. However, they view the box as a place to print alluring pictures and as an effective way to display their product. As EMI (USA) President Sal Licata wrote in *Billboard* magazine, "If we choose to eliminate the 6-by-12 CD package from our marketplace, we will not only reduce our presence there, but with it our punch."

Nevertheless, source reduction remains the top priority in EPA's thinking, as well as in state solid waste management plans. It is a practice harder to stimulate than recycling. The players are much larger; the stakes are high. But as businesses realize that consumers want environmentally friendly products and as state laws begin to emerge requiring various forms of source reduction, the atmosphere should change.

THE RECYCLING ADVISORY COUNCIL

A top priority in EPA's "Agenda for Action" (see Chapter 3), the Recycling Advisory Council (RAC) is a body of 16 recognized leaders from civic and environmental groups, the recycling industry, other businesses and industries, the National Recycling Coalition, and all levels of government. The council's mission is to analyze America's potential for recycling and private initiatives that promote recycling, consistent with a safe and healthy environment. The chairman of the group is Fred Krupp, executive director of the Environmental Defense Fund.

At its first meeting, held in April 1990, the council agreed to focus on three areas:

- Developing markets for secondary materials and for products made from these materials

- Evaluating and recommending fiscal policies to encourage and increase recycling

- Working with manufacturers to foster the development and design of products that can be recycled

The council also has released (but, as of January 15, 1991, had not presented to EPA) a standard definition of recycling, according to spokesperson Edgar Miller. Under this definition "recycling is the diversion of materials from the solid waste stream and the beneficial use of such materials." Recycling is further defined as the diversion of waste material for collection, separation, and processing for use as raw material or feedstock in lieu of or in addition to virgin materials to manufacture goods that otherwise would be made from virgin materials.

The council operates through task forces gathered from over 50 organizations that have volunteered to help. The initial committees will concentrate on paper, plastic, and policy issues. The council operates out of the offices of the National Recycling Coalition, Inc., an umbrella organization. For more information on the council's activities and its relationship to the coalition, readers may contact Edgar Miller by telephone at (202) 625-6410 or write to the counsel (see Associations directory at Appendix A).

MARKETS FOR RECYCLED MATERIALS

According to Leslie Legg, the NSWMA analyst who wrote the recycling report noted above, markets for recycled products, especially newsprint, are clogged, especially in urban areas such as the Northeast. The paper industry is building several newsprint recycling plants, she said, but these will not be on line for another year or two. Meanwhile, she said, demand for newsprint is shrinking. The market for clear glass is strong, but buyers for colored glass are too few.

Transportation costs dictate the economics of recycling, Legg added. In areas near lumber mills, for instance, there may be no shortage of markets for paper. Efforts are being made to site new processing plants near cities, she said, but public opposition to such projects can run high. Further discussion of the markets for individual products is found later in this chapter.

EPA's Procurement Program

The Resource Conservation and Recovery Act (RCRA) of 1976 required EPA and the Department of Commerce to develop and implement, within two years, guidelines for the procurement of recycled materials. Despite this mandate, little was done to encourage the federal government to use recycled materials until 1987, when the Environmental Defense Fund and several other groups sued EPA, asking the court to place the agency on an expedient schedule (*EDF v. EPA*, No. 87-3212 D.C.C.). This case resulted in a consent decree under which the agency would make final the proposed guidelines for recycled paper and explore further categories for study.

The agency then issued the earlier proposed paper guideline in final form, while proposing an amendment to create minimum content standards. Soon thereafter, the agency proposed and then issued guidelines for oil, tires, and insulation materials, as described in greater detail below.

The agency's procurement program has taken on a new life under the leadership of Terry Grogan, chief of the agency's recycling section. In addition to implementing and monitoring the guidelines noted above, the office is working on further guidelines for the building trade, covering the raw materials used in a range of construction products such as plastic piping and doorframes. In the future, the agency hopes to create markets for compost from yard waste and develop specifications for paving material derived from used asphalt rubber, according to Grogan. The latter process already has been tested by several rubber companies, Grogan said. In fact, Oregon may have specifications in place before EPA, as the state's Department of Environmental Quality and the Portland Metropolitan Service District work on a pilot plan to use rubber-modified asphalt concrete in road sections in the Portland area. Using information derived from this experiment, the state hopes to develop specifications for general use.

In addition to this work on future guidelines, EPA plans to reexamine a guideline governing fly ash content that was issued in 1983 but has had little agency attention in recent years, Grogan said.

This move by EPA to implement procurement guidelines can make a significant contribution to the growth of recycling in the United States. The government purchases approximately 2.5 percent of the paper industry's production. The U.S. Government Printing Office alone purchases some 486,000 tons of printing paper per year, including that used in the daily *Congressional Record* and *Federal*

Register, both of which were scheduled in late 1990 to be printed on recycled paper.

EPA's four currently active procurement guidelines cover

- Paper and paper products
- Lubricating oils
- Retread tires
- Building insulation products

The procurement guidelines apply to federal procuring agencies, and to state and local agencies using appropriated federal funds if they spend more than $10,000 a year on the designated item. Thus, if a county government spends more than $10,000 a year on paper, and part of that money is from appropriated federal funds, the county government must follow the procurement guidelines in purchasing paper.

The procurement guidelines require affected agencies and governments to review and revise their specifications and establish an affirmative procurement program for purchasing the designated item to the maximum extent practicable. Typical specifications that should be revised include restrictions requiring virgin materials, exclusions of recovered materials, and unnecessarily restrictive performance standards that preclude the use of items containing recovered materials. However, agencies are not expected to purchase reclaimed materials if their use would unduly jeopardize quality.

An affirmative procurement program should include four components: a preference program, a promotion program, procedures for obtaining and verifying estimates and certifications of recovered materials content, and annual review and monitoring.

RCRA does not direct EPA to enforce the procurement guidelines. Instead, individuals may file suit against an agency for violating or ignoring the procurement provisions. Anyone who is injured by such failure may take civil action, either through EPA's protest procedures, the General Accounting Office protest procedures, or the federal courts.

Individual Procurement Guidelines

EPA so far has issued specific procurement guidelines for paper, lubricating oil, retread tires, and building insulation, as follows:

Paper: The guideline for paper and paper products containing recovered materials was issued in June 1988. Effective one year after that date, the guideline recommends that procuring agencies set their minimum content levels at the highest levels possible but no lower than the levels shown in Table 1.

Table 1
EPA Recommended Minimum Content Standards for Selected Papers and Paper Products

	Minimum percentage of recovered materials	Minimum percentage of postconsumer recovered materials	Minimum percentage of waste paper [1]
Newsprint	—	40	—
High grade bleached printing and writing papers:			
Offset printing	—	—	50
Mimeo and duplicator paper	—	—	50
Writing (stationary)	—	—	50
Office paper (e.g., note pads)	—	—	50
Paper for high-speed copiers	—	—	(2)
Envelopes	—	—	50
Form bond including computer paper and carbonless	—	—	(2)
Book papers	—	—	50
Bond papers	—	—	50
Ledger	—	—	50
Cover stock	—	—	50
Cotton fiber papers	25	—	—
Tissue products:			
Toilet tissue	—	20	—
Paper towels	—	40	—
Paper napkins	—	30	—
Facial tissue	—	5	—
Doilies	—	40	—
Industrial wipers	—	0	—
Unbleached packaging:			
Corrugated boxes	—	35	—
Fiber boxes	—	35	—
Brown papers (e.g., bags)	—	5	—
Recycled paperboard:			
Recycled paperboard products including folding cartons	—	80	—
Pad backing	—	90	—

[1] Waste paper is defined in 40 CFR 250.4 and refers to specific postconsumer and other recovered materials.

EPA stresses that in the case of printing and writing paper, a waste paper content is recommended; for the newsprint, tissue, packaging, and paperboard categories, a postconsumer waste content is used as the standard.

Noting that recycled paper products sometimes are more expensive than their alternatives, the guideline notes that Section 6002 of RCRA allows an agency to reject a recycled item if the price is too high. Moreover, procuring agencies are not expected to tolerate unusual and unreasonable delays in obtaining paper. Performance also must be adequate. Noting a common fear that recycled paper causes difficulty in high-speed presses and copier machines, EPA observes that state agencies with strong recycled materials programs have had good experience with recycled paper. Agencies should consider trial tests of newly procured paper, the guideline advises.

Government agencies also are told to promote the fact that they are seeking to buy recycled paper, establish procedures to verify that paper meets the necessary specifications, and undertake an annual review of program effectiveness.

Lubricating Oils: This guideline, issued June 30 and effective one year later, requires government agencies to purchase re-refined engine lubricating oils, hydraulic fluids, and general purpose gear oils. It recommends that agencies use a minimum recovered materials content standard of 25 percent re-refined oil in the base stock when purchasing these items.

Unlike paper, used oil does not constitute a large percentage by volume of the solid waste stream. However, it contains hazardous constituents and may be contaminated with other hazardous materials, such as solvents or polychlorinated biphenyls. Traditionally, used oil has been used for dust and mosquito control, sometimes with disastrous results. Used oil also may be recycled as a fuel or fuel supplement. However, this application allows the fuel to be reused only once, whereas re-refining allows the oil to be reused many times, EPA observes.

Except for specifying a minimum re-refined oil content, the guideline has no unique specifications. EPA notes that all lubricating oil, whether virgin or re-refined, must meet military specifications or the American Petroleum Institute service levels through testing of the oil package. The list of oils meeting military specifications is maintained by the U.S. Army's Fort Belvoir, Virginia, Research and Development Center. Studies undertaken by EPA in the development of the procurement guideline show that re-refined oils are substantially equivalent to virgin oils, and in some respects actually perform better than their virgin counterpart.

EPA notes that re-refined oil has been criticized because its quality diminishes as the catalysts used during re-refining wear down. While this is true, EPA observes, the same happens to catalysts used in the refining of virgin oil. In both cases, the catalyst must be changed from time to time.

Retread Tires: The scope of the U.S. scrap tire problem is immense. The materials accumulate as an eyesore in rural fields or are deposited in landfills, where they inevitably rise to the top and sometimes spontaneously ignite, creating horrendous polluting fires. As one example, a pile of 4 million tires ignited in Winchester, Virginia, in 1983. It took federal, state, and county government agencies eight months to control the fire at a cost to the federal government alone of $1.2 million, according to an EPA document in support of the procurement guideline.

The states are using a number of tools to manage this scrap tire problem, including increased landfill tipping fees for tires, landfill bans, restriction of tires to monofills, taxes on new tires to raise revenue for scrap tire management, and the construction of waste-to-energy facilities to burn tire chips, EPA observes.

The retread tire guideline, issued November 17, 1988, complements the efforts already being made by many states. The guideline recommends that agencies obtain retreading services for their used tires and purchase retread tires. Retreading services can be purchased in a number of ways, EPA notes, adding that the purchasing agency usually specifies the type of tread desired. The contractor also may be asked to guarantee the tread for a specified mileage.

The GSA is the lead federal agency for these guidelines. As of the end of June 1990, GSA had revised its specification for replacement tires (ZZ-T-381). The agency completed tests of retread tires in order to be ready to implement the guideline by the November 17, 1990, deadline.

Building Insulation: According to EPA, a number of building insulation materials can be manufactured with recovered materials, including cellulose, fiberglass, perlite composite board, plastic foams and boards, and rock wool. All of these products fall within the scope of a guideline issued February 17, 1989. As is the case for all of the guidelines, procuring agencies must have a program in place one year later. As it did for paper, EPA recommended minimum content standards (based on the weight of material in the insulating core only) for recovered materials in building insulation products, as follows:

- Cellulose loose-fill and spray on: 75 percent postconsumer recovered paper.

- Perlite composite board: 23 percent postconsumer recovered paper.

- Plastic foams: 5 percent to 9 percent recovered material depending on the type of foam.

- Rock wool: 50 percent recovered material. (In an advisory sent February 17, 1989, EPA informed procuring agencies that many manufacturers can accomplish 75 percent recovery rates in this process.)

The guideline also advises agencies to place the responsibility for choosing the required insulation products on the designing architect or engineer, whether a contractor or an employee.

Information Sources

Sources on recycled materials markets are increasing as associations, state agencies, and EPA generate new materials on the subject. Some of these information sources are described here.

Markets on the Phone: EPA's Procurement Hotline

EPA has established a procurement hotline to answer questions from government agencies, vendors, and the public concerning its federal procurement program described earlier in this chapter. The agency also is developing lists of manufacturers and vendors. Copies of the lists, as well as the guidelines, can be obtained by calling the hotline at (703) 941-4452.

Markets on Line

A computer bulletin board that began as a means of helping link buyers to markets in Florida has grown to serve recyclers throughout the United States. Commissioned by the state Department of Environmental Regulation (DER), the Florida Recycling Marketing System (FRMS) is scheduled to be operated at least through mid-1991 by Clark, Roumelis & Associates. After that, the system will be operated by the DER, funded further to Clark, Roumelis & Associates, or sold.

Anyone with a computer modem can call the toll-free number to access the bulletin board. FRMS prefers IBM-compatible computers, but others may work on a limited basis. Users can register their name and company in the computer directory. Besides being listed in a directory, users can place a classified advertisement to buy or sell recyclables, free of charge. Those seeking markets or suppliers simply search the advertisements for contacts. The current log-on number is (800) 348-1239. To learn the status of the system after June 1991, contact the FRMS at (904) 576-0478. (This is a type of waste exchange but focuses on nonhazardous waste. Other waste exchanges are listed in Appendix A, Directories.)

Markets in Print

Associations also furnish market information. As noted elsewhere, both the American Paper Institute and the Glass Packaging Institute furnish updated materials reflecting markets in their industries. Another useful source of marketing information is NSWMA's *Waste Age's Recycling Times*, a biweekly news publication (printed on recycled paper) that furnishes, among other items, price information by market region of paper (paid by processors and by end users or mills), aluminum used beverage cans and scrap, glass

Municipal Solid Waste Recycling 183

(paid by processors, dealers, and by end users), plastics, steel cans, and miscellaneous recyclables. The subscription price is $95 per year.

> *Waste Age's Recycling Times*
> National Solid Wastes Management Association
> Suite 1000
> 1730 Rhode Island Ave.
> Washington, DC 20036-3196
> (202) 861-1708 (circulation)

EPA also has a recycling publication, *Reusable News*, published quarterly. This report does not contain current marketing information but does keep readers abreast of market trends and notifies them of the agency's activities and new publications. (See the Bibliography for a list of EPA's manuals on all subjects related to waste management.)

MUNICIPAL RECYCLING PRODUCTS AND MARKETS

States, counties, and municipalities are developing curbside recycling programs and/or drop-off centers faster than markets become available for recyclable materials. The products most frequently recycled include old newspaper and/or mixed paper, aluminum, glass, and plastics. Issues relating to each of these products are discussed here.

Aluminum

Aluminum recycling is now a well-established practice, and thus entails fewer risks and unknown elements than other recycling activities. The United States is the world's largest producer and user of aluminum products, most of which are beverage cans. Because the production of primary aluminum is expensive and energy intensive, the industry has been a willing purchaser of scrap material. There are more than 50 secondary aluminum producers in operation in the United States. Especially impressive is the rate of recovery in this industry. In 1988, 77.9 billion aluminum beverage cans were shipped and 42.5 billion cans were recovered, indicating an aluminum can recovery rate of almost 55 percent. In 1989, the recycling percentage increased to 60.8 percent. In 1990, according to John Dickenson, the Aluminum Association's director of statistical services, the recycling rate increased again, to about 67 percent, based on receipts covering some 95 percent of the market.

Recycling is an integral part of the aluminum industry, Dickenson said. At primary smelters, the valuable alumina has long been salvaged from the waste stream. All waste material from the manufacture of aluminum products is recycled as "new scrap." Used scrap, salvaged from items as diverse as automobiles and home appliances, is marketed by well-established scrap dealers, an "old time business," Dickenson said. A new development is the flourishing used can market, he said, noting that industry spokespersons predict a 75 percent recycling rate for these items within the next few years.

Scrap aluminum prices reflect the strength of this market. Whereas paper prices, including even those of high grades like white ledger and laser-free computer printout, slumped during the summer of 1990, prices for both aluminum cans and other types of aluminum scrap increased.

The Aluminum Association produced, in December 1985, the *Aluminum Recycling Casebook* (see Bibliography), which now is out of date in some respects but contains useful information on the types and costs of various aluminum recycling and trash separation systems.

Paper

Some readers might be surprised to learn that paper recycling is quite an ancient art. According to Robert Mitchell, manager of procurement and industrial relations for the Mobile Paperboard Corp., the Rittenhouse mill near Philadelphia manufactured paper from recycled materials in 1690. As late as 1904, 40 percent of paper was made of recycled materials derived from textiles as well as waste paper. During World War II a new recycling wave hit, when a peak of 35.3 percent recycled material was reached in 1944. After the war, a population tired of stamping on tin cans and bundling old newspapers sent recycling levels to an all-time low.

American Paper Institute Program

With the new national focus on waste problems, the pendulum has swung back. The American Paper Institute, Inc. (API), announced in early 1990 that it has set a new national goal of 40 percent paper recovery and reuse by the end of 1995. Achievement of this goal will require the domestic recycling and export of about 40 million tons of waste paper per year, a 50 percent increase over 1988 levels, according to API. If the 40 percent level is to be reached, the American paper collection infrastructure also must increase, API contends. The infrastructure must be capable not only of recovering large amounts of paper, but of ensuring that the paper is of sufficient quality to be recycled, cleaned, and sorted by grades, the institute notes, adding that success will require state and local governmental cooperation. Markets also will vary, depending on manufacturing processes, mill location, and end product, the study points out. To do its share in reaching the goal, the paper industry has committed itself to expanding recycling capacity in at least 37 facilities and to constructing 8 new mills.

API also has published a book listing paper companies that use recycled paper feedstock and communities and recycling centers that supply the material planning and communications.

The book, called *PaperMatch*, is mailed free of charge to thousands of paper recycling participants, according to Robert T. McKernan, vice president of policy planning and communications. It not only lists user companies but notes their procurement needs, he added. Because the paper recycling industry is growing and changing so rapidly, the book is updated frequently. Copies are available from API by calling (202) 463-2420.

According to McKernan, there are approximately 600 U.S. mills producing pulp, paper, paperboard, or related products, of which some 200 depend almost entirely on waste paper for their raw material. Another 300 use between 20 percent and 50 percent waste paper in their pulping process. During 1988, almost 26 million tons of waste paper were recycled, a recovery rate of 30 percent of all paper consumed. When compared to a 12.5 million ton recovery rate in 1970, this is impressive progress.

The paper recycling business has undergone explosive change in the last three years, McKernan said. Where once demand exceeded supply, the opposite now is true, and some market disruption is inevitable, he continued. The necessary new production capacity will cost "tens of millions of dollars," an expenditure the industry is making, he stressed, but not overnight. He estimates that markets will stabilize in the next five years.

Paper Types

There are 49 types of paper and 31 specialty grades, all of which are not equally valuable as recycled material, according to Mitchell. The main categories are as follows:

- Old newspapers, which are used mostly to make new newsprint and recycled paperboard.

- Old corrugated containers and container plant cuttings (collected now from virtually every major retailer), which are used to make linerboard, corrugated "medium," and recycled paperboard.

- Mixed paper, used almost exclusively for paperboard.

- Pulp substitutes, which include unprinted grades of brown and colored kraft, tabulating cards, white and semibleached sheets and cuttings, and shavings or trim of unprinted grades, also used mostly in paperboard.

- High-grade or de-inking paper, which includes computer printout, office ledgers, coated book and groundwood paper, and bleached sulfate sheets and cuttings. This paper, which can be de-inked profitably, is used to make tissue and printing or writing paper. There can be problems (described below) even with this high-grade paper.

Case Examples

Caithness King Co.: Mitchell's observations concerning the value of various grades may be too conservative. Two new mills planned by Caithness King Co. of Stamford, Connecticut, would de-ink old newspapers and old magazines into a marketable pulp to be sold to paper companies that want to add recycled content without building their own de-inking facilities. The pulp would be sold to producers of value-added groundwood paper products such as phone directory paper, specialty coated paper used for newspaper inserts, and groundwood-containing magazine paper. Publications such as *Time* magazine could handle up to 50 percent of this pulp in their paper, according to Paul Stern, manager of environmental affairs for Caithness King. The technology for this process comes from Europe and Japan, Stern said. The multistage system can manage newspaper and magazine waste, even when they are commingled, he added.

The paper recycling business has both large and small players. While the major paper companies all have stepped up investment in recycling, smaller companies devoted entirely to recycling also have shown impressive growth. Two examples, one of a major investment by James River Corp. and the other of the activities of the Mobile Paperboard Corp. of the Newark Group, provide an indication of the scale of paper recycling activities poised for the 1990s.

James River Corp.: This large company announced, on June 14, 1990, that it would build a $65 million waste office paper recycling plant in Oregon, due for completion in late 1991 or early 1992. The plant will create a major market for waste paper for the entire area west of the Mississippi River to the Pacific Ocean and north into western Canada, according to Charles Warren of the firm's pulp and paper plant in Halsey, Oregon.

The plant will clean and process 450 tons per day of industrial and commercial office waste paper to produce up to 300 tons per day of high-grade pulp. The pulp will be used to manufacture tissue and towels at the Halsey facility, as well as other paper products at the company's other Northwest facilities.

As is the practice at many paper recycling enterprises, James River will blend some of the recycled pulp with virgin pulp to maintain fiber strength. Other products will be derived from 100 percent recycled materials.

This plant was heralded as a welcome addition to western markets, which were inadequate, composed of only small facilities in California and Arizona, Warren said. James River, the third largest paper producer in the United States, has four other U.S. recycling plants, of which this will be the largest.

Mobile Paperboard Corp.: This is an old-timer among recycling plants. Started in the early 1900s, it is the oldest paper mill in Alabama and has become a regional leader in the recycling business. The company receives about 2,000 tons of waste paper per month, thus creating a market to support massive waste paper recycling throughout the Southeast.

The company's capacity was doubled when it purchased from Scott Paper Company (for $1.00) a surplus cylinder boxboard machine. The machine, as reconstructed from Scott components, is capable of producing the full range of industrial grades of recycled paperboard. With state-of-the-art stock preparation, new presses, additional drying capacity, and modern process controls, the machine is twice as productive as its parent. This is the first such installation in the last 15 years and represents a substantial commitment to production of recycled paper products.

Mobile Paperboard serves as a collection center not only for paper, but for aluminum and glass as well. It purchases some 65,000 pounds per month of cans and 25,000 pounds per month of glass, which are sold to Reynolds Metals, Inc., and Owens-Illinois, respectively. The company pays out some $1 million per year to local recycling participants, including schools, churches, and clubs, as well as communities and individuals.

The firm is a subsidiary of the Newark Group, Inc., headquartered in Cranford, New Jersey. The group holds a network of similar paperboard mills, recycled fiber mills, and other packaging companies throughout the United States.

A Market Glut

An example of the vagaries of the old newspaper market is the case of Browning Ferris Industries (BFI). Suddenly, in late 1990, the company had a glut of newspapers that filled its warehouses and was spilling outside. As recently as a year before, the Cincinnati market yielded BFI $25 per ton for BFI's old paper. Once the company's curbside program took hold, the principal buyer, Cincinnati Paperboard Corp., was swamped. Having at one time taken all of the paper BFI could produce, the buyer suddenly dropped the price and then took none at all, according to BFI district recycling manager Bob Case. The company now must decide whether to continue to rely on the shaky local market or take the more expensive option of baling the paper and shipping it elsewhere, he said.

Prices are jittery even for high-quality de-inking paper, partly because mills vary their orders, sometimes preferring virgin pulp at exactly the time when supplies of computer printout have increased through office recycling programs. Laser-printed paper entails a further problem, NSWMA reports. Laser printing contaminates the pulp, causing it to stain recycled paper. As laser printers replace conventional printers in more and more markets, opportunities to recycle computer printout will decrease, primarily because the difference between laser printout and high-quality nonlaser printout is hard to spot.

Plastic Markets

Plastic constitutes some 7.5 percent of the solid waste stream and an even greater disposal problem. The recycling of most plastics after use remains negligible except in the case of two resins, polyethylene terephthalate (PET) and high-density polyethylene, the raw materials of plastic soda bottles and milk jugs. Growth in the recycling of other materials was, until mid-1990, a slow process. However, extensive experimentation has taken place on polystyrene and polyvinyl chloride and has begun to flourish, as described below.

High-density polyethylene, which comes largely from the base cups for PET soft drink containers, can be recycled into lumber substitutes, base cups for soft drink bottles, flower pots, pipes, toys, pails and drums, traffic barrier cones, golf bag liners, kitchen drain boards, milk bottle crates, soft drink bottle carriers, trash cans, and signs.

Similarly, PET can be recycled into an imposing array of products, including strapping, scouring pads, fence posts, parking space bumpers, industrial paints, paint brushes, fiberfill for pillows, ski jackets, sleeping bags, carpet fibers, rope, sails, and tire cord. The material also is used to produce other plastics such as polyol, unsaturated polyester, engineering plastics, and thermoformable sheets.

At the first plastics roundtable of the Institute of Scrap Recycling Industries, held in late summer 1990 in Atlanta, Georgia, speakers were skeptical of claims concerning the processing of plastics other than PET or high-density polyethylene. For these plastics, however, the market appeared to be large. Dennis Sabourin of Wellman, Inc., a plastics recycling firm in Shrewsbury, New Jersey, said his firm could process twice as much as it was receiving. To get more plastic, Wellman has gone into partnership with companies such as Browning-Ferris Industries.

Applications

As shown here, statements concerning the recyclability of various plastic materials are outdated almost as fast as they are made. Increasingly, the complaint is not about the recyclability of plastic materials but the availability of supply. As in the case of glass described below, plastic items, to be desirable as recyclable material, must be uncontaminated, of predictable quality and color, and in orderly supply. Despite such barriers, both the large and the small players within the plastic industry have responded to public opinion with energy and creativeness, as shown in the examples below.

Rubbermaid Commercial Products, Inc.: Rubbermaid estimates that the demand for recycled plastics will continue to grow and that demand will exceed supply during the 1990s, as a result of continued shortages in the availability of recycled materials. The company nevertheless increased its consumption of recycled plastics from the 1990 amount of 1 million pounds per year to more than 5 million pounds per year going into 1991, at which point recycled plastics accounted for 5 percent to 10 percent of all resin consumed in making Rubbermaid's commercial products, according to Charles J. Lancelot of Rubbermaid Commercial Products, Inc., Winchester, Virginia.

The company now has extensively tested plastics recycled from many of the most common postconsumer sources, including high-density polyethylene milk jugs and soda bottle base caps and polystyrene food packaging foam, Lancelot said at an EPA/International Association for Clean Technology conference on pollution prevention held in Washington, D.C., in June 1990.

For example, a number of the company's sidewalk refuse containers are made with up to 25 percent recycled milk jugs, Lancelot said. Rubbermaid plans soon to introduce desk-top accessories made with 10 percent to 25 percent recycled polystyrene packaging foam, he added, noting that several other products can be made with recycled plastics by special order.

Lancelot stressed that the quality and cost of goods made from recycled goods is equal to that of products made from virgin material. The company's use of recycled goods is limited not only by supply but also by other provisions, especially the FDA requirement noted above that limits the use of recycled plastics in items coming into direct contact with food. The best materials, he said, are those coming from large processors who control their sources, run their own cleaning and finishing operations, certify quality and freedom from contaminants, and supply consistent quantities.

Plastic Lumber: One product that can be made from mixed plastics is plastic lumber. For example, AFCO Industries of Alexandria, Louisiana, uses a patented Belgium process to solve problems caused by the various melting points of different plastics. The process operates at a temperature and speed that prevents burning of the lower melting plastics while leaving slower melting plastics partially solid. The unmelted pieces form flakes that migrate to the center of the material, where they do not affect structural strength. According to Bengt Rossby of the company's Syntech Division, the synthetic wood costs about three times as much as top-grade pine lumber but lasts much longer. It is ideally suited for use in moist environments and for construction of fence posts, benches, landscaping components, speed bumps, and highway equipment, he said.

Mixed Plastic Recycling: Technological problems or no, Hammer Plastics Recycling Corp., an Iowa Falls, Iowa, firm that already operates two recycled plastic manufacturing plants handling about 300,000 pounds per month, plans to build 16 more such plants by 1992. Eight of these ventures will be in a joint enterprise with Air & Water Technologies Corp., according to Floyd Hammer, the company's president. As of the end of 1990, some 70 percent of the company's raw materials constituted postindustrial scrap. However, as recycling increases, Hammer expects to use a greater percentage of consumer-generated scrap. The company plans to manufacture a great range of products, including such items as marine pilings, speed bumps, park benches, trash containers, picnic tables, and pallets.

Polystyrene: National Polystyrene Recycling Co. (NPRC), a Lincolnshire, Illinois, firm, has joined with Talco Recycling, Inc., of Corona, California, to open the country's largest polystyrene recycling plant in Southern California. The plant can process 13 million pounds per year of waste from consumer material such as foam plates, cups, trays, peanuts packaging, liners, and other polystyrene containers. Three comparable facilities are under way in San Francisco, Chicago, and Philadelphia.

Eight large producers of polystyrene contributed some $4 million each to launch the NPRC company. The companies are Amoco Chemical Co., ARCO Chemical Co., Chevron Chemical Co., Dow Chemical Co., Fina Oil and Chemical Co., Hunsman Chemical Corp., Mobil Chemical Co., and Polysar, Inc.

NPRC's success hinges on whether it will be able to convince schools, restaurants, and other large-scale consumers of polystyrene to separate and deliver their plastic waste, at their own expense, to the nearest plant. NPRC will pay them market prices, currently four cents, for each pound they contribute, Schneiders said.

Landfill Alternatives, Inc., an Elburn, Illinois, business that recycles used polystyrene cups, has constructed a second plant in Independence, Missouri. The plants make polystyrene granules available for reuse in a variety of products. The company still has difficulty marketing this material but was optimistic enough about markets to start the new plant, which is four times the size of its first, according to James Frank, treasurer and partner. The new plant can process 1 million pounds of postconsumer food service polystyrene and 2 million pounds of nonfood service and postindustrial polystyrene.

Grocery Bags: Some 4,000 grocery stores in North America are serving as collection sites for plastic bags. However, careless recyclers may spoil the market by returning not only bags but an array of other items. Jill Beresford, owner of a large Taunton, Massachusetts, packaging company, claims to have spent thousands of dollars trying to recycle bags, only to find she gets "50 pounds of junk of any given 33 pounds of high-density film." Another problem is that grocery bags may be made of either high-density or low-density polyethylene, which are incompatible in many applications, according to another bag maker.

Greater success was achieved by PLC Eastern, an Oaksville, Ontario, firm that makes trash bags from recycled materials. Because the bags are black, impurities are not as visible. PLC can manufacture these bags from recycled materials at prices comparable to those for virgin materials, according to an NSWMA report.

Glass Markets

The recyclability of glass is now one of the industry's main selling points, according to industry representatives. Especially in competition with plastics, the glassmakers find recyclability a strong marketing tool. For instance, Pepsi-Cola Co. and Hanover Brands, Inc., now display the recycling "G" on the labels of their glass bottles.

Cullet derived from used glass is 100 percent recyclable, in theory at least, according to Chaz Miller, recycling manager for the Glass Packaging Institute (GPI). The deterrent to reaching this goal is not the quality of recycled glass but the dependability of the market, Miller added. Because the price of the silica sands and other raw materials used in glassmaking is relatively low, the amount glass smelters will pay for recycled glass rises very slowly, Miller continued. This price competition also makes it easier for smelters to turn away from the recycling markets if supply is uncertain.

It should be emphasized here that high-quality glass can be made from 100 percent cullet, despite some allegations to the contrary, according to both Chaz Miller and V. David Baker, executive director of the Southeast Glass Recycling Program (a branch of GPI). The important thing is that glass be meticulously sorted to ensure that no colored glass taints clear glass quality. Miller said that the industry's recycling percentages are climbing but still have ample room for improvement as more sophisticated curbside recycling projects take hold. According to the latest statistics, about 30 percent of glass is made from cullet, either from consumer recyclables or from glass generated in-house. This is a 5 percent increase over the last year, Miller said. The industry's expressed goal is 50 percent cullet use, according to GPI.

The industry has set up glass recycling programs spanning more than half of the United States, the institute claims. A list of information sources on glass recycling is included in Appendix A.

Market Example

Sometimes a wedding between two plants can make good economics and good recycling. Ball-InCon Glass Packaging of Seattle, Washington, could not economically increase its use of recycled glass because its Seattle plant lacked an adequate system for accepting the material. Fibres International of Bellevue, Washington, a broad-based recycling firm, saw an opportunity to increase its business. It opened a new plant capable of preparing recycled glass for the furnaces at Ball-InCon's Seattle plant with some left over to be shipped to another plant in Oklahoma. The recycling company was able to negotiate a formal agreement with the packaging company to handle all their recycled cullet, which amounted to more than 19,000 tons in 1990.

OTHER RECYCLING ACTIVITIES AND ISSUES

Recycling has become such a ubiquitous activity that numerous new ideas, applications, and issues emerge constantly. The following brief discussions cover only a few.

Lead Acid Batteries: EPA considers lead to be one of the most dangerous of all pollutants, known to cause neurological disorders, anemia, reproductive defects, and other problems. The battery industry is the user of the majority of the lead consumed in the United States, according to EPA. Currently, 80 percent to 90 percent of these batteries are recycled. However, these amounts fluctuate, and the agency's aim is that all such batteries be recycled. On December 24, 1990, the agency called for comment on whether it would be appropriate to use the negotiated rulemaking procedure to develop rules for battery recycling under the Toxic Substances Control Act. The negotiating committee would need to discuss the best way to accomplish EPA's recycling goal, how the recycling rate can be sustained if the price of virgin lead drops, what market incentives might be used, who should bear the recovery responsibility and costs, and whether any battery recycling methods will adversely affect the competitiveness of the domestic lead industry. The agency notes, in this regard, that the practice of shipping lead acid batteries abroad for recycling could act to pull battery manufacture off shore as well.

Composting: Composting garden and other forms of organic waste is an obvious and increasingly popular method of reducing the stream of organic wastes to landfills. As noted above, EPA may issue guidelines to encourage government procurement of composted material. In fact, many communities already compost waste, selling it or giving it away to citizens or large users such as nurseries or golf courses. In financially healthy communities, the compost may be used to fertilize parks and street borders.

Yard wastes mixed with other organic wastes have substantially reduced the burden on landfills in Delaware. A compacting facility in Wilmington processes approximately 1,000 tons of mixed municipal solid waste each day. Owned by the Delaware Solid Waste Authority and operated by Raytheon Service Co., the facility handles 70 percent of all household waste generated in the state. The compost, consisting primarily of paper, paperboard, food wastes, and other organics, is marketed for use in landscaping and on golf courses and athletic fields.

Asphalt: Cyclean, Inc., a Georgetown, Texas, venture capital firm, has pioneered a process for recycling used asphalt into new asphalt product. According to Carl Hutchison, president of the company, old asphalt constitutes the single largest waste product in the nation. More than 100 million tons are removed from roads and airports each year. Recycling all of this material would not only reduce the burden on waste disposal facilities; it also would save millions of barrels of oil, Hutchison said.

The company makes its recycled product with portable equipment at the location of the old asphalt. Ground asphalt is fed through a screen to ensure uniform size, moved through a conveyor to a preheated dryer where water vapor and dust are removed, mixed with petroleum additives to restore flexibility, and conveyed to a microwave unit where the mixture is heated to about 300°. The resulting product can be sold for $13.00 per ton compared to $18.50 for virgin produce.

Pesticide Buckets: Empty plastic pesticide buckets accumulate on farms throughout Mississippi as well as other states. With the help of an $80,000 EPA grant, the Mississippi Division of Plant Industry (MDPI) carried out a pilot project to collect and recycle these eyesores from Mississippi farms. The plan was to collect and rinse the buckets and ship them to out-of-state recycling plants.

The idea began to spread, and has been taken up by at least 10 states. E.I. du Pont de Nemours & Co. and the National Agricultural Chemical Association now are participating in the effort and hope to broaden the interest to many more chemical companies. Even after the recycling of 130,000 pounds of collected plastic, there remain 13 to 14 million containers in Mississippi alone, according to Bob Brand, senior entomologist with MDPI.

Limits on Environmental Claims: The National Association of Attorneys General has, on several occasions, appealed to Congress, and to EPA and the Federal Trade Commission (FTC), to set guidelines whereby companies may make environmental claims related to their products. Of particular concern to the attorneys general are claims relating to disposability (for example, "degradable" or "recyclable") when the advertised option may not even be available to consumers in the area where the product is sold. A 10-state task force held a series of meetings addressing these concerns and issued a *Green Report* recommending that environmental claims be as specific as possible, substantive, and supported by competent and reliable scientific evidence. The report is available from Don Donahugh at the following address:

> Minnesota Attorney General's Office
> 200 Ford Building
> 117 University Ave.
> St. Paul, MN 55155

The FTC is unlikely to abandon its current case-by-case law enforcement strategy in favor of issuing guidelines, Commissioner Mary L. Azcuenaga told a meeting of the Cosmetic, Toiletry and Fragrance Association in Washington, D.C., on November 15, 1990. Speaking for herself rather than the commission, Azcuenaga acknowledged that deceptive environmental claims may be a barrier to fair competition. However, she continued, an attempt to move toward defined guidelines would be plagued by the lack of generally accepted definitions for terms such as *degradable*, *recyclable*, and *reusable*. She further stated that FTC knows "too little" to issue comprehensive guidelines.

COMMUNITY RECYCLING PROGRAMS

Driven by state waste management plans, community recycling programs are being developed almost daily. They take many forms. Sometimes cities decide to manage their own programs, purchasing the trucks, negotiating contracts, and bargaining for the necessary equipment. More often, communities hire a waste management firm to do the work for them. Two programs are described here. Seattle's record-breaking recycling scheme is complex and depends not on one but two contracted suppliers. The success of the new program in

Fairhope, Alabama is not yet assured. A description of each program brings out many of the pitfalls and the rewards of establishing a workable recycling program.

Seattle's Recycling Program

The Natural Resources Defense Council (NRDC) declared Seattle the "recycling capital of the nation, in terms of both per capita and total tonnage." San Jose, California, is second, according to NRDC.

Seattle had a long history of piecemeal recycling and is known for its strong environmental ethic. Nevertheless, the recycling program, as it is today, is new. The need for improved waste management became clear in 1986, when the city's two landfills began leaking methane gas *off-site*, thereby creating a potential Superfund problem. The city stemmed the emergency by contracting with King County (of which it is a part) to use its landfill, at a hefty increase in costs from $11.00 to $31.50 per ton. It then did an exhaustive study of the feasibility of a waste-to-energy incinerator, only to decide that a comprehensive recycling plan would be quicker and more acceptable to the public, according to Lorie Parker, recycling program manager for Seattle's Solid Waste Utility.

Choosing Recyclers

After seeking competitive bids, the city chose two recycling firms, one to serve the 65,000 eligible households in the more affluent, educated north end of the city and the other to serve the 84,000 households on the south side. Eligible households were all single-family units (which predominate in Seattle) and multiple units of up to four families.

Each recycler has a different method of collection. Recycle America, which serves the northern sector, uses three-compartment bins, in which participants place glass, aluminum, and tin; mixed scrap paper, including junk mail and magazines; and newspaper. Recycle Seattle, a new subsidiary of Rabanco, a local waste collector, serves the south side. This firm collects all of the recyclables in one bin, sorting them later in the sophisticated materials recovery facility described later in this chapter.

A Rough Start

Kick-off time for the new project was mid-December 1987, when the city sent out cards inviting citizens to sign up. The response was poor, so the city made a second mailing in February 1988. This time residents were confused as to whether they needed to sign up twice, Parker said. The city was besieged with 10,000 phone calls in one month. Then, according to Parker, Recycle Seattle had computer trouble leading to the temporary loss of thousands of sign-ups, while Recycle America's processing facility was not ready; its employees spent the first two months in operation sorting trash on a parking lot.

Participation

The city's estimates of participation were way on the low side, Parker said. After a thorough job of promotion, 89.8 percent of eligible residents on the north side signed up, and 67.3 percent of the south side signed on as well. In retrospect, both the city and the recyclers agree that participation would have been even higher if participants had simply been given the necessary containers without being asked to sign up, according to Parker.

Although the program is voluntary, citizens do have financial incentives; if they cut their wastes from two cans to one, they saved nine dollars a month under 1990 rates.

Economics

In 1989 the two recycling firms processed 40,732 tons of material, or 16 percent of the total waste generated. Tonnage to the city landfill was down by about 22 percent. The cost to the city of the recycling program of about $51.50 per ton was greater than current landfill costs but is expected to be more favorable in the future as collections improve and prices for recycled goods increase, Parker said.

The city's marketing efforts achieved mixed results. Local steel and glass companies provide good markets for both of these materials. Old newspaper prices fell from about $60 to $20 per ton and then crept upward again to about $30 per ton as newspapers increased their purchases of recycled newsprint. Plastic markets took little except PET. To help stimulate markets, the city's Solid Waste Utility joined the Chamber of Commerce and the King County Commission on Marketing Recyclables in a nonprofit venture to increase markets for recycled materials, according to Don Kneass, regional recycling manager for Recycle America.

Fairhope, Alabama

Fairhope, with a population slightly in excess of 8,000, considers itself a model southern city. Its preserved downtown section is abloom 12 months a year with flowers that change by season; its immaculate shops market luxuries from antiques to health food to Swiss chocolate; and its virtually unspoiled frontage on Mobile Bay includes almost three miles of park land. With an educated populace, a mixture of local residents and retired northerners, Fairhope has its fair share of "green" citizens who welcome an opportunity to improve the environment. It also has a history of doing things for itself. Citizens already had been asked to sort "clean trash" from "garbage," and yard waste had for several years been sent to a composter, from whence it was used by the city for its landscaping or given away to residents. Therefore, once the idea of establishing a city-wide recycling program took hold, a full-fledged curbside program managed by the city was not long in the making.

Program Development

At first, the development of Fairhope's plan was leisurely. A consultant was hired to calculate the hypothetical costs and benefits of recycling as part of an overall waste management policy; a citizen advisory committee was formed to examine various options before coming up with a plan. However, as is the case everywhere, Fairhope's activities were not isolated. Baldwin County, of which Fairhope is a part, was required by the state to create a 25 percent waste reduction plan to cover unincorporated areas. Neighboring cities were forging ahead with their own plans, in each case contracting with vendors.

Accustomed to leadership, Fairhope decided to act. Months before the advisory committee had completed its agenda, the mayor and city council moved to adopt a plan that would be run by the city, under the direction of the existing sanitation department. The object was to keep the program voluntary—and save money.

The city spent $2,000 to purchase a surplus flatbed truck from the state. Members of the sanitation department constructed and decorated the compartments that would hold the various categories of waste: mixed paper, aluminum and hard plastic, and glass. The cost of this project was about $600.

The truck drives four different routes, each one day per week. Using two newly hired workers, the crew collects and sorts the recycled material as the truck progresses. To make this job easier, residents are encouraged to purchase compartmentalized bins identical to those used in Seattle. Alternatively, they are asked to stratify the categories in their waste bins.

Markets

Markets for these products still are reasonably strong in this area. The paper is sold to Mobile Paper Board (see above) for $30 per ton as this book goes to press. This price will very likely plummet soon, however, as supply grows to exceed demand. The aluminum is sold to Reynolds Metals, Inc., and the glass, which must be accumulated in large quantities, to Owens-Illinois in Atlanta. The community has not found a purchaser for the plastic but gives it to the local Goodwill Industries outlet, which sells it through a middleman to E.I. du Pont de Nemours and Co.

Progress

The program has only been in place since December 1, 1990, but was still was not paying for itself in early March 1991, according to Cindy McBrearty of the citizen advisory committee. At that time participation was running at about 30 percent but was hard to measure because most people do not put out material every week. Moreover, the middle school and several churches still run their own recycling programs as fund raisers. While supportive of the city's efforts, these groups do not want to lose their income, especially from aluminum, which is the most valuable of community-recycled commodities. In fact, the city suspected that some aluminum was being stolen from the curbside bins and adopted a new ordinance declaring such activity a misdemeanor. The bins themselves also have been stolen on occasion, McBrearty said.

The program definitely needs greater participation and better presorting, McBreaty said, adding that more publicity probably would help. If the community cannot boost its participation through these voluntary efforts, it will view other incentives such as reduced garbage collection, higher fees, or, as a last resort, a move to mandatory recycling.

McBrearty said that communities who contract out for recycling must make their programs mandatory to justify the cost, since it is based on full participation. Fairhope chose to do the job itself and keep costs down, hoping to depend on goodwill rather than mandate. Only time will tell whether this community, or any community, can make recycling work on this basis.

As reported at a meeting of the advisory committee on April 25, 1991, the voluntary recycling program was blossoming into a resounding success. Participation had increased to about 40 percent and accounted for an estimated 20 percent by volume of trash generated, still short of the state's mandatory 25 percent waste reduction goal. Paper sales, which garnered only $423.45 in December 1990, increased every month to reach $3,172.60 in April 1991. Total sales revenue was $9,388.40. Aluminum collection and sales also had improved, to reach a total of $706.15. The most satisfying achievement was the city's sale of 23 tons of glass at $60 per ton to the Reynolds facility in Atlanta. The sale garnered $1,380 less a very low shipping fee of $400. The low-cost transportation was furnished by a Fairhope firm that wanted to support the program.

In addition to the sales revenue, the city saved $6,300 in tipping fees.

Municipal Recycling Technologies

There are numerous types and designs of municipal recycling equipment, known generally as materials recovery facilities. They range from simple conveyor belts where workers sort waste manually to sophisticated systems using screening, magnetism, and weight separation to sort materials such as plastic resins and waste paper. The following is but a brief sampling of such technologies. For detailed information, NSWMA would be a good place to start (see Appendix A).

Hybrid Collection Facilities

A hybrid refuse collection facility might increase recycling levels to extraordinary levels. Such a facility has been constructed in Whitmore Lake, Michigan. The new $2.7 million, privately owned "Mister Rubbish Recycling and Solid Waste Processing Facility" receives a community's entire waste load on one tipping floor. The facility extracts, processes, and sells from the mixed waste load all corrugated cardboard, wood, glass, metal, and plastic. The facility also accepts source-separated recyclables. In fact, part of its agenda is to educate the communities it serves to place all their sorted recyclables in one bag, garbage in another, and old newspapers in a third. All of the bags then are collected on the same truck.

Mister Rubbish, funded by Michigan's departments of commerce and natural resources and Waste Management of North America, Inc., can process 300 tons per day. Included in a 25,000-square-foot building are three conveyors leading from the tipping floor, an extruder for the waste, and two balers for plastics and paper. The facility will be operated by two six-worker shifts per day. A tub grinder placed outside processes the wood waste, turning it into uniform chips for landscaping or use as fuel.

Recycle Seattle's Sorter

At Recycle Seattle's new facility, recyclables arrive unsorted. The mixed wastes are conveyed along an elevated belt, first through a screen that removes most of the cans and bottles. They then pass to a blower that separates most of the mixed scrap paper from the heavier cardboard and newspaper; at the end of the line a magnet separates the steel from the aluminum. Workers operate on a platform between these devices, sorting the glass by color and sorting cans and bottles missed by the screen. The sorted materials fall through flexible tubes to bins below. The bins then can be moved as necessary for further processing of the material.

Sorting on the Truck

The new San Diego Recycling Center, geared to process from 300 to 500 tons per day of presorted materials, starts with custom-designed, compartmentalized trucks capable of picking up six types of recyclables at curbside and segregating them en route. When the trucks arrive at the center's computerized scales, they weigh in fully loaded and then are reweighed as each compartment is emptied through trap doors at the bottom of the compartments. In this manner, accurate weights are credited to each municipality using the facility. The weighing facility can accommodate several types of truck, and therefore can be used by many recyclers.

After collection into a separated pit under the scale, the wastes are conveyed through a series of five belts to hand picking stations, storage areas, and finally to the baler. This equipment produces bales of old newspapers, mixed paper, office paper, aluminum, bimetal containers, and two types of plastic. Glass at the facility is not crushed into cullet but separated by color and sold either whole or broken.

Automated Container Recycling

Reverse vending machines accept used aluminum containers and spit out cash. Developed at least partly in response to beverage can deposit requirements, the machines are most commonly seen in major metropolitan areas, including New York, Chicago, Los Angeles, Milwaukee, and Dallas, among others. Experience has shown that the economics of operating these machines is higher in mandatory deposit states. Depending on machine costs and payout, break-even volumes range from 5,000 pounds per month for a medium-sized, indoor machine to 11,000 pounds per month for a large, outdoor machine, according to the Aluminum Association. Such machines handle only aluminum.

Chapter 10

HAZARDOUS WASTE PRETREATMENT REQUIREMENTS

By 1984, when Congress adopted comprehensive amendments to the Resource Conservation and Recovery Act (RCRA), a consensus had been reached that land disposal of untreated hazardous waste, even in reasonably well-managed facilities, creates a continuous threat to groundwater and should be discouraged. The amendments therefore direct the Environmental Protection Agency (EPA) to ban untreated wastes from landfills, injection wells, and impoundments, according to a schedule designed to allow for smooth transition to better waste management. The amendments provide for an exemption for facilities so well designed that there would be no chance of migration into groundwater, a demonstration that is feasible for owners and operators of deep injection wells but probably not for those operating other land disposal facilities, according to Chemical Waste Management, Inc., spokesperson H. Gordon Kenna. For most land applications, pretreatment of the wastes before disposal has become the norm.

In implementing these new RCRA requirements, EPA listed the affected wastes in stages that had run their complete course by June 1, 1990. The affected materials now include solvent-containing wastes, dioxin-containing wastes, California-list wastes, and all other wastes for which pretreatment standards have been adopted–in effect, all hazardous wastes. The hazardous substance lists are discussed in Chapter 2 and shown in full text in Appendix B. The pretreatment standards, which are based either on constituent concentrations or on technology, depending on the ease with which hazardous constituents can be characterized, are shown in Appendix C. More information on these standards is found later in this chapter.

The most obvious impact of the land disposal restrictions is growth and proliferation of pretreatment facilities, a fact that has led to a new series of air pollution regulations, described in Chapter 5. Another more beneficial result in terms of the total environment is an increased interest in source reduction and recycling. The associated costs of enhanced pretreatment, combined with increased fees charged by large multifaceted treatment, storage, and disposal (TSD) facilities (and the states within which they are located), drive generators toward finding less wasteful ways of doing business.

IMPLEMENTATION OF THE LAND DISPOSAL BAN

Despite the fact that all hazardous substances became subject to the land disposal restrictions on the June 1990 date shown above, certain activities could continue for stated periods beyond that date. Those activities with final dates after June 1990 are briefly described here.

Underground Injection: Wastes K049 through K052 and K062, K071, and K104 could be injected in Class I underground injection wells until August 1, 1990; Wastes K016 (at concentrations less than 1 percent) and F007, K011, and K013 (nonwastewaters) could be injected until June 8, 1991. Moreover, wastes may be injected in Class I wells if they do not exhibit any prohibited hazardous waste characteristic (see Chapter 2) at the point of injection. As noted earlier, these wells also are most likely to withstand scrutiny under the no-migration exemption.

Second-Third Wastes: So-called second-third wastes became subject to the general restrictions on June 8, 1989. Within this group, certain categories (known as "soft hammer wastes") were granted effective dates through June 8, 1991. Of particular interest, all wastes contaminated with soil and debris that have a treatment standard based on incineration were banned from land disposal after that date.

Third-Third Wastes: Of these most recently listed wastes, many were subject to the pretreatment standards immediately. Another long list had deadlines of August 8 or November 8, 1990. Those with deadlines stretched to May 1992 are as follows:

- F039 wastes (nonwastewaters)

- K031, K084, K102, and K106 nonwastewaters

- P011, P012, P036, P038, P065, P087, and P092 nonwastewaters

- U136 and U151 nonwastewaters

- If based on waste characteristics alone, D004 nonwastewaters, D008 lead materials stored before secondary smelting, and D009 non-wastewaters

- Inorganic solids as defined in 40 CFR 268.2(a)(7) and RCRA hazardous wastes that contain naturally occurring radioactive materials

- Those wastes listed in 40 CFR 268.12 that are mixed radioactive/hazardous wastes

- Wastes with treatment standards based on incineration, mercury retorting, or vitrification

Jerry F. Vorbach, a chemical engineer with EPA's Office of Solid Waste, developed a summary of the deadline dates as they would apply to contaminated solid and debris from corrective actions under the Comprehensive Environmental Response, Compensation, and Liability Act or RCRA. These wastes come under regulation according to a calendar based on the status of the constituents they contain and the development of applicable treatment standards, Vorbach said. The category of cleanup wastes that remains exempt after June 1991 is "soil and debris contaminated with third-third wastes, or first- or second-third soft hammer wastes that had treatment standards promulgated in the third-third rule, for which the treatment standards are based on incineration, vitrification, or mercury retorting; as well as all inorganic solids debris contaminated with D004-D011 wastes, and all soil and debris contaminated mixed RCRA/radioactive wastes." This extension runs down May 8, 1992 (see above).

The agency also is planning to set separate treatment standards for soil and debris containing hazardous constituents, Vorbach said, noting that the target date for final action of September 1992 will be met.

Surface Impoundment Treatment: Wastes that are otherwise prohibited from land disposal may be treated in surface impoundments provided certain conditions concerning the quality and handling of the residue are met. The impoundment must meet design requirements as shown later in this chapter to ensure no harm to groundwater. It is important to understand that the impoundments must be for treatment rather than for storage or disposal. Evaporation of hazardous constituents as the principal means of treatment is not considered an exempt activity. Moreover, impoundments are subject to new air quality standards described in Chapter 4.

Exemptions from the Land Disposal Restrictions

Certain activities are exempt from the land disposal restrictions because of the waste type, the generator category, or the quality of the land disposal facility. Notably, a variance is available for waste that cannot be treated to a specified concentration standard or handled by a stated technological standard. This demonstration must be made to EPA; wastes exempted in this manner still must be analyzed in accordance with the requirements for all restricted wastes.

Certain generators also are exempt, as follows:

- Small-quantity generators of less than 100 kilograms of nonacute hazardous wastes per month or less than one kilogram of acute hazardous waste per month.

- Farmers disposing of pesticide residues on their land, provided each container is triple rinsed in a manner consistent with the instructions on the pesticide label

Hazardous Waste Pretreatment Requirements

- Those generating wastes identified as hazardous after November 8, 1984, for which EPA has not issued land disposal prohibitions or treatment standards

EPA's Office of Solid Waste has published helpful material on the land disposal restrictions in the form of a six-volume set called *Superfund LDS Guide* (Directives–OIFS.01-06, published July 1989). The six volumes include an overview of the landfill disposal rules (LDR), information on understanding the so-called California Wastes list and the treatment standards applicable to that list, a Superfund LDR treatment guide, and more. To obtain copies, call the RCRA hotline at (800) 424-9346 or (703) 928-9810.

Disposal Facility Extensions

Recognizing that generators of certain listed substances might have difficulty finding a suitable treatment facility, EPA included in its land restriction rule a provision for a compliance extension under carefully drawn circumstances. To qualify, the person wishing an extension must demonstrate the following:

- A nationwide good-faith effort to locate and contract with a TSD facility within the effective date.

- A binding contract to construct or otherwise provide an adequate alternative TSD, with a showing that completion of the facility by the effective date is impossible. The contract must include details of how and when permits will be obtained.

During this extension the generator is exempt from applicable storage restrictions.

No-Migration Exemption Petition

Over and above the limited exemptions described above, individuals may petition EPA to exempt a given land disposal facility from the restriction. Petitioners must demonstrate to the agency's satisfaction that hazardous constituents will not migrate from the unit for as long as the wastes remain hazardous. The demonstration must include waste identification and analysis, site characterization studies, a monitoring plan, and compliance assurance. All information must be accurate and reproducible and approved by EPA. All methods necessary for quality assurance and control must be followed, as described in detail in BNA's *Chemical Substances Control*. An exemption does not relieve the petitioner of its hazardous waste management responsibilities or of its obligation to report immediately should migration occur. The exemption does not apply to liquid hazardous wastes containing polychlorinated biphenyls at concentrations above 500 parts per million. As noted earlier, this exemption is most likely applicable only to deep injection wells.

Waste Characterization

Under the land disposal restrictions, considerable time and resources must be given to waste characterization, as generators and treatment disposal facility managers must demonstrate that a given waste meets standards before disposal. Moreover, the operator of the disposal facility also must test the waste it receives according to a schedule set forth in its waste analysis plan. At the Waste Management, Inc., landfill in Emelle, Alabama, this plan includes sampling every barrel or other container of waste when it arrives at the site and after it is treated before it may be placed in the landfill. The analytical methods and procedures for such testing are discussed in Chapter 2.

TREATMENT STANDARDS

As noted above, EPA has issued concentration-based and technology-based treatment standards for wastes subject to the land disposal restrictions. When wastes with differing treatment standards for a constituent of concern are combined for purposes of treatment, the treatment residue must meet the lowest treatment standard for the constituent of concern. For the purpose of these standards, EPA defines wastewaters as containing less than 1 percent total suspended (filterable) solids and less than 1 percent total organic carbon. All wastes that do not meet this definition are considered nonwastewater.

Concentration-Based Standards

The concentration-based standards are predicated on what EPA determined to be best demonstrated available technology for each treatability group. However, the standards may be met using any technology except dilution, which is not a permissible treatment method.

The concentration tables fall into two categories. The Constituent Concentrations in Waste Extract (CCWE) tables are to be used to determine whether a waste can be disposed of without treatment. The second table, Treatment Standards Expressed as Waste Concentrations, must be used to test waste or treatment residue if it is to be disposed of on land. These tables are in full text at Appendix C.

Land Disposal Prohibitions

The following wastes may not be placed in a landfill in any concentration:

- K004 nonwastewaters disposed of after August 17, 1988, and not generated in the course of treating wastewater forms of these wastes (based on no generation)

- K005 nonwastewaters generated by the process described in the waste listing description, disposed after June 8, 1989, and not generated in the course of treating wastewater forms of these wastes (based on no generation)

- K007 nonwastewaters generated by the process described in the waste listing description, disposed after June 8, 1989, and not generated in the course of treating wastewater forms of these wastes (based on no generation)

- K008 nonwastewaters disposed of after August 17, 1988, and not generated in the course of treating wastewater forms of these wastes (based on no generation)

- K021 nonwastewaters disposed of after August 17, 1988, and not generated in the course of treating wastewater forms of these wastes (based on no generation)

- K025 nonwastewaters disposed of after August 17, 1988, and not generated in the course of treating wastewater forms of these wastes (based on no generation)

- K036 nonwastewaters disposed of after August 17, 1988, and not generated in the course of treating wastewater forms of these wastes (based on no generation)

- K044 (based on reactivity)

Technology-Based Treatment Standards

EPA determined that for many "U" and "P" wastes (see Chapter 2), and for certain other wastes as well, constituent measurements were difficult if not impossible. The agency therefore established technology-based standards for these constituents. Three tables showing the standards appear in Appendix C. The first, very useful table shows a detailed description of the required technologies and their technology codes. Table 2 shows the regulated wastes together with these codes. Table 3 lists the standards for specific radioactive hazardous mixed waste.

STANDARDS FOR PRETREATMENT FACILITIES (40 CFR 265)

EPA has issued permit standards for certain pretreatment facilities, including tanks that treat or store hazardous waste, surface impoundments, waste piles, land treatment, and miscellaneous facilities, described below.

Storage Tanks

Tanks that treat or store hazardous waste are covered by interim status standards supplemented by a few additional permit requirements. Rules issued under the 1984 RCRA amendments require owners and operators to use dual containment and leak detection systems for their tanks to prevent environmental releases. Tanks constructed before the rules were adopted are exempt from these design requirements but are subject to integrity assessments that were due January 12, 1988. Tanks used to store materials that were designated as hazardous after July 14, 1986, also must be assessed, in this case within 12 months of the designation. Guidelines for making these assessments are found in the American Petroleum Institute's *Guide for Inspection of Refinery Equipment*, Chapter 13, "Atmospheric and Low-Pressure Storage Tanks," 4th edition, 1981.

The design standard outlines steps that should be taken to avoid corrosion. As a first step, a qualified professional engineer must certify that the tank system is sound and that the stored wastes are compatible with the tank. Moreover, an expert certified by the National Association of Corrosion Engineers (NACE) must assess whether a new tank whose outer shell comes in contact with water or soil is likely to corrode. Some of the factors to consider include the soil's moisture content, pH, solid sulfides level, and resistivity; the integrity of the tank; and influences of nearby metal structures or electrical facilities. NACE has issued guidelines on corrosion protection that should be available from the corrosion expert.

In addition to design requirements, such facilities are subject to leak inspection obligations and operation and maintenance requirements to prevent spills and overflows. Owners and operators also must develop contingency response plans. The standard also includes information on closure practices, postclosure care, and waste analysis requirements, which are described in detail in BNA's *Chemical Substances Control* binder.

The air pollution control requirements that apply to these facilities are described in Chapter 4.

Surface Impoundments

Surface impoundments, which may be used only as treatment methods under the 1984 amendments, are covered by permit standards that took effect January 26, 1983, at a time when such facilities still were used for storage and disposal as well as treatment.

The standards require that such facilities be designed to protect groundwater, as follows:

- Two or more liners and a leachate collection system

- A maintenance program to control overtopping, runoff, and equipment failure

- Dikes built strong enough to prevent failure

Details of these design requirements are reviewed on a case-by-case basis. Moreover, the double-liner requirement may be waived for certain monofills used at foundries under conditions spelled out in RCRA (see Chapter 1).

Hazardous wastes F020, F021, F022, F023, F026, and F027 (dioxins and furans) may never be placed in impoundments. Ignitable, reactive, or incompatible waste may be so managed only under stringent conditions. To close such facilities, owners or operators must either remove accumulated waste and decontaminate the entire facility or remove liquids only, solidify the residue, cover the facility, and adhere to a maintenance and monitoring program.

Air pollution regulations still in the proposal stage would require these facilities to be covered unless their contents are undisturbed. This stipulation could cause many closures, according to participants at an EPA workshop.

Litigation

A requirement by EPA that companies clean up surface impoundments that have been used to store hazardous waste before they may be reused for storage or disposal of nonhazardous substances was challenged by the Chemical Manufacturers Association in the U.S. Court of Appeals for the District of Columbia Circuit. The plaintiffs argued that RCRA's language and legislative history did not require the closure of all impoundments that had not been modernized. However, the court agreed with EPA that the regulations are in keeping with the act's mandate to prevent seepage into the groundwater and to reduce reliance on land disposal of hazardous wastes *(Chemical Manufacturers Association v. EPA*, CA DC, No. 86-1433, 11/16/90).

Waste Piles

Waste piles, which sometimes are used in the course of pretreatment, are subject to most of the same restrictions as impoundments. They may be either double-lined or single-lined, but in the latter case are subject to intense water quality monitoring obligations. The rule is quite flexible, allowing alternatives to all of the technical requirements if demonstration can be made that groundwater will not be contaminated. Waste piles also are covered by the Phase II air pollution rules for miscellaneous units, which require that emissions be controlled in the same manner as for like facilities, in this case surface impoundments.

Land Treatment Facilities

Unlike the facilities described above, these are open systems designed to allow liquids out. The treatment depends on a number of soil/waste interactions to degrade, transform, and immobilize hazardous constituents. Expressed briefly, such facilities must be subject to a program that includes characterization of the waste being treated and the soil, climate, and topography; the mechanisms used to provide maximum treatment; and a scheme to prevent migration off-site during the worst 24-hour storm that could appear within any 25-year period. The restrictions pertaining to dioxins and furans and to ignitable, reactive, or incompatible wastes are comparable to those applied to surface impoundments. This is a detailed standard and should be consulted in its entirety by anyone operating such a system.

Miscellaneous Facilities

These permit standards are generic, and apply to diverse technologies that are not covered by specific permit standards. Pretreatment facilities subject to these standards include but are not limited to deactivated missile silos other than injection wells that are used to treat, store, or dispose of hazardous wastes; thermal treatment units other than incinerators, boilers, or industrial furnaces; units open burning or open detonating explosive wastes (open burning of hazardous wastes that are not explosive is forbidden); and chemical, physical, or biological treatment units.

Miscellaneous units must meet performance objectives requiring protection of human health and the environment. These objectives are to protect groundwater, surface water (including wetlands), air quality, and soil. Permits are processed on a facility-specific basis. While each of the above objectives must be addressed, specific control requirements may not be necessary if there is no threat of environmental harm. If a miscellaneous facility is similar to another facility subject to permit standards, the compliance plan need identify only the differences that might have deleterious health or environmental effects. The necessary conditions then would be added to the permit requirements applying to the related facility.

These standards do not supersede other restrictions such as the land disposal ban. Anyone injecting waste into the ground, regardless of its nature, must either pretreat the waste or apply for the no-migration exemption.

PRETREATMENT METHODS

The technology-based treatment standards offer an excellent short guide through the assortment of available treatment methods and the chemicals to which they are applicable. For more in-depth information, not only on the technical standards but on the numerical standards as well, refer to the background materials, known as best available technology (BAT) documents, that were published in support of these standards. Such documents have been issued for each waste code shown in the standard and may be obtained by calling the RCRA hotline shown in the Appendix. For ease of access, the BAT documents have been compiled in a book published by Government Institutes (see Bibliography).

Established treatment methods include aerobic biological treatment, batch distillation, carbon adsorption, critical fluid extraction, fractionation, fuel substitution, solvent extraction, steam or air stripping, thin film evaporation, acid leaching, chemical precipitation, electrolytic oxidation (applicable to cyanide), high-temperature metals recovery, ion exchange, metals stabilization, chemical and other forms of oxidation, filtration, and stabilization or encapsulation.

Incineration and retorting also may be considered pretreatment methods but are described separately in Chapter 11.

Used improperly, a number of these techniques could transfer pollution from one environmental medium to another. Distillation units, strippers, extractors, and the like must, under the new regulatory scheme, be closed-loop systems designed so that no hazardous materials migrate to the air or the water.

Bioprocessing Wastes

Biological processes have been used since the 19th century to reduce the organic matter in sewage. A typical effluent treatment plant uses as a secondary treatment method both anaerobic and aerobic biological treatment to reduce levels of soluble organic compounds. This approach does not work against all organics, especially those that are toxic.

More sophisticated microbial systems have been tried in recent years as an advanced method of pretreating hazardous waste. A technique called bioaugmentation, developed in the early 1980s, entails the use of a commercially available bacterial culture to increase the population of microbes treating specific substances such as oils, fats, soaps, detergents, ammonia, and certain hydrocarbons. Bioaugmentation has not been very successful when applied to toxic constituents, according to the literature.

A Prizewinning Invention

A newly formed English company, Viridian Bioprocessing Ltd., won the 1991 Daily Telegraph-Nat/West Clean Technology Award for its new bacterial treatment method that can biodegrade a toxic soup of pollutants, including aromatics such as benzene and toluene; phenols; aliphatic hydrocarbons (hexadecans); heterocyclics (pyridine); hydrocarbons, including oils, fats, and diesel fuel; halogenated alphatics; chloroaromatics; nitroaromatics; polycyclic aromatics; nitrosamines; phthalates; and surfactants, all found in many chemical waste streams.

Viridian holds an exclusive license to market this "microbial custom blend" technology that can degrade all of the toxic components of many specific waste streams.

The company already has applied its technology to the needs of certain U.S. and British clients. It uses a three-stage approach in helping solve waste problems, from an evaluation period that can take as long as six months, to bench scale testing, to turnkey operation. For information on this singular advanced form of bioprocessing, contact Jeremy Wyatt, technical manager, at the following address:

> Viridian Bioprocessing Ltd.
> 114-116 John Wilson Business Park
> Thanet Way
> Whitstable, Kent CT5 3qt
> United Kingdom
> 011-44-0227-77-0505 (telephone)

Solar Evaporation

Many waste streams consist of large quantities of water made hazardous by the presence of small amounts of regulated substances. Large companies may already have means to separate this moisture using pretreatment devices such as those described above. If they can recycle the solids, they save money. Small businesses such as machine shops, farms, agricultural chemical supply companies, crop dusters, golf courses, and medical laboratories also may have highly dilute streams that would be much cheaper to dispose of if in smaller volume.

A solar evaporator developed by the University of Alabama in Huntsville and the Tennessee Valley Authority's National Fertilizer and Environmental Research Center in Muscle Shoals, Alabama, may be the solution. This evaporator uses the sun's energy to accomplish what previously was done using electricity or steam. A 30-square-foot test unit at Banner Machine Co., Inc., in Huntsville, showed the ability to evaporate about 600 gallons of water in a year.

Such an evaporator can be built for about $1,000, less than the cost to ship three 55-gallon barrels of waste, according to Dr. Gerald Guinn, senior scientist for the project.

PRETREATMENT OR RECYCLING

Several of the above treatment methods recycle separated solvents, metals, or other materials back into the process. Thus, there emerges the question as to whether the recycling exemption should apply. In its hazardous waste classifications and its recycling standard, described in Chapter 13, EPA sets forth in regulatory language the method by which this distinction must be made.

Nevertheless, according to Michael Petruska of the regulatory development branch of EPA's Office of Solid Waste, the differentiation between pretreatment and recycling often must be made on a case-by-case basis. The question hinges on whether the activity is part of the production process, in which case all aspects of RCRA, including transportation and storage of the material, do not apply. Using this distinction, spent solvent recovery does not constitute recycling, Petruska said.

In making the distinction, questions may need to be asked concerning the ownership and purpose of the facility, Petruska continued. Where does the company generate its income, through production or waste management? Is it legitimate recycling or a sham to avoid regulation? The location of the facility also makes a difference, he continued. If it is used in conjunction with other waste treatment facilities that require permits, the recycling facility becomes subject to permit requirements as well.

In fact, Petruska continued, some recycling facilities are located off-site and served only by tank trucks. Thus, they can make the claim that they do not store any hazardous waste and that their product returns directly to the process. Firms take this step to avoid the expensive process of obtaining RCRA permits more than to avoid the use of environmentally protective equipment, he said.

There is danger in this approach, however. Because it is off-site and unregulated, such a facility should not be out of mind. Without attention being given to the leak prevention stipulations described above, a recycling facility could end up a hazardous waste site requiring remedial action. In fact, many such facilities already have become Superfund sites.

Chapter 11

DISPOSAL FACILITIES: TECHNICAL STANDARDS, ISSUES, AND GUIDELINES

Whether the waste to be disposed of is garbage, industrial solid waste, special waste, or hazardous waste, its ultimate resting place will be a combustor or the ground. Even when a combustor is used, the residual ash and air pollution control byproducts must be disposed of and may incur more regulations, as described below.

The Environmental Protection Agency (EPA) has issued rules, criteria, and guidelines to cover all such resting places, and for the storage and pretreatment facilities that hold them en route. Technical standards, issues, and guidance concerning disposal facilities, including solid and hazardous waste incinerators, industrial boilers, landfills, and deep injection wells, are included in this chapter. Information on storage and treatment tanks, surface impoundments, wastepiles, recycling units, and miscellaneous facilities can be found in Chapter 10.

SOLID WASTE COMBUSTORS

Garbage-to-energy incinerators, also known as resource recovery facilities, or municipal solid waste combustors, have proliferated in recent years. According to a study released by the Institute for Resource Recovery, the 140 waste-to-energy plants operating in the United States at the end of 1990 produced power equivalent to nearly 27 million barrels of oil per year, or "61 percent of the oil imported from Kuwait, or 12 percent of the oil imported from Iraq prior to the August 1990 invasion." If all of the plants that were under construction during that year eventually come on line, the energy savings could rise to the equivalent of nearly 33 million barrels of oil annually, according to Kent Burton, director of the institute.

According to the study, 14 new combustion plants were either finished or in late stages of construction during 1990, a record-setting year for new waste-to-energy capacity. Burton said 1991 would see a drop in new capacity, with only eight plants capable of burning about 9,000 tons per day scheduled to start operation. Some plans were on hold, Burton said, as state and local governments worked to balance integrated systems that combine waste reduction, recycling, combustion, and land filling (see Chapter 3).

Many critics continue to worry about the environmental effects of these facilities despite allegations on the part of many environmental professionals that the new pollution control technologies are protective of health and the environment. Richard Denison of the Environmental Defense Fund said more attention must be paid to what goes into the incinerators and to ensuring that state-of-the-art equipment is used.

Risks attendant to solid waste combustion are discussed in Chapter 3, while regulations and guidelines concerning air emissions from these facilities are included in Chapter 4. Technical issues are covered here.

Resource Conservation and Recovery Act Guidelines (40 CFR 245)

In view of the environmental concerns expressed above, it is worth noting that in 1976, when Congress enacted the Resource Conservation and Recovery Act (RCRA), energy independence was a sizable issue, just as it may become again in the wake of the Iraq war. Part 245 of the act mandated federal agencies to establish or use combustion to recover energy or resources if they handled more than 100 tons of solid waste per day. If two or more agencies were in the same metropolitan statistical area and each generated 50 tons or more of waste per day, they also were covered by this mandate. Under Subtitle E of RCRA, the Department of Commerce also was supposed to encourage greater commercialization of this technology.

EPA admits to having done little to stimulate resource recovery incineration, largely because its focus was on hazardous waste issues. However, the technology's growth has been so strong without governmental stimulation that it seems unlikely that EPA will devote much time to market development now.

However, the agency did carry out another obligation under Part 245 by issuing codified guidelines for these facilities, which were mandatory for federal facilities and advisory to states in developing their own rules. The guidelines included information on waste separation, site selection and design, water quality control, air quality control, vector prevention, aesthetics, residue management, and recordkeeping.

The source-separation and air pollution control aspects of these guidelines are supplanted by new proposed guidelines that must be adopted by the states over the coming months. Chapter 4 contains descriptions of the standard and the guideline, both of which concern emissions into the air. Other, still pertinent aspects of the earlier guidelines are described here:

Site Selection and Design: The site selected for a combustion facility should be in an area zoned for industrial use and accessible by permanent roads. Environmental and socioeconomic restraints should be taken into account before a site is selected. While sounding straightforward enough, this criterion is unrealistic because the necessary zoning laws simply do not exist in many areas of the United States. In the absence of zoning, irate citizens often challenge new facilities on environmental grounds because that is the only way to fight a development perceived to be inappropriate or undesirable. (For more discussion of facility siting, see Chapter 12.)

Design plans for a new or modified facility should be prepared by a professional engineer who is accountable to the responsible agency or municipality. The types, amounts (by weight and by volume), and characteristics of all solid wastes to be processed should be learned through survey and analysis. The gross calorific value of the wastes also should be determined, to serve as a basis for the design. In designing a facility, such factors as the quantity and characteristics of the waste, variation in waste generation, equipment downtime, and availability of alternative storage, process, or disposal must be considered.

Communities zealous for the income afforded by energy production must take this aspect of the guidance very seriously, especially when crafting waste management plans to conform with EPA's priority objectives of waste reduction and recycling. If waste reduction goals are reached or exceeded, calorific projections could be too high and the income from energy production significantly reduced (see Chapter 3 for more on this subject).

The facility's components should be designed to withstand a breakdown; standby water and power should be available. Instrumentation should be capable of continuously measuring the weight of incoming and outgoing materials; total combustion airflow rates; underfire and overfire airflows and quantitative distribution of each; selected temperatures and pressures in the furnace, along gas passages, in the particulates collection device, and in the stack; electrical power and water consumption of critical units; and rate of operation. As well, the smoke density, the concentration of carbon monoxide, or the concentration of hydrocarbons in the stack gas should be measured. Under the new air regulations and guidelines for these facilities, acid gas monitoring also must take place. Furthermore, measurement of the pH of effluent waters should be considered.

Finally, there should be audible signals to alert personnel of malfunctions and provision for waste sampling and laboratory testing.

Water Quality: All discharged waters must be sufficiently treated to meet the most stringent of applicable water quality standards. Effluent waters should not be discharged indiscriminately. Consideration should be given to recirculation of process waters and to on-site treatment of process and wastewaters before discharge. When excessive contaminants are found, corrective action must be taken.

Vectors: The facility should be designed for ease of cleaning and maintained to prevent vector infestation. A housekeeping schedule should be established requiring that tipping and residue areas be cleaned as spillage occurs and the storage area be emptied at least weekly. Solid waste and residue should not be allowed to accumulate for more than a week.

Aesthetics and Residue: The facility should be attractively designed and landscaped. Residue should be disposed of in an environmentally acceptable manner. The operator should examine the bottom ash at least twice per shift and record the estimated percentage of unburned combustibles. Wet fly ash should be drained before transport and vehicles should be water-tight. While not covered in the guidelines, odors from the tipping, storage, and residue areas are best controlled through use of a *reverse air system.* Such systems virtually eliminate odors in these facilities, which otherwise would create a nuisance even if all of these housekeeping requirements were followed.

Safety: Incinerators must be designed, operated, and maintained in a manner that protects the health and safety of personnel associated with their operation. Pertinent provisions of the Occupational Safety and Health Act of 1970 (OSHA) are applicable. (For information on OSHA requirements, see *Job Safety and Health*, a BNA reference file service.)

Recordkeeping: The owner or operator should keep exhaustive records during the first 12 to 18 months of operation and during periods of high air pollution or upset conditions. All such records must be kept for three years. During routine operation, the guideline lists some 20 "minimum" measurements that should be kept, all of which would be spelled out in the operating permit.

Types of Solid Waste Combustors

There are two major categories of waste-to-energy combustors, mass burn—by far the largest category—and refuse-derived fuel (RDF) combustors, which were popular in the early 1970s but are a less likely choice now. Mass burn systems are simpler to design and more straightforward; they are therefore the choice of waste authorities anxious to have a reliable facility they can understand. There are advantages to RDF systems as well, however, as described below. Other designs include modular systems, fluidized bed combustors, and pyrolysis reactors.

Mass Burn Systems: These incinerators burn everything tipped off the truck, with the exception of large appliances and recyclables such as metal and batteries. They are large and usually handle at least 200 tons per day. Most systems store the waste in a pit and move it toward the boiler(s) with overhead cranes. The excess-air burners are designed to handle this heterogeneous mass of waste. Most feed the waste through a sloping, moving grate designed to agitate the material and mix it with air. A modern system is governed by a computer that precisely controls grate movement, underfire air, and overfire air.

RDF Systems: In the RDF method of waste combustion, mechanical means are used to produce a more homogeneous fuel that can be burned alone or in combination with other fuels. The great advantage of this method, of course, is the flexibility of the fuel once it is processed. It can be burned in dedicated boilers or co-fired with wood or fossil fuels in existing industrial or utility boilers. The fuel can be produced at one location for use at an off-site boiler. In addition to producing energy, the system preprocesses steel and glass that can be sold. However, the quality of these recycled materials is not as good as that of materials removed beforehand.

Modular Systems: These systems are small, factory-built plants, often custom designed to fit a particular application such as the destruction of industrial or infectious waste. The furnaces have two chambers through which the waste is moved with a hydraulic ram. In the primary chamber, the waste is literally vaporized under "starved air" conditions. The gases then are sent to a secondary chamber operating with the amount of air sufficient for destruction of the waste. If combustion conditions in the second chamber are not well regulated, the waste may not be sufficiently burned, in which case ash quantity is increased and energy recovery reduced. Such incinerators were popular at hospitals because they often could meet applicable particulate and opacity emissions standards without the use of control equipment. New state rules governing infectious waste management often include incinerator regulations requiring that these facilities be shut down or retrofitted to meet more stringent air pollution requirements.

Fluidized Beds: These combustors are best known as an environmentally acceptable method of burning high sulfur coal. In that application coal is mixed with limestone in suspension to produce energy while limiting the release of sulfur dioxide. As applied here, garbage is suspended instead of coal. The design may be either a bubbling bed, which keeps the material close to the bottom of the furnace, or a circulating bed, which moves the material around, thus creating more mixing. So far, this technology has been used to burn sewage sludge and specialized industrial waste.

Pyrolysis: This is a more futuristic method of combustion that entails the chemical decomposition of garbage by heat in the absence of oxygen at relatively low temperatures. As applied to municipal solid waste, the chemical reactions could be very complex. The process produces a solid residue, and liquid tar and gas that can be marketed as energy. The technology should not be confused with starved air designs such as the retort incinerators used by some hospitals, which also are called pyrolytic. True pyrolysis has been used abroad but only has been tested in the United States.

Air Pollution Control Technology

The new air pollution regulations and guidelines that apply to municipal solid waste incinerators require a combination of add-on technology and combustion control to reduce emissions of an array of pollutants to a minimum. The add-on equipment must be used to control particulates, metals, and acid gases to include nitrogen dioxide at facilities subject to the new source performance standard noted above. Combustion methods are employed to reduce carbon monoxide, dioxins and furans, and trace amounts of many organics.

Particulates Control: Control of particulates, including metals, can be accomplished through use of a fabric filter (baghouse) or an electrostatic precipitator. Regulators prefer the baghouse because it captures residual gases as they attach to particles in the filter. In fact, the new source performance standard is based on the use of this equipment. However, a multifield electrostatic precipitator also achieves very high levels of control and may be used if it can achieve equivalent efficiency.

Baghouses could most simply be described as huge houses (more like sheds, actually) filled with oversized vacuum cleaner bags. These bags, which can surpass 30 feet in length, are made of a variety of materials; however, for thermal application, they should be made of a synthetic guaranteed to withstand high temperatures. As effluent gases pass through these bags, the dust is held back and periodically shaken into a hopper for collection and removal.

Electrostatic precipitators (ESPs) are preferred by most utilities and many operators of resource recovery facilities because they are in themselves electrical. There also remain lingering doubts over the ability of the filter bags to withstand the high temperatures and heavy wear of a boiler application. ESPs, which are specified in EPA's guidelines as the preferred retrofit technology for existing incinerators, are composed of small-diameter negative electrodes and a grounded positive electrode plate. As effluent gases pass through an ESP, a strong electrical charge from the negative electrodes is picked up by the particles before they pass to the positive plate and are caught. The particulate matter is dislodged from the plates by mechanical means such as vibration with rappers or, in the case of wet precipitators, water. ESPs come in numerous designs and configurations. For details on these and other air pollution control devices, see BNA's *Air Pollution Control* manual.

Acid Gas Control: To control emissions of sulfur dioxide and hydrogen chloride, large new units must be equipped with a dry scrubber, a device equipped to spray a semidry lime (or other sorbent) mixture into the flue gas to absorb acidic gases, which in turn are dried by the hot gases. These devices achieve a very high level of control when paired with a baghouse. At smaller incinerators, the sorbent may be administrated by mechanically simpler dry injection systems.

Disposal Facilities

Nitrous Oxides Control: At large mass-burn incinerators, nitrous oxides, which become nitrogen dioxide in the ambient air, must be controlled by some means of selective noncatalytic injection, whereby ammonia or urea is injected into the gases to neutralize nitrous oxides to nitrogen. Catalysts also can be used for this purpose, but they cost more and their performance is marred if the catalysts are poisoned by the flue gas. NOx emissions from smaller incinerators can be controlled through proper combustion management. (A comprehensive discussion of incinerator NOx control is found in 54 *Federal Register* 243, December 20, 1989.)

Combustion Efficiency: The most important considerations during combustion are known as the three Ts: temperature, turbulence, and time. Depending on the operation, temperature should be set within the range of 1,500 to 2,000°F. The flow of gases should be disrupted so that the gases are mixed with oxygen to induce combustion. The amount of time that the waste is required to be in the furnace is also important, but is often less than two seconds because of the extreme heat. Other important considerations include maintenance, feed rate, number of chambers, pollution control equipment, stack height, start-up and shutdown, and personnel training.

POINTER Because they are stated in terms of emission limitations, neither the new source performance standard nor the hazardous waste incinerator permit standard specifies time and temperature requirements. However, such stipulations appear in many state regulations. Required residence times range from 0.5 second in Mississippi to 3 seconds in Nevada. Normally, both temperature and residence times are specific to the incinerator design and stated in the permit.

Incinerator Ash

Under the Clean Air Act amendments signed November 15, 1990, incinerator ash is exempt from hazardous waste controls for two more years. By that time the reauthorization of RCRA will be well under way, Congress reasoned, and ash will be covered under a revised Subtitle D. According to Doreen Sterling, director of EPA's ash disposal and management section, EPA would welcome additional regulations to foster the safe management of ash as a nonhazardous waste. EPA specifically wants to regulate the handling, storage, transportation, and reuse of ash, Sterling said.

The agency is participating in long-term studies to determine the behavior of ash in a monofill as well as learn any deleterious effects of placing the substance with other garbage. A November 15, 1990, report of findings at a now closed monofill in Woodburn, Oregon, showed increased levels of salts and reduced levels of sulfates at the end of the third year of study. EPA is gratified by the decreased sulfates but concerned that chloride, sodium, and total dissolved solids concentrations have been increasing over successive years of testing, Sterling continued. Salts accelerate the decay of clay-lined landfills, eventually allowing leachate to seep through, she said. As is so often the case, the salt deposits are a manifestation of transferring a pollutant from one part of the environment to the other. According to Sterling, bases added to neutralize the acid gases in incinerator scrubbers increase the amount of salt residue.

Studies also show that leachates from decomposing garbage increase the mobility of heavy metals found in ash, thus indicating a potential need to segregate ash, as well as ensure that the receiving landfill is well lined, Sterling said. On a positive note, the leachate samples were free of dioxins, while soil samples tested below one part per billion, the level recommended for residential soil by the Centers for Disease Control.

The study was financed in 1990 by the U.S. Conference of Mayors' Coalition on Resource Recovery and Environment after EPA's funding was cut. Copies of the report, Municipal Waste Combustion-Ash Leachate Characterization Monofill—Third Year Study, is available for $50 from:

> U.S. Conference of Mayors
> 1620 Eye St., NW
> Washington, DC 20006

HAZARDOUS WASTE INCINERATORS

The path to the development of dedicated hazardous waste incineration facilities has not been an easy one. Combustion of liquids such as polychlorinated biphenyls (PCBs) at sea, for instance, seemed an answer to a policymaker's prayers, until EPA and the waste management industry discovered that citizens held the ocean as too pristine a medium for such activity, even though the waste burden on the waters would have been zero. Land-based incineration projects have fared only marginally better. As late as 1980 there were only three stationary units, a Rollins incinerator in Houston, Texas; a Waste Management, Inc. (formerly owned by SCA), unit in Chicago; and an ENSCO unit in El Dorado, South Carolina. Since then, scattered facilities have been built elsewhere. The optimum size for such units is about 180 million BTU, according to H. Gordon Kenna, community relations manager for Chemical Waste Management, Inc.'s, southern region. The newest permitted incinerator constructed by Chem Waste's parent company, Waste Management, Inc., is a rotary incinerator in Port Arthur, Texas, that is permitted to burn both RCRA and Toxic Substances Control Act (TOSCA) waste (namely PCBs).

Under TOSCA, incinerators burning only PCBs can be constructed without a permit, so long as they operate under the 99.9999 combustion efficiency standard for such facilities. However, Kenna said, few operators would embark on such projects without a permit, preferring to know at the start that the project can go through. Hence, most PCB incinerators will be permitted for specified RCRA wastes as well, he explained.

Incinerator Standards (40 CFR 265)

RCRA hazardous waste may not be incinerated except under rigidly monitored conditions that include technical specifications for the incinerator as well as waste management criteria similar to those that apply to landfills, as follows:

- Waste feed analysis to demonstrate the destructive capabilities of the incinerator, as described below.

- Performance standards for destroying and removing the most hazardous constituents of each waste feed specified in the permit (for these standards, see Chapter 5).

- Incinerator operating conditions and safety features to ensure compliance with performance standards. Among these provisions are that waste feed be withheld when the incinerator is not in steady-state operation, that fugitive emissions be controlled using seals or negative pressure or other appropriate methods, and that the incinerator shut off automatically when there are operational changes.

- Minimum inspection and monitoring obligations, as described in Chapter 4.

- Permit modification procedures to guarantee that operating parameters remain sufficient to meet applicable performance standards. The procedure may be a trial burn or may be based on alternative data. In order to avoid the need for continuous modifications, EPA suggests that permit applications include the broadest possible range of waste that could be destroyed under each set of operating conditions.

- New incinerator provisions that require a period of shakedown and a trial burn, described below.

- Closure stipulations requiring that the site be cleared of all hazardous waste and residues, including ash, scrubber waters, and scrubber.

Waste Exemptions

Certain wastes are exempted from all the incineration requirements except for the need to perform waste analysis and the obligation to remove waste at closure. Such wastes include those that are free of hazardous constituents and are:

- Listed or classified as hazardous solely because they are ignitable, corrosive, or both.

- Listed or classified only because they are reactive, if they will not be burned when other hazardous wastes are present in the combustion zone. Wastes that react with water or that generate toxic gases, vapors, or fumes when exposed to pH conditions between 2 and 12.5 are not exempt.

Wastes also may be exempt if they fall in the above categories but contain hazardous constituents in low concentrations provided EPA makes a finding that the waste is not a threat to human health or the environment.

Waste Analysis

Incinerators are permitted to burn only those wastes for which analysis indicates they are suitable. The waste analysis must be set forth in a plan that includes details on how monitoring and analysis will be carried out. The analysis must be performed in accordance with approved EPA techniques spelled out in SW-846, available from:

> Solid Waste Information
> Environmental Protection Agency
> 26 W. Clair St.
> Cincinnati, OH 45268

Trial Burns

A new incinerator must have a final RCRA permit before start-up. The permit sets conditions for the four phases of the incinerator's operating life: shakedown, trial burn, follow-up, and permanent operation.

During shakedown the incinerator is operated to identify mechanical difficulties and to achieve steady-state conditions before the trial burn is conducted. Shakedown may not last more than 720 hours unless application is made and approved for an extension.

The trial burn must be carried out under conditions demonstrating compliance with the performance standards following an established trial burn plan.

During the follow-up phase, EPA or the applicable state agency prepares the data gathered during the trial burn. The incinerator may operate during this period.

Finally, during the permanent operation phase, the operating conditions must guarantee continued compliance with the standards.

INDUSTRIAL BOILERS AND FURNACES (40 CFR 266, SUBPART H)

Industrial boilers and furnaces combusting hazardous waste for resource recovery were, for a long time, exempt from most RCRA provisions. After much controversy and two phases of proposal, EPA announced, on December 31, 1990, that such facilities would come under regulation for air emissions of metals, hydrogen chloride, and products of incomplete combustion.

Some 1,000 combustion facilities are affected by this rule in some manner. Of these, 75 large industrial furnaces, including cement kilns, and 125 boilers must meet very stringent standards, according to Don Clay, assistant administrator of solid waste and emergency response. Nearly 600 smaller boilers, burning a total of less than 1 percent of the waste, will be exempt from the technical requirements but must comply with recordkeeping and notification obligations.

EPA estimates that about 200 boiler operators may cease to burn hazardous waste fuels rather than install the necessary control equipment. The rule is expected to cost industry as much as $10 million a year, according to EPA. It applies to boilers burning the waste for any purpose, including energy recovery, material recovery, and destruction. Prior to the passage of this rule, such facilities were subject only to a one-time notice requirement; this requirement continues to apply to the marketer of the waste (see Chapter 7). Waste stored at such facilities also is subject to applicable storage requirements.

SOLID WASTE LANDFILLS

In many parts of the United States, any solid waste that is not recycled ends up in a sanitary landfill. Except in areas short on land, this form of disposal remains the least costly, even when advanced pollution control technology is used.

To be termed a sanitary landfill rather than an open dump, an existing landfill must be in compliance with criteria for all land disposal facilities (40 CFR 257), which are described in Chapter 3.

These criteria improved the manner in which waste was managed before their passage in 1976, but were made obsolete by EPA's latest criteria, which were proposed in August 1988 and were still awaiting final approval or disapproval by the Office of Management and Budget in February 1991. The proposed standards would apply to municipal solid waste landfills that handle hazardous wastes from households or small-quantity generators.

The criteria would apply not only to new landfills but also to existing landfills, which must be updated within a specified period after the proposed criteria become final.

The proposed criteria have been controversial since their inception because they were based on acceptable risk rather than on technological considerations. They were faulted at once as being too flexible by the Environmental Defense Fund and too rigid by the Association for State and Territorial Solid Waste Management Officials and the National Solid Wastes Management Association. Briefly, the Environmental Defense Fund called for a uniform requirement that landfills be double-lined, while the associations recommended an approach allowing the states and operators to choose designs based on site-specific conditions, according to the Office of Management and Budget (OMB).

The author learned in telephone interviews during late January that OMB is concerned with the costs of protecting groundwater from landfill leachates. The costs are estimated to fall on homeowners, amounting to some $10 to $15 per year, agency officials estimate. These costs are considered unduly high at a time when many states are complaining that they lack funding to implement federal regulations, EPA officials added. They could not determine how long it would be before the rule would be made final. "It's conceivable it could take two weeks, two months, or two years," one top official said.

Siting Landfills

The task of siting a new landfill, never an easy one, has been made more difficult in recent years by the uncertainty of the Part D criteria described above. Long before they finally were proposed in 1988, the new rules were known and discussed to the extent that neither states nor waste management professionals felt comfortable ignoring their impending provisions. Despite this uncertainty, Durward Jackson, owner of Waste Away Group (a Waste Management, Inc., partner), managed to open and begin operation of the Salem Waste Disposal Center in Lee County, Alabama, which should meet the new criteria in whatever form they finally take. Technical aspects of the landfill are described here, as they give a good illustration of how to design a modern municipal landfill. In fact, according to the company, it is the only privately owned landfill to be recognized by EPA as a "profile of success" of the "federally supported public-private partnerships initiative." The organization of the project as a partnership and the successful manner in which this partnership dealt with citizens' concerns are described in Chapter 12.

The Salem Waste Disposal Center

As first conceived, the new landfill that would serve the needs of communities in and near Lee County, Alabama, would be equipped with a 40-mil, high-density polyethylene liner. This, in combination with the geological characteristics of the site, was considered more than adequate to prevent migration into the environment. However, as early as 1985, when the landfill accepted its first load of waste, the proposed regulation was on the horizon, Jackson said. The company therefore abandoned its first liner system, replacing it with a 60-mil polyethylene material, geo-net and geo-textile membrane that represents a forefront in design comparable to only five or six landfills across the country, according to the company's director of landfill operations, Rock Payne. This design doubled development costs to roughly $100,000 per acre, Jackson said, but allowed for superior leachate flow.

The site's schematic hill-and-valley leachate collection system encompasses 3,500 linear feet of PVC pipe running around and through the landfill to collection tanks. The system allows no more than 12 inches of leachate to build up at any time.

The facility is divided into 10-acre cells that are developed annually. Before a cell accepts garbage, three feet of dry material blanket the liner. When the cell is full, a final cover of 42 inches of soil (compared to the current state requirement of 24 inches) caps each cell. Other safeguards include six groundwater monitoring wells, of which two are up-gradient and four down-gradient. Far exceeding state regulations, this monitoring system tests for 70 pollutant profiles.

Salem also claims to have the only Alabama solid waste landfill with a National Pollutants Discharge and Elimination System permit and a stormwater collection and filtration system. The landfill also incorporates a methane gas monitoring and eventual recovery program and a hazardous and infectious waste screening program, designed by Payne, that is used as a model by state regulators for all Alabama landfills. The company also requires that all operators be certified by the Governmental Refuse Collection and Disposal Association (now known as the Solid Waste Association of North America; see Directories).

Building on the success of this landfill, Waste Away has signed a contract with the Brundidge (Alabama) City Council to build a similar regional facility. The company will include at this installation an on-site recycling center that will divert at least 25 percent of the waste arriving at the landfill back into the manufacturing process. This will complement local recycling efforts, according to the company.

HAZARDOUS WASTE LANDFILLS

As discussed in some detail in Chapter 9, landfills no longer may be the resting place of untreated hazardous waste. Nevertheless, such facilities still accept large quantities of pretreated hazardous waste. Moreover, they receive a variety of materials associated with hazardous waste, such as drained and cleaned transformers, discarded packaging materials, incinerator ash, and industrial solid waste.

The most important aspect of hazardous waste landfill management is protection of the earth and its underlying groundwater and neighboring surface water bodies such as lakes and streams. With the enactment of the land disposal ban, increased attention must be given at these facilities to waste testing and to storage while such testing transpires. At every stage of the way, the waste must be accounted for, sheltered from the weather, and sampled both before and after treatment. These and other aspects of landfill management are illustrated at the Chemical Waste Management Emelle, Alabama, facility, the largest of its kind, which is described in some detail below.

Groundwater Protection Standard (40 CFR 264)

The groundwater permit standards for hazardous waste facilities apply to surface impoundments, waste piles, land treatment units, and landfills that accept hazardous wastes after January 26, 1982, and may apply to miscellaneous facilities when appropriate.

Monitoring programs at such facilities must include a sufficient number of wells at appropriate locations and at varying depths to yield representative samples from the uppermost aquifer. The samples must include representations of uncontaminated background water and the quality of groundwater passing the point of compliance. The system also must detect migration of contaminants to the uppermost aquifer and must be adequate to detect migration from all compliance points at the facility.

Allowable hazardous waste constituent concentrations are written into a facility's permit and normally may not exceed background levels set for 14 drinking water constituents under the Safe Drinking Water Act and any other limits necessary to protect human health and the environment.

The monitoring program has three phases: detection monitoring, which reveals whether leachate is entering the groundwater; compliance monitoring, which is required to determine whether leakage has caused the constituent concentration to be exceeded; and corrective action designed to bring the facility back into compliance. Corrective action entails either removal of the hazardous constituents or treatment in place.

The 1984 amendments mandate corrective action measures for all facilities seeking hazardous waste permits. This sweeping provision applies to any solid waste management unit, including inactive units, at any treatment, storage, and disposal facility seeking permits. EPA construes this requirement to include any unit from which hazardous constituents might migrate, even when the units were intended for management only of nonhazardous solid waste.

Permit Standards for Hazardous Waste Landfills (40 CFR 2640)

Under the permit standard, each new landfill, each new landfill unit at an existing facility, each replacement unit, and each lateral expansion of an existing unit must be equipped with a double liner and leachate collection system or the equivalent thereof. In other words, no new activity may take place at such landfills unless they are so equipped. Existing landfills without liners or with single-liner systems need not be retrofit to meet the double-liner standard. As provided under RCRA, certain monofills are exempt from this requirement.

The standards also require:

- An inspection to ensure that liners and covers maintain their integrity and that leachate collection and removal systems function properly.
- Recordkeeping to map out each cell and its contents.
- Special handling for ignitable, reactive, or incompatible waste; liquid waste; and restricted wastes.
- Closure and postclosure technology to include a cover no less permeable than the liner system or the natural subsoils. The system must be maintained and monitored according to a postclosure plan.

Landfill Design Proposal

EPA proposed, in early 1986, to develop regulations governing technical aspects of leak detection systems and other design aspects of hazardous landfills. The proposed rules also would require that the lower liner be composed of a composite material, according to Kenneth Shuster, a special assistant in the Solid Waste Office who is responsible for writing the final rule. This, in addition to a companion proposal to ban containerized liquid hazardous wastes from landfills, was shelved for more than two years, Shuster said; now, however, the agency is under court order to complete the package. According to the current schedule, the technology standards will be final in September 1992 and the containerized liquid ban in July 1994.

Shuster said a cursory investigation of current practices at new landfills showed that most already are using technologies along the lines of the proposed standards. However, he said, containerized liquids continue to be deposited in these facilities.

The Emelle Landfill

The Emelle Landfill, located in rural Sumter County not far from the Alabama/Mississippi border, has frequently been in the news over the past few years. This state-of-the-art facility is America's largest and is, by any standard, very well run. It also is a political football, used to give Alabama some clout over national waste management issues and, some argue, the governor an opportunity to take a risk-free environmental stance.

As noted elsewhere, Alabama has been a leader in organizing states that import hazardous waste, trying to exert pressure on those without facilities to take more decisive action. "Why should 'Alabama the Beautiful' (substitute South Carolina, Illinois, Idaho) be the waste dump of the nation?" is the resounding cry.

As shown by the following case example, as well as those in Chapter 13, politics can lead to very poor waste management planning. It is difficult to understand why a meticulously managed hazardous waste management facility, concealed behind rows of trees in the middle of nowhere, should elicit such outrage in a state that actively solicits all other business, much of which becomes the source of the very waste that is so controversial.

The fees paid for waste dumped at Emelle accrue not only to the state but also to the surrounding communities, the nearest of which is five miles from the facility. The tiny community of Emelle has 48 registered voters but now has a modern city hall and playground facility, paid for by taxes from Chemical Waste Management, Inc. (CWM), according to Kenna. Emelle receives 2 percent of the fees paid to the facility. Two larger communities, each several miles away, receive 10 percent of the revenue. The facility also creates over 400 jobs for people in the area.

Site Selection

The Emelle site was chosen on the basis of its geology. It was, in fact, one of about ten areas cited as favorable by a 1973 EPA report to Congress. The facility rests on the Selma Chalk, a massive and stable homogeneous geologic unit stretching across central Alabama and Mississippi. The first water-bearing formation occurs at a depth of about 700 to 900 feet below the landfill. Known as the Eutaw formation, this water is naturally high in total dissolved solids and chloride and is not considered potable. Other aquifers lie still deeper in the earth, Kenna said, adding that only the lowermost of these—some 2,000 feet below ground—contains water acceptable for drinking. According to CWM, no negative environmental impact on groundwater resources is projected to occur in at least 10,000 years. Comparing the chalk formation to the white cliffs of Dover and the chalk under the western Sahara, the company asserts that there are few places in the world with a geologic setting so favorable for containment of wastes.

Other generally accepted criteria for landfill siting, all of which characterize Emelle, are as follows:

- Low population density and low alternative land use
- Absence of floodplains, depressions, and excessive slopes
- Good transportation access (preferably near an interstate highway)
- Reasonable proximity to industrial sources of hazardous waste (in this case not only Alabama, but Louisiana)

Landfill Design

As is the case with any permitted facility, Emelle does not depend on geology alone for groundwater protection. Each cell is equipped with a landfill liner system composed of two separate composite liners and two leachate collection systems, with an underlying pressure relief mechanism. Leachate, which is primarily contaminated rainwater, is collected for treatment and disposal. No liquid waste materials are placed in the landfill.

The landfill composition is as follows: starting from the bottom are a foot of sand, three feet of compacted chalk topped by a 60-mil, high-density polyethylene liner, a second foot of sand, 1.5 feet of compacted chalk covered by a second 60-mil polyethylene liner and a protective fabric, one foot of gravel and a second filter fabric, and, finally, another 1.5 feet of chalk. The water collection system captures moisture from the two lower layers of sand and from the one-inch layer of gravel.

As are all well-managed landfills, the facility is divided into compartments that are further mapped out according to waste type. When filled, each compartment is closed following requirements described above. Grass grows on these formations but no dense vegetation, as they must remain accessible for monitoring and maintenance, Kenna said. The waste management facility is surrounded by 27,000 acres of land, he continued, of which only 500 are intended for landfill development. The remainder is managed for wildlife, he said.

Monitoring System

In addition to the deep well systems that monitor water quality of the Eutaw formation, the landfills are surrounded by about 50 shallow monitoring wells that penetrate between 50 feet and 100 feet into the upper zone of the chalk formation. These wells draw very little water but serve as an early detection system to indicate contaminant migration. Even though some are within five feet of disposal trenches, no waste migration has ever been confirmed at any of these wells, according to the company. Finally, more remote monitoring takes place at a stream some six miles from the facility. This stream also is the receptacle of output from rainwater settling ponds that surround the lower elevation of the facility. This clean water is released only after it has been tested.

Laboratory Facility

The recently expanded laboratory at Emelle tests samples of every container of waste received at the facility. If it proves to be adequately pretreated as represented by the generator, the waste may go directly to the landfill, but only after a gatekeeper checks to make sure the necessary forms are in hand.

If treated at Emelle, the waste is tested again before disposal. Finally, if the laboratory finds that the waste differs in any way from that represented on the manifest, EPA and the state are notified and the waste returned to the generator.

This laboratory also performs all of the monitoring noted above, following methods spelled out in applicable rules. The state Department of Environmental Management (ADEM) and EPA also check results of the facility monitoring system either in conjunction with CWM or independently. ADEM has its own portable offices at the site.

Ancillary Activities

Although remaining CWM's largest landfill facility, Emelle is not its most diverse treatment, storage, and disposal facility. However, it does house certain ancillary facilities, including solvent recovery, fuel blending, a very large stabilization shed, and PCB services capable of removing the material from transformers and capacitors and land filling the solids. The recovered solvents return to specified companies, the blended fuels are sent for combustion in a cement kiln, and the liquid PCB is manifested to a permitted incinerator. The company has plans, so far still on the drawing board, to construct such an incinerator at Emelle.

The compound also includes a wastewater treatment plant that treats waste generated at the offices and cafeteria for use in washing trucks, a process that must take place after every trip into the landfill. The truck-washing wastewater, together with runoff from storage tanks and other potentially hazardous sources, is shipped for treatment elsewhere.

Worker Protection and Housekeeping

Much of the bad press concerning landfills of the past has generated from facilities vastly different from Emelle. Not only was industrial hazardous waste often placed in technologically inferior landfills; little care was given to the protection of workers handling such materials. Kenna said that a factor in North Carolina's inability to site such a facility is the mismanagement of a defunct facility owned by Caldwell Systems, Inc. Workers at this operation actually did suffer neurological damage. Testimony revealed that inspection, supervision, and worker protection at the site were nonexistent, Kenna said, adding that on slow days the workers would stand in the middle of the dump and have sludge fights.

There are no sludge fights at Emelle. According to company records, the accident rate at the facility is very low. Each year the management claims to spend approximately $5,000 per employee for protective clothing and health monitoring activities. A team of health specialists trains employees and directs their adherence to safety standards. Each new employee must participate in an eight-hour orientation safety training course. Further training occurs throughout employees' careers. All employees also attend monthly safety meetings, during which job-specific information is presented in addition to general safety and operational procedures.

A visit to the facility revealed that employees indeed seemed well trained. They were clothed appropriately for their tasks, wore safety masks and hard hats even at sites that were minimally hazardous, and behaved in a manner indicating that they took their work seriously. A training session was in progress while we were there.

The site is designed to reduce contamination and runoff. Stored waste and trucks containing unloaded wastes are under roof. On-site roadways are continuously swept and sprayed if necessary. Empty ground is planted.

As noted above, no truck leaves the hazardous area of the facility without first being washed. As an additional precaution against mishap, the company exceeds federal Department of Transportation and Alabama state regulations in many aspects of maintenance, training, and driver experience. For instance, federal law requires that drivers be at least 21 years old, whereas the company demands that they be at least 25 with a minimum of 3 years' experience in driving commercial vehicles. As would be the case at any well-managed facility, the trucks are subject to a strict inspection and maintenance program and must be placarded, carry a manifest describing their load, and be equipped with response and protective gear.

UNDERGROUND INJECTION WELLS (40 CFR 144, 146, 148, and 265)

Emelle sends waste to a Class I underground injection well in Texas that can accept waste forbidden from disposal in a landfill. Such facilities are subject to certain, but not all, aspects of the land disposal ban. Moreover, they often are in such deep, confined land formations that the no-migration demonstration is relatively easy to make. Unless covered by an exemption, such facilities may not receive dioxins, untreated solvents numbered F001 through F005 on the hazardous waste lists, wastes and sludges containing heavy metals or arsenic, highly acidic liquids or those containing 50 or more parts per million of PCBs, or halogenated organic compounds.

Injection wells are regulated under both the Safe Drinking Water Act and RCRA. EPA overlapped these statutes because complete reliance on the drinking water protection program did not cover other environmental effects or provide for a federally enforceable interim status period.

Class I wells are those in which hazardous wastes are injected beneath the lowest formation having underground sources of drinking water within one-quarter mile of the well site; hence, the ease with which the no-migration demonstration can be made. In former years, hazardous waste could be injected in Class IV wells, which are those receiving waste in or above formations having underground sources of drinking water within one-quarter mile. The 1984 amendments prohibit the disposal of wastes into these wells, except for very narrowly defined treated water reinjected in the course of a corrective action under RCRA. Many states had similar prohibitions in place before the federal government had done so.

Chapter 12

SITING WASTE FACILITIES: AN ENDLESS PURSUIT

The question "Where will we put it?" now dominates all other discussion of planning for future waste disposal capacity. It matters not whether the proposed facility is to be a solid waste landfill or a massive new hazardous waste storage, treatment, and disposal (TSD) facility; opposition will surface and, in many cases, drown even a worthwhile project. As case studies in this and the following chapter will show, solid waste management facilities still are being permitted, sometimes even with community blessing. The siting of comprehensive hazardous waste facilities, however, has become next to impossible.

The only recently permitted virgin comprehensive hazardous waste facility is in Colorado. Ready to receive waste, it stands empty, waiting for transactions to be final in the sale of the facility because developer Browning-Ferris Industries decided to pull out of the hazardous waste business entirely. In announcing this decision, the company cited more stringent and expensive environmental regulations as one cause. However, the company also cited large penalties for alleged noncompliance and recent state decisions that denied permits as reasons for dropping its hazardous waste operations. For more about the process through which the Colorado facility was permitted, see Chapter 13.

In an August 1989 report advocating a regional approach to hazardous waste management in California, the Southern California Hazardous Waste Management Authority found that some projects fail for good reasons. The report indicated that proponents often select a site without adequate environmental assessment and/or care being given to neighborhood compatibility. Some developers select only one site for consideration, make all major investment and design decisions before working with government and the public, hold project decisions and past performance records "close to the vest," and view citizens as "ignorant, obstructive, and determined to defeat the project." According to the Environmental Protection Agency's (EPA) *Sites for Our Solid Waste, A Guidebook for Effective Public Involvement*, this traditional siting process, sometimes called the "Decide, Announce, Defend model," is obsolete.

The California report also criticizes governments for being heavy handed. Particularly damaging is the state or federal decisionmaker who moves headlong into a project without bringing local government in on the ground floor. The community automatically goes on the defensive, sharing with the citizens the perception that both have been deliberately excluded.

CITIZEN ACTIVIST ORGANIZATIONS

While conceding that many projects and their advocates are flawed, the California report's strongest criticism is toward citizen groups, which increasingly portray all projects as evil. The status quo "is defended as perfection" and "nothing is ever safe enough in their eyes." By taking extreme and often disparate views, citizens "veto any progress" and fail to negotiate solutions or acceptable tradeoffs. Thus, emotion rather than intelligent policy making dominates far too much waste management planning.

It was another California report, prepared in 1984 for the state Waste Management Board by Cerrell Associates, that played a large part in the growth of these citizen groups, which seem bent on crying "not in my backyard" (NIMBY). The Cerrel report noted that hazardous waste management projects were more likely to be successfully sited if their proponents chose to locate in rural areas where the residents were older, had an educational level of high school or lower, had low incomes, were Catholic, were politically conservative with a free-market orientation, and had occupations that were "nature exploitive," such as farming, ranching, or mining.

Needless to say, this report generated outrage, particularly in the Catholic press, according to Will Collette, national organizing director of the Citizens Clearinghouse for Hazardous Wastes, a national organization that coordinates citizen activism in this area. Collette and other citizen activists contend that nearly every proposal to site a landfill or hazardous waste facility meets the criteria set forth in the Cerrell report and that anger over the perceived injustices fuels greater local opposition.

Blacks also feel especially harmed by past waste management practices. For example, the Bordeau Action Committee, an association of some 600 African-American residents of Nashville, Tennessee, charged, in a suit filed March 12, 1990, that the continued operation of the Bordeau landfill beyond its scheduled closing date represents unconstitutional racial discrimination. More specifically, the suit charged that "the placement of the...sanitary landfill was and is consistent with a national racially discriminatory trend that has resulted in more than 70 percent of all such landfills existing in Afro-American communities."

Citizens Clearinghouse

The philosophy of the Citizens Clearinghouse for Hazardous Waste exemplifies the depth of feeling of some NIMBY activists. For instance, an April 1990 clearinghouse publication asserted that almost every waste site is a disaster waiting to happen and that each new site allows "polluters to keep polluting." Reiterating the charge that such facilities usually are located in rural and/or poor communities, the clearinghouse said it does not hesitate to help NIMBY activists "because most people quickly evolve from NIMBY to NIABY (not in anyone's back yard)."

Collette noted that, as of the end of 1989, there were 6,300 active citizen NIMBY groups, some fighting new siting efforts and others protesting those already in place (see below). Collette said the coalition does not accept the premise that landfills or other facilities must be sited at all. Such advocates claim that if industry recycled its waste and made every available effort to minimize waste, new facilities would not be needed. Farsighted as this stance may seem, some large companies have shown signs of agreeing with these advocates, as described in Chapter 5.

HOW CITIZENS VIEW RISK

In a paper presented at the June 1990 annual meeting of the Air & Waste Management Association, Betty K. Jensen of Public Service Electric and Gas Co., Newark, New Jersey, and Richard A. Jensen of Hofstra University differentiated between the risk concept of scientists and that of society at large. To a scientist, the authors claim, risk perceptions take into account the probability that an event will occur, the probability that toxic substances will be released by that event, the probable quantity released, the probability of exposure, and the likelihood of adverse human health or environmental effects. Not only does the concept of risk itself imply uncertainty, the risk calculations also reflect big uncertainties, the authors observe.

The layman asks only if something is safe. This lack of understanding of risk analysis leads many to demand a risk-free society at all costs without an appreciation of what that really means, the authors contend. Moreover, as noted in the EPA guidebook, those unfamiliar with technical issues have an inherent distrust in equipment and, more and more frequently, the regulators and consultants that try to explain it to them. According to EPA, citizens view risk on a personal basis, asking whether the risk is voluntary or imposed, whether they can do anything to lower their own risks, and whether they live close to the facility and are therefore unjustly exposed.

The Jensen paper further notes that disagreements about risk cannot be expected to disappear when conflicting evidence is presented. Strong initial views resist change because "subsequent information is processed through a filter consisting of the initial views," the authors explain. New information that counters these perceptions is often dismissed as "unreliable, erroneous, or unrepresentative."

With these observations in mind, EPA advises developers to convey what is known about the environmental and health risks associated with a new disposal facility and about the precautions being taken to manage these risks. Information also must be provided on a range of other siting issues such as property values, air quality, noise, and traffic. The agency further advises against assuming that risk communication is a win-or-win proposition. It is a mistake to assume that developing a risk communication plan is easy or will guarantee success; however, lack of such a plan could most assuredly kill even a good project, EPA observes.

Public Concerns

A paper authored by staff members of Roy F. Weston, Inc., *Public Involvement: Moving Beyond Public Relations*, lists concerns that shape community attitudes toward industry:

- Concern about risks to family and personal health from site emissions into the air and water, accidents, and transportation of hazardous substances to and from the site

- Fear that a site's proximity will hurt the neighborhood

- A feeling of powerlessness in monitoring and controlling potentially hazardous releases

- A perception that neither industry nor regulators can be trusted

- Uncertainty created by conflicting statements from authorities and scientists as to how much risk a particular substance or activity poses

Today, the NIMBY syndrome is stronger than ever, the Weston authors assert, noting that even facilities that have operated for long periods of time in peace with their neighbors face increasing scrutiny. This phenomenon occurred at Emelle, Alabama, when a few citizens, who had long lived in peace with the enormous landfill as a neighbor, suddenly became hostile, at one point lining up at the gate to block incoming trucks. It was this agitation that triggered the state's tougher stance with regard to the amount of waste sent to the landfill, discussed in Chapter 11. According to H. Gordon Kenna, community relations manager for Chemical Waste Management, Inc.'s, southern operations, the local citizens involved in the protest were few, but their numbers were augmented by outsiders.

According to Kenna, Chemical Waste Management has repeatedly invited its critics to tour the facility, but they refuse to come. Rather than see the enemy at first hand, they base their protest on what is handed on to them from other organizations, he charged. He added, however, that the agitation seems to have abated.

Changing Rules and Perceptions

Not all concerns raised by citizens are unjustified. Numerous waste-to-energy facilities were permitted in the earlier part of the 1980s amid assurances by environmental regulators that operational stipulations in combination with a well-designed electrostatic precipitator would be sufficient to protect the health of neighboring citizens. Such a facility was built in downtown Baltimore without any significant opposition.

Now, only a few years later, EPA proposes to require much more, as described in Chapter 4. Moreover, the agency will require that earlier waste-to-energy plants be retrofitted. Even then they will not be as clean-burning as new incinerators are expected to be; they merely will be better controlled than was considered adequate not many years ago. Similarly, the once seemingly sufficient standards for solid waste landfills now are found to be inadequate. Serious seepage into groundwater has occurred from these earlier facilities, leading EPA to propose regulations requiring that all landfills undergo rigorous risk assessment and be technologically almost as foolproof as hazardous waste landfills. Is it any wonder, then, that citizens view askance attempts by regulators to persuade them that any given control method is enough?

RULES OF RISK COMMUNICATION

Vincent T. Covello, director of the Center for Risk Communication at Columbia University and president of the Society for Risk Analysis, and Frederick W. Allen, associate director of EPA's Office of Policy Analysis, compiled seven rules of risk communication that may improve relations among various groups in forums where waste management is at issue. Although many of the rules seem obvious, they continually are violated, according to the authors, and should be studied with care.

Rule 1: Accept and Involve the Public as a Legitimate Partner

People and communities have a right to participate in decisions that affect their lives, property, and the things they value. Demonstrate respect for this principle by involving the community at every step of the way. Include all parties with a stake in the issue. Government employees must remember that they work for the public.

The goal of risk communication should not be to defuse public concerns or to avoid taking necessary action; instead, it should be to produce an informed public that cares but is reasonable and thoughtful enough to seek an equitable solution.

Rule 2: Plan Carefully and Evaluate Your Efforts

When the need to communicate with citizens first emerges, set out clear, explicit risk communication objectives such as the following:

- Determine whether you have sufficient information to discuss the risks. If not, acquire such information before proceedings begin.

- Convey information that will motivate individuals to take responsible action, stimulate response to emergencies, or contribute to the resolution of conflict.

- Classify and segment the various groups in your audience, aiming communications at specific subgroups.

- Recruit people who are skilled at presenting materials and interacting with groups.

- Train your staff in communication skills and reward outstanding performance.

- Learn from your mistakes.

There is no such entity as "the public." Instead, there are many publics, each with its own interests, needs, concerns, priorities, and preferences. Different risk-communication goals, audiences, and media require different communication strategies.

Rule 3: Listen to the Public's Specific Concerns

Avoid making assumptions about what people know, think, or want done with regard to your proposal. Use techniques such as interviews, group meetings, and surveys to learn what people think. Make sure all parties are heard. Identify with your audience, putting yourself in its place. Recognize people's emotions, and be aware that groups may have hidden agendas or political reservations. Realize that projects may take on a symbolic importance that exceeds any real risk.

People in the community often are more worried about such issues as trust, credibility, competence, control, whether the risk is voluntary, fairness, caring, and compassion than about mortality statistics and the details of risk assessment.

Rule 4: Be Honest, Frank, and Open

State your credentials, but do not always expect to be trusted on that basis. When discussing the risks associated with the project, lean toward sharing more information rather than less. If you do not know an answer, do not speculate; if you are uncertain or know that the data are not entirely reliable, say so. Tell people you will seek the information requested. Identify worst-case risk estimates as such, and cite ranges of risk estimates when you can.

Trust and credibility are hard to obtain; once lost, they are almost impossible to regain.

Rule 5: Coordinate and Collaborate with Other Reliable Sources

Allies can be a real help in pushing a project forward. Try to issue communications jointly with other trustworthy sources, such as university scientists, physicians, or trusted local officials, including environmental regulators.

Few things are likely to ruin risk communication efforts more than public disagreements among so-called experts.

Rule 6: Meet the Needs of the Media

Be open and accessible to reporters, who are the prime transmitters of information on risks. Furnish information tailored to the various media, such as graphics and other visual aids for television. Do not hesitate to respond to their stories with praise or criticism, as warranted. Try to build up relations of trust with specific editors and reporters.

The media usually are more interested in politics than in actual risk, in simplicity more than in complexity, and in danger more than in safety.

Rule 7: Speak Clearly and With Compassion

Avoid jargon; instead, use simple and nontechnical language. Be sensitive to local norms in speech and dress. Use vivid, descriptive language to breathe life into technical data but avoid using distant, abstract, unfeeling knowledge about deaths, injuries, or illnesses. Acknowledge in your behavior the fears, outrage, and helplessness that some in your audience may feel but avoid mistakes that could aggravate these attitudes. When attempting to place risks into perspective, remember that people's willingness to accept risk is greater if the risk is voluntary, controllable, and familiar.

Regardless of how well you communicate risk information, some people will not be satisfied. Always acknowledge that any illness, injury, or death is a tragedy and recognize that people may indeed understand complex risk information even if they do not agree with you.

SITE CONSIDERATIONS

The revelation that landfills are usually located in rural, underdeveloped areas should come as no surprise to environmental professionals because of recommendations set forth in a 1973 EPA Office of Solid Waste Report to Congress. Much of the report was concerned with geology, which dictated, for instance, the Emelle site. However, the report also recommended that landfills be in areas of low population on land of little potential value. If no other criterion existed, this "low alternative land use" provision created a probability that landfills would be built on poor land populated mostly by poor people, especially in the South.

According to Kenna, these criteria have been reexamined in light of recent criticisms. Perhaps it does make more sense to place the facilities near the companies that generate the waste, he said. This stance might be appropriate for incineration facilities, he noted, but when planning landfills, geology must be a factor. EPA's standards and criteria concerning facility siting are set forth in appropriate chapters elsewhere in this book.

Planners should remember that in areas without adequate zoning or land use laws, citizens will cite environmental considerations any time they oppose a facility, regardless of its actual effect. If they can find valid issues, their arguments are that much stronger. EPA's siting rules are sketchy at best. Would-be developers must probe deeper in order to anticipate as much as possible what well-led citizens are likely to find. For instance:

- Is the area likely to be inhabited by a species protected by the Endangered Species Act? This controversial law has blocked more than one project. Efforts in Congress to weaken its provisions have failed, as lawmakers stand firm, declaring that if the provisions derail certain projects, that is their purpose.

Siting Waste Facilities: An Endless Pursuit

- Is the facility on or near a watershed that either is in itself important or empties into environmentally sensitive bodies of water?

- Is there any evidence that the site is in a floodplain or near a seismic fault? Citizens are aware that the federal hazardous waste permit standards as well as many state laws specifically forbid the construction of hazardous waste facilities in such areas. Planners therefore must conduct careful geologic research in order to be sure that no such allegation can be made. At the stalled project in Mobile, Arizona, described in the next chapter, citizens charged the developers of placing the facility on both a 100-year floodplain and a seismic fault.

- Is there an adequate land buffer between the facility and its nearest neighbor? If not, is the facility on or near other industrial facilities? TSDs surrounded by green space and screened by trees and shrubbery are not only less obtrusive but also environmentally more compatible. If the active part of a facility is surrounded by acres of land under the owner/operator's control, there is a greater opportunity to control migration of effluent off the plant site. Moreover, the buffer ensures that dwellings are at least some distance from the point of disposal. The Emelle facility is a good example of this kind of planning.

Conversely, a waste management facility, especially an incinerator, treatment, or recycling facility, is far more likely to be acceptable if placed near other industry. For instance, a garbage-to-energy incinerator under construction in Huntsville, Alabama, and described below, is sited on the grounds of the Redstone Arsenal, which also plans to purchase its power.

Lessons from Successful Sitings

EPA's solid waste facility siting guidebook bases its advice on information from numerous case studies. Some of the lessons learned are as follows:

- *Successful siting efforts require both political and technical expertise by public officials and citizens:* In their effort to force improved technology at a proposed hazardous waste site near Denver, Colorado, the Concerned Citizens of Eastern Colorado discovered that expert help was very hard to find, according to president Pam Whelden. The citizens were continuously overwhelmed with the legal and technical power displayed by the landfill developers, she explained (see Chapter 13 for more on this case study). To help mitigate this sense of powerlessness, Wisconsin allows waste managers to provide grants to community representatives to hire their own consultants, according to EPA.

- *The various segments of the public should be consulted at every stage of the decision:* EPA notes that as site planning progresses, public involvement will ebb and flow. As months stretch into years, some drop by the wayside, only to return as the project reaches its final stages. The agency warns that citizens who come on the scene at its later stages assume that nothing happened before they began participating. These new arrivals want to reexamine all of the decisions made during the preceding months; it might have been better to have sought these people out and brought them in at the start. Good documentation also is essential.

- *Successful sitings require an informed opposition and a good risk communication program:* This might include briefings, feature stories in newspapers, mailings, news conferences, or newsletters. With regard to newspaper stories, the manual states that the article will be written as the editor sees fit; "the project proponent has no control over how the story is presented—except to provide full information." This statement is broad and not necessarily accurate. In the first place, newspapers differ in their attitudes toward industrial development and so-called "progress." If developers assume that all reporters are ignorant and that they are the enemy, they convey that fact, often acting as if they have a great deal to hide when, in fact, they are merely frightened at how their ideas will be interpreted. It is imperative to provide the information that reporters need to write a balanced story, and to provide it up front. If reporters feel they need to pry out a story, they move into an investigative mode, which results in far more combative journalism than is likely to occur if information is readily available.

- *The siting process must be flexible:* All characteristics are negotiable. EPA observes that each of its case studies indicates that a flexible attitude is essential. Most important, developers must often go beyond what they know is technically adequate just to quell citizens' fears. For instance, a landfill in Fulton County, New York, included monitoring wells even though the hydrogeological study indicated that there was no risk of groundwater contamination. Similarly, at a regional landfill in Northampton, Massachusetts, neighbors negotiated a restriction limiting the number of disposal trips for haulers from outlying communities to one per week.

- *Planning and communication strategies should be reevaluated throughout the life of the project:* Developers soon will discover that some techniques do not work and should be abandoned. Equally important, they must be prepared to try something else. Siting waste management facilities is a difficult and complex process, EPA notes, and even experienced practitioners face unpredictable obstacles requiring new skills and strategies.

- *The state plays an important role in the siting process:* The state can support projects through outright grants and loans, technical support of its own, and the enactment of rules that favor sound waste management.

SITE STUDIES

EPA includes in its guidebook siting experiences of two solid waste facilities, a landfill in Maricopa County, Arizona, and a resource recovery facility in Hempstead, New York.

Maricopa County Landfill

The need for a new landfill to serve Phoenix became apparent when negotiations began in 1984 to close the existing privately owned landfill. County officials did not envision much opposition to the project because the proposed siting area consisted of desert or undeveloped farmland, according to EPA. When the county presented its inventory of possible sites, however, it was confronted by several hundred angry residents at the first public meeting.

Only then did the county initiate a public involvement program, as well as expand the site study area. A citizen advisory committee was formed of 28 people, including representatives from local municipalities, neighborhoods, the real estate community, farming, water interests, and others. A five-member steering committee was made up of representatives of Maricopa County, the City of El Mirage (the site of the existing landfill), and the Arizona State Department of Health Services. There also were numerous public meetings.

The new effort allowed the citizens and the developers to work toward consensus. An initial list of 24 sites was reduced to 7, which underwent more intense review. The final site, roughly 10 miles from the edge of the northwestern metropolitan area, was chosen with very little opposition. The planners learned, according to EPA, that site selection is "not simply a technical study, but a social process." The county supervisor said that the goal was to arrive at a consensus that was not only environmentally sound, but "one that is socially acceptable."

The county also learned that its concerns differed from those of the citizens. Whereas the county was especially worried about future land use, the citizens were most concerned about possible contamination of their drinking water wells. The designers addressed these fears by including a leachate collection system in the landfill design and banning disposal of liquid bulk waste at the site.

Hempstead Resource Recovery Facility

In 1984, when public officials in Hempstead, Long Island, New York, contemplated redevelopment of a refuse-derived fuel incinerator that had been closed by EPA several years earlier, they faced an uphill battle. A Solid Waste Advisory Committee formed in the early 1980s in response to problems from the previous incinerator harbored animosity toward members of the town board because of the struggle over management of the old incinerator, according to EPA.

However, something needed to be done. Hempstead's population of 750,000 generated over 2,000 tons of solid waste per day. Some of this waste was shipped to Pennsylvania for disposal at a cost of $110 per ton. The rest was going to the nearby Oceanside landfill, scheduled for closure in June 1989. Therefore, the old committee, augmented by citizens of Oceanside who demanded that the landfill be closed immediately, agreed to work with the board to site a new, environmentally acceptable waste recovery facility.

Site selection was relatively simple. Political expediency dictated that the old site be used. The town already owned the land and had only to negotiate the purchase of the closed facility. Adjacent property included a harness track, a shopping center, a six-lane highway, and a park. The nearest residential neighbors were about one quarter of a mile away. Community leaders accepted this site designation and concentrated their energies on safety design issues.

To reduce animosity, the committee and board members asked the public works commissioner to act as mediator, since he was a member of both bodies. The committee met monthly to discuss issues and resolve disputes. Invited speakers regularly explained technologies, risks, and options; an expert from Stonybrook University worked for the committee free of charge. In addition, the forum allowed residents from near the landfill and the incinerator to express a broad range of related community concerns. Committee members therefore felt as if they were well represented and could make an informed decision.

The design that resulted is a mass-burn incinerator capable of processing 3,350 tons per day. The citizens were able to negotiate successfully for a preferred stack height, scrubbers, and a baghouse to control air emissions. They also negotiated a recycling program and open access to monitoring data. The 700 tons per day of ash residue produced by the facility is shipped to a landfill in upstate New York.

PUBLIC/PRIVATE PARTNERSHIPS

The experience described so far in this chapter illustrates the importance of bringing community leaders into the development of facilities that will serve their citizens. One way in which this can be done is through the formation of a public/private partnership, whereby the community has considerable control over the planning of the facility while a private company has responsibility for the technical details.

Public/private partnerships to construct waste-to-energy combustion facilities have become the norm rather than the exception. With the inception of the new proposed Part D rules for landfills, which add immeasurably to the costs of such facilities, public/private partnerships to construct landfills also may seem an intelligent choice.

Ogden Projects of New Jersey, a leading firm in the waste-to-energy business, builds all of its plants under contract with municipalities.

Partnership to Build a Landfill

Alabama has been the site of two such partnerships in recent years, a landfill in Lee County (described in detail in Chapter 10) and a waste-to-energy incinerator near Huntsville. Each project survived community opposition, at least in part because it was a public/private partnership. When such a partnership functions well, the private waste company provides the know-how concerning site selection and facility design, while the public entity can help in gaining community support.

The story of how the Lee County landfill came to be built illustrates how this relationship works. When the county sanitary landfill was nearing capacity in the early 1980s, a solid waste authority was established to study the feasibility of an incinerator. The idea encountered citizen opposition, however, and the authority disbanded. The City of Opelika then attempted to site a new landfill but decided against the idea after again encountering strong citizen opposition.

Alabama law places primary responsibility for managing solid waste on the counties. After the failure in Opelika, Lee County seemed backed to the wall. Aware that it had neither the expertise to build a landfill nor the desire to anger citizens further, the county entered into a contract with Waste Away, Inc., which purchased an acceptable site and designed and built the landfill, taking care that in all aspects it would meet not only current permit provisions but also the intent of the new Part D provisions, which had been aired as early as 1984. Both the company and the County Commission held meetings with the citizens to help them understand that the landfill would be safely managed. According to Waste Away, citizen protests still occurred but, because the site was chosen by the company rather than the commission, there was less political backlash.

Partnership for an Incinerator

The incineration facility, a partnership between the Huntsville Solid Waste Disposal Authority and Ogden Martin Systems, Inc., of Huntsville, went on line four months ahead of schedule, according to Eddie Coker, director of the authority. Ogden designed, constructed, and will operate the 690 tons-per-day facility.

The idea seemed blessed from the start. Before deciding upon the project, the city conducted a thorough study, funded by EPA, on how best to solve its solid waste disposal problem. Notably, Huntsville was among the first cities in Alabama also to have a strong recycling plan. The site choice was felicitous. The incinerator was built on property leased from the U.S. Army's Redstone Arsenal—in other words, on land already dedicated to a variety of potentially dangerous uses, set apart from any community, and publicly owned.

In turn, the partnership sells steam from the recovery unit to the arsenal. In order to meet the terms of the contract, which requires uninterrupted supply, the incinerator was designed to combust landfill gas, natural gas, and other fuels in conjunction with the municipal waste.

The facility was funded through issuance of fixed-rate taxable bonds worth $112 million. The insured AAA bonds were backed by garbage tipping fees and revenue from the sale of the steam. Thus, members of the community had an opportunity to invest in the facility. As a further means to quell resistance, the partnership formed a citizen's advisory committee to keep everyone informed throughout the permitting and construction process. Ironically, the greatest resistance was not on environmental grounds but on cost. The individual monthly fees increased from $5.00 to $7.50, with the potential of increasing to $12.50. In the long run, however, disposal costs in Huntsville should be lower than in cities that did not plan for future solid waste disposal, Coker said.

SITING ON AN INDIAN RESERVATION

In recent years waste management companies have flocked to Indian reservations, aware that many have vast, remote lands that are suitable for development as waste sites. Reservations also typically have populations in need of jobs, a history of poor waste management that will cost all tribal councils combined at least $35 million to rectify, and favorable tax status. According to a special report published by BNA, some 16 tribes have been approached by waste management companies in quest of 20 different projects. Of these, 5 were under construction until 2 were jettisoned because of citizen opposition, 5 are under negotiation, and 8 were rejected by the reservations.

For the reasons noted above, siting a waste management facility on a reservation may seem favorable both to the waste company and to an impoverished tribe. In fact, reservation siting can quickly become as difficult as siting anywhere else. At the reservation level, outside groups as diverse as neighborhood associations and Greenpeace or the Sierra Club may mount very effective opposition. Tribes sometimes disagree among themselves, thus killing a potential project. At the federal level, the Bureau of Indian Affairs (BIA) is the trustee of these lands and will not be pushed into approving projects that could harm the environment.

"We get some real snakes coming through," according to George Farris, BIA chief of environmental services. He said that some are very surprised to discover that the bureau requires completion of a detailed environmental impact statement that costs upwards of $300,000 and takes 12 to 18 months to complete. Undercapitalized companies are overwhelmed by this obstacle, he said. Nevertheless, a large company with sufficient money to operate such a facility responsibly should be able to pay the price, according to Elliot Cooper, vice president of Waste Tech Services, Inc., a Colorado-based waste management company interested in developing on Indian lands.

California Statute

A law adopted by California in 1990 (AB 3477) prohibits Indians from developing waste disposal sites on reservations without making a demonstration that no harm could come to communities or individuals outside the reservation. The law is based on a three-part legal test set forth by the U.S. Supreme Court in 1983 when it approved a California law prohibiting sales of liquor on reservations (*Rice v. Rehner,* 463 U.S. 713, 77 LEd2d 961). Tribes may lose their right to sovereignty under certain conditions. In this case, California based its position on the fact that groundwater and air do not stop at reservations' boundaries and that the state therefore has jurisdiction to protect its citizens.

REDUCING LIABILITY EXPOSURE

While most of this chapter involves the siting of new facilities, some consideration also must be given to waste-related risks attendant to the purchase of an existing plant or of land that has had prior use. "Buyer beware" must be the watchword, lest liability for past environmental transgressions be passed on to unsuspecting purchasers. The common sense rule, "know what you're buying," often is ignored by property buyers, according to David J. Hayes of Latham & Watkins, a Washington, D.C., law firm. He said some buyers falsely assume that the less they know about a piece of property, the easier they could prove in a court challenge under Superfund that they were "innocent buyers," and therefore not at fault.

According to Hayes, closing one's eyes is not a good defense. The stakes are too high to risk the liability of a hazardous waste cleanup, he said. He advises clients to look beyond the four corners of the property and include other liabilities the seller may have. For instance, a seller might have sent waste off-site to a facility that later became a Superfund site. In that case a buyer could inadvertently assume responsibility for off-site problems, he said. Liability also may occur if the seller closed operations several years earlier without taking proper long-term precautions. Hayes and other speakers at a District of Columbia Bar Association luncheon cautioned buyers not to depend entirely on consultants. While consultation is necessary, the buyer (and the buyer's lawyer) must be privy to all records, including information about off-site and closed facilities owned by the seller.

The seller also must attend to environmental liabilities, according to Timothy A. Vanderver, Jr., of Patton, Boggs & Blow. The temptation to push dirt under the rug may be strong, Vanderver said, but lawyers would not be comfortable with a transaction entered into by a seller ignorant of the risks. The seller should seek a clear assignment of environmental liabilities but should not be expected to provide a blanket warranty to the lender, he added. If it becomes clear that cleanup is necessary, the seller may want to carry it out by a set date instead of right away, he said. As a general rule, he added, buyers will want cleanups done to a higher standard than sellers.

State Laws Governing Transactions

Aware of the litigation that could ensue over environmental liability, states gradually are adopting laws requiring that an environmental audit take place before property is transferred.

New Jersey's Environmental Cleanup Responsibility Act (ECRA) was the first, and remains the model for such laws. Under this controversial provision, hazardous wastes must be cleaned up before industrial properties are sold. More specifically, upon sale, transfer, or closing of industrial establishments having a Standard Industrial Classification number within 22-39 inclusive, 46-49 inclusive, 51, and 76, and that in any way used or generated hazardous substances or waste, owners must obtain approval of a cleanup plan or a negative determination prior to completion of the transaction. The law (NJAC 7:1-4 et seq.) is carried out by the state Bureau of Industrial Site Evaluation, which enforces strict time schedules and charges fees.

Chapter 13

HAZARDOUS WASTE FACILITY SITING CASE STUDIES

All too often, rational waste management planning is eclipsed by the dim prospects of siting necessary hazardous waste treatment, storage, and disposal (TSD) facilities over the coming years. Solid waste landfills and incinerators continue to be permitted but at a slower pace. As described in the previous chapter, citizens increasingly question even modest proposals, alleging that waste reduction and recycling should take care of everything, an allegation dismissed by most environmental professionals as unrealistic.

The difficulties surrounding the management of hazardous waste are even more pronounced. The Comprehensive Environmental Response, Compensation, and Liability Act (CERCLA) requirement that each state contribute its share toward creating sufficient waste management capacity to carry us into the next century has proved hard to meet. Massachusetts has been trying for years to locate a hazardous waste facility to no avail. Florida has been equally unsuccessful. Historically, Florida has exported its waste to the Chemical Waste Management, Inc. (CWM), landfill in Emelle, Alabama, but was banned from doing so under Alabama's firm prohibition against the receipt of waste from states without approved capacity assurance plans (CAPs).

The argument that enough hazardous waste disposal capacity exists without the need for massive new sites is not entirely specious, despite the many closures that have occurred. Waste minimization is an attractive idea not only to environmentalists but to businesses as well. Moreover, currently permitted facilities are not all operating at capacity. As described below, the new facility in Colorado sat vacant for some time, waiting for a buyer. The Emelle landfill has capacity stretching well into the next century, with its largest constraint the state's limitations on the amount of waste that may be deposited there, according to CWM spokesman H. Gordon Kenna. Waste Management also has expansion programs under way at many facilities it owns. It has developed plans for new incinerators at Model City, New York; Emelle; Port Arthur, Texas; and Kettleman Hills, California. The company's ability to treat waste and to dispose of polycyclic biphenyls (PCBs) also is expanding.

The problem, however, is that waste management has become highly politicized. States and localities that have hosted such facilities through the years are increasingly unwilling to carry all of the burden, even when the geology is favorable and past problems have been minimal. The perception grows that new areas, and perhaps different kinds of people, should start bearing some of the nation's hazardous waste burden. The federalist way of doing things in the United States comes into play. On one hand, state citizens bridle at the idea of accepting massive quantities of hazardous waste from other states. On the other hand, several courts have ruled that restrictions against such transport are unconstitutional because they limit interstate trade.

Federalist thinking undoubtedly prompted Congress to include the CERCLA provision requiring that each state play some part in providing TSD capacity. The Environmental Protection Agency (EPA) has been unwilling to enforce these provisions as rigorously as some importing states would like, however. Moreover, just as bans are found to be unconstitutional barriers to commerce, some states, most notably Missouri, argue that the federal CAP requirements also inhibit interstate commerce and are equally unconstitutional. So far, however, neither Missouri nor any other state has filed suit on this issue.

This chapter includes three case studies, each of which shows how political issues combine with genuine citizen concerns to wreak havoc on facility planning, even when it is at its most conscientious. When planning is not conscientious, the results can be disastrous. In each of the cases described here, a strong factor in the difficulties encountered is some element of weak, inadequate regulation in the past. The first is the account of the newly permitted, currently empty hazardous waste landfill in Colorado. The second involves North Carolina, which has failed in its attempts to locate a site, thus reneging on its promise to contribute to the southeastern states' CAP. The third describes a comprehensive new hazardous waste facility in Arizona that is under construction, partially permitted, and stalled by a storm of opposition that erupted in June 1990, 10 years after the site-selection studies began.

THE COLORADO SAGA

One morning in October 1980, Pam Whelden noticed three huge piles of dirt forming in a field adjacent to her farm near Last Chance, Colorado. Upon investigation, she learned that the holes from which the dirt had been extracted were to become receptacles for hazardous waste by Highway 36 Land Development Co., a subsidiary of Browning Ferris Industries (BFI) of Colorado. There had been no public hearing or other means of sharing information with the citizens. Yet the landfill had not been done in secret. Both the Colorado Department of Health (CDH) and U.S. EPA Region IX had given it a go-ahead, according to Kenneth Niswonger, project officer for CDH. What Whelden did not know at that time was that a very important deadline was looming. Under the Resource Conservation and Recovery Act of 1976 (RCRA), facilities that were in existence on November 19, 1980, were eligible for an interim status permit, which meant less rigorous technological controls than would be required were the landfill to be built after that date, according to Richard Foster of Cockrell, Quinn, and Creighton, one of two attorneys that represented the citizens through the years of litigation that would follow Whelden's discovery. This statement was confirmed through material supplied by BFI.

Formation of a Citizens Group

"My first instinct was to call the governor," Whelden said. When that failed to bring satisfaction, she contacted the county and learned that they also were concerned. "Luckily, someone in the county had enough sense to get a court injunction to prevent further progress on the fill," Whelden observed. A citizens group, Concerned Citizens of Eastern Colorado (CCEC), was formed, with Whelden as president. Some time passed while the new group had a series of meetings, first with CDH and then with the Adams County Zoning Commission and the County Board of Commissioners. According to Joe French, of French & Stone in Boulder, Colorado (the citizens' other attorney), zoning was the tool by which the CCEC hoped to prevail.

County Approval

The group first persuaded the county board and zoning commission to take their side and defeat the project, Whelden and the attorneys said. However, after an election, new commissioners reversed the votes of their predecessors and approved the special zoning permit that was required, French explained.

French said the only factor that changed the commission's mind was politics. Confirming this perception, BFI notes that the atmosphere had changed considerably between June 1982, when the application was denied, and August 1983, when the commission changed its vote. First, in June 1982, the state's only other hazardous waste disposal facility, the Lowry Landfill in Arapahoe County, closed. More importantly, perhaps, Highway 36 finally commenced the public relations work that should have preceded the first hole in the ground. The company made some 100 slide presentations during those months to local and industry groups, thus gaining some support.

State law also changed in June 1983, when the general assembly amended the Hazardous Waste Act to empower the governor to select a state siting commission if a facility had not been sited by December 31, 1983. Finally, several important conditions were attached to the certificate issued by the commission, the following among them:

- Adams County has the power to approve the fee schedule and the hours of operation for the facility.

- The county will receive 2 percent of the facility's annual gross revenues.

- BFI must purchase emergency response vehicles and equip a hazardous materials vehicle for the county as well as train the appropriate county employees.

- BFI must give preference to Adams County for its supplies and services whenever possible and give county residents preference in hiring.

While these changes were persuasive to the commissioners, they did not alter the viewpoint of the CCEC, which continued its fight. Already, the citizens had won an important battle. By stalling activities beyond the deadline, they ensured that, when built, the landfill would be subject to final permit rules. Thus, Niswonger said, the citizens prevented "an environmental disaster from occurring."

"As a direct result of their action," he added, the company now would have to meet the minimum technology requirements of the permit regulations described in Chapter 10.

Following their defeat before the zoning commission, the citizens filed suit in the state district court against the county and BFI, Whelden said. The suit lingered on and was costly, she continued. Despite this long effort, which drained their resources but educated them as well, the citizens had too little evidence to prove wrongdoing on the part of the county or BFI, she said. By this time, BFI had assembled a team of very competent lawyers who were well prepared and persuasive, French added.

Issuance of the Permit

Once over this hurdle, BFI applied for a Part B permit to EPA that was returned with a notice of deficiency. Before this could be resolved, however, EPA authorized Colorado to manage its own program starting in November 1984. When BFI applied to the state, it received a deficiency notice there as well. Finally, in mid-1985, the company submitted an application that was "substantially complete," and public hearings began.

According to Tennell Roberts, a public health engineer with the department, the hearings process was "unprecedented." As the department completed each section of the draft permit, it held a public hearing to obtain comment. The complete draft permit was finally released in June 1986, and became subject to still more comment that did not close until November of that year. The final permit was issued on February 2, 1987.

The CCEC had not given up. They filed an administrative appeal against this action (*CCEC v. DOC and Highway 36*, HE 88-03, 1987). Among other arguments, the group charged that the plan for the facility could not afford 1,000 years' protection of the aquifers as required by state law and that the geological study was insufficient, Whelden said. CCEC was especially concerned that runoff from the facility would not contaminate their drinking water. "These aquifers are their lifeline," French explained.

Whelden said CCEC hired a local water expert but still had insufficient expertise. They called all over the United States to find a better qualified environmental engineer but without success. As it was, they spent over $250,000, she said, which is now almost paid off through bake sales and similar enterprises, an amazing feat in light of the fact that fewer than 250 people live within a 10-mile radius of the facility.

The appeal was filed on April 1, 1987. The administrative law judge decided, however, that BFI could begin construction while waiting for the final ruling. The hearing was held in September 1989, and a settlement, which included some additional protections for the citizens, was reached in February 1990.

Facility Design

A March 2, 1987, EPA press release described the facility as of "a different dimension than older land disposal facilities." The permit includes many precautions to ensure that "the wastes which go into the secure landfill cells will stay there," the press release said.

A. W. (Gus) Cummings, Jr., site manager, gave the following reasons for selecting this as an ideal location for a hazardous waste facility:

- The geology is suitable; underlying the site is a 4,000-foot layer of impermeable Pierre shale.
- There are no bedrock aquifers under the site.
- The site contains low permeability soils.
- An abundance of clay on the property is suitable for construction of the clay liners.
- The negligible groundwater on the site is nonpotable.
- The property is located in an area of low seismic activity.

The facility will use 325 acres within a 5,760-acre parcel owned by the developers. It has facilities for storage oil and solvent, solidification, and land disposal of solid materials. It is permitted to accept some 98,000 tons of waste a year for treatment that should arrive in an average of thirteen 20-ton truckloads per day. According to the state CAP, the facility will need to accept wastes from beyond Colorado's border. Likely exporting states are Kansas, Nebraska, New Mexico, and Wyoming.

The permit allows for the construction of 16 disposal cells, with a total capacity of 2.5 million cubic yards. Two have been excavated so far, one equipped with liners and leachate/leak detection systems and the second still incomplete. Each cell will be 630 feet long, 330 feet wide, and 40 feet deep, with a capacity of 158,000 cubic yards. At the base of each cell is a three-foot layer of clay overlain by an 80-mil plastic liner topped by three bands of textile materials (Geotextile, Geonet, Geotextile). Above this are three more feet of clay, a second 80-mil liner, a one-inch sand blanket, more textile liner, and a final one-inch soil layer. The leak detection system will collect and remove any liquid that has permeated the primary synthetic and clay liner.

Other facets of facility management are comparable to those carried out at the Emelle, Alabama, landfill, described in Chapter 10, though they are described by Cummings as "well in excess of regulatory requirements." Among the obligations that came as a result of opposition by CCEC are the following:

- An extensive groundwater monitoring scheme requiring a total of 111 monitoring wells, "in spite of the fact that the site is on 4,000 feet of impervious Pierre shale with no bedrock aquifer"
- A redesign of the surface water management plan to handle runoff from a 24-hour, 500-year storm event, or twice the 100-year rainstorm, whichever is more protective
- A random sampling of every 20th truckload of waste to ensure generating honesty, a requirement that will add $7 to each cubic yard of waste disposed
- "Rigorous controls on the type of wastes accepted," with a requirement that the toxicity characteristic leaching procedure be used to test waste prior to acceptance as well as prior to on-site transfers

The citizens also won the right to inspect the monitoring system themselves, Whelden said.

Sale of the Landfill

Upon settlement of the CCEC appeal in early 1990, it seemed that the 10-year progression from the first disputed hole in the ground to the final state-of-the-art landfill was complete. This was not to be so, however. Two months after the settlement, in April 1990, BFI announced that it was going out of the hazardous waste management business and would concentrate instead on solid waste disposal and recycling activities. In fact, it had acquired a bad reputation in hazardous waste management, having had a well-publicized history of haphazard custodianship of landfills it operated in New York, Ohio, and Indiana. The company is the second largest solid waste management company in the United States, following Waste Management, Inc.

The new landfill, the first to be permitted solely under the Hazardous Waste Amendments of 1984, was put up for sale. If the company expected an immediate offer, it was disappointed. The process began in June 1990, when sales proposals were sent to potential buyers. There were no quick offers as one might have expected given the seeming attractiveness of a fully permitted, large hazardous waste site. Many bidders expressed concerns over the income projections included in the prospectus, claiming they were too high. Based on its large capacity and the lack of restrictions on out-of-state waste, the facility could be lucrative indeed, according to industry sources. However, the facility is remote and far from the nearest rail line. There seemed to be great difficulty in projecting even how quickly demand within Colorado would grow.

The company originally resisted offering guarantees on how much waste the site could take because it wanted to close the books on the hazardous waste business, according to industry sources. However, when the final offer came, it included a provision to tie total compensation to the site's earnings.

The final sale came in early 1991. A new company, Concord Resources, Inc., announced on February 19, 1991, that it would buy the Highway 36 Land Development Co. from BFI. Concord is an emerging waste facilities venture formed by OHM Corp. of Findlay, Ohio, and Philadelphia-based Consolidated Rail Corp. (Conrail), according to the company's announcement. In addition to including the guarantees noted above, the sale price, which was not disclosed by the purchasers, is reported to be some 20 percent lower than BFI had projected.

This is the second purchase by the new venture, which for the first time brings a railroad into the waste management business. OHM has been in the business for more than 20 years and is a major contractor with the federal Superfund program. Indicative of its plans to become a model company, Concord chose a former EPA deputy assistant administrator, Swep T. Davis, as the chief executive officer. The company's public affairs officer, who will play a sizable role in its efforts to engage citizen support for its future siting plans—which currently center in Pennsylvania—is William J. Green, a former deputy secretary for the Pennsylvania Department of Environmental Resources. The company also has acquired Stablex Canada, Inc., a hazardous waste treatment and disposal facility near Montreal.

Lessons Learned

Whelden, a spokesperson for the citizens, said the most important lesson she learned over the past 10 years of advocacy is that citizens and would-be developers must stay "in some kind of relationship." It is "hard to build up trust, but you can't keep saying no, without finding solutions to problems," she said, noting that if the citizens had not fought, they never would have gained so much. Some are still "hateful," she said, unwilling even now to accept the compromise that ultimately became necessary. Whelden, who lives only three miles from the site, and whose drinking wells are in the path contamination would take should it occur, said she recognizes that such facilities must be built somewhere. She still wishes it had been somewhere else but recognizes that the permit conditions, which are extensive, will protect her property insofar as technical guarantees can be made.

Foster had two observations:

- Engineers are optimistic about the effectiveness of technological solutions; lawyers, on the other hand, are pessimistic, looking for the worst that might happen.

- One of the mistakes that developers make is to treat citizen groups as ignorant. They educate themselves; litigating issues that might have been resolved through effective communication is expensive.

In a prepared paper, Cummings notes several conclusions that can be made from this experience. He states, above all, that the permitting process is lengthy and costly, with no assurance of success. He said public opposition to siting a well-designed facility remains intense, adding that within the same week that final permits were issued to Highway 36, a Colorado legislative committee killed a bill admittedly designed to stop construction of the project.

As observed in Chapter 12, he found that public expectations are high; their attitude might be summed up as "In a space age society, why can't we simply eliminate hazardous waste?" he said. Government agencies "are hampered by the public's unrealistic demands for risk-free solutions," while few companies "have the resources and patience to undertake the permitting process, if Highway 36 is to be considered a representative example."

He concludes that such efforts still must be made because the waste service industry must avoid the "short-sighted trap of believing that the continued use of older, substandard facilities is an effective alternative in the long run."

While these largely negative observations hold true in many instances, the lesson that may be drawn from this case study is that citizens do not like to be made fools of. BFI admittedly tried to rush in with a substandard facility to escape more stringent rules that would take effect after a known deadline. The company did not seek citizen support until after it already had made enemies. It completely failed to take seriously the concerns of the residents most likely to be affected by the proposed activities. Even after it received the necessary permits and the well-designed landfill was ready for use, the company continued to characterize the citizens' demands as excessive, a no-win stance that alienates rather than unites.

ARIZONA'S STALLED HAZARDOUS WASTE FACILITY

Arizona started planning a hazardous waste facility in 1977, when the Department of Health Services (DHS) selected a contractor to prepare a preliminary report on the selection of a site. Subsequent reports and hydrologic studies were completed in 1978. Based on these purely scientific studies, the department selected a site in Yuma County. At the first public meeting held to advise the residents of this tentative decision, the opposition was extreme, according to a case history compiled by the Arizona Department of Environmental Quality (ADEQ), a 1987 outgrowth of the old DHS.

The opposition was sufficient to kill that first siting effort. Instead, the legislature enacted a new State Hazardous Waste Siting Act (ARS 36-2801), which required the DHS to conduct a study and provide recommendations following specified criteria. The law also required that a public hearing be conducted before a site could be recommended to the legislature. Upon completing a new analysis, the DHS conducted the necessary hearing. There were 368 persons attending, among whom 53 gave oral testimony and 200 submitted written comments.

Selection of a Site

The DHS then transmitted a report to the legislature on December 31, 1980. The report evaluated 11 sites based on environmental, social, economic, and institutional criteria, including transportation risks associated with the importation of waste, according to ADEQ. The report recommended a site in Yuma County, along Interstate 10, but added that two other sites, one of which was in the Rainbow Valley area in southern Maricopa County near the community of Mobile, also were satisfactory. The Mobile site, rather than the site at Yuma, was selected by the legislature, which codified its decision on February 26, 1981.

The DHS was instructed to purchase the site, which was on land owned by the federal Bureau of Land Management (BLM). Because this was determined to be a major federal action, an Environmental Impact Statement (EIS) was required. The U.S. EPA was selected as lead agency; the BLM and DHS were designated as support. The League of Women Voters was chosen to initiate two scoping meetings, which attracted some 60 people in Mobile and 45 people in Phoenix. In the final EIS issued in July 1983, the BLM supported the site proposal as presented. The EPA identified a number of environmental impacts associated with this alternative and recommended mitigation measures, which would be included in the permits. The recommendation was based on a representative facility because the specifications for the actual facility had not yet been drawn up.

BLM's proposed decision to sell the land required yet again public notice, which this time drew 1,185 signatures in opposition to the Mobile site. Despite this outcry, the bureau, on February 3, 1984, issued a final decision to continue with the sale of the site. The approval period for that decision ended on March 10, 1984. There were no appeals filed.

Facility Design

While the land transfer process was still going on, the DHS board reviewed two proposals to develop the site. On July 5, 1983, they unanimously recommended the selection of ENSCO Corp., one of two bidders, to construct a privately financed, "high-technology" facility that would rely on high-temperature incineration supplemented with other processes capable of serving both Arizona and out-of-state generators.

With many other issues remaining to be negotiated, the final contract for the facility was not signed until January 7, 1986. Under this agreement the company was to "submit complete permit applications for the following," according to the ADEQ:

- A storage section to include hazardous waste treatment in above-ground tanks; surface impoundments, if the above-ground tanks were insufficient; and storage units for containerized wastes

- An array of treatment facilities including neutralization, fixation, solidification, incineration, and evaporation

- A landfill

The contract also allowed the contractor to seek approval for substitute chemical, physical, or biological treatment methods or further landfill capacity. Interestingly, the contract required ENSCO to conduct special educational programs and services for area generators of small quantities of hazardous waste. Other obligations taken on by the company included monitoring, liability insurance, and postclosure terms.

Permit Activity

Subsequently, ENSCO asked for more, including the staged construction of three incinerators, the first of which was to be dedicated to PCB destruction, and increased landfill capacity to handle a projected operating rate of 100,000 cubic yards annually. The ADEQ approved construction of the third incinerator only on an as-needed basis and reduced the allowable landfill capacity to 50,000 cubic yards per year. Permits then were issued covering air emissions from the facility, the PCB incinerator (under the Toxic Substances Control Act), groundwater protection, and solid waste disposal. However, at the time the permits were issued, the state lacked statutory authority to hold hearings on proposed air quality permits, thereby opening an avenue for later challenge when the necessary regulations were adopted in September 1989.

The issuance of these mid-1988 permits allowed construction to begin on portions of the facility. However, four proposed permits remained: the revised air quality installation permit noted above, a hazardous waste operating permit from both Arizona and the federal EPA, and an additional toxic waste facility permit.

Hearings

Three hearings were scheduled in mid-1990 on DEQ and EPA proposals to issue these permits, in Mobile on May 7, 1990, in Phoenix on June 20, and in Tucson on June 21.

Pent-up anger concerning the mammoth site and the owners' intention to import out-of-state waste erupted at these hearings. The Mobile hearing was disrupted by protests; 18 activists were arrested. Following these outbursts, Governor Rose Mofford, on June 6, ordered a reassessment of the facility. Meanwhile, the state legislature began considering a bill (SB 1311) that would limit the plant's ability to accept out-of-state wastes.

The hearing in Phoenix drew an estimated 2,500 people, voicing both opposition and support of the project. Detractors made extravagant claims. Ben Chaiken, spokesperson for the Arizona Lung Association, pointed out that the facility would have the potential to incinerate "tens of thousands of pounds" of hazardous solid and liquid wastes per hour." He then attested that EPA cites hazardous waste treatment and disposal facilities as a "major source of toxic air pollutants resulting in excess cancer, genetic mutations, birth defects, and serious and acute respiratory diseases."

Michael Gregory, spokesperson for the Grand Canyon Chapter of the Sierra Club, asserted that the monitoring proposals were inadequate, that there would be excessively high limits for toxic emissions, inadequate risk assessment, inadequate control technology, poor engineering practices, and inadequate emergency procedures. Finally, Pamela Swift, chair of the Toxic Waste Investigative Group, said the ADEQ violated the state's hazardous waste disposal siting law (and EPA's) by placing the facility on a 100-year floodplain and a seismic fault. The department also bypassed the Maricopa County special use permit process by failing to hold a hearing on the permit, she said.

In a February 13, 1991, telephone interview, Norm Weiss, assistant director of the ADEQ, said little progress has been made since the time of the disruptive hearings. Certain valid technical problems were raised at the hearing, he conceded, that will be addressed when final permits are issued. However, the most controversial issue is waste importation, Weiss said, adding that it was not aired early enough in the process.

Moreover, there have been three governors and many changes in the state legislature since the first plans were presented, he said. The citizens' protests therefore reached new listeners, he continued, who now must reexamine all of the issues and make their own decision, especially on whether to reduce the scale of the facility, which then would change the economics and could scuttle the whole project.

Weiss said many of the environmental charges were indeed specious. There is an inactive fault beneath a portion of the facility but not a seismic fault, as defined in the regulations. Similarly, there are portions of the square-mile site that are in the 100-year floodplain, but no facilities will be built in these areas. However, the claims concerning emissions from the incinerators bear examining, he said, in view of the state's commitment to "a very conservative one-in-a-million risk factor."

Asked whether many of the protestors were "not in my backyard" (NIMBY) activists, Weiss said Mobile itself has only about 50 citizens, spread over a wide area. In Arizona, however, people have a "300-square-mile backyard"—some extend this even farther, to "not on the planet earth." And so another acronym—NOPE—is born.

THE CASE OF NORTH CAROLINA

Nowhere were the seeming barriers to achieving a viable CAP plan greater than in North Carolina. The state's old Hazardous Waste Treatment Commission, after making numerous unsuccessful attempts to locate a disposal site, was restricted from further site-selection activities under a moratorium adopted in June 1988.

A second impediment to site development was a 1987 law prohibiting the discharge of any effluent from a new hazardous waste facility upstream of a drinking water source—even if treated and subject to a National Pollutant Discharge Elimination System (NPDES) permit—unless the dilution ratio was 1:1,000 or less. This law halted a plan by GSX, Inc. (now Laidlaw Environmental) to construct a treatment facility in Laurinburg, Scott County. Arguing that the law was arbitrary, the Hazardous Waste Treatment Council filed a petition for EPA to withdraw North Carolina's RCRA authority. After some delay, EPA concluded that the state's authority could not be withdrawn because "the NPDES is not perfect and exceedances are allowed," so this law gives an extra measure of protection, according to Linda W. Little, executive director of the Governor's Waste Management Board.

Even while agreeing that the dilution ratio was arbitrary, the court said the law was justified by the benefits, Little said. The company has challenged this decision in the U.S. Circuit Court of Appeals for the D.C. Circuit.

While its stringent laws and site-selection ban were hindering new capacity development, the state had lost its existing treatment, storage, or disposal capacity through closures. Its sole offering at CAP planning meetings was its exemplary waste minimization program, Pollution Prevention Pays, which predated most other state and federal programs.

The state therefore needed to take decisive action. Its first step was to create a new Hazardous Waste Management Commission to replace the old treatment commission, and to give it authority to site, design, construct, and operate hazardous waste management facilities for the state. Within four months of its creation, the commission entered into a CAP sharing agreement with Alabama, Kentucky, South Carolina, and Tennessee that would require North Carolina to construct and operate a 50,000 tons-per-year rotary kiln incinerator, a 15,000 tons-per-year solvent recovery unit, and a 10,000 tons-per-year ash landfill.

Search for a Facility Site

After developing site-selection criteria, which, among other things, would avoid constructing a new facility in counties that had poor experiences in the past, the commission designated ThermalKEM as the operator of any facility built. It focused on two sites, one in Granville County and the other on the line between Iredell and Rowan County. When they tried to access the sites for testing, however, irate citizens turned them away. The governor refused to remove the citizens even though this was private land, according to an official state history of these events.

Following this fiasco, the commission turned its attention to state-owned properties, asking the consulting firm, PEI, to review 246 such properties with regard to statutory requirements, state and federal rules, and commission criteria. After performing on-site testing and holding hearings in Granville, Iredell, Rowan, and Johnston counties, the commission turned its attention to a site in Butner County, where it designated the state-owned Umstead Farm Unit as the most suitable site for the incinerator complex. Because the land was state owned, the commission needed approval from another state agency, the Council of State, to transfer the site from the Department of Agriculture. The council denied the request. According to Little, this was a political decision, with the two Republicans on the council favoring the idea and seven Democrats voting it down. The commission has not selected any other sites. Instead, it awaits action by the state legislature to end the impasse over Umstead Farm, Little said.

County Initiatives

The commission has welcomed county initiatives, however, and three counties have shown some interest. Northhampton County, which is close to making a favorable decision, fits exactly the picture painted by Cerrell Associates as a typical waste facility site (see Chapter 12). It is in a rural, poor area located along Interstate 95, with a population about 60 percent black. The county has lost 10 percent of its citizens because it has few jobs and "some of the worst schools in the state," Little said, adding that 40 percent of the remaining county citizens commute elsewhere to work.

The proposed incinerator complex would offer 200 to 300 new jobs and would double the county's $3.5 million income, thus providing money for much needed schools and health facilities, Little said. As this book goes to press, the mixed-race county council has voted 2 to 2 to accept the facility; the fifth, deciding member is reportedly in favor of the facility but has been too ill to come to meetings and vote, according to several state officials.

Burden of Past Mistakes

Not the least among North Carolina's difficulties in achieving public acceptance of its proposed incineration complex is past mismanagement. Most notably, an incinerator system owned by Caldwell County but leased out to a local operator was so poorly managed that personnel at the site showed health effects that are still being analyzed by the Agency for Toxic Disease Registry.

EPA was not blameless in this instance, Little said. The agency used the facility as a depository for torpedo fuels generated during the cleanup of a navy facility. The agency was seen as looking the other way while continuing to use the facility, even though it was known to be poorly run and potentially dangerous, Little explained. It eventually closed in 1989, unable to meet the requirements for a final permit.

The media also have contributed to North Carolina's difficulties, Little said, citing a television documentary called "Fire in the Mountains" that documents all the worst that can happen at a carelessly managed facility. Similarly, a Greenpeace film called "The Rush to Burn" contains many discrepancies and is "an invitation to participate in civil disobedience," Little charged, noting that "not managing waste at all is much worse than using the technologies of the time, even if they eventually become outmoded."

APPENDIX A

DIRECTORIES

EPA Protection Agency Office of the Administrator 289
EPA Regional PCB Disposal Office 293
EPA Hotlines 294
U.S. EPA Regional Pollution Prevention Offices 295
Federal Pollution Prevention Research Contacts 297
State Waste Management Programs 298
State Government Technical/Financial Assistance Programs .. 303
State Pollution Prevention Contacts 307
Associations 317
Major Waste Exchanges Operating in North America 320

ENVIRONMENTAL PROTECTION AGENCY OFFICE OF THE ADMINISTRATOR

Waterside Mall, 401 M St. S.W.
Washington, D.C. 20460

[**Editor's Note:** Call the agency locater service, (202) 382-2090, if you experience difficulty in reaching a particular office.]

Administrator: (202) 382-4700

Deputy Administrator: (202) 382-4711

Assistant Administrator for International Activities: (202) 382-4870
Associate Administrator for Regional Operations and State/Local Operations: (202) 382-4724
Chief Administrative Law Judge: (202) 382-4860
Director, Civil Rights: (202) 382-4575
Director, Office of Small and Disadvantaged Business Utilization: (703) 557-7777
Small Business Ombudsman: (202) 557-1938

Director, Science Advisory Board: (202) 382-4126
Associate Administrator for Congressional and Administrative Affairs: (202) 382-5200
Deputy Director, Legislative Affairs: (202) 382-5414
Director, Press Division: (202) 382-4355
Director, External Relations and Education: (202) 382-4454
Associate Administrator for Communications and Public Affairs: (202) 382-7963

Office of the Inspector General

Inspector General: (202) 382-3137

Deputy Inspector General: (202) 382-4112
Assistant Inspector General, Office of Audits: (202) 382-4106

Assistant Inspector General, Office of Investigations: (202) 382-4109

Office For Administration and Resources Management

Assistant Administrator: (202) 382-4600

Deputy Assistant Administrator: (202) 382-4151
Director, Grants Administration Division: (202) 382-5240
Director, Facilities Management Services Division: (202) 382-2030

Office of the Comptroller: (202) 475-9674

Director, Office of Administration: (202) 475-8400

Office of Policy, Planning, and Evaluation

Assistant Administrator: (202) 382-4332

Deputy Assistant Administrator: (202) 382-4332

Director, Office of Policy Analysis: (202) 382-4034

Director, Office of Regulation Management and Evaluation: (202) 382-4001

Office For Enforcement

Assistant Administrator: (202) 382-4134

Deputy Assistant Administrator: (202) 382-4134

Director Criminal Division: (202) 382-4134

Director, Office of Enforcement Policy: (202) 382-4134

Director, Office of Compliance Analysis and Program Operations: (202) 382-4140

Associate Enforcement Counsel for Waste: (202) 382-3050

Associate Enforcement Counsel for Pesticides and Toxic Substances: (202) 382-4544

Office of the General Counsel

General Counsel: (202) 475-8040

Deputy General Counsel: (202) 475-8064

Deputy General Counsel for Litigation and Regional Operations: (202) 475-8067

Associate General Counsel for Solid Waste and Emergency Response: (202) 382-7706

Associate General Counsel, Pesticides and Toxic Substances: (202) 382-7505

Office of Solid Waste and Emergency Response

Assistant Administrator: (202) 382-4610

Toll-free RCRA, Superfund Hotline
1-800-424-9346
382-3000 in the Washington, D.C. area

Deputy Assistant Administrator: (202) 382-4610

Director, Office of Waste Programs Enforcement: (202) 382-4814

Director, Office of Solid Waste: (202) 382-4627

Director, Characterization and Assessment Division: (202) 382-4637

Director, Permits and State Programs Division: (202) 475-7276

Director, Underground Storage Tanks Programs: (202) 382-4756

Director, Office of Emergency and Remedial Response: (202) 382-2180

Director, Office of Policy Analysis Staff: (202) 382-2186

Director, CERCLA Enforcement Division: (202) 382-4812

Director, RCRA Enforcement Division: (202) 382-4823

Director, Hazardous Site Control Division: (202) 308-8313

Director, Hazardous Site Evaluation Division: (202) 475-8602

Office of Pesticides and Toxic Substances

Assistant Administrator: (202) 382-2902

Deputy Assistant Administrator: (202) 382-2910
Director, Office of Toxic Substances: (202) 382-3810
Director, Existing Chemical Assessment Division: (202) 382-3442
Director, Office of Compliance Monitoring: (202) 382-3807
Director, Compliance Division: (202) 382-3807
Director, Exposure Evaluation Division: (202) 382-3866
Director, Economics and Technology Division: (202) 382-3667
Director, Chemical Control Division: (202) 382-3749
Director, Information Management Division: (202) 382-3938
Director, Office of Pesticide Programs: (703) 557-7090
Director, Program Management & Support Division: (703) 557-2440
Director, Biological & Economic Analysis Division: (703) 308-8200
Director, Environmental Fate and Effects Division: (703) 557-7695
Director, Registration Division: (703) 557-5447
Director, Health and Environmental Review Division: (202) 382-4241

TSCA Assistance Office

Director: (202) 382-3790

TSCA Hotline (202) 554-1404

Office of Research and Development

Assistant Administrator for Research and Development: (202) 382-7676

Deputy Assistant Administrator: (202) 382-7676
Director, Office of Research Program Management: (202) 382-7500
Director, Office of Exploratory Research: (202) 382-5750
Director, Office of Health and Environmental Assessment: (202) 382-7317
Director, Office of Environmental Engineering and Technology Demonstration: (202) 382-2600
Director, Office of Environmental Processes and Effects Research: (202) 382-5950
Director, Office of Health Research: (202) 382-5900
Director, Modeling, Monitoring Systems, and Quality Assurance: (202) 382-5767
Director, Office of Technology Transfer and Regulatory Support: (202) 382-7669

Regional Offices

Region I—Massachusetts, Maine, Rhode Island, Connecticut, New Hampshire, Vermont

Room 2203, John F. Kennedy Federal Building, Boston, MA 02203, (617) 565-3715

Region II—New York, New Jersey, Virgin Islands, Puerto Rico

Room 900, 26 Federal Plaza, New York, NY, 10278, (212) 264-2525

Region III—Pennsylvania, Delaware, District of Columbia, Maryland, Virginia, West Virginia

841 Chestnut Building, Philadelphia, PA. 19107, (215) 597-9800

Region IV—Alabama, Florida, Georgia, Kentucky, Mississippi, North Carolina, South Carolina,

345 Courtland Street, N.E., Atlanta, GA 30365, (404) 347-4727

Region V—Illinois, Indiana, Michigan, Minnesota, Ohio, Wisconsin

230 South Dearborn Street, Chicago, IL 60604, (312) 353-2000

Region VI—Arkansas, Louisiana, New Mexico, Oklahoma, Texas

1445 Ross Ave., Dallas, TX 75202, (214) 655-6444

Region VII—Iowa, Kansas, Missouri, Nebraska

726 Minnesota Avenue, Kansas City, KS 66101, (913) 351-7006

Region VIII—Montana, North Dakota, South Dakota, Utah, Wyoming, Colorado

Suite 1300, 999 18th Street, One Denver Place, Denver, CO 80202-2413, (303) 293-1603

Region IX—Arizona, California, Hawaii, Nevada, Guam, American Samoa

215 Fremont Street, San Francisco, CA 94105, (415) 556-6608

Region X—Alaska, Idaho, Oregon, Washington

1200 6th Avenue, Seattle, WA 98101, (206) 442-5810

U.S. EPA REGIONAL PCB DISPOSAL OFFICES

Region I
(Connecticut, Maine, Massachusetts, New Hampshire, Rhode Island, Vermont)
Air Management Division
John F. Kennedy Federal Building
Boston, MA 02203
(617) 565-3279

Region II
(New Jersey, New York, Puerto Rico, Virgin Islands)
Air and Waste Management Division
26 Federal Plaza
New York, NY 10278
(212) 264-8682

Region III
(Delaware, District of Columbia, Maryland, Pennsylvania, Virginia, West Virginia)
Air Toxics and Radiation Management Division (3AT31)
841 Chestnut Street
Philadelphia, PA 19107
(215) 597-7668

Region IV
(Alabama, Florida, Georgia, Kentucky, Mississippi, North Carolina, South Carolina, Tennessee)
Title III and Toxics Section
345 Courtland Street, N.E.
Atlanta, GA 30365
(404) 347-3864

Region V
(Illinois, Indiana, Michigan, Minnesota, Ohio, Wisconsin)
Pesticides and Toxic Substances Branch (5SPT-7)
230 South Dearborn Street
Chicago, IL 60604
(312) 886-6087

Region VI
(Arkansas, Louisiana, New Mexico, Oklahoma, Texas)
Hazardous Waste Management Division
Allied Bank Tower
1445 Ross Avenue
Dallas, TX 75202-2733
(214) 655-6700

Region VII
(Iowa, Kansas, Missouri, Nebraska)
Air and Toxics Division
726 Minnesota Avenue
Kansas City, KS 66101
(913) 551-7020

Region VIII
(Colorado, Montana, North Dakota, South Dakota, Utah, Wyoming)
Toxic Substances Branch
Denver Place
999 18th Street, Suite 500
Denver, CO 80202-2405
(303) 293-1732

Region IX
(Arizona, California, Hawaii, Nevada, American Samoa, Guam)
Pesticides and Toxics Branch
75 Hawthorne Street
San Francisco, CA 94105
(415) 744-1093

Region X
(Alaska, Idaho, Oregon, Washington)
Air and Toxic Substances Branch
1200 Sixth Avenue
Seattle, WA 98101
(206) 553-7369

ENVIRONMENTAL PROTECTION AGENCY HOTLINES

Several offices supported by the Environmental Protection Agency operate information hotlines to help individuals find quick answers to questions concerning waste management. Other EPA telephone numbers are shown in the agency directory that also is in Appendix A. More detailed descriptions of the programs covered by these hotlines are described in applicable chapters of this book.

The available hotlines are as follows:

Resource Conservation and Recovery Act Hotline: (800) 424-9346; in Washington, D.C., (202) 382-3000. This hotline responds to general questions concerning compliance with the hazardous waste provisions of RCRA.

Solid Waste Hotline: (800) 67-SWITCH. This hotline, as its name implies, fields questions and offers information about municipal and industrial nonhazardous solid waste management. Funded by EPA and operated by the Solid Waste Association of North America (SWANA), formerly the Governmental Refuse Collection & Disposal Association, this information clearinghouse also has on-line information available through modems at (301) 585-0204. Questions may be faxed to SWITCH at (301) 585-0297.

Pollution Prevention Hotline: (703) 821-4800. This number yields further information on a variety of services offered to promote this program.

Pollution Prevention Information Exchange System Hotline (PPIES): (703) 506-1025. This number plugs callers directly into EPA's computerized pollution prevention information bank.

EPA Procurement Hotline: (703) 941-4452. As its name implies, this office yields current information on federal recycled or reclaimed materials procurement needs.

Small Business Ombudsman Hotline: (800) 368-5888. This hotline answers questions from small businesses on all environmental matters. In addition to explaining regulatory provisions, the hotline offers information on grant or loan availability and recycling assistance and serves as a waste reduction information exchange.

U.S. EPA REGIONAL POLLUTION PREVENTION OFFICES

REGION I

Pollution Prevention Program
U.S. EPA Region I
Room 2203 (PAS-2300)
John F. Kennedy Federal Building
Boston, MA 02203
Manager: (617) 565-1155
FTS: 835-1155
Assistant Manager: (617) 835-4523
FTS: 835-4523

REGION II

Office of Program Management
Policy and Program Integration Branch
U.S. EPA Region II
26 Federal Plaza
New York, NY 10278
Chief: (212) 264-4296

Hazardous Waste Program
Air and Waste Management Division
U.S. EPA Region II
26 Federal Plaza
New York, NY 10278
(212) 264-2377
FTS: 264-2377

REGION III

Environmental Assessment Branch
Environmental Services Division
U.S. EPA Region III
841 Chesnut Building (3ES43)
Philadelphia, PA 19107
Regional Coordinator: (215) 597-9384
FTS: 597-9834

REGION IV

Pollution Prevention Program
Policy, Planning, and Evaluation Branch
Office of Policy Management
U.S. EPA Region IV
345 Courtland Street, NE
Atlanta, GA 30365
Manager: (404) 257-7109
FTS: 257-7109

REGION V

Planning and Budgeting Branch
Policy and Management Division
U.S. EPA Region V
230 South Dearborn Street (5MA-14)
Chicago, IL 60604
Pollution Prevention Coordinator: (312) 886-1019
FTS: 886-1019

Waste Management Division
U.S. EPA Region V
230 South Dearborn Street (5H)
Chicago, IL 60604
(312) 886-6942
FTS: 886-6942

REGION VI

Policy, Planning and Integration Branch
Management Division
U.S. EPA Region VI
1445 Ross Avenue (6M-P)
Dallas, TX 75270
Chief: (214) 655-6444
FTS: 255-6444

REGION VI (continued)

Planning and Evaluation Section
Management Division
U.S. EPA Region VI
1445 Ross Avenue (6M–PP)
Dallas, TX 75270
Chief: (214) 655–6444
FTS: 255–6444

REGION VII

RCRA Branch
Policy Office
U.S. EPA Region VII
726 Minnesota Avenue
Kansas City, KS 66101
Chief: (913) 236-2800
FTS: 757–2800

REGION VIII

Policy Office
U.S. EPA Region VIII
999 18th Street, Suite 500
Denver, CO 80202–2405
Chief: (303) 293–1456
FTS: 330–1456
Program Analyst: (303) 293-1454
FTS: 330-1454

FEDERAL POLLUTION PREVENTION RESEARCH CONTACTS

Please feel free to contact the organizations listed below for more information on the various elements of the EPA Pollution Prevention Research Program.

Pollution Prevention Research Chief	Harry Freeman	(513) 569-7529
Programs in General		
Process Research Programs	Ivars Licis	(513) 569-7634
Products Research Programs	Mary Ann Curran	(513) 569-7837
Pollution Prevention Technical Assistance	Garry Howell	(513) 569-7756
WRITE State Programs		
Connecticut	Lisa Brown	(513) 569-7634
California	Lisa Brown	(513) 569-7634
New Jersey	Johnny Springer	(513) 569-7542
Illinois	Paul Randall	(513) 569-7673
Minnesota	Teresa Harten	(513) 569-7565
Washington	Ivars Licis	(513) 569-7634
Erie County, NY	Paul Randall	(513) 569-7673
WREAFS	Jim Bridges	(513) 569-7683
Waste Minimization Assessments	Mary Ann Curran	(513) 569-7837
	Brian Westfall	(513) 569-7755
Pollution Prevention Information Clearinghouse (PPIC)	Dave Stephan	(513) 569-7896
American Institute for Pollution Prevention (AIPP)	Dave Stephan	(513) 569-7896
Conference, Seminars	Ken Stone	(513) 569-7474

Correspondence should be addressed to:

Pollution Prevention Research Branch
Risk Reduction Engineering Laboratory
26 W. Martin Luther King Drive
Cincinnati, OH 45268

Source: EPA

STATE WASTE MANAGEMENT PROGRAMS

Alabama Department of Environmental
  Management
Land Division
1751 Congressman W.L. Dickinson
  Drive
Montgomery, AL 36130
Chief: (205) 271-7730

Alaska Department of Environmental
  Conservation
Division of Environmental Quality
Solid and Hazardous Waste
  Management Section
P.O. Box O
Juneau, AK 99811-1800
Chief: (907) 465-2671

Arizona Department of Environmental
  Quality
Office of Waste Programs
2005 North Central
Phoenix, AZ 85004
Chief: (602) 257-2318

Arkansas Department of Pollution
  Control and Ecology
Solid and Hazardous Waste Divisions
8001 National Drive
P.O. Box 8913
Little Rock, AR 72219
Chief, Solid Waste: (501) 562-7444
Chief, Hazardous Waste:
  (501) 570-2891

California Department of Health
  Services
Toxic Substances Control Program
400 P Street
P.O. Box 942734-7320
Sacramento, CA 9234-7320
Deputy Director: (916) 323-9723
Chief, Integrated Waste Management
  Board: (916) 322-3330

Colorado Department of Health
  Hazardous Materials and Waste
  Management Division
4210 East 11th Avenue
Denver, CO 80220
Director: (303) 331-4830

Connecticut Department of
  Environmental Protection
Bureau of Waste Management
165 Capitol Avenue
Hartford, CT 06106
Bureau Chief: (203) 566-8476

Delaware Department of Natural
  Resources and Environmental
  Control
Waste Management Section, Air and
  Waste Management Division
89 Kings Highway
P.O. Box 1401
Dover, DE 19903
Administrator: (302) 739-3672

District of Columbia Department of
  Consumer and Regulatory Affairs
Environmental Control Division
Pesticides and Hazardous Waste
  Management Branch
2100 Martin Luther King, Jr. Avenue,
  SE
Washington, DC 20020
Branch Chief: (202) 404-1167
Department of Public Works Office
  of Recycling: (202) 939-7192

Florida Department of Environmental
  Regulation
Division of Waste Management
2600 Blair Stone Road
Tallahassee, FL 32399-2400
Director: (904) 487-3299

Appendix A: Directories 299

Georgia Department of Natural
  Resources
Environmental Protection Division
Land Protection Branch
205 Butler Street S.E.
Suite 1154, East Tower
Atlanta, GA 30334
Chief: (404) 656-2833

Hawaii Department of Health
Environmental Management Division
Five Waterfront Plaza
500 Ala Moana Boulevard, Suite 250
Honolulu, HI 96813
Chief, Solid and Hazardous Waste
  Branch: (808) 543-8225
Chief, Hazard Evaluation and
  Emergency Response Office:
  (808) 543-8248

Idaho Department of Health and
  Welfare
Division of Environmental Quality
Hazardous Materials Bureau
1410 North Hilton Street
Boise, ID 83706
Chief: (208) 334-5879

Illinois Environmental Protection
  Agency
Division of Land Pollution Control
2200 Churchill Road
P.O. Box 19276
Springfield, IL 62794-9276
Division Manager: (217) 785-9407

Indianapolis Department of
  Environmental Management
Office of Solid and Hazardous Waste
  Management
105 South Meridian Street
Indianapolis, IN 46255
Assistant Commissioner:
  (317) 232-3210

Iowa Department of Natural Resources
Environmental Protection Division
900 East Grand Avenue
Henry A. Wallace Building

Des Moines, IA 50319-0034
Administrator, Waste Management:
  (515) 281-8975

Kansas Department of Health and
  Environment
Division of Environment
Bureau of Air and Waste Management
Forbes Field, Building 740
Topeka, KS 66620
Division Director: (913) 296-1593
Chief, Solid Waste Section:
  (913) 295-1590
Chief, Hazardous Waste Section:
  (913) 296-1607

Kentucky Department for
  Environmental Protection
Division of Waste Management
Frankfort Office Park
18 Reilly Road
Frankfort, KY 40601
Director: (502) 564-6716

Louisiana Department of
  Environmental Quality
Office of Solid and Hazardous Waste
P.O. Box 44307
Baton Rouge, LA 79894-4307
Assistant Secretary: (504) 342-9099

Maine Department of Environmental
  Protection
State House Station 17
Augusta, ME 04333
Director, Solid Waste Bureau:
  (207) 582-8740

Maryland Department of the
  Environment
Hazardous & Solid Waste
  Management Administration
2500 Broening Highway
Baltimore, MD 21224
Acting Director: (301) 631-3304

Massachusetts Department of
  Environmental Protection
Bureau of Waste Prevention

Division of Solid Waste Management
One Winter Street
4th Floor
Boston, MA 02108
Assistant Commissioner, Bureau of
  Waste Prevention: (617) 292-5953
Assistant Commissioner, Bureau of
  Waste Site Cleanup: (617) 292-5648

Michigan Department of Natural
  Resources
Waste Management Division
P.O. Box 30241
Lansing, MI 48909
Chief: (517) 373-9523 or
  (517) 373-2730

Minnesota Office of Waste
  Management
1150 Energy Lane
St. Paul, MN 55108
Director: (612) 649-5403

Minnesota Pollution Control Agency
520 Lafayette Road, North
St. Paul, MN 55155
Director, Ground Water and Solid
  Waste Division: (612) 296-7777
Director, Hazardous Waste Division:
  (612) 643-3402

Mississippi Department of Natural
  Resources
Bureau of Pollution Control
2380 Highway 80 West
P.O. Box 10385
Jackson, MS 39289
Chief, Hazardous Waste Division:
  (601) 961-5171
Chief, Ground Water Protection
  Division: (601) 961-5171

Missouri Department of Natural
  Resources
Environmental Quality Division
Waste Management Program
205 Jefferson Street
Jefferson City, MO 65102
Director: (314) 751-3176

Montana Department of Health and
  Environmental Sciences
Solid and Hazardous Waste Bureau
Cogswell Building
Helena, MT 59620
Chief: (406) 444-2821

Nebraska Department of
  Environmental Control
Land Quality Division
P.O. Box 98922
301 Centennial Mall South
Lincoln, NE 68509–8922
Chief: (402) 471-4210

Nevada Division of Environmental
  Protection
Bureau of Waste Management
123 West Nye Lane
Room 120
Carson City, NV 89710
Chief: (702) 687-5872

New Hampshire Department of
  Environmental Services
Waste Management Division
6 Hazen Drive
Concord, NH 03301–6509
Director: (603) 271-2905

New Jersey Department of
  Environmental Protection
Division of Solid Waste Management
840 Bear Tavern Road
CN 414
Trenton, NJ 08625
Director: (609) 530-8591

Division of Hazardous Waste
  Management
CN 028
Acting Director: (609) 292-1250

Division of Hazardous Site Mitigation
CN 413
Director: (609) 984-2902

New Mexico Health and Environment
  Department

Environmental Improvement Division
Waste Management Branch
1190 Francis Drive
Santa Fe, NM 87503
Deputy Director: (505) 827-2835

New York Department of
  Environmental Conservation
Division of Solid Waste
50 Wolf Road
Albany, NY 12233-4010
Director, Division of Solid Waste:
  (518) 457-6603
Director, Division of Hazardous
  Substances Regulation:
  (518) 457-6934

North Carolina Department of
  Environment, Health, and
  Natural Resources Division of Solid
  Waste Management
P.O. Box 27687
Raleigh, NC 27611-7687
Director: (919) 733-4996

North Dakota Department of Health
  Division of Waste Management
1200 Missouri Avenue, Room 302
Box 5520
Bismarck, ND 58502-5520
Director: (701) 224-2366

Ohio Environmental Protection Agency
1800 WaterMark Drive
P.O. Box 1049
Columbus, OH 43266-0149
Chief, Division of Solid and
  Hazardous Waste Management:
  (614) 644-2958
Chief, Division of Emergency and
  Remedial Response: (614) 644-2924

Oklahoma Department of Health
P.O. Box 53551
1000 N.E. 10th Street
Oklahoma City, OK 73152
Chief, Industrial Waste Service:
  (405) 271-7047

Chief, Solid Waste Service:
  (405) 271-7159

Oregon Department of Environmental
  Hazardous and Solid Waste Division
811 SW Sixth Avenue
Portland, OR 97204
Administrator: (503) 229-5356
Administrator, Environmental
  Cleanup: (503) 229-5254

Pennsylvania Department of
  Environmental Resources
Bureau of Waste Management
P.O. Box 2063, Fulton Building
200 North Third Street
Harrisburg, PA 17105-2063
Director: (717) 787-9870

Rhode Island Department of
  Environmental Management
Division of Air and Hazardous
  Materials
291 Promenade Street
Providence, RI 02908
Chief: (401) 277-2808

South Carolina Department of Health
  and Environmental Control
Bureau of Solid and Hazardous Waste
  Management
2600 Bull Street
Columbia, SC 29201
Chief: (803) 734-5164

South Dakota Department of Water
  and Natural Resources
Division of Environmental Regulation
Foss Building
523 East Capitol
Pierre, SD 57501
Director: (605) 773-3153

Tennessee Department of Health and
  Environment
Division of Solid Waste Management
Customs House, 4th Floor
701 Broadway

Nashville, TN 37247–3530
Director: (615) 741-3424

Texas Department of Health
Bureau of Solid Waste Management
1100 West 49th Street
Austin, TX 78756–3199
Chief: (512) 458-7271

Texas Water Commission
Hazardous and Solid Waste Division
P.O. Box 13087, Capitol Station
Austin, TX 78711
Director: (512) 463-7760

Utah Department of Health
Division of Environmental Health
Bureau of Solid and Hazardous Waste
288 North 1460 West
P.O. Box 16690
Salt Lake City, UT 84116–0690
Director: (801) 538-6170

Vermont Department of Environmental
  Conservation
Hazardous Materials Management
  Division
103 South Main Street
Waterbury, VT 05676
Deputy Commissioner:
  (802) 244-8755
Director, Solid Waste: (802) 244-7831

Virginia Department of Waste
  Management
101 North 14th Street

11th Floor
Richmond, VA 23219
Executive Director: (804) 225-2999

Washington Department of Ecology
Waste Management Programs
Mail Stop PV–11
Olympia, WA 98504–8711
Manager, Solid and Hazardous Waste
  Program: (206) 459-6316
Assistant Director, DEC:
  (206) 459-6029

West Virginia Department of
  Commerce, Labor and
  Environmental Resources
Division of Natural Resources
Waste Management Section
Charleston, WV 25301
Acting Chief: (304) 348-5929

Wisconsin Department of Natural
  Resources
Division for Environmental Quality
Bureau of Solid and Hazardous Waste
  Management
P.O. Box 7921
Madison, WI 53707
Director: (608) 266-1327

Wyoming Department of
  Environmental Quality Division
  of Solid Waste
122 West 25th Street
Cheyenne, WY 82002
Manager: (307) 777-7752

STATE GOVERNMENT TECHNICAL/FINANCIAL ASSISTANCE PROGRAMS

The following states have programs that offer technical and/or financial assistance in the areas of waste minimization and treatment.

ALABAMA
Hazardous Material Management
 and Resource Recovery Program
University of Alabama
P.O. Box 6373
Tuscaloosa, AL 35487-6373
(202) 345-8401

ALASKA
Alaska Health Project
Waste Reduction Assistance
 Program
431 West Seventh Avenue
Suite 101
Anchorage, AK 99501
(907) 276-2864

ARKANSAS
Arkansas Industrial Development
 Commission
One State Capitol Mall
Little Rock, AR 72201
(501) 371-1370

CALIFORNIA
Alternative Technology Section
Toxic Substances Control Division
California State Department of
 Health Services
714/744P Street
Sacramento, CA 94234-7320
(916) 324-1807

CONNECTICUT
Connecticut Hazardous Waste
 Management Service
Suite 360
900 Asylum Avenue
Hartford, CT 06105
(203) 244-2007

Connecticut Department of
 Economic Development
210 Washington Street
Hartford CT 06106
(203) 566-7196

GEORGIA
Hazardous Waste Technical
 Assistance Program
Georgia Institute of Technology
Georgia Technical Research Institute
Environmental Health and Safety
 Division
O'Keefe Building, Room 027
Atlanta, GA 30332
(404) 894-3806

Environmental Protection Division
Georgia Department of Natural
 Resouces
Floyd Towers East, Suite 1154
205 Bulter Street
Atlanta, CA 30334
(404) 656-2833

ILLINOIS
Hazardous Waste Research and
 Information Center
Illinois Department of Energy and
 Natural Resources
1808 Woodfield Drive
Savoy, IL 61874
(217) 333-8940

INDIANA
Environmental Management and
 Education Program
Young Graduate House, Room 120
Purdue University
West Lafayette, IN 47907
(317) 494-5036

INDIANA (continued)
Indiana Department of
  Environmental Management
Office of Technical Assistance
P.O. Box 6015
105 South Meridian Street
Indianapolis, IN 46206-6015
(317) 232-8172

IOWA
Iowa Department of Natural
  Resources
Air Quality and Solid Waste
  Protection Bureau
Wallace State Office Building
900 East Grand Avenue
Des Moines, IA 50319-0034
(515) 281-8690

Center for Industrial Research and
  Service
205 Engineering Annex
Iowa State University
Ames, IA 50011
(515) 294-3420

KANSAS
Bureau of Waste Management
Department of Health and
  Environment
Forbes Field, Building 730
Topeka, KS 66620
(913) 296-1607

KENTUCKY
Division of Waste Management
Natural Resources and
  Environmental Protection Cabinet
18 Reilly Road
Frankfort, KY 40601
(502) 564-6716

LOUISIANA
Department of Environmental
  Quality
Office of Solid and Hazardous
  Waste
P.O. Box 44307
Baton Rouge, LA 70804
(504) 342-1354

MARYLAND
Maryland Hazardous Waste
  Facilities Siting Board
60 West Street, Suite 200A
Annapolis, MD 21401
(301) 974-3432

Maryland Environmental Service
2020 Industrial Drive
Annapolis, MD 21401
(301) 269-3291
(800) 492-9188 (in Maryland)

MASSACHUSETTS
Office of State Waste Management
Department of Environmental
  Management
100 Cambridge Street, Room 1094
Boston, MA 02202
(617) 727-3260

Source Reduction Program
Massachusetts Department of
  Environmental Quality
  Engineering
1 Winter Street
Boston, MA 02202
(617) 292-5982

MICHIGAN
Resource Recovery Section
Department of Natural Resources
P.O. Box 30028
Lansing, MI 48909
(517) 373-0540

MINNESOTA
Minnesota Pollution Control Agency
Solid and Hazardous Waste Division
520 Lafayette Road
St. Paul, MN 55155
(612) 296-6300

Minnesota Technical Assistance
  Program

W-140 Boynton Health Service
University of Minnesota
Minneapolis, MN 55455
(612) 625-9677
(800) 247-0015 (in Minnesota)

Minnesota Waste Management
  Board
123 Thorson Center
7323 Fifty-Eighth Avenue North
Crystal, MN 55428
(612) 536-0816

MISSOURI
State Environmental Improvement
  and Energy Resources Agency
P.O. Box 744
Jefferson City, MO 65102
(314) 751-4919

NEW JERSEY
New Jersey Hazardous Waste
  Facilities Siting Commission
Room 614
28 West State Street
Trenton, NJ 08608
(609) 292-1459
(609) 292-1026

Hazardous Waste Advisement
  Program
Bureau of Regulation and
  Classification
New Jersey Department of
  Environmental Protection
401 East State Street
Trenton, NJ 08625

NEW YORK
New York State Environmental
  Facilities
Corporation
50 Wolf Road
Albany, NY 12205
(518) 457-3273

NORTH CAROLINA

Pollution Prevention Pays Program
Department of Natural Resources
  and Community Development
P.O. Box 27687
512 North Salisbury Street
Raleigh, NC 27611
(919) 733-7015

Governor's Waste Management
  Board
325 North Salisbury Street
Raleigh, NC 27611
(919) 733-9020

Technical Assistance Unit
Solid and Hazardous Waste
  Management Branch
North Carolina Department of
  Human Resources
P.O. Box 2091
306 North Wilmington Street
Raleigh, NC 27602
(919) 733-2178

OHIO
Division of Solid and Hazardous
  Waste Management
Ohio Environmental Protection
  Agency
P.O. Box 1049
1800 WaterMark Drive
Columbus, OH 43266-1049
(614) 466-4286

OKLAHOMA
Industrial Waste Elimination
  Program
Oklahoma State Department of
  Health
P.O. Box 53551
Oklahoma City, OK 73152
(405) 271-7353

OREGON
Oregon Hazardous Waste Reduction
  Program
Department of Environmental
  Quality
811 Southwest Sixth Avenue
Portland, OR 97204
(503) 229-5913

PENNSYLVANIA
Pennsylvania Technical Assistance
  Program
501 F. Orvis Keller Building
University Park, PA 16802
(814) 865-0427

Bureau of Waste Management
Pennsylvania Department of
  Environmental Resources
P.O. Box 2063
Fulton Building
3rd and Locust Streets
Harrisburg, PA 17120
(717) 787-6239

Center of Hazardous Material
  Research
320 William Pitt Way
Pittsburgh, PA 15238
(412) 826-5320

RHODE ISLAND
Ocean State Cleanup and Recycling
  Program
Rhode Island Department of
  Environmental Management
9 Hayes Street
Providence, RI 02908-5003
(401) 277-3434
(800) 253-2674 (in Rhode Island)

Center of Environmental Studies
Brown University P.O. Box 1943
135 Angell Street
Providence, RI 02912
(401) 863-3449

TENNESSEE
Center for Industrial Services
102 Alumni Hall
University of Tennessee
Knoxville, TN 37996
(615) 974-2456

VIRGINIA
Office of Policy and Planning
Virginia Department of Waste
  Management
11th Floor, Monroe Building
101 North 14th Street
Richmond, VA 23219
(804) 225-2667

WASHINGTON
Hazardous Waste Section
Mail Stop PV-11
Washington Department of Ecology
Olympia, WA 98504-8711
(206) 459-6322

WISCONSIN
Bureau of Solid Waste Management
Wisconsin Department of Natural
  Resources
P.O. Box 7921
101 South Webster Street
Madison, WI 53707
(608) 266-2699

WYOMING
Solid Waste Management Program
Wyoming Department of
  Environmental Quality
Herschler Building, 4th Floor, West
  Wing
122 West 25th Street
Cheyenne, WY 82002
(307) 777-7752

STATE POLLUTION PREVENTION CONTACTS

ALABAMA

Daniel E. Cooper
Land Division
Alabama Department of Environmental Management
7751 Congressman W.L. Dickenson Drive
Montgomery, AL 36130
(205) 271-7730

John E. Moeller
Project Director, Regulatory Information Service
Hazardous Materials Management and Resource Recovery (HAMMARR)
241 Mineral Industries Building
University of Alabama
P.O. Drawer G
Tuscaloosa, AL 35487-9644
(205) 348-4878

ALASKA

Dennis Kelso
Commissioner
Alaska Department of Environmental Conservation
P.O. Box O
Juneau, AK 99811-1800
(907) 465-2600

David Kidd
Environmental Engineer
Alaska Health Project
431 W. 7th, Suite 101
Anchorage, AK 99501
(907) 276-2864

ARKANSAS

Mike Bates
Acting Chief, Hazardous Waste Division
Arkansas Department of Pollution Control and Ecology
P.O. Box 9583
Little Rock, AR 72219
(501) 562-7444

ARIZONA

Stephanie Wilson
Office of Waste and Water Quality Management
Arizona Department of Environmental Quality
2005 N. Central Ave., Room 304
Phoenix, AZ 85004
(602) 257-6917

CALIFORNIA

Kim Wilhelm
Toxic Substances Control Division
Alternative Technology Section
California Department of Health Services
714/744 P Street
Sacramento, CA 95234-7320
(916) 324-1807

Loma Dobrovolny
California Waste Exchange
Alternative Technology Services
California Department of Health Services
714/744 P Street
Sacramento, CA 95234-7320
(916) 324-1807

COLORADO

Neil Kolwey
Colorado Department of Health
4210 East 11th Avenue
Denver, CO 80220
(303) 331-4830

COLORADO (continued)

Dr. Harry Edwards
Department of Mechanical
  Engineering
Colorado State University
Fort Collins, CO 80523
(303) 491-6558

CONNECTICUT

Dick Barlow
Waste Management Bureau
Connecticut Department of
  Environmental Protection
18-20 Trinity Street
Hartford, CT 06106
(203) 566-3476

Frederic W. Kaeser
Manager, Technical Services
Connecticut Hazardous Waste
  Management Services
Suite 360
900 Asylum Avenue
Hartford, CT 06105-1904
(203) 244-2007

DELAWARE

Andrea Farrella
Hazardous Waste Management Section
Delaware Department of Natural
  Resources and Environmental
  Control
P.O. Box 1401
Dover, DE 19903
(302) 736-3822

DISTRICT OF COLUMBIA

George Jenkins
Recycling Coordinator, Office of
  Recycling
D.C. Department of Public Works
8th Floor
2000 14th Street, N.W.
Washington, DC 20009
(202) 939-7116

FLORIDA

Janeth A. Campbell
Environmental Supervisor
Waste Reduction Assistance Program
Florida Department of Environmental
  Regulation
Twin Towers Office Building
2600 Blair Stone Road
Tallahassee, FL 32399-2400
(904) 488-0300

Dr. Jim Bryant
Director
Center for Training, Research and
  Education for Environmental
  Occupations
Division of Continuing Education
University of Florida
3900 S.W. 63rd Boulevard
Gainesville, FL 32608
(904) 392-9570

GEORGIA

Susan Hendricks
Environmental Specialist, Hazardous
  Waste Information and Education
  Program
Environmental Protection Division
Georgia Department of Natural
  Resources
Floyd Tower East, Suite 1154
2054 Butler Street, S.E.
Atlanta, GA 30334
(404) 656-7802

Jim Walsh
Environmental Sciences and
  Technology Division
O'Keefe Building
Georgia Technical Research Institute
Atlanta, GA 30332
(404) 894-3412

HAWAII

Grace Marcos
Solid and Hazardous Waste Branch
Hawaii Department of Health
645 Halekaulia Street
2nd Floor
Honolulu, HI 96813
(808) 548-2270

IDAHO

John Moeller
Idaho Hazardous Materials Bureau
450 W. State Street
Boise, ID 83720
(208) 334-5926

ILLINOIS

Michael Hays
Pollution Prevention Coordinator
Illinois Environmental Protection
 Agency
P.O. Box 19276
M/C 31
Springfield, IL 62794
(217) 785-0833

Dr. David L. Thomas
Director
Hazardous Waste Research and
 Information Center
Illinois Department of Energy and
 Natural Resources
1808 Woodfield Drive
Savoy, IL 61874
(217) 333-8940

INDIANA

Harry Davis
Office of Technical Assistance
Indiana Department of Environmental
 Management
105 South Meridian Street
Indianapolis, IN 46225
(317) 232-8172

Mike Dalton
Office of Solid and Hazardous Waste
 Management
Indiana Department of Environmental
 Management
105 South Meridian Street
Indianapolis, IN 46225
(317) 232-8884

IOWA

Tom Blewett
Environmental Specialist, Waste
 Management Authority
Division
Iowa Department of Natural Resources
Wallace State Office Building
Des Moines, IA 50319
(515) 281-8489

John Konefes
Director
Iowa Waste Reduction Center
75 BRC
University of Northern Iowa
Cedar Falls, IA 50614-0185
(319) 273-2079
(800) 422-3109

KANSAS

Tom Gross
Kansas Department of Health and
 Environment
Forbes Field, Building 730
Topeka, KS 66620
(913) 296-1603

KENTUCKY

Russ Barnett
Kentucky Department for
 Environmental Protection
18 Reilly Road
Frankfort, KY 40601
(502) 564-2150

KENTUCKY (continued)

Joyce St. Clair
Executive Director
Kentucky Partners
Room 213, Ernst Hall
University of Louisville
Louisville, KY 40292
(502) 588-7260

LOUISIANA

Nicholas Achee
Alternate Technologies Research and
  Development
Office of the Secretary
Louisiana Department of
  Environmental Quality
P.O. Box 44066
Baton Rouge, LA 70804
(504) 342-1254

MAINE

Scott Whittier
Director, Licensing and Enforcement
  Branch
Bureau of Oil and Hazardous
  Materials Control
Maine Department of Environmental
  Protection
State House, Station 17
Augusta, ME 04333
(207) 289-2651

Ann Pistell
Maine Department of Environmental
  Protection
State House, Station 17
Augusta, ME 04333
(207) 289-7871

Sandy Tate
Maine Department of Environmental
  Protection
State House, Station 17
Augusta, ME 04333
(207) 582-8740

State House, Station 17
Augusta, ME 04333

George McDonald
Director, Office of Waste Reduction
  and Recycling
Maine Office of Economic and
  Community Development
State House, Station 130
Augusta, ME 04333
(207) 289-6800

MARYLAND

William Sloan
Executive Director
Maryland Environmental Service
2020 Industrial Drive
Annapolis, MD 21401
(301) 974-7291

Travis Walton
Director, Technology Extension
  Service
Engineering Research Center
University of Maryland
College Park, MD 20742
(301) 454-1941

MASSACHUSETTS

Kathleen A. Porter
Manager, Source Reduction Program
Massachusetts Department of
  Environmental Management
100 Cambridge Street
Boston, MA 02202
(617) 727-3260

Manik Roy
Coordinator, Source Reduction Policy
  Program
Massachusetts Department of
  Environmental Management
1 Winter Street
Boston, MA 02108
(617) 292-5982

MICHIGAN

Lois R. Debacker
Office of Waste Reduction Services
Michigan Department of Commerce
  and Natural Resources
309 North Washington, Suite 103
Lansing, MI 48909
(517) 335-1178

MINNESOTA

Ed Meyer
Minnesota Pollution Control Agency
520 Lafayette Road
St. Paul, MN 55155
(612) 643-3496

Nancy Misera
Minnesota Pollution Control Agency
520 Lafayette Road
St. Paul, MN 55155
(612) 643-3497

Cindy McComas
Director
Minnesota Technical Assistance
  Program (MnTAP)
Box 197 Mayo Building
420 Delaware Street S.E.
University of Minnesota
Minneapolis, MN 55455
(612) 625-9471

David Cera
Minnesota Office of Waste
  Management
1350 Energy Lane
St. Paul, MN 55108
(612) 649-5742

Kevin McDonald
Minnesota Office of Waste
  Management
1350 Energy Lane
St. Paul, MN 55108
(612) 649-5744

MISSISSIPPI

Tom Whitten
Director, Waste Minimization
  Program
Mississippi Department of Natural
  Resources
P.O. Box 10385
Jackson, MS 39209
(601) 961-5241

Dr. Caroline Hill
Dr. Don Hill
Mississippi Technical Assistance
  Program
Chemical Engineering Department
Mississippi State University
P.O. Drawer CN
Mississippi State, MS 39762
(601) 325-8454

MISSOURI

Charles Hayes
Waste Management Program
Division of Environmental Quality
Missouri Department of Natural
  Resources
P.O. Box 176
Jefferson City, MO 65102
(314) 751-3176

Steven Mahfood
Director
Environmental Improvement and
  Energy Resource Authority
225 Madison Street
P.O. Box 744
Jefferson City, MO 65102
(314) 751-4919

MONTANA

Bill Potts
Solid and Hazardous Waste Bureau
Montana Department of Health and
  Environmental Sciences

MONTANA (continued)

Cogswell Building
Room B-201
Helena, MT 59620
(406) 444-2821

NEBRASKA

Lorraine Cope
Hazardous Waste Department
Nebraska Department of
  Environmental Control
P.O. Box 98922
Lincoln, NE 68509
(402) 471-4217

NEVADA

Verne Rosse
Director, Waste Management Program
Nevada Division of Environmental
  Protection
Capitol Complex
201 South Fall Street
Carson City, NV 89710
(702) 885-5872

David Humke
Business Development Associate
Nevada Small Business Development
  Center
Room 411
Department of Business
  Administration
University of Nevada
Reno, NV 89557
(702) 784-1717

Curtis Framel
Manager, State Energy Conservation
  Program
Nevada Energy Program
Office of Community Services
Capitol Complex
201 South Fall Street
Carson City, NV 89710
(702) 885-4420

NEW HAMPSHIRE

Vincent Perrelli
Waste Management Division
New Hampshire Department of
  Environmental Services
6 Hazen Drive
Concord, NH 03301
(603) 271-2902

Sharon Yergeau
Waste Management Division
New Hampshire Department of
  Environmental Services
6 Hazen Drive
Concord, NH 03301
(603) 271-2918

NEW JERSEY

Sanat Bhavsar
Kevin Gashlin
Division of Hazardous Waste
  Management
Hazardous Waste Advisement
  Program
New Jersey Department of
  Environmental Protection
401 East State Street (CN028)
Trenton, NJ 08625
(609) 292-8341

Jean Herb
Division of Science and Research
Hazardous Waste Advisement
  Program
New Jersey Department of
  Environmental Protection
401 East State Street (CN409)
Trenton, NJ 08625
(609) 984-5339

NEW MEXICO

John Gould
Environmental Improvement Division
New Mexico Hazardous Waste Bureau

P.O. Box 968
Sante Fe, NM 87504-0968
(505) 827-2925

NEW YORK

John Lanotti
Director, Bureau of Hazardous Waste
  Program Development
New York State Department of
  Environmental Conservation
50 Wolf Road
Albany, NY 12233
(518) 457-7267

Thomas J. Lynch
Chief, Waste Reduction
Implementation Section
New York State Department of
  Environmental Conservation
50 Wolf Road
Albany, NY 12233
(518) 485-8400

Harold Snow
Environmental Facilities Corporation
50 Wolf Road
Albany, NY 12205
(518) 457-4138

NORTH CAROLINA

Gary Hunt
Pollution Prevention Pays Program
North Carolina Department of Natural
  Resources and Community
  Development
P.O. Box 27687
Raleigh, NC 27611-7687
(919) 733-7015

Bill Meyer
Solid Waste Division
North Carolina Department of Natural
  Resources
P.O. Box 27687
Raleigh, NC 27611-7687
(919) 733-4996

NORTH DAKOTA

Neil Knatterud
Division of Hazardous Waste
  Management and Special Studies
North Dakota Department of Health
1200 Missouri Ave, Room 302
Bismarck, ND 58502-5520
(701) 224-2366

OHIO

Anthony Sasson
Manager, RCRA Technical Assistance
Division of Solid and Hazardous
  Waste Management
Ohio Environmental Protection
Agency
P.O. Box 1049
1800 Watermark Drive
Columbus, OH 43266-0149
(614) 644-2967

Jeff Shick
State Coordinator
Ohio Department of Development
Ohio Technology Transfer
  Organization (OTTO)
77 South High Street, 26th Floor
Columbus, OH 43255-0330
(614) 466-4292

Dawn Palmieri
Environmental Liaison
Ohio Department of Development
Ohio Technology Transfer
  Organization (OTTO)
77 South High Street, 26th Floor
Columbus, Ohio 43255-0330
(614) 644-9336

OKLAHOMA

Robert Rabatine
Environmental Program Administrator
Waste Management Service

OKLAHOMA (continued)

Oklahoma State Department of Health
1000 Northeast 10th Street
Oklahoma City, OK 73152
(405) 271-5338

OREGON

Marianne Fitzgerald
David Rozell
Hazardous Waste Reduction Program
Oregon Department of Environmental
  Quality
811 SW Sixth
Portland, OR 97204-1390
(503) 229-5913

PENNSYLVANIA

Keith Kerns
Chief, Division of Waste
  Minimization and Planning
Pennsylvania Department of
  Environmental Resources
P.O. Box 2063
Harrisburg, PA 17105-2063
(717) 787-7382

Greg Harder
Division of Waste Minimization and
  Planning
Pennsylvania Department of
  Environmental Resources
P.O. Box 2063
Harrisburg, PA 17120
(717) 787-7382

William Arble
Pennsylvania Technical Assistance
  Program (PENNTAP)
1527 William Street
University Park, PA 16801
(814) 865-1914

RHODE ISLAND

Victor Bell
Office of Environmental Coordination
Rhode Island Department of
  Environmental Management
83 Park Street
Providence, RI 02903
(401) 277-3434

Eugene Pepper
Rhode Island Department of
  Environmental Management
83 Park Street
Providence, Rhode Island 02903
(401) 277-3434

SOUTH CAROLINA

Jeffrey P. deBessonet
Manager, Waste Minimization Section
Bureau of Solid and Hazardous Waste
  Management
South Carolina Department of Health
  and Environmental Control
2600 Bull Street
Columbia, SC 29201
(803) 734-5191

SOUTH DAKOTA

Vonni Kallemeyn
Division of Air Quality and Solid
  Waste
South Dakota Department of Water
  and Natural Resources
Joe Foss Building, Room 416
523 E. Capital Ave.
Pierre, SD 57501
(605) 773-3153

TENNESSEE

Jim Ault
Bureau of Environment
Tennessee Department of Health and
  Environment
150 9th Avenue, North
Nashville, TN 37219-3657
(615) 741-3657

Carrol Duggan
Projects Manager

Waste Technology Program
Tennessee Valley Authority
2F71B Old City Hall Building
601 West Summit Hill Drive
Knoxville, TN 37901
(615) 632-3160

George Smelcer
Center for Industrial Services
University of Tennessee
226 Capitol Boulevard Building
Suite 401
Nashville, TN 37219
(615) 242-2456

TEXAS

Cheryl Wilson
Coordinator
Resource Exchange Network for
   Eliminating Waste
Texas Water Commission
P.O. Box 13087, Capitol Station
Austin, TX 78711-3087
(512) 463-7773

UTAH

Rusty Lundberg
Chief, Planning and Program
   Development
Bureau of Solid and Hazardous Waste
   Management
Utah Department of Health
P.O. Box 16690
288 North 1460 West Street
Salt Lake City, UT 84116-0690
(801) 538-6170

VERMONT

Gary Gulka
Chief, Hazardous Waste Management
   Section
Vermont Agency of Natural Resources
103 South Main Street
Waterbury, VT 05676
(802) 244-8702

Constance Leach
Chief, Recycling and Resource
   Conservation
Vermont Agency of Natural Resources
103 South Main Street
Waterbury, VT 05676
(802) 244-7831

VIRGINIA

Harry Gregori
Virginia Department of Waste
   Management
Monroe Building, 11th Floor
101 North 14th Street
Richmond, VA 23219
(804) 225-2667

WASHINGTON

Jay Shepard
Unit Supervisor, Office of Waste
   Reduction
Washington Department of Ecology
Olympia, WA 98504
(206) 459-6302

WEST VIRGINIA

Michael Dorsey
Assistant Chief
Compliance Monitoring Unit
Waste Management Division
West Virginia Department of Natural
   Resources
1260 Greenbrier Street
Charleston, WV 25311
(304) 348-5935

WISCONSIN

Pat Walsh
Community Dynamics Institute
University of Wisconsin - Extension
529 Lowell Hall
610 Langdon Street

Madison, WI 53703
(608) 262-8179

Kate Cooper
Recycling Coordinator, Bureau of
 Solid and Hazardous Waste
 Management
Wisconsin Department of Natural
 Resources
101 South Webster Street
Box 7921
Madison, WI 53707-7921
(608) 267-7565

Lynn Persson
Hazardous Waste Reduction and
 Recycling Coordinator
Bureau of Solid and Hazardous Waste
 Management
Wisconsin Department of Natural
 Resources
Box 7921 (SW/3)
Madison, WI 53703-7921
(608) 262-8179

John Cain
Pollution Prevention Coordinator
Office of Technical Services
Wisconsin Department of Natural
 Resources
P.O. Box 7921
Madison, WI 53707
(608) 266-9259

WYOMING

David Finley
Manager, Solid Waste Management
 Program
Wyoming Department of
 Environmental Quality
122 West 25th Street
Herschler Building
Cheyenne, WY 82002
(307) 777-7752

ASSOCIATIONS

Air & Waste Management Association
P.O. Box 2861
Pittsburgh, PA 15230
(412) 232-3444

The Aluminum Association, Inc.
818 Connecticut Avenue, NW
Washington, DC 20006
(202) 862-5100

Aluminum Recycling Association
900 17th Street, NW
Washington, DC 20006

American Academy of Environmental Engineers
132 Holiday Court, #206
Annapolis, MD 21401
(301) 266-3311

American Arbitration Association
140 West 51st Street
New York, NY 10020
(212) 484-4000

American Chemical Society
1155 16th Street, NW
Washington, DC 20036
(202) 872-4600

American Industrial Health Council
1330 Connecticut Avenue, NW
Suite 300
Washington, DC 20019
(202) 659-0060

American Institute of Chemical Engineers
1901 L Street, NW
Suite 804
Washington, DC 20036
(202) 223-0650

American Paper Institute
260 Madison Avenue
New York, NY 10016
(212) 340-0626

American Paper Institute
1250 Connecticut Avenue, NW
Suite 210
Washington, DC 20036
(202) 463-2420

Association of State and Territorial Solid Waste Management Officials
444 North Capitol Street, NW
Suite 388
Washington, DC 20001
(202) 624-7875

Automotive Dismantlers and Recyclers of America
1000 Vermont Avenue, NW
Washington, DC 20005
(202) 628-4634

Center for the Environment and Natural Resources
Council of State Governments
P.O. Box 11910, Iron Works Pike
Lexington, KY 40578
(606) 231-1866

Chemical Manufacturers Association
2501 M St., NW
Washington, DC 20037
(202) 887-1100

Citizens for a Better Environment
33 East Congress, Suite 523
Chicago, IL 60605
(312) 939-1530

Coalition for Responsible Waste Incineration
1330 Connecticut Avenue, NW
Suite 300
Washington, DC 20036
(202) 659-0060

Coalition on Resource Recovery and the Environment
U.S. Conference of Mayors
1620 Eye Street, NW
Washington, DC 20006
(202) 293-7330

The Conservation Foundation
1250 24th Street, NW
Washington, DC 20037
(202) 293-4800

The Council for Solid Waste Solutions
A Program of The Society of the Plastics Industry, Inc.
1275 K Street, NW
Suite 400
Washington, DC 20005
(202) 371-5319

Environmental Action
1525 New Hampshire Avenue, NW
Suite 731
Washington, DC 20036
(202) 833-1845

Environmental Defense Fund
257 Park Avenue South
New York, NY 10010
(212) 686-4191

Environmental Health Science Programs
Box 612
440 East 26th Street
New York, NY 10010
(212) 481-4357

Environmental Industry Council
1825 K Street, NW
Suite 210
Washington, DC 20006
(202) 944-8500

Environmental Information Center
48 West 38th Street
New York, NY 10018
(212) 944-8500

Environmental Policy Institute
218 D Street, SE
Washington, DC 20006
(202) 544-2600

Glass Packaging Institute
1801 K Street NW, Suite 1105-L
Washington, DC 20006
(202) 782-1280

Governmental Refuse Collection & Disposal Association
(see Solid Waste Association of North America)

Hazardous Materials Advisory Council
1012 14th Street, NW
Suite 907
Washington, DC 20005
(202) 783-7460

Hazardous Waste Treatment Council
1440 New York Avenue, N.W.
Suite 310
Washington, DC 20005
(202) 783-0870

Institute of Scrap Iron and Steel
1627 K Street, NW
Washington, DC 20006
(202) 466-4050

National Association of Attorneys General
444 North Capitol Street
Washington, DC 20001
(202) 628-0435

National Association of Corrosion Engineers
P.O. Box 218340
Houston, TX 77218
(713) 492-0535

National Association of Environmental Professionals
P.O. Box 9400
Washington, DC 20016
(703) 683-3746

Appendix A: Directories

National Association of Recycling Industries, Inc.
330 Madison Avenue
New York, NW 10017
(212) 867-7330

National Association of State Development Agencies
Hall of States, Suite 611
444 North Capitol Street, NW
Washington, DC 20001
(202) 624-5411

National Conferences of State Legislatures
444 North Capitol Street, NW
Suite 500
Washington, DC 20001
(202) 624-5400

National Environmental Development Association
1440 New York Avenue, NW
Suite 300
Washington, DC 20005
(202) 683-1230

National Governors' Association
Hall of the States
444 North Capitol Street
Washington, DC 20001
(202) 624-5300

National Recycling Coalition Inc. and Recycling Advisory Council
1101 30th Street, NW
Suite 305
Washington, DC 20007
(202) 625-6409

National Resource Recovery Association
U.S. Conference of Mayors
1620 Eye Street, NW
Washington, DC 20006
(202) 293-7330

National Solid Wastes Management Association
Suite 1000

1730 Rhode Island Avenue, NW
Washington, DC 20036
(202) 659-4613

Natural Resources Defense Council
1350 New York Avenue, NW
Suite 300
Washington, DC 20005

Northeast Waste Management Officials' Association
85 Merrimac Street
Boston, MA 02114
(617) 367-8558

Public Risk Management Association
1117 North 19th Street, Suite 900
Arlington, VA 22209
(703) 528-7701

Sierra Club
730 Polk Street
San Francisco, CA 94109
(415) 776-2211

Spill Control Association of America
100 Renaissance Center, Suite 1575
Detroit, MI 48243
(313) 567-0500

Solid Waste Association of North America
P.O. Box 7219
8401 Dixon Avenue, Suite 4
Silver Spring, MD 20910
(301) 585-2898

Synthetic Organic Chemical Manufacturers Association
1330 Connecticut Avenue, NW
Suite 300
Washington, DC 20036
(202) 659-0060

New York office:
1075 Central Park Avenue
Scarsdale, NY 10583
(914) 725-1492

MAJOR WASTE EXCHANGES OPERATING IN NORTH AMERICA

Alabama Waste Exchange
William J. Herz
The University of Alabama
P.O. Box 870203
Tuscaloosa, AL 35487-0203
(205) 348-5889
FAX: (205) 348-8573

Alberta Waste Material Exchange
William C. Kay
Alberta Research Council
P.O. Box 8330
Postal Station F
Edmonton, Alberta
Canada T6H 5X2
(403) 450-5408

British Columbia Waste Exchange
Lynn Deegan
2150 Maple Street
Vancouver, B.C
Canada V6J 3T3
(604) 731-7222

California Waste Exchange
Robert McCormick
Department of Health Services
Toxic Substances Control Division
Alternative Technology Section
P.O. Box 942732
Sacramento, CA 94234-7320
(916) 324-1807

Canadian Chemical Exchange*
Philippe La Roche
P.O. Box 1135
Ste. Adele, Quebec
Canada JOR 1LO
(514) 229-6511

Canadian Waste Materials Exchange
ORTECH International
Dr. Robert Laughlin
2395 Speakman Drive

Mississauga, Ontario
Canada L5K 1B3
(416) 822-4111 Ext. 265

Enstar Corporation*
Mr. J.T. Engster
P.O. Box 189
Latham, NY 12110
(518) 785-0470

Great Lakes Waste Exchange
Kay Ostrowski
400 Ann St. N.E., Suite 201-A
Grand Rapids, MI 49504-2054
(616) 363-3262

Indiana Waste Exchange
Susan Scrogham
P.O. Box 1220
Indianapolis, IN 46206
(317) 634-2142

Industrial Materials Exchange
(IMEX)
Jerry Henderson
172 20th Avenue
Seattle, WA 98122
(206) 296-4633
FAX: (206) 296-0188

Industrial Materials Exchange Service
Diane Shockey
P.O. Box 19276
Springfield, IL 62794-9276
(217) 782-0450
FAX: (217) 524-4193

Industrial Waste Information Exchange
William E. Payne
New Jersey Chamber of Commerce
5 Commerce Street
Newark, NJ 07102
(201) 623-7070

Manitoba Waste Exchange
James Ferguson
c/o Biomass Energy Institute, Inc.
1329 Niakwa Road
Winnipeg, Manitoba
Canada R2J 3T4
(204) 257-3891

Montana Industrial Waste Exchange
Don Ingles
Montana Chamber of Commerce
P.O. Box 1730
Helena, MT 59624
(406) 422-2405

New Hampshire Waste Exchange
Gary J. Olson
c/o NHRRA
P.O. Box 721
Concord, NH 03301
(603) 224-6996

Northeast Industrial Waste Exchange
Lewis Cutler
90 Presidential Plaza, Suite 122
Syracuse, NY 13202
(315) 422-6572
FAX: (315) 422-9051

Ontario Waste Excahnge
ORTECH International
Wanda Varangu
2395 Speaman Drive
Mississauga, Ontario
Canada L5K 1B3
(416) 822-4111 Ext. 512

Pacific Materials Exchange
Bob Smee
South 3707 Godfrey Boulevard
Spokane, WA 99204
(509) 623-4244

Peel Regional Waste Exchange
Glen Milbury
Regional Municipality of Peel
10 Peel Center Drive
Brampton, Ontario
Canada L6T 4B9
(416) 791-9400

RENEW
Cheryl Wilson
Texas Water Commission
P.O. Box 13087
Austin, TX 76711-3087
(512) 463-7773
FAX: (512) 463-8317

Southeast Waste Exchange
Mary McDaniel
Urban Institute
UNCC Station
Charlotte, NC 28223
(704) 547-2370

Southern Waste Information Exchange
Eugene B. Jones
P.O. Box 960
Tallahassee, FL 32302
(800) 441-SWIX (7949)
(904) 644-5516
FAX: (904) 574-6704

Wastelink, Division of Tencon Inc.
Mary E. Malotke
140 Wooster Pike
Milford, OH 45150
(513) 248-0012
FAX: (513) 248-1094

*For Profit Waste Information Exchange

Source: EPA

APPENDIX B

HAZARDOUS WASTE TABLES

Hazardous Waste—Nonspecific and Specific Source 325
Discarded Commercial Chemical Products—(Toxic) 335
Discarded Commercial Chemical Products—(Acute) 343
Basis for Listing Hazardous Wastes 347
List of Hazardous Constituents 351

HAZARDOUS WASTE—NONSPECIFIC AND SPECIFIC SOURCES

Hazardous Waste From Nonspecific Sources

Industry and EPA hazardous waste No.	Hazardous waste	Hazard code
Generic:		
F001	The following spent halogenated solvents used in degreasing: tetrachloroethylene, trichloroethylene, methylene chloride, 1,1,1-trichloroethane, carbon tetrachloride, and chlorinated fluorocarbons; all spent solvent mixtures/blends used in degreasing containing, before use, a total of ten percent or more (by volume) or one or more of the above halogenated solvents or those solvents listed in F002, F004, and F005; and still bottoms from the recovery of these spent solvents and spent solvent mixtures.	(T)
F002	The following spent halogenated solvents: tetrachloroethylene, methylene chloride, trichloroethylene, 1,1,1-trichloroethane, chlorobenzene, 1,1,2-trichloro-1,2,2-trifluoroethane, orthodichlorobenzene, trichlorofluoro-methane, and 1,1,2-trichloroethane; all spent solvent mixtures/blends containing, before use, a total of ten percent or more (by volume) of one or more of the above halogenated solvents or those listed in F001, F004, or F005; and still bottoms from the recovery of these spent solvents and spent solvent mixtures.	(T)
F003	The following spent nonhalogenated solvents: xylene, acetone, ethyl acetate, ethyl benzene, ethyl ether, methyl isobutyl ketone, n-butyl alcohol, cyclohexanone, and methanol; all spent solvent mixtures/blends containing, before use, only the above spent nonhalogenated solvents; and all spent solvent mixtures/blends containing, before use, one or more of the above nonhalogenated solvents, and, a total of ten percent or more (by volume) of one or more of those solvents listed in F001, F002, F004, and F005; and still bottoms from the recovery of these spent solvents and spent solvent mixtures.	(I)*
F004	The following spent nonhalogenated solvents: cresols and cresylic acid, and nitrobenzene; all spent solvent mixtures/blends containing, before use, a total of ten percent or more (by volume) of one or more of the above nonhalogenated solvents or those solvents listed in F001, F002, and F005; and still bottoms from the recovery of these spent solvents and spent solvent mixtures.	(T)

Industry and EPA hazardous waste No.	Hazardous waste	Hazard code
F005	The following spent nonhalogenated solvents: toluene, methyl ethyl ketone, carbon disulfide, isobutanol, pyridine, benzene, 2-ethoxyethanol, and 2-nitropropane; all spent solvent mixtures/blends containing, before use, a total of ten percent or more (by volume) of one or more of the above nonhalogenated solvents or those solvents listed in F001, F002, or F004; and still bottoms from the recovery of these spent solvents and spent solvent mixtures.	
F006	Wastewater treatment sludges from electroplating operations except from the following processes: (1) sulfuric acid anodizing of aluminum; (2) tin plating on carbon steel; (3) zinc plating (segregated basis) on carbon steel; (4) aluminum or zinc-aluminum plating on carbon steel; (5) cleaning/stripping associated with tin, zinc and aluminum plating on carbon steel; and (6) chemical etching and milling of aluminum.	(T)
F007	Spent cyanide plating bath solutions from electroplating operations.	(R, T)
F008	Plating bath residues from the bottom of plating bath from electroplating operations where cyanides are used in the process (except for precious metals electroplating plating bath sludges).	(R, T)
F009	Spent stripping and cleaning bath solutions from electroplating operations where cyanides are used in the process.	(R, T)
F010	Quenching bath residues from oil baths from metal heat treating operations where cyanides are used in the process.	(R, T)
F011	Spent cyanide solutions from salt bath pot cleaning from metal heat treating operations.	(R, T)
F012	Quenching waste water treatment sludges from metal heat treating operations where cyanides are used in the process.	(T)
F019	Wastewater treatment sludges from the chemical conversion coating of aluminum except for zirconium phosphating in aluminum can washing when such phosphating is an exclusive conversion coating process.	(T)
F020	Wastes (except wastewater and spent carbon from hydrogen chloride purification) from the production or manufacturing use (as a reactant, chemical intermediate, or component in a formulating process) of tri- or tetrachlorophenol, or of intermediates used to produce their pesticide derivatives. (This listing does not include wastes from the production of Hexachlorophene from highly purified 2,4,5-trichlorophenol.).	(H)
F021	Wastes (except wastewater and spent carbon from hydrogen chloride purification) from the production or manufacturing use (as a reactant, chemical intermediate, or component in a formulating process) of pentachlorophenol, or of intermediates used to produce its derivatives.	(H)

Appendix B: Hazardous Waste Tables

Industry and EPA hazardous waste No.	Hazardous waste	Hazard code
F022	Wastes (except wastewater and spent carbon from hydrogen chloride purification) from the manufacturing use (as a reactant, chemical intermediate, or component in a formulating process) of tetra-, penta-, or hexachlorobenzenes under alkaline conditions.	(H)
F023	Wastes (except wastewater and spent carbon from hydrogen chloride purification) from the production of materials on equipment previously used for the production or manufacturing use (as a reactant, chemical intermediate, or component in a formulating process) of tri- and tetrachlorophenols. (This listing does not include wastes from equipment used only for the production or use of Hexachlorophene from highly purified 2,4,5-trichlorophenol.).	(H)
F024	Wastes, including but not limited to, distillation residues, heavy ends, tars, and reactor clean-out wastes from the production of certain chlorinated aliphatic hydrocarbons by free radical catalyzed processes. These chlorinated aliphatic hycrocarbons are those having carbon chain lengths ranging from one to and including five, with varying amounts and positions of chlorine substitution. (This listing does not include wastewaters, wastewater treatment sludges, spent catalysts, and wastes listed in §261.31 or §261.32).	(T)
F025	Condensed light ends, spent filter acids, and spent desiccant wastes from the production of certain chlorinated aliphatic hydrocarbons, by free radical catalyzed processes. These chlorinated aliphatic hydrocarbons are those having carbon chain lengths from one to and including five, with varying amounts and positions of chlorine substitution.	(T)
F026	Wastes (except wastewater and spent carbon from hydrogen chloride purification) from the production of materials on equipment previously used for the manufacturing use (as a reactant, chemical intermediate, or component in a formulating process) of tetra-, penta-, or hexachlorobenzene under alkaline conditions.	(H)
F027	Discarded unused formulations containing tri-, tetra-, or pentachlorophenol or discarded unused formulations containing compounds derived from these chlorophenols. (This listing does not include formulations containing Hexachlorophene synthesized from prepurified 2,4,5-trichlorophenol as the sole component.).	(H)
F028	Residues resulting from the incineration or thermal treatment of soil contaminated with EPA Hazardous Waste Nos. F020, F021, F022, F023, F026, and F2027.	(T)

Industry and EPA hazardous waste No.	Hazardous waste	Hazard code
F032	Wastewaters, process residuals, preservative drippage, and spent formulations from wood preserving processes generated at plants that currently use or have previously used chlorophenolic formulations (except potentially cross-contaminated wastes that have had the F032 waste code deleted in accordance § 261.35 of this chapter and where the generator does not resume or inititate use of chlorophenolic formulations). This listing does not include K001 bottom sediment sludge from the treatment of wastewater from wood preserving processses that use creosole and/or pentachlorophenol.	(T)
F034	Wastewaters, process residuals, preservative drippage, and spent formulations from wood preserving processes generated at plants that use creosote formulations. This listing does not include K001 bottom sediment sludge from the treatment of wastewater from wood preserving processes that use creosote and/or pentachlorophenol.	(T)
F035	Wastewaters, process residuals, preservative drippage, and spent formulations from wood preserving processes generated at plants that use inorganic preservatives containing arsenic or chromium. This listing does not include K001 bottom sediment sludge from the treatment of wastewater from wood preserving processes that use creosote and/or pentachlorophenol.	(T)
F037	Petroleum refinery primary oil/water/solids separation sludge—Any sludge generated from the gravitational separation of oil/water/solids during the storage or treatment of process wastewaters and oily cooling wastewaters from petroleum refineries. Such sludges include, but are not limited to, those generated in: oil/water/solids separators; tanks and impoundments; ditches and other conveyances; sumps; and stormwater units receiving dry weather flow. Sludge generated in stormwater units that do not receive dry weather flow, sludges generated from noncontact once-through cooling waters segregated for treatment from other process or oily cooling waters, sludges generated in aggressive biological treatment units as defined in §261.31(b)(2) (including sludges generated in one or more additional units after wastewaters have been treated in aggressive biological treatment units) and K051 wastes are not included in this listing.	(T)

Appendix B: Hazardous Waste Tables

Industry and EPA hazardous waste No.	Hazardous waste	Hazard code
F038	Petroleum refinery secondary (emulsified) oil/water/solids separation sludge—Any sludge and/or float generated from the physical and/or chemical separation of oil/water/solids in process wastewaters and oily cooling wastewaters from petroleum refineries. Such wastes include, but are not limited to, all sludges and floats generated in: induced air flotation (IAF) units, tanks and impoundments, and all sludges generated in DAF units. Sludges generated in stormwater units that do not receive dry weather flow, sludges generated from non-contact once-through cooling waters segregated for treatment from other process or oily cooling waters, sludges and floats generated in aggressive biological treatment units as defined in §262.31(b)(2) (including sludges and floats generated in one or more additional units after wastewaters have been treated in aggressive biological treatment units) and F037, K048, and K051 wastes are not included in this listing.	(T)
F039	Leachate resulting from the treatment, storage, or disposal of wastes classified by more than one waste code under Supart D, or from a mixture of wastes classified under Subparts C and D of this part. (Leachate resulting from the management of one or more of the following EPA Hazardous Wastes and no other hazardous waste retains its hazardous waste code(s): F020, F021, F022, F023, F026, F027, and/or F028).	(T)

*(I,T) should be used to specify mixtures containing ignitable and toxic constituents.

Hazardous Waste From Specific Sources

Industry and EPA hazardous waste No.	Hazardous waste	Hazard code
Wood Preservation:		
K001	Bottom sediment sludge from the treatment of wastewaters from wood preserving processes that use creosote and/or pentachlorophenol	(T)
Inorganic Pigments:		
K002	Wastewater treatment sludge from the production of chrome yellow and orange pigments	(T)
K003	Wastewater treatment sludge from the production of molybdate orange pigments	(T)
K004	Wastewater treatment sludge from the production of zinc yellow pigments	(T)
K005	Wastewater treatment sludge from the production of chrome green pigments	(T)
K006	Wastewater treatment sludge from the production of chrome oxide green pigments (anhydrous and hydrated)	(T)
K007	Wastewater treatment sludge from the production of iron blue pigments	(T)
K008	Oven residue from the production of chrome oxide green pigments	(T)
Organic Chemicals:		
K009	Distillation bottoms from the production of acetaldehyde from ethylene	(T)
K010	Distillation side cuts from the production of acetaldehyde from ethylene	(T)
K011	Bottom stream from the wastewater stripper in the production of acrylonitrile	(R, T)
K013	Bottom stream from the acetonitrile column in the production of acrylonitrile	(R, T)
K014	Bottoms from the acetonitrile purification column in the production of acrylonitrile	(T)
K015	Still bottoms from the distillation of benzyl chloride	(T)
K016	Heavy ends or distillation residues from the production of carbon tetrachloride	(T)
K017	Heavy ends (still bottoms) from the purification column in the production of epichlorohydrin	(T)
K018	Heavy ends from the fractionation column in ethyl chloride production	(T)
K019	Heavy ends from the distillation of ethylene dichloride in ethylene dichloride production	(T)
K020	Heavy ends from the distillation of vinyl chloride in vinyl chloride monomer production	(T)
K021	Aqueous spent antimony catalyst waste from fluoromethanes production	(T)
K022	Distillation bottom tars from the production of phenol/acetone from cumene	(T)
K023	Distillation light ends from the production of phthalic anhydride from naphthalene	(T)
K024	Distillation bottoms from the production of phthalic anhydride from naphthalene	(T)
K025	Distillation bottoms from the production of nitrobenzene by the nitration of benzene	(T)
K026	Stripping still tails from the production of methyl ethyl pyridines	(T)
K027	Centrifuge and distillation residues from toluene diisocyanate production	(R,T)
K028	Spent catalyst from the hydrochlorinator reactor in the production of 1,1,1-trichloroethane	(T)

Appendix B: Hazardous Waste Tables

Industry and EPA hazardous waste No.	Hazardous waste	Hazard code
K029	Waste from the product steam stripper in the production of 1,1,1-trichloroethane	(T)
K030	Column bottoms or heavy ends from the combined production of trichloroethylene and perchloroethylene	(T)
K083	Distillation bottoms from aniline production	(T)
K085	Distillation or fractionation column bottoms from the production of chlorobenzenes	(T)
K093	Distillation light ends from the production of phthalic anhydride from ortho-xylene	(T)
K094	Distillation bottoms from the production of phthalic anhydride from ortho-xylene	(T)
K095	Distillation bottoms from the production of 1,1,1-trichloroethane	(T)
K096	Heavy ends from the heavy ends column from the production of 1,1,1-trichloroethane	(T)
K103	Process residues from aniline extraction from the production of aniline	(T)
K104	Combined wastewater streams generated from nitrobenzene/aniline production	(T)
K105	Separated aqueous stream from the reactor product washing step in the production of chlorobenzenes	(T)
K107	Column bottoms from product separation from the production of 1,1-dimethylhydrazine (UDMH) from carboxylic acid hydrazines	(C,T)
K108	Condensed column overheads from product separation and condensed reactor vent gases from the production of 1,1-dimethylhydrazine (UDMH) from carboxylic acid hydrazides	(I,T)
K109	Spent filter cartridges from product purification from the production of 1,1-dimethylhydrazine (UDMH) from carboxylic acid hydrazides	(T)
K110	Condensed column overheads from intermediate separation from the production of 1,1-dimethylhydrazine (UDMH) from carboxylic acid hydrazides	(T)
K111	Product washwaters from the production of dinitrotoluene via nitration of toluene	(C,T)
K112	Reaction by-product water from the drying column in the production of toluenediamine via hydrogenation of dinitrotoluene	(T)
K113	Condensed liquid light ends from the purification of toluenediamine in the production of toluenediamine via hydrogenation of dinitrotoluene	(T)
K114	Vicinals from the purification of toluenediamine in the production of toluenediamine via hydrogenation of dinitrotoluene	(T)
K115	Heavy ends from the purification of toluenediamine in the production of toluenediamine via hydrogenation of dinitrotoluene	(T)
K116	Organic condensate from the solvent recovery column in the production of toluene diisocyanate via phosgenation of toluenediamine	(T)
K117	Wastewater from the reactor vent gas scrubber in the production of ethylene dibromide via bromination of ethene	(T)

Industry and EPA hazardous waste No.	Hazardous waste	Hazard code
K118	Spent adsorbent solids from purification of ethylene dibromide in the production of ethylene dibromide via bromination of ethene	(T)
K119	Still bottoms from the purification of ethylene dibromide in the production of ethylene dibromide via bromination of ethene	(T)
Inorganic Chemicals:		
K071	Brine purification muds from the mercury cell process in chlorine production where separately prepurifed brine is not used	(T)
K073	Chlorinated hydrocarbon waste from the purification step of the diaphragm cell process using graphite anodes in chlorine production	(T)
K106	Wastewater treatment sludge from the mercury cell process in chlorine production	(T)
Pesticides:		
K031	By-product salts generated in the production of MSMA and cacodylic acid	(T)
K032	Wastewater treatment sludge from the production of chlordane	(T)
K033	Wastewater and scrub water from the chlorination of cyclopentadiene in the production of chlordane	(T)
K034	Filter solids from the filtration of hexachlorocyclopentadiene in the production of chlordane	(T)
K035	Wastewater treatment sludges generated in the production of creosote	(T)
K036	Still bottoms from toluene reclamation distillation in the production of disulfoton	(T)
K037	Wastewater treatment sludges from the production of disulfoton	(T)
K038	Wastewater from the washing and stripping of phorate production	(T)
K039	Filter cake from the filtration of diethylphosphorodithioic acid in the production of phorate	(T)
K040	Wastewater treatment sludge from the production of phorate	(T)
K041	Wastewater treatment sludge from the production of toxaphene	(T)
K042	Heavy ends or distillation residues from the distillation of tetrachlorobenzene in the production of 2,4,5-T	(T)
K043	2,6-Dichlorophenol waste from the production of 2,4-D	(T)
K097	Vacuum stripper discharge from the chlordane chlorinator in the production of chlordane	(T)
K098	Untreated process wastewater from the production of toxaphene	(T)
K099	Untreated wastewater from the production of 2,4-D	(T)
K123	Process wastewater (including supernates, filtrates, and washwaters) from the production of ethylenebisdithiocarbamic acid and its salt.	(T)
K124	Reactor vent scrubber water from the production of ethylenebisdithiocarbamic acid and its salts.	(C,T)

Appendix B: Hazardous Waste Tables

Industry and EPA hazardous waste No.	Hazardous waste	Hazard code
K125	Filtration evaporation, and centrifugation solids from the production of ethylene-bisdithiocarbamic acid and its salts.	(T)
K126	Baghouse dust and floor sweepings in milling and packaging operations from the production or formulation of ethylenebisdithiocarbamic acid and its salts.	(T)
K131	Wastewater from the reactor and spent sulfuric acid from the acid dryer from the production of methyl bromide.	(C, T)
K132	Spent absorbent and wastewater separator solids from the production of methyl bromide.	(T)
Explosives:		
K044	Wastewater treatment sludges from the manufacturing and processing of explosives	(R)
K045	Spent carbon from the treatment of wastewater containing explosives	(R)
K046	Wastewater treatment sludges from the manufacturing, formulation and loading of lead-based irritating compounds	(T)
K047	Pink/red water from TNT operations	(R)
Petroleum Refining		
K048	Dissolved air flotation (DAF) float from the petroleum refining industry	(T)
K049	Slop oil emulsion solids from the petroleum refining industry	(T)
K050	Heat exchanger bundle cleaning sludge from the petroleum refining industry	(T)
K051	API separator sludge from the petroleum refining industry	(T)
K052	Tank bottoms (leaded) from the petroleum refining industry	(T)
Iron and Steel:		
K061	Emission control dust/sludge from the primary production of steel in electric furnaces	(T)
K062	Spent pickle liquor generated by steel finishing operations of facilities within the iron and steel industry (SIC Codes 331 and 332)	(C,T)
Primary copper:		
K064	Acid plant blowdown slurry/sludge resulting from the thickening of blowdown slurry from primary copper production.	(T)
Primary lead:		
K065	Surface impoundment solids contained in and dredged from surface impoundments at primary lead smelting facilities	(T)
Primary zinc:		
K066	Sludge from treatment of process wastewater and/or acid plant blowdown from primary zinc production.	(T)
Primary aluminum:		
K088	Spent potliners from primary aluminum reduction.	(T)
Ferroalloys:		
K090	Emission control dust or sludge from ferrochromium-silicon production.	(T)
K091	Emission control dust or sludge from ferrochromium production.	(T)
Secondary Lead:		

Industry and EPA hazardous waste No.	Hazardous waste	Hazard code
K069	Emission control dust/sludge from secondary lead smelting. (NOTE: This listing is stayed administratively for sludge generated from secondary acid scrubber systems. The stay will remain in effect until further administrative action is taken. If EPA takes further action effecting this stay, EPA will publish a notice of the action in the *Federal Register*.	(T)
K100	Waste leaching solution from acid leaching of emission control dust/sludge from secondary lead smelting...	(T)
Veterinary Pharmaceuticals:		
K084	Wastewater treatment sludges generated during the production of veterinary pharmaceuticals from arsenic or organo-arsenic compounds ...	(T)
K101	Distillation tar residues from the distillation of aniline-based compounds in the production of veterinary pharmaceuticals from arsenic or organo-arsenic compounds	(T)
K102	Residue from the use of activated carbon for decolorization in the production of veterinary pharmaceuticals from arsenic or organo-arsenic compounds	(T)
Ink Formulation:		
K086	Solvent washes and sludges, caustic washes and sludges, or water washes and sludges from cleaning tubs and equipment used in the formulation of ink from pigments, driers, soaps, and stabilizers containing chromium and lead..	(T)
Coking:		
K060	Ammonia still lime sludge from coking operations	(T)
K087	Decanter tank tar sludge from coking operations	(T)

DISCARDED COMMERCIAL CHEMICAL PRODUCTS—
Toxics

Any commercial chemical product, manufacturing chemical intermediate, or off-specification commercial chemical product having the generic name on this list is considered a hazardous waste if discarded or intended for discard, and is subject to the small quantity generator exclusion as defined in BNA's *Chemical Substances Control*, beginning at p. 241:971.

The primary hazardous properties of these materials are indicated by the letters T (toxicity), R (reactivity), I (ignitability), and C (corrosivity). Absence of a letter indicates that the compound is only listed for toxicity.

(List begins next page)

Hazardous waste No.	Chemical abstracts No.	Substance		Hazardous waste No.	Chemical abstracts No.	Substance
U001	75-07-0	Acetaldehyde (I)		U021	92-87-5	Benzidine
U034	75-87-6	Acetaldehyde, trichloro-		U202	81-07-2	1,2-Benzisothiazol-3(2H)-one, 1,1-dioxide, & salts
U187	62-44-2	Acetamide, N-(4-ethoxyphenyl)-		U203	94-59-7	1,3-Benzodioxole, 5-(2-propenyl)-
U005	53-96-3	Acetamide, N-9H-fluoren-2-yl-		U141	120-58-1	1,3-Benzodioxole, 5-(1-propenyl)-
U240	94-75-7	Acetic acid, (2,4-dichlorophenoxy)-, salts & esters		U090	94-58-6	1,3-Benzodioxole, 5-propyl-
U112	141-78-6	Acetic acid ethyl ester (I)		U064	189-55-9	Benzo[rst]pentaphene
U144	301-04-2	Acetic acid, lead(2+) salt		U248	181-81-2	2H-1-Benzopyran-2-one, 4-hydroxy-3-(3-oxo-1-phenyl-butyl)-, & salts, when present at concentrations of 0.3% or less
U214	563-68-8	Acetic acid, thallium(1+) salt				
see F027	93-76-5	Acetic acid, (2,4,5-trichlorophenoxy)-		U022	50-32-8	Benzo[a]pyrene
U002	67-64-1	Acetone (I)		U197	106-51-4	p-Benzoquinone
U003	75-05-8	Acetonitrile (I,T)		U023	98-07-7	Benzotrichloride (C,R,T)
U004	98-86-2	Acetophenone		U085	1464-53-5	2,2'-Bioxirane
U005	53-96-3	2-Acetylaminofluorene		U021	92-87-5	[1,1'-Biphenyl]-4,4'-diamine
U006	75-36-5	Acetyl chloride (C,R,T)		U073	91-94-1	[1,1'-Biphenyl]-4,4'-diamine, 3,3'-dichloro-
U007	79-06-1	Acrylamide		U091	119-90-4	[1,1'-Biphenyl]-4,4'-diamine, 3,3'-dimethoxy-
U008	79-10-7	Acrylic acid (I)		U095	119-93-7	[1,1'-Biphenyl]-4,4'-diamine, 3,3'-dimethyl-
U009	107-13-1	Acrylonitrile		U225	75-25-2	Bromoform
U011	61-82-5	Amitrole		U030	101-55-3	4-Bromophenyl phenyl ether
U012	62-53-3	Aniline (I,T)		U128	87-68-3	1,3-Butadiene, 1,1,2,3,4,4-hexachloro-
U136	75-60-5	Arsinic acid, dimethyl-		U172	924-16-3	1-Butanamine, N-butyl-N-nitroso-
U014	492-80-8	Auramine		U031	71-36-3	1-Butanol (I)
U015	115-02-6	Azaserine		U159	78-93-3	2-Butanone (I,T)
U010	50-07-7	Azirino[2',3':3,4]pyrrolo[1,2-a]indole-4,7-dione, 6-amino-8-[[(aminocarbonyl)oxy]methyl]-1,1a,2,8,8a,8b-hexahydro-8a-methoxy-5-methyl-,[1aS-(1aalpha,8beta,8aalpha,8balpha)]-		U160	1338-23-4	2-Butanone, peroxide (R,T)
				U053	4170-30-3	2-Butenal
				U074	764-41-0	2-Butene, 1,4-dichloro- (I,T)
				U143	303-34-4	2-Butenoic acid, 2-methyl-, 7-[[2,3-dihydroxy-2-(1-methoxyethyl)-3-methyl-1-oxobutoxy]methyl]-2,3,5,7a-tetrahydro-1H-pyrrolizin-1-yl ester,[1S-[1alpha(Z),7(2S*,3R*),7aalpha]]-
U157	56-49-5	Benz[j]aceanthrylene, 1,2-dihydro-3-methyl-				
U016	225-51-4	Benz[c]acridine				
U017	98-87-3	Benzal chloride		U031	71-36-3	n-Butyl alcohol (I)
U192	23950-58-5	Benzamide, 3,5-dichloro-N-(1,1-dimethyl-2-propynyl)-		U136	75-60-5	Cacodylic acid
U018	56-55-3	Benz[a]anthracene		U032	13765-19-0	Calcium chromate
U094	57-97-6	Benz[a]anthracene, 7,12-dimethyl-		U238	51-79-6	Carbamic acid, ethyl ester
U012	62-53-3	Benzenamine (I,T)		U178	615-53-2	Carbamic acid, methylnitroso-, ethyl ester
U014	492-80-8	Benzenamine, 4,4'-carbonimidoylbis[N,N-dimethyl-		U097	79-44-7	Carbamic chloride, dimethyl-
U049	3165-93-3	Benzenamine, 4-chloro-2-methyl-, hydrochloride		U114	111-54-6	Carbamodithioic acid, 1,2-ethanediylbis-, salts & esters
U093	60-11-7	Benzenamine, N,N-dimethyl-4-(phenylazo)-				
U328	95-53-4	Benzenamine, 2-methyl-				

Appendix B: Hazardous Waste Tables

U353	106-49-0	Benzenamine, 4-methyl-
U158	101-14-4	Benzenamine, 4,4'-methylenebis[2-chloro-
U222	636-21-5	Benzenamine, 2-methyl-, hydrochloride
U181	99-55-8	Benzenamine, 2-methyl-5-nitro-
U019	71-43-2	Benzene (I,T)
U038	510-15-6	Benzeneacetic acid, 4-chloro-alpha-(4-chlorophenyl)-alpha-hydroxy-, ethyl ester
U030	101-55-3	Benzene, 1-bromo-4-phenoxy-
U035	305-03-3	Benzenebutanoic acid, 4-[bis(2-chloroethyl)amino]-
U037	108-90-7	Benzene, chloro-
U221	25376-45-8	Benzenediamine, ar-methyl-
U028	117-81-7	1,2-Benzenedicarboxylic acid, bis(2-ethylhexyl) ester
U069	84-74-2	1,2-Benzenedicarboxylic acid, dibutyl ester
U088	84-66-2	1,2-Benzenedicarboxylic acid, diethyl ester
U102	131-11-3	1,2-Benzenedicarboxylic acid, dimethyl ester
U107	117-84-0	1,2-Benzenedicarboxylic acid, dioctyl ester
U070	95-50-1	Benzene, 1,2-dichloro-
U071	541-73-1	Benzene, 1,3-dichloro-
U072	106-46-7	Benzene, 1,4-dichloro-
U060	72-54-8	Benzene, 1,1'-(2,2-dichloroethylidene)bis[4-chloro-
U017	98-87-3	Benzene, (dichloromethyl)-
U223	26471-62-5	Benzene, 1,3-diisocyanatomethyl- (R,T)
U239	1330-20-7	Benzene, dimethyl- (I,T)
U201	108-46-3	1,3-Benzenediol
U127	118-74-1	Benzene, hexachloro-
U056	110-82-7	Benzene, hexahydro- (I)
U220	108-88-3	Benzene, methyl-
U105	121-14-2	Benzene, 1-methyl-2,4-dinitro-
U106	606-20-2	Benzene, 2-methyl-1,3-dinitro-
U055	98-82-8	Benzene, (1-methylethyl)- (I)
U169	98-95-3	Benzene, nitro-
U183	608-93-5	Benzene, pentachloro-
U185	82-68-8	Benzene, pentachloronitro-
U020	98-09-9	Benzenesulfonic acid chloride (C,R)
U020	98-09-9	Benzenesulfonyl chloride (C,R)
U207	95-94-3	Benzene, 1,2,4,5-tetrachloro-
U061	50-29-3	Benzene, 1,1'-(2,2,2-trichloroethylidene)bis[4-chloro-
U247	72-43-5	Benzene, 1,1'-(2,2,2-trichloroethylidene)bis[4-methoxy-
U023	98-07-7	Benzene, (trichloromethyl)-
U234	99-35-4	Benzene, 1,3,5-trinitro-

U062	2303-16-4	Carbamothioic acid, bis(1-methylethyl)-, S-(2,3-dichloro-2-propenyl) ester
U215	6533-73-9	Carbonic acid, dithallium(1+) salt
U033	353-50-4	Carbonic difluoride
U156	79-22-1	Carbonochloridic acid, methyl ester (I,T)
U033	353-50-4	Carbon oxyfluoride (R,T)
U211	56-23-5	Carbon tetrachloride
U034	75-87-6	Chloral
U035	305-03-3	Chlorambucil
U036	57-74-9	Chlordane, alpha & gamma isomers
U026	494-03-1	Chlornaphazin
U037	108-90-7	Chlorobenzene
U038	510-15-6	Chlorobenzilate
U039	59-50-7	p-Chloro-m-cresol
U042	110-75-8	2-Chloroethyl vinyl ether
U044	67-66-3	Chloroform
U046	107-30-2	Chloromethyl methyl ether
U047	91-58-7	beta-Chloronaphthalene
U048	95-57-8	o-Chlorophenol
U049	3165-93-3	4-Chloro-o-toluidine, hydrochloride
U032	13765-19-0	Chromic acid H$_2$CrO$_4$, calcium salt
U050	218-01-9	Chrysene
U051		Creosote
U052	1319-77-3	Cresol (Cresylic acid)
U053	4170-30-3	Crotonaldehyde
U055	98-82-8	Cumene (I)
U246	506-68-3	Cyanogen bromide (CN)Br
U197	106-51-4	2,5-Cyclohexadiene-1,4-dione
U056	110-82-7	Cyclohexane (I)
U129	58-89-9	Cyclohexane, 1,2,3,4,5,6-hexachloro-, (1alpha,2alpha,3beta,4alpha,5alpha,6beta)-
U057	108-94-1	Cyclohexanone (I)
U130	77-47-4	1,3-Cyclopentadiene, 1,2,3,4,5,5-hexachloro-
U058	50-18-0	Cyclophosphamide
U240	94-75-7	2,4-D, salts & esters
U059	20830-81-3	Daunomycin
U060	72-54-8	DDD
U061	50-29-3	DDT
U062	2303-16-4	Diallate
U063	53-70-3	Dibenz[a,h]anthracene
U064	189-55-9	Dibenzo[a,i]pyrene

Hazardous waste No.	Chemical abstracts No.	Substance	Hazardous waste No.	Chemical abstracts No.	Substance
U066	96-12-8	1,2-Dibromo-3-chloropropane	U116	96-45-7	Ethyleneethiourea
U069	84-74-2	Dibutyl phthalate	U076	75-34-3	Ethylidene dichloride
U070	95-50-1	o-Dichlorobenzene	U118	97-63-2	Ethyl methacrylate
U071	541-73-1	m-Dichlorobenzene	U119	62-50-0	Ethyl methanesulfonate
U072	106-46-7	p-Dichlorobenzene	U120	206-44-0	Fluoranthene
U073	91-94-1	3,3'-Dichlorobenzidine	U122	50-00-0	Formaldehyde
U074	764-41-0	1,4-Dichloro-2-butene (I,T)	U123	64-18-6	Formic acid (C,T)
U075	75-71-8	Dichlorodifluoromethane	U124	110-00-9	Furan (I)
U078	75-35-4	1,1-Dichloroethylene	U125	98-01-1	2-Furancarboxaldehyde (I)
U079	156-60-5	1,2-Dichloroethylene	U147	108-31-6	2,5-Furandione
U025	111-44-4	Dichloroethyl ether	U213	109-99-9	Furan, tetrahydro-(I)
U027	108-60-1	Dichloroisopropyl ether	U125	98-01-1	Furfural (I)
U024	111-91-1	Dichloromethoxy ethane	U124	110-00-9	Furfuran (I)
U081	120-83-2	2,4-Dichlorophenol	U206	18883-66-4	Glucopyranose, 2-deoxy-2-(3-methyl-3-nitrosoureido)-D-
U082	87-65-0	2,6-Dichlorophenol			
U084	542-75-6	1,3-Dichloropropene	U206	18883-66-4	D-Glucose, 2-deoxy-2-[[(methylnitrosoamino)-carbonyl]amino]-
U085	1464-53-5	1,2:3,4-Diepoxybutane (I,T)			
U108	123-91-1	1,4-Diethyleneoxide	U126	765-34-4	Glycidylaldehyde
U028	117-81-7	Diethylhexyl phthalate	U163	70-25-7	Guanidine, N-methyl-N'-nitro-N-nitroso-
U086	1615-80-1	N,N'-Diethylhydrazine	U127	118-74-1	Hexachlorobenzene
U087	3288-58-2	O,O-Diethyl S-methyl dithophosphate	U128	87-68-3	Hexachlorobutadiene
U088	84-66-2	Diethyl phthalate	U130	77-47-4	Hexachlorocyclopentadiene
U089	56-53-1	Diethylstilbesterol	U131	67-72-1	Hexachloroethane
U090	94-58-6	Dihydrosafrole	U132	70-30-4	Hexachlorophene
U091	119-90-4	3,3'-Dimethoxybenzidine	U243	1888-71-7	Hexachloropropene
U092	124-40-3	Dimethylamine (I)	U133	302-01-2	Hydrazine (R,T)
U093	60-11-7	p-Dimethylaminoazobenzene	U086	1615-80-1	Hydrazine, 1,2-diethyl-
U094	57-97-6	7,12-Dimethylbenz[a]anthracene	U098	57-14-7	Hydrazine, 1,1-dimethyl-
U095	119-93-7	3,3'-Dimethylbenzidine	U099	540-73-8	Hydrazine, 1,2-dimethyl-
U096	80-15-9	alpha,alpha-Dimethylbenzylhydroperoxide (R)	U109	122-66-7	Hydrazine, 1,2-diphenyl-
U097	79-44-7	Dimethylcarbamoyl chloride	U134	7664-39-3	Hydrofluoric acid (C,T)
U098	57-14-7	1,1-Dimethylhydrazine	U134	7664-39-3	Hydrogen fluoride (C,T)
U099	540-73-8	1,2-Dimethylhydrazine	U135	7783-06-4	Hydrogen sulfide
U101	105-67-9	2,4-Dimethylphenol	U135	7783-06-4	Hydrogen sulfide H_2S
U102	131-11-3	Dimethyl phthalate	U096	80-15-9	Hydroperoxide, 1-methyl-1-phenylethyl- (R)
U103	77-78-1	Dimethyl sulfate	U116	96-45-7	2-imidazolidinethione
U105	121-14-2	2,4-Dinitrotoluene	U137	193-39-5	Indeno[1,2,3-cd]pyrene

Appendix B: Hazardous Waste Tables

Code	CAS	Name	Code	CAS	Name
U106	606-20-2	2,6-Dinitrotoluene	U190	85-44-9	1,3-Isobenzofurandione
U107	117-84-0	Di-n-octyl phthalate	U140	78-83-1	Isobutyl alcohol (I,T)
U108	123-91-1	1,4-Dioxane	U141	120-58-1	Isosafrole
U109	122-66-7	1,2-Diphenylhydrazine	U142	143-50-0	Kepone
U110	142-84-7	Dipropylamine (I)	U143	303-34-4	Lasiocarpine
U111	621-64-7	Di-n-propylnitrosamine	U144	301-04-2	Lead acetate
U041	106-89-8	Epichlorohydrin	U146	1335-32-6	Lead, bis(acetato-O)tetrahydroxytri-
U001	75-07-0	Ethanal (I)	U145	7446-27-7	Lead phosphate
U174	55-18-5	Ethanamine, N-ethyl-N-nitroso-	U146	1335-32-6	Lead subacetate
U155	91-80-5	1,2-Ethanediamine, N,N-dimethyl-N'-2-pyridinyl-N'-2-thenylmethyl)-	U129	58-89-9	Lindane
			U163	70-25-7	MNNG
U067	106-93-4	Ethane, 1,2-dibromo-	U147	108-31-6	Maleic anhydride
U076	75-34-3	Ethane, 1,1-dichloro-	U148	123-33-1	Maleic hydrazide
U077	107-06-2	Ethane, 1,2-dichloro-	U149	109-77-3	Malononitrile
U131	67-72-1	Ethane, hexachloro-	U150	148-82-3	Melphalan
U024	111-91-1	Ethane, 1,1'-[methylenebis(oxy)]bis[2-chloro-	U151	7439-97-6	Mercury
U117	60-29-7	Ethane, 1,1'-oxybis-(I)	U152	126-98-7	Methacrylonitrile (I, T)
U025	111-44-4	Ethane, 1,1'-oxybis[2-chloro-	U092	124-40-3	Methanamine, N-methyl- (I)
U184	76-01-7	Ethane, pentachloro-	U029	74-83-9	Methane, bromo-
U208	630-20-6	Ethane, 1,1,1,2-tetrachloro-	U045	74-87-3	Methane, chloro- (I, T)
U209	79-34-5	Ethane, 1,1,2,2-tetrachloro-	U046	107-30-2	Methane, chloromethoxy-
U218	62-55-5	Ethanethioamide	U068	74-95-3	Methane, dibromo-
U226	71-55-6	Ethane, 1,1,1-trichloro-	U080	75-09-2	Methane, dichloro-
U227	79-00-5	Ethane, 1,1,2-trichloro-	U075	75-71-8	Methane, dichlorodifluoro-
U359	110-80-5	Ethanol, 2-ethoxy-	U138	74-88-4	Methane, iodo-
U173	1116-54-7	Ethanol, 2,2'-(nitrosoimino)bis-	U119	62-50-0	Methanesulfonic acid, ethyl ester
U004	98-86-2	Ethanone, 1-phenyl-	U211	56-23-5	Methane, tetrachloro-
U043	75-01-4	Ethene, chloro-	U153	74-93-1	Methanethiol (I, T)
U042	110-75-8	Ethene, (2-chloroethoxy)-	U225	75-25-2	Methane, tribromo-
U078	75-35-4	Ethene, 1,1-dichloro-	U044	67-66-3	Methane, trichloro-
U079	156-60-5	Ethene, 1,2-dichloro-, (E)-	U121	75-69-4	Methane, trichlorofluoro-
U210	127-18-4	Ethene, tetrachloro-	U036	57-74-9	4,7-Methano-1H-indene, 1,2,4,5,6,7,8,8-octachloro-2,3,3a,4,7,7a-hexahydro-
U228	79-01-6	Ethene, trichloro-	U154	67-56-1	Methanol (I)
U112	141-78-6	Ethyl acetate (I)	U155	91-80-5	Methapyrilene
U113	140-88-5	Ethyl acrylate (I)	U142	143-50-0	1,3,4-Metheno-2H-cyclobuta[cd]pentalen-2-one, 1,1a,3,3a,4,5,5,5a,5b,6-decachlorooctahydro-
U238	51-79-6	Ethyl carbamate (urethane)	U247	72-43-5	Methoxychlor
U117	60-29-7	Ethyl ether (I)	U154	67-56-1	Methyl alcohol (I)
U114	111-54-6	Ethylenebisdithiocarbamic acid, salts & esters	U029	74-83-9	Methyl bromide
U067	106-93-4	Ethylene dibromide	U186	504-60-9	1-Methylbutadiene (I)
U077	107-06-2	Ethylene dichloride			
U359	110-80-5	Ethylene glycol monoethyl ether			
U115	75-21-8	Ethylene oxide (I,T)			

Hazardous waste No	Chemical abstracts No.	Substance		Hazardous waste No	Chemical abstracts No	Substance
U045	74-87-3	Methyl chloride (I,T)		See F027	87-86-5	Phenol, pentachloro-
U156	79-22-1	Methyl chlorocarbonate (I,T)		U156	58-90-2	Phenol, 2,3,4,6-tetrachloro-
U226	71-55-6	Methyl chloroform		See F027		
U157	56-49-5	3-Methylcholanthrene		U158	95-95-4	Phenol, 2,4,5-trichloro-
U158	101-14-4	4,4'-Methylenebis(2-chloroaniline)		See F027	88-06-2	Phenol, 2,4,6-trichloro-
U068	74-95-3	Methylene bromide				
U080	75-09-2	Methylene chloride		U150	148-82-3	L-Phenylalanine, 4-[bis(2-chloroethyl)amino]-
U159	78-93-3	Methyl ethyl ketone (MEK) (I,T)		U145	7446-27-7	Phosphoric acid, lead(2+) salt (2:3)
U160	1338-23-4	Methyl ethyl ketone peroxide (R,T)		U087	3288-58-2	Phosphorodithioic acid, O,O-diethyl S-methyl ester
U138	74-88-4	Methyl iodide		U189	1314-80-3	Phosphorus sulfide (R)
U161	108-10-1	Methyl isobutyl ketone (I)		U190	85-44-9	Phthalic anhydride
U162	80-62-6	Methyl methacrylate (I,T)		U191	109-06-8	2-Picoline
U161	108-10-1	4-Methyl-2-pentanone (I)		U179	100-75-4	Piperidine, 1-nitroso-
U164	56-04-2	Methylthiouracil		U192	23950-58-5	Pronamide
U010	50-07-7	Mitomycin C		U194	107-10-8	1-Propanamine (I,T)
U059	20830-81-3	5,12-Naphthacenedione, 8-acetyl-10-[8-amino-2,3,6-triodeoxy)-alpha-L-lyxo-hexopyranosyl)oxy]-7,8,9,10-tetrahydro-6,8,11-trihydroxy-1-methoxy-,		U111	621-64-7	1-Propanamine, N-nitroso-N-propyl-
				U110	142-84-7	1-Propanamine, N-propyl- (I)
				U066	96-12-8	Propane, 1,2-dibromo-3-chloro-
U167	134-32-7	1-Naphthalenamine		U083	78-87-5	Propane, 1,2-dichloro-
U168	91-59-8	2-Naphthalenamine		U149	109-77-3	Propanedinitrile
U026	494-03-1	Naphthalenamine, N,N-bis(2-chloroethyl)-		U171	79-46-9	Propane, 2-nitro- (I,T)
U165	91-20-3	Naphthalene		U027	108-60-1	Propane, 2,2'-oxybis[2-chloro-
U047	91-58-7	Naphthalene, 2-chloro-		U193	1120-71-4	1,3-Propane sultone
U166	130-15-4	1,4-Naphthalenedione		See F027	93-72-1	Propanoic acid, 2-(2,4,5-trichlorophenoxy)-
U236	72-57-1	2,7-Naphthalenedisulfonic acid, 3,3'-[(3,3'-dimethyl[1,1'-biphenyl]-4,4'-diyl)bis(azo)]bis[5-amino-4-hydroxyl-, tetrasodium salt		U235	126-72-7	1-Propanol, 2,3-dibromo-, phosphate (3:1)
				U167	78-83-1	1-Propanol, 2-methyl- (I,T)
U166	130-15-4	1,4-Naphthoquinone		U168	67-64-1	2-Propanone (I)
U167	134-32-7	alpha-Naphthylamine		U002	79-06-1	2-Propenamide
U168	91-59-8	beta-Naphthylamine		U007	542-75-6	1-Propene, 1,3-dichloro-
U217	10102-45-1	Nitric acid, thallium(1+) salt		U084		
U169	98-95-3	Nitrobenzene (I,T)				

Appendix B: Hazardous Waste Tables

U170	100-02-7	p-Nitrophenol	U243	1888-71-7	1-Propene, 1,1,2,3,3,3-hexachloro-
U171	79-46-9	2-Nitropropane (I,T)	U009	107-13-1	2-Propenenitrile
U172	924-16-3	N-Nitrosodi-n-butylamine	U152	126-98-7	2-Propenenitrile, 2-methyl- (I,T)
U173	1116-54-7	N-Nitrosodiethanolamine	U008	79-10-7	2-Propenoic acid (I)
U174	55-18-5	N-Nitrosodiethylamine	U113	140-88-5	2-Propenoic acid, ethyl ester (I)
U176	759-73-9	N-Nitroso-N-ethylurea	U118	97-63-2	2-Propenoic acid, 2-methyl-, ethyl ester
U177	684-93-5	N-Nitroso-N-methylurea	U162	80-62-6	2-Propenoic acid, 2-methyl-, methyl ester (I,T)
U178	615-53-2	N-Nitroso-N-methylurethane	U194	107-10-8	n-Propylamine (I,T)
U179	100-75-4	N-Nitrosopiperidine	U083	78-87-5	Propylene dichloride
U180	930-55-2	N-Nitrosopyrrolidine	U148	123-33-1	3,6-Pyridazinedione, 1,2-dihydro-
U181	99-55-8	5-Nitro-o-toluidine	U196	110-86-1	Pyridine
U193	1120-71-4	1,2-Oxathiolane, 2,2-dioxide	U191	109-06-8	Pyridine, 2-methyl-
U058	50-18-0	2H-1,3,2-Oxazaphosphorin-2-amine, N,N-bis(2-chloroethyl)tetrahydro-, 2-oxide	U237	66-75-1	2,4-(1H,3H)-Pyrimidinedione, 5-[bis(2-chloroethyl)amino]-
U115	75-21-8	Oxirane (I,T)	U164	56-04-2	4(1H)-Pyrimidinone, 2,3-dihydro-6-methyl-2-thioxo-
U126	765-34-4	Oxiranecarboxyaldehyde	U180	930-55-2	Pyrrolidine, 1-nitroso-
U041	106-89-8	Oxirane, (chloromethyl)-	U200	50-55-5	Reserpine
U182	123-63-7	Paraldehyde	U201	108-46-3	Resorcinol
U183	608-93-5	Pentachlorobenzene	U202	81-07-2	Saccharin, & salts
U184	76-01-7	Pentachloroethane	U203	94-59-7	Safrole
U185	82-68-8	Pentachloronitrobenzene (PCNB)	U204	7783-00-8	Selenious acid
See F027	87-86-5	Pentachlorophenol	U204	7783-00-8	Selenium dioxide
			U205	7488-56-4	Selenium sulfide
U161	108-10-1	Pentanol, 4-methyl-	U205	7488-56-4	Selenium sulfide SeS$_2$ (R,T)
U186	504-60-9	1,3-Pentadiene (I)	U015	115-02-6	L-Serine, diazoacetate (ester)
U187	62-44-2	Phenacetin	See F027	93-72-1	Silvex (2,4,5-TP)
U188	108-95-2	Phenol			
U048	95-57-8	Phenol, 2-chloro-	U206	18883-66-4	Streptozotocin
U039	59-50-7	Phenol, 4-chloro-3-methyl-	U103	77-78-1	Sulfuric acid, dimethyl ester
U081	120-83-2	Phenol, 2,4-dichloro-	U189	1314-80-3	Sulfur phosphide (R)
U082	87-65-0	Phenol, 2,6-dichloro-	See F027	93-76-5	2,4,5-T
U089	56-53-1	Phenol, 4,4'-(1,2-diethyl-1,2-ethenediyl)bis-, (E)-	U207	95-94-3	1,2,4,5-Tetrachlorobenzene
U101	105-67-9	Phenol, 2,4-dimethyl-	U208	630-20-6	1,1,1,2-Tetrachloroethane
U052	1319-77-3	Phenol, methyl-	U209	79-34-5	1,1,2,2-Tetrachloroethane
U132	70-30-4	Phenol, 2,2'-methylenebis[3,4,6-trichloro-	U210	127-18-4	Tetrachloroethylene
U170	100-02-7	Phenol, 4-nitro-			

Hazardous waste No.	Chemical abstracts No.	Substance
See F027	58-90-2	2,3,4,6-Tetrachlorophenol
U213	109-99-9	Tetrahydrofuran (I)
U214	563-68-8	Thallium(I) acetate
U215	6533-73-9	Thallium(I) carbonate
U216	7791-12-0	Thallium(I) chloride
U216	7791-12-0	Thallium chloride TlCl
U217	10102-45-1	Thallium(I) nitrate
U218	62-55-5	Thioacetamide
U153	74-93-1	Thiomethanol (I,T)
U244	137-26-8	Thioperoxydicarbonic diamide [(H₂N)C(S)]₂S₂, tetramethyl-
U219	62-56-6	Thiourea
U244	137-26-8	Thiram
U220	108-88-3	Toluene
U221	25376-45-8	Toluenediamine
U223	26471-62-5	Toluene diisocyanate (R,T)
U328	95-53-4	o-Toluidine
U353	106-49-0	p-Toluidine
U222	636-21-5	o-Toluidine hydrochloride
U011	61-82-5	1H-1,2,4-Triazol-3-amine
U227	79-00-5	1,1,2-Trichloroethane

[1] CAS Number given for parent compound only.

Hazardous waste No.	Chemical abstracts No.	Substance
U228	79-01-6	Trichloroethylene
U121	75-69-4	Trichloromonofluoromethane
See F027	95-95-4	2,4,5-Trichlorophenol
See F027	88-06-2	2,4,6-Trichlorophenol
U234	99-35-4	1,3,5-Trinitrobenzene (R,T)
U182	123-63-7	1,3,5-Trioxane, 2,4,6-trimethyl-
U235	126-72-7	Tris(2,3-dibromopropyl) phosphate
U236	72-57-1	Trypan blue
U237	66-75-1	Uracil mustard
U176	759-73-9	Urea, N-ethyl-N-nitroso-
U177	684-93-5	Urea, N-methyl-N-nitroso-
U043	75-01-4	Vinyl chloride
U248	[1] 81-81-2	Warfarin, & salts, when present at concentrations of 0.3% or less
U239	1330-20-7	Xylene (I)
U200	50-55-5	Yohimban-16-carboxylic acid, 11,17-dimethoxy-18-[(3,4,5-trimethoxybenzoyl)oxy]-, methyl ester, (3beta,16beta,17alpha,18beta,20alpha)-
U249	1314-84-7	Zinc phosphide Zn₃P₂, when present at concentrations of 10% or less

DISCARDED COMMERCIAL CHEMICAL PRODUCTS—
Acutely Hazardous Wastes

The following commercial chemical products or manufacturing chemical intermediates are hazardous wastes if they are discarded or intended for discard, and include off-specification variants and the residue and debris from the cleanup of spills of these chemicals. These chemicals also are considered hazardous when they are mixed with waste oil or used oil or other material and applied to the land for dust suppression or road treatment (see *BNA's Chemical Substances Control* beginning at p. 241:501 for more information).

A substance having the generic name listed herein is considered to be acutely hazardous if discarded and is subject to the small quantity generator exclusion as defined in the chapter beginning at p. 241:971.

The primary hazardous properties of these substances are indicated by the letters T (toxicity) and R (reactivity). Absence of a letter indicates that the compound only is listed for acute toxicity.

(List begins next page)

Hazardous waste No.	Chemical abstracts No.	Substance	Hazardous waste No.	Chemical abstracts No.	Substance
P023	107-20-0	Acetaldehyde, chloro-	P018	357-57-3	Brucine
P002	591-08-2	Acetamide, N-(aminothioxomethyl)	P045	39196-18-4	2-Butanone, 3,3-dimethyl-1-(methylamino)-0-[methylamino)carbonyl] oxime
P057	640-19-7	Acetamide, 2-fluoro-	P021	592-01-6	Calcium cyanide
P068	62-74-8	Acetic acid, fluoro-sodium salt	P021	592-01-8	Calcium cyanide (Ca(CN)
P002	591-08-2	1 Acetyl-2-thiourea	P022	75-15-0	Carbon disulfide
P003	107-02-8	Acrotein	P095	75-44-5	Carbonic dichloride
P070	116-06-3	Aldicard	P023	107-20-0	Chloroacetaldehyde
P004	309-00-2	Aldrin	P024	106-47-8	p-Chloroaniline
P005	107-18-6	Allyl alcohol	P026	5344-82-1	1-(o-Chlorophenyl)thiourea
P006	20859-73-8	Aluminum phosphide (R,1)	P027	542-76-7	3-Chloropropionitrile
P007	2763-96-4	5-(Aminomethyl)-3-isoxazolol	P029	544-92-3	Copper cyanide
P008	604-24-5	4-Aminopyridine	P029	544-92-3	Copper cyanide Cu(CN)
P009	131-74-8	Ammonium picrate (R)	P030		Cyanides (soluble cyanide salts), not otherwise specified
P119	7803-55-6	Ammonium vanadate			
P099	506-61-6	Argentate(1-), bis(cyano-C) potassium	P031	460-19-5	Cyanogen
P010	7778-39-4	Arsenic acid H_3AsO_4	P033	506-77-4	Cyanogen chloride
P012	1327-53-3	Arsenic oxide As_2O_3	P033	506-77-4	Cyanogen chloride (CN)Cl
P011	1303-28-2	Arsenic oxide As_2O_5	P034	131-89-5	2-Cyclohexyl-4, 6-dinitrophenol
P011	1303-28-2	Arsenic pentoxide	P016	542-88-1	Dichloromethyl ether
P012	1327-53-23	Arsenic trioxide	P036	696-28-6	Dichlorophenylarsine
P038	692-42-2	Arsine, diethyl-	P037	60-57-1	Dieldrin
P036	696-28-6	Arsenous dichloride, phenyl-	P038	692-42-2	Diethylarsine
P054	151-56-4	Azindine	P041	311-45-5	Diethyl-p-nitrophenyl phosphate
P007	75-55-8	Azindine, 2-methyl-	P040	297-97-2	O, O-Diethyl O-pyrazinyl phosphorothioate
P013	542-62-1	Barium cyanide			
P024	106-47-8	Benzenamine, 4-chloro-	P043	55-91-4	Diisopropylfluorophosphate (DFP)
P077	100-01-6	Benzenamine, 4-nitro-	P004	309-00-2	1,4,5,8-Dimethanonaphthalene, 1,2,3,4,10,10-hexachloro-1,4,4a,5,8,8a,-hexahydro-,-(1alpha, 4alpha, 4abeta, 5alpha, 8alpha, 8abeta)-
P028	100-44-7	Benzene, (chloromethyl)-			
P042	51-43-4	1,2 Benzenediol, 4-[1-hydroxy-2-methlytaminolethyl]-,(R)-			
P046	122-09-8	Benzeneethanamine, alpha, alpha-dimethyl	P060	465-73-6	1,4,5,8-Dimethanonaphthalene, 1,2,3,4,10,10-hexachloro-1,4,4a,5,8,8a,-hexahydro-,-(1alpha, 4alpha, 4abeta, 5beta, 8beta, 8abeta)-
P014	108-98-5	Benzenethiol			
P001	181-81-2	2H-1-Benzopyran-2-one, 4-hydroxy-3-(3-oxo-1-phenyl-butyl), & salts, when present at concentrations greater than 0.3%	P037	60-57-1	2,7:3,6-Dimethanonaphthl 2,3-bjoxirene, 3,4,5,6,9,9-hexachloro-1a,2,2a,3,6,6a,7,7a -octahydro-, (1aalpha, 2beta, 2aalpha, 3beta, 6beta, 6aalpha, 7beta, 7aalpha)-
P028	100-44-7	Benzyl chloride			
P015	7440-41-7	Beryllium			
P017	598-31-2	Bromoacetone			

Appendix B: Hazardous Waste Tables

Hazardous waste No.	Chemical abstracts No.	Substance	Hazardous waste No.	Chemical abstracts No.	Substance
P051	72-20-8	2,7,3,6-Dimethanonaphth [2,3-b]oxirene, 3,4,5,6,9,9-hexachloro-1a,2,2a,3,6,6a,7,7a-octahydro-, (1aalpha, 2beta, 2abeta, 3alpha, 6alpha, 6abeta, 7beta, 7aalpha)-, & metabolites	P082	62-75-9	Methanamine, N-methyl-N-nitroso-
			P064	624-83-9	Methane, isocyanato-
			P016	542-88-1	Methane, oxybis(chloro-
			P112	509-14-8	Methane, tetranitro-(R)
			P118	75-70-7	Methanethiol, trichloro-
			P050	115-29-7	6,9-Methano-2,4,3-benzodioxathiepin, 6,7,8,9,10,10-hexachloro-1,5,5a,6,9,9a-hexahydro-3-oxide
P044	60-51-5	Dimethoate	P059	76-44-8	4,7-Methano-1H-indene, 1,4,5,6,7,8,8-heptachloro-3a,4,7,7a-tetrahydro-
P046	122-09-8	alpha,alpha-Dimethylphenethylamine			
P047	534-52-1	4,6-Dinitro-o-cresol & salts			
P048	51-28-5	2,4-Dinitrophenol	P066	16752-77-5	Methomyl
P020	88-85-7	Dinoseb	P068	60-34-4	Methyl hydrazine
P085	152-16-9	Diphosphoramide, octamethyl	P064	624-83-9	Methyl isocyanate
P111	107-49-3	Diphosphoric acid, tetraethyl ester	P069	75-86-5	2-Methyllactonitrile
P039	298-04-4	Disulfoton	P071	298-00-0	Methyl parathion
P049	541-53-7	Dithiobiuret	P072	86-88-4	alpha-Naphthylthiourea
P050	115-29-7	Endosulfan	P073	13463-39-3	Nickel carbonyl
P088	145-73-3	Endothall	P073	13463-39-3	Nickel carbonyl Ni(CO)₄ (T-4)-
P051	72-20-8	Endrin, & metabolites	P074	557-19-7	Nickel cyanide
P051	72-20-8	Endrin	P074	557-19-7	Nickel cyanide Ni(CN)₂
P042	51-43-4	Epinephrine	P075	154-11-5	Nicotine, & salts
P031	460-19-5	Ethanedinitrile	P076	10102-43-9	Nitric oxide
P066	16752-77-5	Ethanimidothioic acid, N(methylamino)carbonyltoxyl, methyl ester	P077	100-01-6	p-Nitroaniline
			P078	10102-44-0	Nitrogen dioxide
			P076	10102-43-9	Nitrogen oxide NO
			P078	10102-44-0	Nitrogen oxide NO₂
P101	107-12-0	Ethyl cyanide	P081	55-63-0	Nitroglycerine (R)
P054	151-66-4	Ethyleneimine	P082	62-75-9	N-Nitrosodimethylamine
P097	52-65-7	Famphur	P084	4549-40-0	N-Nitrosomethylvinylamine
P056	7782-41-4	Fluorine	P085	152-16-9	Octamethylpyrophosphoramide
P057	640-19-7	Fluoroacetamide	P087	20816-12-0	Osmium oxide OsO₄ (T-4)-
P058	62-74-8	Fluoroacetic acid, sodium salt	P087	20816-12-0	Osmium tetroxide
P065	628-86-4	Fulminic acid, mercury(2) salt (R,T)	P088	145-73-3	7-Oxabicyclo[2.2.1]heptane-2,3-dicarboxylic acid
P059	76-44-8	Heptachlor			
P062	767-58-4	Hexaethyl tetraphosphate	P089	56-88-2	Parathion
P116	79-19-6	Hydrazinecarbothioamide	P034	131-89-5	Phenol, 2-cyclohexyl-4,6-dinitro-
P068	60-34-4	Hydrazine, methyl	P048	51-28-5	Phenol, 2,4-dinitro-
P063	74-90-8	Hydrocyanic acid	P047	1534-52-1	Phenol, 2-methyl-4,6-dinitro-, & salts
P063	74-90-8	Hydrogen cyanide	P020	88-85-7	Phenol, 2-(1-methylpropyl)-4,6-dinitro-
P096	7803-51-2	Hydrogen phosphide	P009	131-74-8	Phenol, 2,4,6-trinitro-, ammonium salt (R)
P060	465-73-6	Isodrian			
P007	2763-96-4	3(2H)-Isoxazolone, 5-(aminomethyl)			
P092	62-38-4	Mercury (acetate-O)phenyl-			
P065	628-66-4	Mercury fulminate (R,T)			

Waste Management Guide

Hazardous waste No.	Chemical abstracts No.	Substance	Hazardous waste No.	Chemical abstracts No.	Substance
P092	62-38-4	Phenylmercury acetate	P114	12039-52-0	Selenious acid, dithallium(1+) salt
P093	103-85-5	Phenylthiourea			
P094	298-02-2	Phorate	P103	630-10-4	Selenourea
P095	75-44-5	Phosgene	P104	506-64-9	Silver cyanide
P096	7803-51-2	Phosphine	P104	506-64-9	Silver cyanide Ag(CN)
P041	311-45-5	Phosphoric acid, diethyl 4-nitrophenyl ester	P105	26628-22-8	Sodium azide
P039	298-04-4	Phosphorodithioic acid, O,O-diethyl S-[2-(ethylthio)ethyl] ester	P106	143-33-9	Sodium cyanide
			P106	143-33-9	Sodium cyanide Na(CN)
P094	298-02-2	Phosphorodithioic acid, O,O-diethyl S-[(ethylthio)methyl] ester	P108	157-24-9	Strychnidin-10-one, & salts
			P018	357-57-3	Strychnidin-10-one, 2,3-dimethoxy-
P044	60-51-5	Phosphorodithioic acid, O,O-dimethyl S-[2-(methyl-amino)-2-oxoethyl] ester	P108	157-24-9	Strychnine, & salts
			P115	7446-18-6	Sulfuric acid, dithallium(1+) salt
P043	55-91-4	Phosphorodithioic acid, bis(1-methylethyl) ester	P109	3689-24-5	Tetraethyldithiopyrophosphate
			P110	78-00-2	Tetraethyl lead
P089	56-38-2	Phosphorodithioic acid, O,O-diethyl O-(4-nitrophenyl) ester	P111	107-49-3	Tetraethyl pyrophosphate
			P112	509-14-8	Tetranitromethane (R)
P040	297-97-2	Phosphorothioic acid, O,O-diethyl O-pyrazinyl ester	P062	757-58-4	Tetraphosphoric acid, hexaethyl ester
			P113	1314-32-5	Thallic oxide
P097	52-85-7	Phosphorothioic acid, O-[4](dimethylamino)sulfonyl[phenyl]O,O-dimethyl ester	P113	1314-32-5	Thallium oxide Tl$_2$O$_3$
			P114	12039-52-0	Thallium(I) selenite
			P115	7446-18-6	Thallium(I) sulfate
P071	298-00-0	Phosphorothioic acid, O,O-dimethyl O-(4-nitrophenyl) ester	P109	3689-24-5	Thiodiphosphoric acid, tetraethyl ester
P110	78-00-2	Plumbane, tetraethyl-	P045	39196-18-4	Thiofanox
P098	151-50-8	Potassium cyanide	P049	541-53-7	Thioimidodicarbonic diamide [(H$_2$N)C(S)]$_2$NH
P098	151-50-8	Potassium cyanide K(CN)			
P099	506-61-6	Potassium silver cyanide	P014	108-98-5	Thiophenol
P070	116-06-3	Propanal, 2-methyl-2-(methylthio)-, O-[(methylamino)carbonyl]oxime	P116	79-19-6	Thiosemicarbazide
			P026	5344-82-1	Thiourea, (2-chlorophenyl)-
P101	107-12-0	Propanenitrile	P072	86-88-4	Thiourea, 1-naphthalenyl-
P027	542-76-7	Propanenitrile, 3-chloro-	P093	103-85-5	Thiourea, phenyl-
P069	75-86-5	Propanenitrile, 2-hydroxy-2-methyl-	P123	8001-35-2	Toxaphene
P081	55-63-0	1,2,3-Propanetriol, trinitrate (R)	P118	75-70-7	Trichloromethanethiol
P017	598-31-2	2-Propanone, 1-bromo-	P119	7803-55-6	Vanadic acid, ammonium salt
P102	107-19-7	Propargyl alcohol	P120	1314-62-1	Vanadium oxide V$_2$O$_5$
P003	107-02-8	2-Propenal	P120	1314-62-1	Vanadium pentoxide
P005	107-18-6	2-Propen-1-ol	P084	4549-40-0	Vinylamine, N-methyl-N-nitroso-
P067	75-55-8	1,2-Propylenimine	P001	181-81-2	Warfarin, & salts, when present at concentrations greater than 0.3%
P102	107-19-7	2-Propyn-1-ol			
P008	504-24-5	4-Pyridinamine	P121	557-21-1	Zinc cyanide
P075	154-11-5	Pyridine, 3-(1-methyl-2-pyrrolidinyl)-, (S)-, & salts	P121	557-21-1	Zinc cyanide ZN(CN)$_2$
			P122	1314-84-7	Zinc phosphide Zn$_3$P$_2$, when present at concentrations greater than 10% (R,T)

BASIS FOR LISTING HAZARDOUS WASTES

EPA hazardous waste No.	Hazardous constituents for which listed
F001	Tetrachloroethylene, methylene chloride, trichloroethylene, 1,1,1-trichloroethane, carbon tetrachloride, chlorinated fluorocarbons.
F002	Tetrachloroethylene, methylene chloride, trichloroethylene, 1,1,1-trichloroethane, 1,1,2-trichloroethane, chlorobenzene, 1,1,2-trichloro-1,2,2-trifluoroethane, ortho-dichlorobenzene, trichlorofluoromethane.[8]
F003	N.A.
F004	Cresols and cresylic acid, nitrobenzene.
F005	Toluene, methyl ethyl ketone, carbon disulfide, isobutanol, pyridine, 2-ethoxyethanol, benzene, 2-nitropropane.[8]
F006	Cadmium, hexavalent chromium, nickel, cyanide (complexed).
F007	Cyanide (salts).
F008	Cyanide (salts).
F009	Cyanide (salts).
F010	Cyanide (salts).
F011	Cyanide (salts).
F012	Cyanide (complexed).
F019	Hexavalent chromium, cyanide (complexed).
F020	Tetra- and pentachlorodibenzo-p-dioxins; tetra and pentachlorodi-benzofurans; tri- and tetrachlorophenols and their chlorophenoxy derivative acids, esters, ethers, amine and other salts.
F021	Penta- and hexachlorodibenzo-p-dioxins; penta- and hexachlorodibenzofurans; pentachlorophenol and its derivatives.
F022	Tetra-, penta-, and hexachlorodibenzo-p-dioxins; tetra-, penta-, and hexachlorodibenzofurans.
F023	Tetra-, and pentachlorodibenzo-p-dioxins: tetra- and pentachlorodibenzofurans; tri- and tetrachlorophenols and their chlorophenoxy derivative acids, esters, ethers, amine and other salts.
F024	Chloromethane, dichloromethane, trichloromethane, carbon tetrachloride, chloroethylene, 1,1-dichloroethane, 1,2-dichloroethane, trans-1-2-dichloroethylene, 1,1-dichloroethylene, 1,1,1-trichloroethane, 1,1,2-trichloroethane, trichloroethylene, 1,1,1,2-tetrachloroethane, 1,1,2,2-tetrachloroethane, tetrachloroethylene, pentachloroethane, hexachloroethane, allyl chloride (3-chloropropene), dichloropropane, dichloropropene, 2-chloro-1,3-butadiene, hexachloro-1,3-butadiene, hexachlorocyclopentadiene, hexachlorocyclohexane, benzene, chlorobenzene, dichlorobenzenes, 1,2,4-trichlorobenzene, tetrachlorobenzene, pentachlorobenzene, hexachlorobenzene, toluene, naphthalene
F025	Chloromethane, dichloromethane, trichloromethane, carbon tetrachloride, chloroethylene, 1,1-dichloroethane, 1,2-dichloroethane, trans-1,2-dichloroethylene, 1,1-dichloroethylene, 1,1,1-trichloroethane, 1,1,2-trichloroethane, trichloroethylene, 1,1,1,2-tetrachloroethane, 1,1,2,2,-tetrachloroethane, tetrachloroethylene, pentachloroethane, hexachloroethane, allyl chloride (3-chloropropene), dichloropropane, dichloropropene, 2-chloro-1,3-butadiene, hexachloro-1,3-butadiene, hexachlorocyclopentadiene, hexachlorocyclohexane, benzene, chlorobenzene, dichlorobenzenes, 1,2,4-trichlorobenzene, tetrachlorobenzene, pentachlorobenzene, hexachlorobenzene, toluene, naphthalene.

EPA hazardous waste No.	Hazardous constituents for which listed
F026	Tetra-, penta-, and hexachlorodibenzo-p-dioxins; tetra-, penta-, and hexachlorodibenzofurans.
F027	Tetra-, penta-, and hexachlorodibenzo-p-dioxins; tetra-, penta-, and hexachlorodibenzofurans; tri-, tetra-, and pentachlorophenols and their chlorophenoxy derivative acids, esters, ethers, amine and other salts.
F028	Tetra-, penta-, and hexachlorodibenzo-p-dioxins; tetra-, penta-, and hexachlorodibenzofurans; tri-, tetra-, and pentachlorophenols and their chlorophenoxy derivative acids, esters, ethers, amine and other salts.
F032	Benz(a)anthracene, benzo(a)pyrene, dibenz(a,h)anthracene, indeno(1,2,3-cd)pyrene, pentachlorophenol, arsenic, chromium, tetra-, penta-, hexa, heptachlorodibenzo-p-dioxins, tetra-, penta-, hexa-, heptachlorodibenzofurans.
F034	Benz(a)anthracene, benzo(k)fluoroanthene, benzo(a)pyrene, dibenz(a,h)anthracene, indeno(1,2,3-dc)pyrene, napthalene, arsenic, chromium.
F035	Arsenic, chromium, lead.
F037	Benzene, benzo(a)pyrene, chrysene, lead, chromium.[8]
F038	Benzene, benzo(a)pyrene, chrysene, lead, chromium.[8]
F039	All constituents for which treatment standards are specified for multi-source leachate (wastewaters and nonwastewaters) under 40 CFR 268.43(a), Table CCW.[7]
K001	Pentachlorophenol, phenol, 2-chlorophenol, p-chloro-m-cresol, 2,4-dimethylphenyl, 2,4-dinitrophenol, trichlorophenols, tetrachlorophenols, 2,4-dinitrophenol, creosote, chrysene, naphthalene, fluoranthene, benzo(b)fluoranthene, benzo(a)pyrene, indeno(1,2,3-cd)pyrene, benz(a)anthracene, dibenz(a)anthracene, acenaphthalene.
K002	Hexavalent chromium, lead.
K003	Hexavalent chromium, lead.

EPA hazardous waste No.	Hazardous constituents for which listed
K004	Hexavalent chromium.
K005	Hexavalent chromium, lead.
K006	Hexavalent chromium.
K007	Cyanide (complexed), hexavalent chromium.
K008	Hexavalent chromium.
K009	Chloroform, formaldehyde, methylene chloride, methyl chloride, paraldehyde, formic acid.
K010	Chloroform, formaldehyde, methylene chloride, methyl chloride, paraldehyde, formic acid, chloroacetaldehyde.
K011	Acrylonitrile, acetonitrile, hydrocyanic acid.
K013	Hydrocyanic acid, acrylonitrile, acetonitrile.
K014	Acetonitrile, acrylamide.
K015	Benzyl chloride, chlorobenzene, toluene, benzotrichloride.
K016	Hexachlorobenzene, hexachlorobutadiene, carbon tetrachloride, hexachloroethane, perchloroethylene.
K017	Epichlorohydrin, chloroethers [bis(chloromethyl) ether and bis (2-chloroethyl) ethers], trichloropropane, dichloropropanols.
K018	1,2-dichloroethane, trichloroethylene, hexachlorobutadiene, hexachlorobenzene.
K019	Ethylene dichloride, 1,1,1-trichloroethane, 1,1,2-trichloro ethane, tetrachloroethanes (1,1,2,2-tetrachloroethane and 1,1,1,2-tetrachloroethane), trichloroethylene, tetrachloroethylene, carbon tetrachloride, chloroform, vinyl chloride, vinylidene chloride.
K020	Ethylene dichloride, 1,1,1-trichloroethane, 1,1,2-trichloro ethane, tetrachloroethanes (1,1,2,2-tetrachloroethane and 1,1,1,2-tetrachloroethane), trichloroethylene, tetrachloroethylene, carbon tetrachloride, chloroform, vinyl chloride, vinylidene chloride.
K021	Antimony, carbon tetrachloride, chloroform.
K022	Phenol, tars (polycyclic aromatic hydrocarbons).
K023	Phthalic anhydride, maleic anhydride.
K024	Phthalic anhydride, 1,4-naphthoquinone.

EPA hazardous waste No.	Hazardous constituents for which listed
K025	Meta-dinitrobenzene, 2,4-dinitrotoluene.
K026	Paraldehyde, pyridines, 2-picoline.
K027	Toluene diisocyanate, toluene-2,4-diamine.
K028	1,1,1-trichloroethane, vinyl chloride.
K029	1,2-dichloroethane, 1,1,1-trichloroethane, vinyl chloride, vinylidene chloride, chloroform
K030	Hexachlorobenzene, hexachlorobutadiene, hexachloroethane, 1,1,1,2-tetrachloroethane, 1,1,2,2-tetrachloroethane, ethylene dichloride.
K031	Arsenic.
K032	Hexachlorocyclopentadiene.
K033	Hexachlorocyclopentadiene.
K034	Hexachlorocyclopentadiene.
K035	Creosote, chrysene, naphthalene, fluoranthene benzo(b) fluoranthene, benzo(a)pyrene, indeno(1,2,3-cd) pyrene, benzo(a)anthracene, dibenzo(a)anthracene, acenaphthalene.
K036	Toluene, phosphorodithioic and phosphoro-thioic acid esters.
K037	Toluene, phosphorodithioic and phosphoro-thioic acid esters.
K038	Phorate, formaldehyde, phosphorodithioic and phosphorothioic acid esters.
K039	Phosphorodithioic and phosphorothioic acid esters.
K040	Phorate, formaldehyde, phosphorodithioic and phosphorothioic acid esters.
K041	Toxaphene.
K042	Hexachlorobenzene, ortho-dichlorobenzene.
K043	2,4-dichlorophenol, 2,6-dichlorophenol, 2,4,6-trichlorophenol.
K044	N.A.
K045	N.A.
K046	Lead.
K047	N.A.
K048	Hexavalent chromium, lead.
K049	Hexavalent chromium, lead.
K050	Hexavalent chromium.
K051	Hexavalent chromium, lead.
K052	Lead.
K060	Cyanide, napthalene, phenolic compounds, arsenic.
K061	Hexavalent chromium, lead, cadmium.
K062	Hexavalent chromium, lead.
K064	Lead, cadmium.

EPA hazardous waste No.	Hazardous constituents for which listed
K065	Lead, cadmium.
K066	Lead, cadmium.
K069	Hexavalent chromium, lead, cadmium.
K071	Mercury.
K073	Chloroform, carbon tetrachloride, hexachloroethane, trichlorethane, tetrachloroethylene, dichloroethylene, 1,1,2,2-tetrachloroethane.
K083	Aniline, diphenylamine, nitrobenzene, phenylenediamine.
K084	Arsenic.
K085	Benzene, dichlorobenzenes, trichlorobenzenes, tetrachlorobenzenes, pentachlorobenzene, hexachlobenzene, benzyl chloride.
K086	Lead, hexavalent chromium.
K087	Phenol, naphtalene.
K088	Cyanide (complexes).
K090	Chromium.
K091	Chromium.
K093	Phtalic anhydride, maleic anhydride.
K094	Phtalic anhydride.
K095	1,1,2-trichloreothane, 1,1,1,2-tetrachloroethane 1,1,2,2-tetrachloroethane.
K096	1,2-dichloroethane, 1,1,1-trichloroethane, 1,1,2-trichloroethane.
K097	Chlordane, heptachlor.
K098	Toxaphene.
K099	2,4-dichlorophenol, 2,4,6-trichlorophenol.
K100	Hexavalent chromium, lead, cadmium.
K101	Arsenic.
K102	Arsenic.
K103	Aniline, nitrobenzene, phenylenediamine.
K104	Aniline, benzene, diphenylamine, nitrobenzene, phenylenediamine.
K105	Benzene, monochlorobenzene, dichlorobenzenes, 2,4,6-trichlorophenol.
K106	Mercury.
K107	1,1-Dimethylhydrazine (UDMH).[6]
K108	1,1-Dimethylhydrazine (UDMH).[6]
K109	1,1-Dimethylhydrazine (UDMH).[6]
K110	1,1-Dimethylhydrazine (UDMH).[6]
K111	2,4-Dinitrotoluene.[1]
K112	2,4-Toluenediamine, o-toluidine, p-toluidine, aniline.[1]

EPA hazardous waste No.	Hazardous constituents for which listed
K113	2,4-Toluenediamine, *o*-toluidine, *p*-toluidine, aniline.[1]
K114	2,4-Toluenediamine, *o*-toluidine, *p*-toluidine.
K115	2,4-Toluenediamine.[1]
K116	Carbon tetrachloride, tetrachloroethylene, chloroform, phosgene.[1]
K117	Ethylene dibromide.[2]
K118	Ethylene dibromide.[2]
K123	Ethylene thiourea.[4]
K124	Ethylene thiourea.[4]
K125	Ethylene thiourea.[4]
K126	Ethylene thiourea.[4]
K131	Dimethyl sulfate, Methyl bromide.[5]
K132	Methyl bromide.[5]
K136	Ethylene dibromide.[2]

[1] 50 FR 42936, Oct. 23, 1985, effective April 23, 1986.
[2] 51 FR 5327, Feb. 13, 1986, effective Aug. 13, 1986.
[3] 51 FR 6537, Feb. 25, 1986, effective Aug. 25, 1986.
[4] 51 FR 37725, Oct. 24, 1986.
[5] 54 FR 41402, Oct. 6, 1989, effective April 6, 1990.
[6] 55 FR 18496, May 2, 1990, effective Nov. 2, 1990.
[7] 55 FR 22520, June 1, 1990, effective May 8, 1990.
[8] 55 FR 46354, Nov. 2, 1990, effective May 2, 1991.

N.A. — Waste is hazardous because it fails the test for the characteristic of ignitability, corrosivity, or reactivity.

LIST OF HAZARDOUS CONSTITUENTS

The following list of hazardous constituents have been shown in reputable scientific studies to have toxic, carcinogenic, mutagenic, or teratogenic effects on humans or other life forms, and include substances identified as carcinogens by EPA's Carcinogen Assessment Group.

(List begins next page)

Waste Management Guide

Common name	Chemical abstracts name	Chemical abstracts No.	Hazardous waste No.
Acetonitrile	Same	75-05-8	U003
Acetophenone	Ethanone, 1-phenyl-	98-86-2	U004
2-Acetylaminofluarone	Acetamide, N-9H-fluoren-2-yl-	53-96-3	U005
Acetyl chloride	Same	75-36-5	U006
1-Acetyl-2-thiourea	Acetamide, N-(aminothioxomethyl)-	591-08-2	P002
Acrolein	2-Propenal	107-02-8	P003
Acrylamide	2-Propenamide	79-06-1	U007
Acrylonitrile	2-Propenenitrile	107-13-1	U009
Aflatoxins	Same	1402-68-2	
Aldicarb	Propanal, 2-methyl-2-(methylthio)-, O-[(methylamino)carbonyl]oxime	116-06-3	P070
Aldrin	1,4,5,8-Dimethanonaphthalene, 1,2,3,4,10,10-hexachloro-1,4,4a,5,8,8a-hexahydro-, (1alpha,4alpha,4abeta,5alpha,8alpha,8abeta)-	309-00-2	P004
Allyl alcohol	2-Propen-1-ol	107-18-6	P005
Aluminum phosphide	Same	20859-73-8	P006
4-Aminobiphenyl	[1,1'-Biphenyl]-4-amine	92-67-1	
5-(Aminomethyl)-3-isoxazolol	3(2H)-Isoxazolone, 5-(aminomethyl)-	2763-96-4	P007
4-Aminopyridine	4-Pyridinamine	504-24-5	P008
Amitrole	1H-1,2,4-Triazol-3-amine	61-82-5	U011
Ammonium vanadate	Vanadic acid, ammonium salt	7803-55-6	P119
Aniline	Benzenamine	62-53-3	U012
Antimony	Same	7440-36-0	
Antimony compounds, N.O.S.[1]			
Aramite	Sulfurous acid, 2-chloroethyl 2-[4-(1,1-dimethylethyl)phenoxy]-1-methylethyl ester	140-57-8	
Arsenic	Same	7440-38-2	
Arsenic compounds, N.O.S.[1]			
Arsenic acid	Arsenic acid H₃AsO₄	7778-39-4	P010
Arsenic pentoxide	Arsenic oxide As₂O₅	1303-28-2	P011
Arsenic trioxide	Arsenic oxide As₂O₃	1327-53-3	P012
Auramine	Benzenamine, 4,4'-carbonimidoylbis[N,N-dimethyl	492-80-8	U014
Azaserine	L-Serine, diazoacetate (ester)	115-02-6	U015
Barium	Same	7440-39-3	
Barium compounds, N.O.S.[1]			
Barium cyanide	Same	542-62-1	P013
Benz[c]acridine	Same	225-51-4	U016
Benz[a]anthracene	Same	56-55-3	U018
Benzal chloride	Benzene, (dichloromethyl)-	98-87-3	U017
Benzene	Same	71-43-2	U019
Benzenearsonic acid	Arsonic acid, phenyl-	98-05-5	
Benzidine	[1,1'-Biphenyl]-4,4'-diamine	92-87-5	U021
Benzo[b]fluoranthene	Benz[e]acephenanthrylene	205-99-2	

Appendix B: Hazardous Waste Tables 353

Benzo[j]fluoranthene	Same	205-82-3	
Benzo[a]pyrene	Same	50-32-8	U022
p-Benzoquinone	2,5-Cyclohexadiene-1,4-dione	106-51-4	U197
Benzotrichloride	Benzene, (trichloromethyl)-	98-07-7	U023
Benzyl chloride	Benzene, (chloromethyl)-	100-44-7	P028
Beryllium	Same	7440-41-7	P015
Beryllium compounds, N.O.S.[1]			
Bromoacetone	2-Propanone, 1-bromo-	598-31-2	P017
Bromoform	Methane, tribromo-	75-25-2	U225
4-Bromophenyl phenyl ether	Benzene, 1-bromo-4-phenoxy-	101-55-3	U030
Brucine	Strychnidin-10-one, 2,3-dimethoxy-	357-57-3	P018
Butyl benzyl phthalate	1,2-Benzenedicarboxylic acid, butyl phenylmethyl ester	85-68-7	
Cacodylic acid	Arsinic acid, dimethyl-	75-60-5	U136
Cadmium	Same	7440-43-9	
Cadmium compounds, N.O.S.[1]			
Calcium chromate	Chromic acid H$_2$CrO$_4$, calcium salt	13765-19-0	U032
Calcium cyanide	Calcium cyanide Ca(CN)$_2$	592-01-8	P021
Carbon disulfide	Same	75-15-0	P022
Carbon oxyfluoride	Carbonic difluoride	353-50-4	U033
Carbon tetrachloride	Methane, tetrachloro-	56-23-5	U211
Chloral	Acetaldehyde, trichloro-	75-87-6	U034
Chlorambucil	Benzenebutanoic acid, 4-[bis(2-chloroethyl)amino]-	305-03-3	U035
Chlordane	4,7-Methano-1H-indene, 1,2,4,5,6,7,8,8-octachloro-2,3,3a,4,7,7a-hexahydro-	57-74-9	U036
Chlordane (alpha and gamma isomers)			
Chlorinated benzenes, N.O.S.[1]			
Chlorinated ethane, N.O.S.[1]			
Chlorinated fluorocarbons, N.O.S.[1]			
Chlorinated naphthalene, N.O.S.[1]			
Chlorinated phenol, N.O.S.[1]			
Chlornaphazin	Naphthalenamine, N,N'-bis(2-chloroethyl)-	494-03-1	U026
Chloroacetaldehyde	Acetaldehyde, chloro-	107-20-0	P023
Chloroalkyl ethers, N.O.S.[1]			
p-Chloroaniline	Benzenamine, 4-chloro-	106-47-8	P024
Chlorobenzene	Benzene, chloro-	108-90-7	U037
Chlorobenzilate	Benzeneacetic acid, 4-chloro-alpha-(4-chlorophenyl)-alpha-hydroxy-, ethyl ester	510-15-6	U038

Common name	Chemical abstracts name	Chemical abstracts No.	Hazardous waste No.
p-Chloro-m-cresol	Phenol, 4-chloro-3-methyl-	59-50-7	U039
2-Chloroethyl vinyl ether	Ethene, (2-chloroethoxy)-	110-75-8	U042
Chloroform	Methane, trichloro-	67-66-3	U044
Chloromethyl methyl ether	Methane, chloromethoxy-	107-30-2	U046
beta-Chloronaphthalene	Naphthalene, 2-chloro-	91-58-7	U047
o-Chlorophenol	Phenol, 2-chloro-	95-57-8	U048
1-(o-Chlorophenyl)thiourea	Thiourea, (2-chlorophenyl)-	5344-82-1	P026
Chloroprene	1,3-Butadiene, 2-chloro-	126-99-8	
3-Chloropropionitrile	Propanenitrile, 3-chloro-	542-76-7	P027
Chromium	Same	7440-47-3	
Chromium compounds, N.O.S.¹			
Chrysene	Same	218-01-9	U050
Citrus red No. 2	2-Naphthalenol, 1-[(2,5-dimethoxyphenyl)azo]-	6358-53-8	
Coal tar creosote	Same	8007-45-2	
Copper cyanide	Copper cyanide CuCN.	544-92-3	P029
Creosote	Same		U051
Cresol (Cresylic acid)	Phenol, methyl-	1319-77-3	U052
Crotonaldehyde	2-Butenal	4170-30-3	U053
Cyanides (soluble salts and complexes) N.O.S.¹			P030
Cyanogen	Ethanedinitrile.	460-19-5	P031
Cyanogen bromide	Cyanogen bromide (CN)Br.	506-68-3	U246
Cyanogen chloride	Cyanogen chloride (CN)Cl.	506-77-4	P033
Cycasin	beta-D-Glucopyranoside, (methyl-ONN-azoxy)methyl	14901-08-7	
2-Cyclohexyl-4,6-dinitrophenol	Phenol, 2-cyclohexyl-4,6-dinitro-	131-89-5	P034
Cyclophosphamide	2H-1,3,2-Oxazaphosphorin-2-amine, N,N-bis(2-chloroethyl)tetrahydro-, 2-oxide	50-18-0	U058
2,4-D	Acetic acid, (2,4-dichlorophenoxy)-	94-75-7	U240
2,4-D, salts, esters			U240
Daunomycin	5,12-Naphthacenedione, 8-acetyl-10-[(3-amino-2,3,6-trideoxy-alpha-L-lyxo-hexopyranosyl)oxy]-7,8,9,10-tetrahydro-6,8,11-trihydroxy-1-methoxy-, (8S-cis)-	20830-81-3	U059
DDD	Benzene, 1,1'-(2,2-dichloroethylidene)bis[4-chloro-	72-54-8	U060
DDE	Benzene, 1,1'-(dichloroethenylidene)bis[4-chloro-	72-55-9	
DDT	Benzene, 1,1'-(2,2,2-trichloroethylidene)bis[4-chloro-	50-29-3	U061
Dialate	Carbamothioic acid, bis(1-methylethyl)-, S-(2,3-dichloro-2-propenyl) ester	2303-16-4	U062
Dibenz[a,h]acridine	Same	226-36-8	
Dibenz[a,j]acridine	Same	224-42-0	

Appendix B: Hazardous Waste Tables

Name	Synonym	CAS No.	Waste Code
Dibenz[a,h]anthracene	Same	53-70-3	U063
7H-Dibenzo[c,g]carbazole	Same	194-59-2	
Dibenzo[a,e]pyrene	Naphtho[1,2,3,4-def]chrysene	192-65-4	
Dibenzo[a,h]pyrene	Dibenzo[b,def]chrysene	189-64-0	
Dibenzo[a,i]pyrene	Benzo[rst]pentaphene	189-55-9	U064
1,2-Dibromo-3-chloropropane	Propane, 1,2-dibromo-3-chloro-	96-12-8	U066
Dibutyl phthalate	1,2-Benzenedicarboxylic acid, dibutyl ester	84-74-2	U069
o-Dichlorobenzene	Benzene, 1,2-dichloro-	95-50-1	U070
m-Dichlorobenzene	Benzene, 1,3-dichloro-	541-73-1	U071
p-Dichlorobenzene	Benzene, 1,4-dichloro-	106-46-7	U072
Dichlorobenzene, N.O.S.[1]	Benzene, dichloro-	25321-22-6	
3,3'-Dichlorobenzidine	[1,1'-Biphenyl]-4,4'-diamine, 3,3'-dichloro-	91-94-1	U073
1,4-Dichloro-2-butene	2-Butene, 1,4-dichloro-	764-41-0	U074
Dichlorodifluoromethane	Methane, dichlorodifluoro-	75-71-8	U075
Dichloroethylene, N.O.S.[1]	Dichloroethylene	25323-30-2	
1,1-Dichloroethylene	Ethene, 1,1-dichloro-	75-35-4	U078
1,2-Dichloroethylene	Ethene, 1,2-dichloro-, (E)-	156-60-5	U079
Dichloroethyl ether	Ethane, 1,1'-oxybis[2-chloro-	111-44-4	U025
Dichloroisopropyl ether	Propane, 2,2'-oxybis[2-chloro-	108-60-1	U027
Dichloromethoxy ethane	Ethane, 1,1'-[methylenebis(oxy)]bis[2-chloro-	111-91-1	U024
Dichloromethyl ether	Methane, oxybis[chloro-	542-88-1	P016
2,4-Dichlorophenol	Phenol, 2,4-dichloro-	120-83-2	U081
2,6-Dichlorophenol	Phenol, 2,6-dichloro-	87-65-0	U082
Dichlorophenylarsine	Arsonous dichloride, phenyl-	696-28-6	P036
Dichloropropane, N.O.S.[1]	Propane, dichloro-	26638-19-7	
Dichloropropanol, N.O.S.[1]	Propanol, dichloro-	26545-73-3	
Dichloropropene, N.O.S.[1]	1-Propene, dichloro-	26952-23-8	
1,3-Dichloropropene	1-Propene, 1,3-dichloro-	542-75-6	U084
Dieldrin	2,7:3,6-Dimethanonaphth[2,3-b]oxirene, 3,4,5,6,9,9-hexachloro-1a,2,2a,3,6,6a,7,7a-octahydro-, (1aalpha,2beta,2aalpha,3beta,6beta,6aalpha,7beta,7aalpha)-	60-57-1	P037
1,2,3,4-Diepoxybutane	2,2'Bioxirane	1464-53-5	U085
Diethylarsine	Arsine, diethyl-	692-42-2	P038
1,4-Diethyleneoxide	1,4-Dioxane	123-91-1	U108
Diethylhexyl phthalate	1,2-Benzenedicarboxylic acid, bis(2-ethylhexyl) ester	117-81-7	U028
N,N-Diethylhydrazine	Hydrazine, 1,2-diethyl-	1615-80-1	U086
O,O-Diethyl S-methyl dithiophosphate	Phosphorodithioic acid, O,O-diethyl S-methyl ester	3288-58-2	U087
Diethyl-p-nitrophenyl phosphate	Phosphoric acid, diethyl 4-nitrophenyl ester	311-45-5	P041
Diethyl phthalate	1,2-Benzenedicarboxylic acid, diethyl ester	84-66-2	U088
O,O-Diethyl O-pyrazinyl phosphorothioate	Phosphorothioic acid, O,O-diethyl O-pyrazinyl ester	297-97-2	P040
Diethylstilbesterol	Phenol, 4,4'-(1,2-diethyl-1,2-ethenediyl)bis-, (E)-	56-53-1	U089
Dihydrosafrole	1,3-Benzodioxole, 5-propyl-	94-58-6	U090
Diisopropylfluorophosphate (DFP)	Phosphorofluoridic acid, bis(1-methylethyl) ester	55-91-4	P043

356 Waste Management Guide

Common name	Chemical abstracts name	Chemical abstracts No.	Hazardous waste No
Dimethoate	Phosphorodithioic acid, O,O-dimethyl S-[2-(methylamino)-2-oxoethyl] ester	60-51-5	P044
3,3'-Dimethoxybenzidine	[1,1'-Biphenyl]-4,4'-diamine, 3,3'-dimethoxy-	119-90-4	U091
p-Dimethylaminoazobenzene	Benzenamine, N,N-dimethyl-4-(phenylazo)-	60-11-7	U093
7,12-Dimethylbenz[a]anthracene	Benz[a]anthracene, 7,12-dimethyl-	57-97-6	U094
3,3'-Dimethylbenzidine	[1,1'-Biphenyl]-4,4'-diamine, 3,3'-dimethyl-	119-93-7	U095
Dimethylcarbamoyl chloride	Carbamic chloride, dimethyl-	79-44-7	U097
1,1-Dimethylhydrazine	Hydrazine, 1,1-dimethyl-	57-14-7	U098
1,2-Dimethylhydrazine	Hydrazine, 1,2-dimethyl-	540-73-8	U099
alpha,alpha-Dimethylphenethylamine	Benzeneethanamine, alpha,alpha-dimethyl-	122-09-8	PC46
2,4-Dimethylphenol	Phenol, 2,4-dimethyl-	105-67-9	U101
Dimethyl phthalate	1,2-Benzenedicarboxylic acid, dimethyl ester	131-11-3	U102
Dimethyl sulfate	Sulfuric acid, dimethyl ester	77-78-1	U103
Dinitrobenzene, N.O.S.[1]	Benzene, dinitro-	25154-54-5	
4,6-Dinitro-o-cresol	Phenol, 2-methyl-4,6-dinitro-	534-52-1	P047
4,6-Dinitro-o-cresol salts			P047
2,4-Dinitrophenol	Phenol, 2,4-dinitro-	51-28-5	P048
2,4-Dinitrotoluene	Benzene, 1-methyl-2,4-dinitro-	121-14-2	U105
2,6-Dinitrotoluene	Benzene, 2-methyl-1,3-dinitro-	606-20-2	U106
Dinoseb	Phenol, 2-(1-methylpropyl)-4,6-dinitro-	88-85-7	P020
Di-n-octyl phthalate	1,2-Benzenedicarboxylic acid, dioctyl ester	117-84-0	U017
Diphenylamine	Benzenamine, N-phenyl-	122-39-4	
1,2-Diphenylhydrazine	Hydrazine, 1,2-diphenyl-	122-66-7	U109
Di-n-propylnitrosamine	1-Propanamine, N-nitroso-N-propyl-	621-64-7	U111
Disulfoton	Phosphorodithioic acid, O,O-diethyl S-[2-(ethylthio)ethyl] ester	298-04-4	P039
Dithiobiuret	Thioimidodicarbonic diamide [(H₂N)C(S)]₂NH	541-53-7	P049
Endosulfan	6,9-Methano-2,4,3-benzodioxathiepin, 6,7,8,9,10,10-hexachloro-1,5,5a,6,9,9a-hexahydro-, 3-oxide	115-29-7	P050
Endothall	7-Oxabicyclo[2.2.1]heptane-2,3-dicarboxylic acid	145-73-3	P088
Endrin	2,7,3,6-Dimethanonaphth[2,3-b]oxirene, 3,4,5,6,9,9-hexachloro-1a,2,2a,3,6,6a,7,7a-octahydro-, (1aalpha,2beta,2abeta,3alpha,6alpha,6abeta,7beta,7aalpha)-	72-20-8	P051
Endrin metabolites			P051
Epichlorohydrin	Oxirane, (chloromethyl)-	106-89-8	U041
Epinephrine	1,2-Benzenediol, 4-[1-hydroxy-2-(methylamino)ethyl]-, (R)-	51-43-4	P042
Ethyl carbamate (urethane)	Carbamic acid, ethyl ester	51-79-6	U238
Ethyl cyanide	Propanenitrile	107-12-0	P101
Ethylenebisdithiocarbamic acid	Carbamodithioic acid, 1,2-ethanediylbis-	111-54-6	U114
Ethylenebisdithiocarbamic acid, salts and esters			U114
Ethylene dibromide	Ethane, 1,2-dibromo-	106-93-4	U067

Appendix B: Hazardous Waste Tables

Ethylene dichloride	Ethane, 1,2-dichloro-	107-06-2	U077
Ethylene glycol monoethyl ether	Ethanol, 2-ethoxy-	110-80-5	U359
Ethyleneimine	Aziridine	151-56-4	P054
Ethylene oxide	Oxirane	75-21-8	U115
Ethylenethiourea	2-Imidazolidinethione	96-45-7	U116
Ethylidene dichloride	Ethane, 1,1-dichloro-	75-34-3	U076
Ethyl methacrylate	2-Propenoic acid, 2-methyl-, ethyl ester	97-63-2	U118
Ethyl methanesulfonate	Methanesulfonic acid, ethyl ester	62-50-0	U119
Famphur	Phosphorothioic acid, O-[4-[(dimethylamino)sulfonyl]phenyl] O,O-dimethyl ester	52-85-7	P097
Fluoranthene	Same	206-44-0	U120
Fluorine	Same	7782-41-4	P056
Fluoroacetamide	Acetamide, 2-fluoro-	640-19-7	P057
Fluoroacetic acid, sodium salt	Acetic acid, fluoro-, sodium salt	62-74-8	P058
Formaldehyde	Same	50-00-0	U122
Formic acid	Same	64-18-6	U123
Glycidylaldehyde	Oxiranecarboxyaldehyde	765-34-4	U126
Halomethanes, N.O.S.¹			
Heptachlor	4,7-Methano-1H-indene, 1,4,5,6,7,8,8-heptachloro-3a,4,7,7a-tetrahydro-	76-44-8	P059
Heptachlor epoxide	2,5-Methano-2H-indeno[1,2-b]oxirene, 2,3,4,5,6,7,7-heptachloro-1a,1b,5,5a,6,6a-hexahydro-, (1aalpha,1bbeta,2alpha,5alpha,5abeta,6beta,6aalpha)-	1024-57-3	
Heptachlor epoxide (alpha, beta, and gamma isomers)			
Hexachlorobenzene	Benzene, hexachloro-	118-74-1	U127
Hexachlorobutadiene	1,3-Butadiene, 1,1,2,3,4,4-hexachloro-	87-68-3	U128
Hexachlorocyclopentadiene	1,3-Cyclopentadiene, 1,2,3,4,5,5-hexachloro-	77-47-4	U130
Hexachlorodibenzo-p-dioxins			
Hexachlorodibenzofurans			
Hexachloroethane	Ethane, hexachloro-	67-72-1	U131
Hexachlorophene	Phenol, 2,2'-methylenebis[3,4,6-trichloro-	70-30-4	U132
Hexachloropropene	1-Propene, 1,1,2,3,3,3-hexachloro-	1888-71-7	U243
Hexaethyl tetraphosphate	Tetraphosphoric acid, hexaethyl ester	757-58-4	P062
Hydrazine	Same	302-01-2	U133
Hydrogen cyanide	Hydrocyanic acid	74-90-8	P063
Hydrogen fluoride	Hydrofluoric acid	7664-39-3	U134
Hydrogen sulfide	Hydrogen sulfide H₂S	7783-06-4	U135
Indeno[1,2,3-cd]pyrene	Same	193-39-5	U137
Isobutyl alcohol	1-Propanol, 2-methyl-	78-83-1	U140
Isodrin	1,4,5,8-Dimethanonaphthalene, 1,2,3,4,10,10-hexachloro-1,4,4a,5,8,8a-hexahydro-, (1alpha,4alpha,4abeta,5beta,8beta,8abeta)-	465-73-6	P060

358 Waste Management Guide

Common name	Chemical abstracts name	Chemical abstracts No.	Hazardous waste No.
Isosafrole	1,3-Benzodioxole, 5-(1-propenyl)-	120-58-1	U141
Kepone	1,3,4-Metheno-2H-cyclobuta[cd]pentalen-2-one, 1,1a,3,3a,4,5,5,5a,5b,6-decachlorooctahydro-	143-50-0	U142
Lasiocarpine	2-Butenoic acid, 2-methyl-, 7-[[2,3-dihydroxy-2-(1-methoxyethyl)-3-methyl-1-oxobutoxy]methyl]-2,3,5,7a-tetrahydro-1H-pyrrolizin-1-yl ester, [1S-[1alpha(Z),7(2S*,3R*),7aalpha]]-	303-34-1	4143
Lead	Same	7439-92-1	
Lead compounds, N.O.S.[1]			
Lead acetate	Acetic acid, lead(2+) salt	301-04-2	U144
Lead phosphate	Phosphoric acid, lead(2+) salt (2:3)	7446-27-7	U145
Lead subacetate	Lead, bis(acetato-O)tetrahydroxytri-	1335-32-6	U146
Lindane	Cyclohexane, 1,2,3,4,5,6-hexachloro-, (1alpha,2alpha,3beta,4alpha,5alpha,6beta)-	58-89-9	U129
Maleic anhydride	2,5-Furandione	108-31-6	U147
Maleic hydrazide	3,6-Pyridazinedione, 1,2-dihydro-	123-33-1	U148
Malononitrile	Propanedinitrile	109-77-3	U149
Melphalan	L-Phenylalanine, 4-[bis(2-chloroethyl)amino]-	148-82-3	U150
Mercury	Same	7439-97-6	U151
Mercury compounds, N.O.S.[1]			
Mercury fulminate	Fulminic acid, mercury(2+) salt	628-86-4	P065
Methacrylonitrile	2-Propenenitrile, 2-methyl-	126-98-7	U152
Methapyrilene	1,2-Ethanediamine, N,N-dimethyl-N'-2-pyridinyl-N'-(2-thenylmethyl)-	91-80-5	U155
Methomyl	Ethanimidothioic acid, N-[[(methylamino)carbonyl]oxy]-, methyl ester	16752-77-5	P066
Methoxychlor	Benzene, 1,1'-(2,2,2-trichloroethylidene)bis[4-methoxy-	72-43-5	U247
Methyl bromide	Methane, bromo-	74-83-9	U029
Methyl chloride	Methane, chloro-	74-87-3	U045
Methyl chlorocarbonate	Carbonochloridic acid, methyl ester	79-22-1	U156
Methyl chloroform	Ethane, 1,1,1-trichloro-	71-55-6	U226
3-Methylcholanthrene	Benz[j]aceanthrylene, 1,2-dihydro-3-methyl-	56-49-5	U157
4,4'-Methylenebis(2-chloroaniline)	Benzenamine, 4,4'-methylenebis[2-chloro-	101-14-4	U158
Methylene bromide	Methane, dibromo-	74-95-3	U068
Methylene chloride	Methane, dichloro-	75-09-2	U080
Methyl ethyl ketone (MEK)	2-Butanone	78-93-3	U159
Methyl ethyl ketone peroxide	2-Butanone, peroxide	1338-23-4	U160
Methyl hydrazine	Hydrazine, methyl-	60-34-4	P068
Methyl iodide	Methane, iodo-	74-88-4	U138
Methyl isocyanate	Methane, isocyanato-	624-83-9	P064
2-Methyllactonitrile	Propanenitrile, 2-hydroxy-2-methyl-	75-86-5	P069
Methyl methacrylate	2-Propenoic acid, 2-methyl-, methyl ester	80-62-6	U162
Methyl methanesulfonate	Methanesulfonic acid, methyl ester	66-27-3	

Appendix B: Hazardous Waste Tables 359

Substance	CAS No.	Waste No.
Methyl parathion	298-00-0	P071
Methylthiouracil	56-04-2	U164
Mitomycin C	50-07-7	U010
Phosphorothioic acid, O,O-dimethyl O-(4-nitrophenyl) ester		
4(1H)-Pyrimidinone, 2,3-dihydro-6-methyl-2-thioxo-		
Azirino[2',3':3,4]pyrrolo[1,2-a]indole-4,7-dione, 6-amino-8-[[(aminocarbonyl)oxy]methyl]-1,1a,2,8,8a,8b-hexahydro-8a-methoxy-5-methyl-, [1aS-(1aalpha,8beta,8aalpha,8balpha)]-.		
MNNG	70-25-7	U163
Mustard gas	505-60-2	
Guanidine, N-methyl-N'-nitro-N-nitroso-		
Ethane, 1,1'-thiobis[2-chloro-		
Naphthalene	91-20-3	U165
1,4-Naphthoquinone	130-15-4	U166
alpha-Naphthylamine	134-32-7	U167
beta-Naphthylamine	91-59-8	U168
alpha-Naphthylthiourea	86-88-4	P072
1,4-Naphthalenedione		
1-Naphthalenamine		
2-Naphthalenamine		
Thiourea, 1-naphthalenyl-		
Nickel	7440-02-0	
Same		
Nickel compounds, N.O.S.[1]		
Nickel carbonyl	13463-39-3	P073
Nickel cyanide	557-19-7	P074
Nicotine	54-11-5	P075
Nickel carbonyl Ni(CO)₄, (T-4)-		
Nickel cyanide Ni(CN)₂		
Pyridine, 3-(1-methyl-2-pyrrolidinyl)-, (S)-		
Nicotine salts		P075
Nitric oxide	10102-43-9	P076
p-Nitroaniline	100-01-6	U077
Nitrobenzene	98-95-3	U169
Nitrogen dioxide	10102-44-0	P078
Nitrogen oxide NO		
Benzenamine, 4-nitro-		
Benzene, nitro-		
Nitrogen oxide NO₂		
Nitrogen mustard	51-75-2	
Ethanamine, 2-chloro-N-(2-chloroethyl)-N-methyl-		
Nitrogen mustard, hydrochloride salt		
Nitrogen mustard N-oxide	126-85-2	
Nitrogen mustard, N-oxide, hydrochloride salt		
Ethanamine, 2-chloro-N-(2-chloroethyl)-N-methyl-, N-oxide		
Nitroglycerin	55-63-0	P081
p-Nitrophenol	100-02-7	U170
2-Nitropropane	79-46-9	U171
1,2,3-Propanetriol, trinitrate		
Phenol, 4-nitro-		
Propane, 2-nitro-		
Nitrosamines, N.O.S.[1]	35576-91-1D	
N-Nitrosodi-n-butylamine	924-16-3	U172
N-Nitrosodiethanolamine	1116-54-7	U173
N-Nitrosodiethylamine	55-18-5	U174
N-Nitrosodimethylamine	62-75-9	P082
1-Butanamine, N-butyl-N-nitroso-		
Ethanol, 2,2'-(nitrosoimino)bis-		
Ethanamine, N-ethyl-N-nitroso-		
Methanamine, N-methyl-N-nitroso-		
N-Nitroso-N-ethylurea	759-73-9	U176
N-Nitrosomethylethylamine	10595-95-6	
N-Nitroso-N-methylurea		U177
N-Nitroso-N-methylurethane	684-93-5	U178
Urea, N-ethyl-N-nitroso-		
Ethanamine, N-methyl-N-nitroso-		
Urea, N-methyl-N-nitroso-		
Carbamic acid, methylnitroso-, ethyl ester	615-53-2	
N-Nitrosomethylvinylamine	4549-40-0	P084
Vinylamine, N-methyl-N-nitroso-		

Waste Management Guide

Common name	Chemical abstracts name	Chemical abstracts No.	Hazardous waste No.
N-Nitrosomorpholine	Morpholine, 4-nitroso-	59-89-2	
N-Nitrosonornicotine	Pyridine, 3-(1-nitroso-2-pyrrolidinyl)-, (S)-	16543-55-8	
N-Nitrosopiperidine	Piperidine, 1-nitroso-	100-75-4	U179
N-Nitrosopyrrolidine	Pyrrolidine, 1-nitroso-	930-55-2	U180
N-Nitrososarcosine	Glycine, N-methyl-N-nitroso-	13256-22-9	
5-Nitro-o-toluidine	Benzenamine, 2-methyl-5-nitro-	99-55-8	U181
Octamethylpyrophosphoramide	Diphosphoramide, octamethyl-	152-16-9	P085
Osmium tetroxide	Osmium oxide OsO₄, (T-4)-	20816-12-0	P087
Paraldehyde	1,3,5-Trioxane, 2,4,6-trimethyl-	123-63-7	U182
Parathion	Phosphorothioic acid, O,O-diethyl O-(4-nitrophenyl) ester	56-38-2	P089
Pentachlorobenzene	Benzene, pentachloro-	608-93-5	U183
Pentachlorodibenzo-p-dioxins			
Pentachlorodibenzofurans			
Pentachloroethane	Ethane, pentachloro-	76-01-7	U184
Pentachloronitrobenzene (PCNB)	Benzene, pentachloronitro-	82-68-8	U185
Pentachlorophenol	Phenol, pentachloro-	87-86-5	See F027
Phenacetin	Acetamide, N-(4-ethoxyphenyl)-	62-44-2	U187
Phenol	Same	108-95-2	U188
Phenylenediamine	Benzenediamine	25265-76-3	
Phenylmercury acetate	Mercury, (acetato-O)phenyl-	62-38-4	P092
Phenylthiourea	Thiourea, phenyl-	103-85-5	P093
Phosgene	Carbonic dichloride	75-44-5	P095
Phosphine	Same	7803-51-2	P096
Phorate	Phosphorodithioic acid, O,O-diethyl S-[(ethylthio)methyl] ester	298-02-2	P094
Phthalic acid esters, N.O.S.[1]			
Phthalic anhydride	1,3-Isobenzofurandione	85-44-9	U190
2-Picoline	Pyridine, 2-methyl-	109-06-8	U191
Polychlorinated biphenyls, N.O.S.[1]			
Potassium cyanide	Potassium cyanide K(CN)	151-50-8	P098
Potassium silver cyanide	Argentate(1-), bis(cyano-C)-, potassium	506-61-6	P099
Pronamide	Benzamide, 3,5-dichloro-N-(1,1-dimethyl-2-propynyl)-	23950-58-5	U192
1,3-Propane sultone	1,2-Oxathiolane, 2,2-dioxide	1120-71-4	U193
n-Propylamine	1-Propanamine	107-10-8	U194
Propargyl alcohol	2-Propyn-1-ol	107-19-7	P102
Propylene dichloride	Propane, 1,2-dichloro-	78-87-5	U083
1,2-Propylenimine	Aziridine, 2-methyl-	75-55-8	P067
Propylthiouracil	4(1H)-Pyrimidinone, 2,3-dihydro-6-propyl-2-thioxo-	51-52-5	
Pyridine	Same	110-86-1	U196
Reserpine	Yohimban-16-carboxylic acid, 11,17-dimethoxy-18-[(3,4,5-trimethoxybenzoyl)oxy]-, methyl ester, (3beta,16beta,17alpha,18beta,20alpha)-	50-55-5	U200

Appendix B: Hazardous Waste Tables

Resorcinol	1,3-Benzenediol	108-46-3	U201
Saccharin	1,2-Benzisothiazol-3(2H)-one, 1,1-dioxide	81-07-2	U202
Saccharin salts			U202
Safrole	1,3-Benzodioxole, 5-(2-propenyl)-	94-59-7	U203
Selenium	Same	7782-49-2	
Selenium compounds, N.O.S.¹			
Selenium dioxide	Selenious acid	7783-00-8	U204
Selenium sulfide	Selenium sulfide SeS₂	7488-56-4	U205
Selenourea	Same	630-10-4	P103
Silver	Same	7440-22-4	
Silver compounds, N.O.S.¹			
Silver cyanide	Silver cyanide Ag(CN)	506-64-9	P104
Silvex (2,4,5-TP)	Propanoic acid, 2-(2,4,5-trichlorophenoxy)-	93-72-1	See F027
Sodium cyanide	Sodium cyanide Na(CN)	143-33-9	P106
Streptozotocin	D-Glucose, 2-deoxy-2-[[(methylnitrosoamino)carbonyl]amino]-	18883-66-4	U206
Strychnine	Strychnidin-10-one	57-24-9	P108
Strychnine salts			P108
TCDD	Dibenzo[b,e][1,4]dioxin, 2,3,7,8-tetrachloro-	1746-01-6	U207
1,2,4,5-Tetrachlorobenzene	Benzene, 1,2,4,5-tetrachloro-	95-94-3	
Tetrachlorodibenzo-p-dioxins			
Tetrachlorodibenzofurans			
Tetrachloroethane, N.O.S.¹	Ethane, tetrachloro-, N.O.S.	25322-20-7	
1,1,1,2-Tetrachloroethane	Ethane, 1,1,1,2-tetrachloro-	630-20-6	U208
1,1,2,2-Tetrachloroethane	Ethane, 1,1,2,2-tetrachloro-	79-34-5	U209
Tetrachloroethylene	Ethene, tetrachloro-	127-18-4	U210
2,3,4,6-Tetrachlorophenol	Phenol, 2,3,4,6-tetrachloro-	58-90-2	See F027
Tetraethyldithiopyrophosphate	Thiodiphosphoric acid, tetraethyl ester	3689-24-5	P109
Tetraethyl lead	Plumbane, tetraethyl-	78-00-2	P110
Tetraethyl pyrophosphate	Diphosphoric acid, tetraethyl ester	107-49-3	P111
Tetranitromethane	Methane, tetranitro-	509-14-8	P112
Thallium	Same	7440-28-0	
Thallium compounds, N.O.S.¹			
Thallic oxide	Thallium oxide Tl₂O₃	1314-32-5	P113
Thallium(I) acetate	Acetic acid, thallium(1+) salt	563-68-8	U214
Thallium(I) carbonate	Carbonic acid, dithallium(1+) salt	6533-73-9	U215
Thallium(I) chloride	Thallium chloride TlCl	7791-12-0	U216
Thallium(I) nitrate	Nitric acid, thallium(1+) salt	10102-45-1	U217
Thallium selenite	Selenious acid, dithallium(1+) salt	12039-52-0	P114

Common name	Chemical abstracts name	Chemical abstracts No.	Hazardous waste No.
Thallium(I) sulfate	Sulfuric acid, dithallium(1+) salt	7446-18-6	P115
Thioacetamide	Ethanethioamide	62-55-5	U218
Thiofanox	2-Butanone, 3,3-dimethyl-1-(methylthio)-, O-[(methylamino)carbonyl] oxime	39196-18-4	P045
Thiomethanol	Methanethiol	74-93-1	U153
Thiophenol	Benzenethiol	108-98-5	P014
Thiosemicarbazide	Hydrazinecarbothioamide	79-19-6	P116
Thiourea	Same	62-56-6	U219
Thiram	Thioperoxydicarbonic diamide [(H$_2$N)C(S)]$_2$S$_2$, tetramethyl-	137-26-8	U244
Toluene	Benzene, methyl-	108-88-3	U220
Toluenediamine	Benzenediamine, ar-methyl-	25376-45-8	U221
Toluene-2,4-diamine	1,3-Benzenediamine, 4-methyl-	95-80-7	
Toluene-2,6-diamine	1,3-Benzenediamine, 2-methyl-	823-40-5	
Toluene-3,4-diamine	1,2-Benzenediamine, 4-methyl-	496-72-0	
Toluene diisocyanate	Benzene, 1,3-diisocyanatomethyl-	26471-62-5	U223
o-Toluidine	Benzenamine, 2-methyl-	95-53-4	U328
o-Toluidine hydrochloride	Benzenamine, 2-methyl-, hydrochloride	636-21-5	U222
p-Toluidine	Benzenamine, 4 methyl-	106-49-0	U353
Toxaphene	Same	8001-35-2	P123
1,2,4-Trichlorobenzene	Benzene, 1,2,4-trichloro-	120-82-1	
1,1,2-Trichloroethane	Ethane, 1,1,2-trichloro-	79-06-5	U227
Trichloroethylene	Ethene, trichloro-	79-01-6	U228
Trichloromethanethiol	Methanethiol, trichloro-	75-70-7	P118
Trichloromonofluoromethane	Methane, trichlorofluoro-	75-69-4	U121
2,4,5-Trichlorophenol	Phenol, 2,4,5-trichloro-	95-35-4	See F027
2,4,6-Trichlorophenol	Phenol, 2,4,6-trichloro-	88-06-2	See F027
2,4,5-T	Acetic acid, (2,4,5-trichlorophenoxy)-	93-76-5	See F027
Trichloropropane, N.O.S.[1]			
1,2,3-Trichloropropane	Propane, 1,2,3-trichloro-	25735-29-9	
O,O,O-Triethyl phosphorothioate	Phosphorothioic acid, O,O,O-triethyl ester	96-18-4	
1,3,5-Trinitrobenzene	Benzene, 1,3,5-trinitro-	126-68-1	U234
Tris(1-aziridinyl)phosphine sulfide	Aziridine, 1,1',1''-phosphinothioylidynetris-	99-35-4	
Tris(2,3-dibromopropyl) phosphate	1-Propanol, 2,3-dibromo-, phosphate (3:1)	52-24-4	U235
Trypan blue	2,7-Naphthalenedisulfonic acid, 3,3'-[(3,3'-dimethyl[1,1'-biphenyl]-4,4'-diyl)bis(azo)]-bis[5-amino-4-hydroxy-, tetrasodium salt	126-72-7	U236
		72-57-1	
Uracil mustard	2,4-(1H,3H)-Pyrimidinedione, 5-[bis(2-chloroethyl)amino]-	66-75-1	U237

Vanadium pentoxide		
Vanadium oxide V₂O₅	1314-62-1	P120
Vinyl chloride		
Ethene, chloro	75-01-4	U043
Warfarin		
2H-1-Benzopyran-2-one, 4-hydroxy-3-(3-oxo-1-phenylbutyl)-, when present at concentrations less than 0.3%.	81-81-2	U248
Warfarin		
2H-1-Benzopyran-2-one, 4-hydroxy-3-(3-oxo-1-phenylbutyl)-, when present at concentrations greater than 0.3%.	81-81-2	P001
Warfarin salts, when present at concentrations less than 0.3%.		U248
Warfarin salts, when present at concentrations greater than 0.3%.		P001
Zinc cyanide		
Zinc cyanide Zn(CN)₂	557-21-1	P121
Zinc phosphide		
Zinc phosphide Zn₃P₂, when present at concentrations greater than 10%	1314-84-7	P122
Zinc phosphide		
Zinc phosphide Zn₃P₂, when present at concentrations of 10% or less	1314-84-7	U249

¹ The abbreviation N.O.S. (not otherwise specified) signifies those members of the general class not specifically listed by name in this appendix.

APPENDIX C

PRETREATMENT STANDARDS

Land Disposal Restrictions: Concentation-Based Treatment
   Standards 367
   Policy Guide 367
   Application of Policy 367
Table CCWE (Constituent Concentrations in Waste Extract) . . 368
Land Disposal Prohibitions 401
   Table 1: Land Disposal Restriction: Technology-Based
      Treatment Standards 402
   Table 2: Technology Codes and Description of
      Technology-Based Standards 405
   Table 3: Technology-Based Standards by RCRA
      Waste Code 414

LAND DISPOSAL RESTRICTION: CONCENTRATION-BASED TREATMENT STANDARDS

POLICY GUIDE

The RCRA land disposal regulations (40 CFR 268) prohibit disposal of hazardous wastes before treatment. EPA, in developing land ban regulations, also issued treatment standards and storage prohibitions for those wastes.

These standards and prohibitions, as well as a variance and an exemption pertaining to surface impoundments, correspond to land disposal restrictions for specific wastes. BNA's *Chemical Substances Control* explains how the land disposal regulation is structured and the specific wastes that are affected. This section explains the treatment standards for those individual wastes.

The full test of EPA's land disposal ban regulations can be found in BNA's *Environment Reporter* at Federal Regulations 6.

APPLICATION OF POLICY

Treatment Standards

Restricted wastes may be land disposed without further treatment only if an extract of the waste, the treatment residual, or a concentration of the waste developed using the Toxicity Characteristic Leaching Procedure (TCLP) (found in BNA's *Environment Reporter*, in Appendix I to part 268 in the chapter beginning at page 161:2201) does not exceed a specified value. These values are shown in the Constituent Concentrations in Waste Extract (CCWE) tables that follow for any hazardous constituent, extract, or concentration listed for the waste. If, on the other hand, a total analysis of the waste indicates that individual contaminants are either absent from the waste or present in such low concentrations that they do not exceed regulatory thresholds, the TCLP need not be run. A restricted waste for which a treatment technology is specified (see below) may be land disposed after it is treated using that specified technology or an equivalent treatment method approved by EPA.

Treatment standards for first-third wastes are based on the performance levels achievable by the best demonstrated available technology identified for each treatability group. EPA emphasizes that any technology not otherwise prohibited (i.e., impermissible dilution) may be used to meet the concentration-based treatment standards.

No generator, transporter, handler, or owner/operator of a treatment, storage, or disposal facility can in any way dilute a restricted waste or the residual from treatment of a restricted waste as a substitute for treatment to comply with these requirements, or to circumvent or avoid the effective date of a land disposal prohibition.

Impermissible dilution is mixing a waste that does not require treatment or that does not aid in treatment to dilute hazardous constituents into a larger volume of wastes to lower constituent concentrations. However, aggregation of waste streams for centralized treatment is permitted as a form of mixing that facilitates treatment. (This is not the same as aggregation points designed to avoid a prohibition.)

For treatment standard purposes, EPA defines wastewaters as wastes that contain less than 1 percent total organic carbon (TOC) and less than 1 percent total suspended solids (i.e. total filterable solids). Wastes that do not meet the definition are considered nonwastewater.

Standards expressed as concentrations in waste extract —

Table CCWE identifies the restricted wastes and the concentrations of their associated hazardous constituents which may not be exceeded by the extract of a waste or waste treatment residual developed using the TCLP method if the waste is to be disposed of on land.

When wastes with differing treatment standards for a constituent of concern are combined for purposes of treatment, the treatment residue must meet the lowest treatment standard for the constituent of concern, except that mixtures of high and low zinc nonwastewater K061 are subject to the treatment standard for high zinc K061.

TABLE CCWE — CONSTITUENT CONCENTRATIONS IN WASTE EXTRACT

F001-F005 spent solvents	Concentration (in mg/l)	
	Wastewaters containing spent solvents	All other spent solvent wastes
Acetone	0.05	0.59
n-Butyl alcohol	5.0	5.0
Carbon disulfide	1.05	4.81
Carbon tetrachloride	.05	.96
Chlorobenzene	.15	.05
Cresols (and cresylic acid)	2.82	.75
Cyclohexanone	.125	.75
1,2-Dichlorobenzene	.65	.125
Ethyl acetate	.05	.75
Ethylbenzene	.05	.053
Ethyl ether	.05	.75
Isobutanol	5.0	5.0
Methanol	.25	.75
Methylene chloride	.20	.96
Methyl ethyl ketone	0.05	0.75
Methyl isobutyl ketone	0.05	0.33
Nitrobenzene	0.66	0.125
Pyridine	1.12	0.33

TABLE CCWE — CONSTITUENT CONCENTRATIONS IN WASTE EXTRACT

F001-F005 spent solvents	Concentration (in mg/l)	
	Wastewaters containing spent solvents	All other spent solvent wastes
Tetrachloroethylene	0.079	0.05
Toluene	1.12	0.33
1,1,1-Trichloroethane	1.05	0.41
1,1,2-Trichloro-1,2,2-trifluoroethane	1.05	0.96
Trichloroethylene	0.062	0.091
Trichlorofluoromethane	0.05	0.96
Xylene	0.05	0.15

F006 nonwastewaters (see also Table CCW in § 268.43)	Concentration (in mg/l)
Cadmium	0.066
Chromium (Total)	5.2
Lead	.51
Nickel	.32
Silver	.072
Cyanides (Total)	[Reserved]

F007, F008, and F009 nonwastewaters (see also Table CCW in § 268.43)	Concentration (in mg/l)
Cadmium	0.066
Chromium (Total)	5.2
Lead	0.51
Nickel	0.32
Silver	0.072

F011 and F012 nonwastewaters (see also Table CCW in § 268.43)	Concentration (in mg/l)
Cadmium	0.066
Chromium (Total)	5.2
Lead	0.51
Nickel	0.32
Silver	0.072

F019 nonwastewaters (see also Table CCW in § 268.43)	Concentration (in mg/l)
Chromium	5.2

Appendix C: Pretreatment Standards

F024 nonwastewaters (see also Table CCW in § 268.43)	Concentration (in mg/l)
Chromium (Total)	Reserved.
Nickel	Reserved.

F020-F023 and F026-F028 dioxin containing wastes	Concentration
HxCDO — All Herachlorodibenzo-p-dioxins	< 1 ppb
HxGDF — All Hexachlorodibenzofurans	< 1 ppb
PeCDD — All Pentachlorodibenzo-p-dioxins	< 1 ppb
PeCDF — All Pentachlorodibenzofurans	< 1 ppb
TCDD — All Tetrachlorodibenzo-p-dioxins	< 1 ppb
TCDF — All Tetrachlorodibenzofurans	< 1 ppb
2,4,5-Trichlorophenol	< 0.05 ppm
2,4,6-Trichlorophenol	< 0.05 ppm
2,3,4,6-Tetrachlorophenol	< 0.10 ppm
Pentachlorophenol	< 0.01 ppm

F039 nonwastewaters (see also Table in § 268.43)	Concentration (in mg/l)
Antimony	0.23
Arsenic	5.0
Barium	52
Cadmium	0.066
Chromium (Total)	5.2
Lead	0.51
Mercury	0.025
Nickel	0.32
Selenium	5.7
Silver	0.072

K001 nonwastewaters (see also Table in § 268.43)	Concentration (in mg/l)
Lead	0.51

K002-K005, K006 (anhydrous), K007 and K008 nonwastewaters (see also Table in § 268.43)	Concentration (in mg/l)
Chromium (Total)	0.094
Lead	0.37

K006 (hydrated) nonwastewaters (see also Table in § 268.43)	Concentration (in mg/l)
Chromium (Total)	5.2

K015 nonwastewaters (see also Table in § 268.43)	Concentration (in mg/l)
Chromium	1.7
Lead	0.2

K021 nonwastewaters (see also Table in § 268.43)	Concentration (in mg/l)
Antimony	0.23

K022 nonwastewaters (see also Table CCW in § 268.43)	Concentration (in mg/l)
Chromium (Total)	5.2
Nickel	0.32

K028 nonwastewaters (see also Table CCW in § 268.43)	Concentration (in mg/l)
Chromium (Total)	0.073
Lead	0.021
Nickel	0.088

K031 nonwastewaters (see also Table CCW in § 268.43)	Concentration (in mg/l)
Arsenic	5.6

K046 nonwastewaters (Nonreactive Subcategory)	Concentration (in mg/l)
Lead	0.18

K048, K049, K050, K051 and K052 nonwastewaters (see also Table CCW in § 268.43)	Concentration (in mg/l)
Chromium (Total)	1.7
Nickel	0.20

K061 nonwastewaters (Low Zinc Subcategory—less than 15% total zinc)	Concentration (in mg/l)
Cadmium	0.14
Chromium (Total)	5.2

K061 nonwastewaters (Low Zinc Subcategory—less than 15% total zinc)	Concentration (in mg/l)
Lead	0.24
Nickel	0.32

K061 nonwastewaters (High Zinc Subcategory—greater than or equal to 15% total zinc)	Concentration (in mg/l)
Antimony	2.1
Arsenic	0.055
Barium	7.6
Beryllium	0.014
Cadmium	0.19
Chromium (Total)	0.33
Lead	0.37
Mercury	0.009
Nickel	5
Silenium	0.16
Silver	0.3
Thallium	0.078
Vanadium	Reserved
Zinc	5.3

K062 nonwastewaters	Concentration (in mg/l)
Chromium (Total)	0.094
Lead	0.37

K069 nonwastewaters (Calcium Sulfate Subcategory)	Concentration (in mg/l)
Cadmium	014.
Lead	0.24

K071 nonwastewaters (Low Mercury Subcategory—less 16 mg/kg Mercury)	Concentration (in mg/l)
Mercury	0.025

K086 nonwastewaters (Solvent Washes Subcategory) see also Table CCW in § 268.43)	Concentration (in mg/l)
Chromium (Total)	0.094
Lead	.37

K087 nonwastewaters (see also Table CCW in § 268.43)	Concentration (in mg/l)
Lead	0.51

K100 nonwastewaters (see also Table CCW in § 268.43)	Concentration Concentration (in mg/l)
Cadmium	0.066
Chromium (Total)	5.2
Lead	0.51

K101 and K102 nonwastewaters (see also Table CCW in § 268.43)	Concentration (in mg/l)
Arsenic	5.6

K106 nonwastewaters (Low Mercury Subcategory)—less than 260 mg/kg Mercury—residues from RMERC)	Concentration (in mg/l)
Mercury	0.20

K106 nonwastewaters (Low Mercury Subcategory)—less than 260 mg/kg Mercury—that are not residues from RMERC)	Concentration (in mg/l)
Mercury	0.025

K115 nonwastewaters (see also Table CCW in § 268.43)	Concentration (in mg/l)
Nickel	0.32

P010-P012, P036, P038 nonwastewaters (see also Table CCW in § 268.43)	Concentration (in mg/l)
Arsenic	5.6

P013 nonwastewaters (see also Table CCW in § 268.43)	Concentration (in mg/l)
Barium	52

Appendix C: Pretreatment Standards

P065 and P092 nonwastewaters (Low Mercury Subcategory)—less than 260 mg/kg Mercury—residues from RMERC)	Concentration (in mg/l)
Mercury	0.20

P065 and P092 nonwastewaters (Low Mercury Subcategory)—less than 260 mg/kg Mercury—that are not residues from RMERC)	Concentration (in mg/l)
Mercury	0.025

P073 and P074 nonwastewaters (see also Table CCW in § 268.43)	Concentration (in mg/l)
Nickel	0.32

P099 and P104 nonwastewaters (see also Table CCW in § 268.43)	Concentration (in mg/l)
Silver	0.072

P103 and P114 nonwastewaters (see also Table CCW in § 268.43)	Concentration (in mg/l)
Selenium	5.7

P110 nonwastewaters (see also Table CCW in § 268.43)	Concentration (in mg/l)
Lead	0.51

U032 nonwastewaters (see also Table CCW in § 268.43)	Concentration (in mg/l)
Chromium (Total)	0.094

U051 and U144-U146 nonwastewaters (see also Table CCW in § 268.43)	Concentration (in mg/l)
Lead	0.51

U151 nonwastewaters (Low Mercury Subcategory)—less than 260 mg/kg Mercury—residues from RMERC)	Concentration (in mg/l)
Mercury	0.20

U151 nonwastewaters (Low Mercury Subcategory)—less than 260 mg/kg Mercury—that are not residues from RMERC)	Concentration (in mg/l)
Mercury	0.025

U204 and U205 nonwastewaters (see also Table CCW in § 268.43)	Concentration (in mg/l)
Selenium	5.7

Treatment Standards Expressed As Waste Concentrations

The following Constituent Concentrations in Wastes (CCW) table identifies the restricted wastes and concentrations of their associated hazardous constituents that may not be exceeded by the waste or treatment residual (not an extract of such waste or residual) if the waste or residual is to be disposed of on land.

TABLE CCW—CONSTITUENT CONCENTRATIONS IN WASTES

F001, F002, F003, F004 and F005 wastewaters (Pharmaceutical Industry)	Concentration (in mg/l)
Methylene chloride	0.44

F006 nonwastewaters (see also Table CCWE in § 268.41)	Concentration (in mg/kg)
Cyanides (Total)	590
Cyanides (Amenable)	30

F006 wastewaters (see also Table CCWE in § 268.41)	Concentration (in mg/l)
Cyanides (Total)	1.2
Cyanides (Amenable)	0.86
Cadmium	1.6
Chromium	0.32

F006 wastewaters (see also Table CCWE in § 268.41)	Concentration (in mg/l)
Lead	0.040
Nickel	0.44

F007, F008, and F009 nonwastewaters (see also Table CCWE in § 268.41)	Concentration (in mg/kg)
Cyanides (Total)	590
Cyanides (Amenable)	30

F007, F008, and F009 wastewaters (see also Table CCWE in § 268.41)	Concentration (in mg/l)
Cyanides (Total)	1.9
Cyanides (Amenable)	0.10
Chromium (Total)	0.32
Lead	0.04
Nickel	0.44

F010 nonwastewaters	Concentration (in mg/kg)
Cyanides (Total)	1.5

F010 wastewaters	Concentration (in mg/l)
Cyanides (Total)	1.9
Cyanides (Amenable)	0.10

F011 and F012 nonwastewaters[1]	Concentration (in mg/kg)
Cyanides (Total)	110
Cyanides (Amenable)	9.1

[1] Effective December 8, 1989; from July 8, 1989 until December 8, 1989, these wastes are subject to the same treatment standards as F007, F008, and F009 nonwastewaters (see also Table CCWE in §268.41).

F011 and F012 wastewaters (see also Table CCWE in § 268.41)	Concentration (in mg/l)
Cyanides (Total)	1.9
Cyanides (Amenable)	0.10
Chromium (Total)	0.32
Lead	0.04
Nickel	0.44

F019 wastewaters (see also Table CCWE in § 268.41)	Concentration (in mg/l)
Cyanides (Total)	1.2
Cyanides (Amenable)	0.86
Chromium (Total)	0.32

F019 nonwastewaters (see also Table CCWE in § 268.41)	Concentration (in mg/kg)
Cyanides (Total)	590
Cyanides (Amenable)	30

F024 nonwastewaters (see also Table CCWE in § 268.41)	Concentration (in mg/kg)
2-Chloro-1,3-butadiene	0.28
3-Chloropropene	0.28
1,1-Dichloroethane	0.014
1,2-Dichloroethane	0.014
1,2-Dichloropropane	0.014
cis-1,3-Dichloropropene	0.014
trans-1,3-Dichloropropene	0.014
Bis(2-ethylhexyl)phthalate	0.036
Hexachloroethane	0.036

F024 wastewaters (see also Table CCWE in § 268.41)	Concentration (in mg/l)
2-Chloro-1,3-butadiene	0.28
3-Chloropropene	0.28
1,1-Dichloroethane	0.014
1,2-Dichloroethane	0.014
1,2-Dichloropropane	0.014
cis-1,3-Dichloropropene	0.014
trans-1,3-Dichloropropene	0.014
Bis(2-ethylhexyl)phthalate	0.036
Hexachloroethane	0.036
Chromium (Total)	0.35
Nickel	0.47

F025 nonwastewaters (Light ends subcategory	Concentration (in mg/kg)
Chloroform	6.2
1,2-Dichloroethane	6.2
1,1-Dichloroethylene	6.2
Methylene chloride	31
Carbon tetrachloride	6.2
1,1,2-Trichloroethane	6.2
Trichloroethylene	5.6
Vinyl chloride	33

Appendix C: Pretreatment Standards

F025 nonwastewaters (Spent filter/aids and desicants subcategory)	Concentration (in mg/l)
Chloroform	0.046
Methylene chloride	0.089
Carbon tetrachloride	0.057
1,1,2-Trichloroethane	0.054
Trichloroethylene	0.054
Vinyl chloride	0.27
Hexachlorobenzene	0.055
Hexachloroethane	0.055

F039 nonwastewaters (see also Table CCWE in § 268.41)	Concentration (in mg/kg)
Acetone	160
Acenaphtalene	3.4
Acenaphthene	4.0
Acenophenone	9.7
2-Acetylaminofluoroene	140
Acrylonitrile	84
Aldrin	0.066
Aniline	14
Anthracene	4.0
Aroclor 1016	0.92
Aroclor 1221	0.92
Aroclor 1232	0.92
Aroclor 1242	0.92
Aroclor 1248	0.92
Aroclor 1254	1.8
Aroclor 1260	1.8
alph-BHC	0.066
beta-BHC	0.066
delta-BHC	0.066
gamma-BHC	0.066
Benzene	36
Benzo(a)anthracene	8.2
Benzo(b)fluoanthene	3.4
Benzo(k)fluoanthene	3.4
Benzo(g,h,i)perylene	1.5
Benzo(a)pyrene	8.2
Bromodichloromethane	15
Bromoform	15
Bromomethane (methyl bromide)	15
4-Bromophenyl phenyl ether	15
n-Butyl alcohol	2.6
Butyl benzyl phthalate	7.9
2-sec-Butyl-4,6-dinitrophenol	2.5
Carbon tetrachloride	5.6
Chlordane	0.13
p-Chloroaniline	16
Chlorobenzene	5.7
Chlorodibromomethane	16
Chlorethane	6.0
bis(2-Chloroethoxy) ethane	7.2
bis(2-Chloroethyl) ether	7.2
Chloroform	5.6
bis(2-Chloroisopropyl) ether	7.2
p-Chloro-m-cresol	14
Chloromethane (Methyl chloride)	33
2-Chloronaphthalene	5.6

F039 nonwastewaters (see also Table CCWE in § 268.41)	Concentration (in mg/kg)
2-Chlorophenol	5.7
3-Chloropropene	28
Chrysene	8.2
o-Cresol	5.6
Cresol (m- and p-isomers)	3.2
1,2-Dibromo-3-chloropropane	15
1,2-Dibromoethane (Ethylene dibromide)	15
Dibromomethane	15
2,4-Dichlorophenoxyacetic acid (2,4-D)	10
o,p'-DDD	0.087
p,p'-DDD	0.087
o,p'-DDE	0.087
p,p'-DDE	0.087
o,p'-DDT	0.087
p,p'-DDT	0.087
Dibenzo(a,h)anthracene	8.2
m-Dichlorobenzene	6.2
o-Dichlorobenzene	6.2
p-Dichlorobenzene	6.2
Dichlorodifluoromethane	7.2
1,1-Dichloroethane	7.2
1,2-Dichloroethane	7.2
1,1-Dichloroethylene	33
trans-1,3-Dichloropropene	33
2,4-Dichlorophenol	14
2,6-Dichlorophenol	14
2,4-Dichloropropane	18
cis-1,3-Dichloropropene	18
trans-1,3-Dichloropropene	18
Dieldrin	0.13
Diethyl phthalate	28
2,4-Dimethyl phenol	14
Dimethyl phthalate	28
Di-n-butyl phthalate	28
1,4-Dinitrobenzen	2.3
4,6-Dinitro-o-cresol	160
2,4-Dinitrophenol	160
2,4-Dinitrotoluene	140
2,6-Dinitrotoluene	28
Di-n-octyl phthalate	28
Di-n-propylnitrosoamine	14
1,4-Dioxane	170
Disulfoton	6.2
Endosulfan I	0.066
Endosulfan II	0.13
Endosulfan sulfate	0.13
Endrin	0.13
Endrin aldehyde	0.13
Ethyl acetate	33
Ethyl benzene	6.0
Ethyl ether	160
bis(2-Ethylhexyl) phthalate	28
Ethyl methacrylate	160
Famphur	15
Fluoranthene	8.2
Fluorene	4.0
Fluorotrichloromethane	33
Heptachlor	0.066
Heptachlor epoxide	0.066

Waste Management Guide

F039 nonwastewaters (see also Table CCWE in § 268.41)	Concentration (in mg/kg)
Hexachlorobenzene	37
Hexachlorbutadiene	28
Hexachlorocyclopentadiene	3.6
Hexachlorodibenzo-furans	0.001
Hexachlorodibenzo-p-dioxins	0.001
Hexachloroethane	28
Hexachloropropene	28
Indeno(1,2,3-c,d)pyrene	8.2
Iodomethane	65
Isobutanol	170
Isodrin	0.066
Isosafrole	2.6
Kepone	0.13
Methacrylonitrile	84
Methapyrilene	1.5
Methoxychlor	0.18
3-Methylcholanthrene	15
4,4-Methylene-bis-(2-chloroaniline)	35
Methylene chloride	33
Methyl ethel ketone	36
Methyl isobutol ketone	33
Methyl methacrylate	160
Methyl parathion	4.6
Naphthalene	3.1
p-Nitroanilene	28
Nitrobenze	14
5-Nitro-o-toluidine	28
4-Nitrophenol	29
N-Nitrosodiethylamine	28
N-Nitroso-di-n-butylamine	17
N-Nitrosomethylethylamine	2.3
N-Nitrosomorpholine	2.3
N-Nitrosopiperidine	35
N-Nitrosopyrrolidine	35
Parathion	4.6
Pentachlorobenzene	37
Pentachlorodibenzo-furans	0.001
Pentachlorodibenzo-p-dioxins	0.001
Pentachloronitrobenzene	4.8
Pentachloronitrophenol	7.4
Phenacetin	16
Phenanthrene	3.1
Phenol	6.2
Phorate	4.6
Propanenitrile (ethyl cyanide)	360
Promamide	1.5
Pyrene	8.2
Pyridine	16
Safrole	22
Silvex (2,4,5-TP)	7.9
2,4,5-T	7.9
1,2,4,5-Tetrachlorobenzene	19
Tetrachlorodibenzo-furans	0.001
Tetrachlorodibenzo-p-dioxins	0.001
1,1,1,2-Tetrachloroethane	42
1,1,2,2-Tetrachloroethane	42
Tetrachloroethene	5.6
2,3,4,6-Tetrachlorophenol	37
Toluene	28
Toxaphene	1.3
1,2,4-Trichlorobenzen	19

F039 nonwastewaters (see also Table CCWE in § 268.41)	Concentration (in mg/kg)
1,1,1-Trichloroethane	5.6
1,1,2-Trichloroethane	5.6
Trichloroethylene	5.6
2,4,5-Trichlorophenol	37
2,4,6-Trichlorophenol	37
1,2,3-Trichloropropane	28
1,1,2-Trichloro-1,2,2-trifluoro-ethane	28
Vinyl chloride	33
Xylene(s)	28
Cyanides (total)	1.8

F039 wastewaters (see also Table CCWE in § 268.41)	Concentration (in mg/l)
Acetone	0.28
Acenaphtalene	0.59
Acenaphthene	0.59
Acetonitrile	0.17
Acenophenone	0.010
2-Acetylaminofluoroene	0.059
Acrylonitrile	0.24
Aldrin	0.021
4-Aminobiphenyl	0.13
Aniline	0.81
Anthracene	0.059
Aroclor 1016	0.013
Aroclor 1221	0.014
Aroclor 1232	0.013
Aroclor 1242	0.017
Aroclor 1248	0.013
Aroclor 1254	0.014
Aroclor 1260	0.014
alph-BHC	0.00014
beta-BHC	0.00014
delta-BHC	0.023
gamma-BHC	0.0017
Benzene	0.14
Benzo(a)anthracene	0.059
Benzo(b)fluoanthene	0.055
Benzo(k)fluoanthene	0.059
Benzo(g,h,i)perylene	0.0055
Benzo(a)pyrene	0.061
Bromodichloromethane	0.35
Bromoform	0.63
Bromomethane (methyl bromide)	0.11
4-Bromophenyl phenyl ether	0.055
n-Butyl alcohol	5.6
Butyl benzyl phthalate	0.017
2-sec-Butyl-4,6-dinitrophenol	0.066
Carbon tetrachloride	0.057
Carbon disulfide	0.014
Chlordane	0.0033
p-Chloroaniline	0.46
Chlorobenzene	0.057
Chlorobenzilate	0.10
Chlorodibromomethane	0.057
Chlorethane	0.27
bis(2-Chloroethoxy) methane	0.036
bis(2-Chloroethyl) ether	0.033

F039 wastewaters (see also Table CCWE in § 268.41)	Concentration (in mg/l)	F039 wastewaters (see also Table CCWE in § 268.41)	Concentration (in mg/l)
2-Chloroethyl vinyl ether	0.057	Ethyl benzene	0.57
Chloroform	0.046	Ethyl ether	0.12
bis(2-Chloroisopropyl) ether	0.055	bis(2-Ethylhexyl) phthalate	0.28
p-Chloro-m-cresol	0.018	Ethyl methacrylate	0.14
Chloromethane (Methyl chloride)	0.19	Ethylene oxide	0.12
2-Chloronaphthalene	0.055	Famphur	0.017
2-Chlorophenol	0.044	Fluoranthene	0.068
3-Chloropropene	0.036	Fluorene	0.059
Chrysene	0.059	Fluorotrichloromethane	0.020
o-Cresol	0.11	Heptachlor	0.012
Cresol (m- and p-isomers)	0.77	Heptachlor epoxide	0.016
Cyclohexanone	0.36	Hexachlorobenzene	0.055
1,2-Dibromo-3-chloropropane	0.11	Hexachlorbutadiene	0.055
1,2-Dibromoethane (Ethylene dibromide)	0.028	Hexachlorocyclopentadiene	0.057
		Hexachlorodibenzo-furans	0.000063
Dibromomethane	0.11	Hexachlorodibenzo-p-dioxins	0.000063
2,4-Dichlorophenoxyacetic acid (2,4-D)	0.72	Hexachloroethane	0.055
		Hexachloropropene	0.035
o,p'-DDD	0.023	Indeno(1,2,3-c,d)pyrene	0.0055
p,p'-DDD	0.023	Iodomethane	0.019
o,p'-DDE	0.031	Isobutanol	5.6
p,p'-DDE	0.031	Isodrin	0.021
o,p'-DDT	0.0039	Isosafrole	0.081
p,p'-DDT	0.0039	Kepone	0.0011
Dibenzo(a,h)anthracene	0.055	Methacrylonitrile	0.24
m-Dichlorobenzene	0.036	Methapyrilene	0.081
o-Dichlorobenzene	0.088	Methoxychlor	0.025
p-Dichlorobenzene	0.090	3-Methylcholanthrene	0.0055
Dichlorodifluoromethane	0.23	4,4-Methylene-bis-(2-chloroaniline)	0.50
1,1-Dichloroethane	0.059	Methylene chloride	0.089
1,2-Dichloroethane	0.21	Methyl ethyl ketone	0.28
1,1-Dichloroethylene	0.025	Methyl isobutol ketone	0.14
trans-1,3-Dichloropropene	0.054	Methyl methacrylate	0.14
2,4-Dichlorophenol	0.044	Methyl methanate	0.018
2,6-Dichlorophenol	0.044	Methyl parathion	0.014
2,4-Dichloropropane	0.85	Naphthalene	0.059
cis-1,3-Dichloropropene	0.036	2-Naphtylamine	0.52
trans-1,3-Dichloropropene	0.036	p-Nitroanilene	0.028
Dieldrin	0.017	Nitrobenze	0.068
Diethyl phthalate	0.20	5-Nitro-o-toluidine	0.32
p-Dimethylaminoazobenzene	0.13	4-Nitrophenol	0.12
2,4-Dimethyl phenol	0.036	N-Nitrosodiethylamine	0.40
Dimethyl phthalate	0.047	N-Nitrosodimethylamine	0.40
Di-n-butyl phthalate	0.057	N-Nitroso-di-n-butylamine	0.40
1,4-Dinitrobenzen	0.32	N-Nitrosomethylethylamine	0.40
4,6-Dinitro-o-cresol	0.28	N-Nitrosomorpholine	0.40
2,4-Dinitrophenol	0.12	N-Nitrosopiperidine	0.013
2,4-Dinitrotoluene	0.32	N-Nitrosopyrrolidine	0.013
2,6-Dinitrotoluene	0.55	Parathion	0.017
Di-n-octyl phthalate	0.017	Pentachlorobenzene	0.055
Di-n-propylnitrosoamine	0.40	Pentachlorodibenzo-furans	0.000035
1,2-Diphenyl hydrazine	0.087	Pentachlorodibenzo-p-dioxins	0.000063
1,4-Dioxane	0.12	Pentachloronitrobenzene	0.055
Disulfoton	0.017	Pentachloronitrophenol	0.089
Endosulfan I	0.023	Phenacetin	0.081
Endosulfan II	0.029	Phenanthrene	0.059
Endosulfan sulfate	0.029	Phenol	0.039
Endrin	0.0028	Phorate	0.021
Endrin aldehyde	0.025	Propanenitrile (ethyl cyanide)	0.24
Ethyl acetate	0.34	Promamide	0.093
Ethyl cyanide	0.24	Pyrene	0.067

F039 wastewaters (see also Table CCWE in § 268.41)	Concentration (in mg/l)
Pyridine	0.014
Safrole	0.081
Silvex (2,4,5-TP)	0.72
2,4,5-T	0.72
1,2,4,5-Tetrachlorobenzene	0.055
Tetrachlorodibenzo-furans	0.000063
Tetrachlorodibenzo-p-dioxins	0.000063
2,3,7,8-Tetrachlorodibenzo-p-dioxin	0.000063
1,1,1,2-Tetrachloroethane	0.057
1,1,2,2-Tetrachloroethane	0.057
Tetrachloroethene	0.056
2,3,4,6-Tetrachlorophenol	0.030
Toluene	0.080
Toxaphene	0.0095
1,2,4-Trichlorobenzen	0.055
1,1,1-Trichloroethane	0.054
1,1,2-Trichloroethane	0.054
Trichloroethylene	0.054
2,4,5-Trichlorophenol	0.18
2,4,6-Trichlorophenol	0.035
1,2,3-Trichloropropane	0.85
1,1,2-Trichloro-1,2,2-trifluoro-ethane	0.057
Vinyl chloride	0.027
Xylene(s)	0.32
Cyanides (total)	1.2
Cyanides (amenable)	0.86
Fluoride	35
Sulfide	14
Antimony	1.9
Arsenic	5.0
Barium	1.2
Beryllium	0.82
Cadmium	0.20
Chromium (total)	0.27
Copper	1.3
Lead	0.28
Mercury	0.15
Nickel	0.55
Selenium	0.82
Silver	0.29
Vanadium	0.042

K001 nonwastewaters (see also Table CCWE in § 268.41)	Concentration (in mg/kg)
Naphthalene	1.5
Pentachlorophenol	1.5
Phenanthrene	1.5
Pyrene	1.5
Toluene	28
Xylenes	33

K001 wastewaters	Concentration (in mg/l)
Naphthalene	0.15
Pentachlorophenol	0.031

K001 wastewaters	Concentration (in mg/l)
Phenanthrene	0.031
Pyrene	0.028
Toluene	0.028
Xylenes	0.032
Lead	0.037

K002, K003, K004, K006 and K008 wastewaters (see also Table CCWE in § 268.41	Concentration (in mg/l)
Chromium (Total)	2.9
Lead	3.4

K005 and K007 wastewaters (see also Table CCWE in § 268.41)	Concentration (in mg/l)
Chromium (Total)	2.9
Lead	3.4
Cyanides (Total)	0.74

K009 and K010 nonwastewaters	Concentration (in mg/kg)
Chloroform	6.0

K009 and K010 wastewaters	Concentration (in mg/l)
Chloroform	0.10

K011, K013, and K014 nonwastewaters	Concentration (in mg/kg)
Acetonitrile	1.8
Acrylonitrile	1.4
Acrylamide	23
Benzene	0.03
Cyanides (Total)	57

K011, K013, and K014 wastewaters	Concentration (in mg/l)
Acetonitrile	38
Acrylonitrile	0.06
Acrylamide	19
Benzene	0.02
Cyanides (Total)	21

Appendix C: Pretreatment Standards

K015 nonwastewaters	Concentration (in mg/l)
Anthracene	3.4
Benzal chloride	6.2
Benzo (b and/or K) fluoranthene	3.4
Phenanthrene	3.4
Toluene	6.0

K015 wastewaters	Concentration (in mg/l)
Anthracene	1.0
Benzal chloride	0.28
Benzo (b and/or K) fluoranthene	0.29
Phenanthrene	0.27
Toluene	0.15
Chromium (Total)	0.32
Nickel	0.44

K016 nonwastewaters	Concentration (in mg/kg)
Hexachlorobenzene	28
Hexachlorobutadiene	5.6
Hexachlorocyclopentadiene	5.6
Hexachloroethane	28
Tetrachloroethene	6.0

K016 wastewaters	Concentration (in mg/l)
Hexachlorobenzene	0.033
Hexachlorobutadiene	.007
Hexachlorocyclopentadiene	.007
Hexachloroethane	.033
Tetrachloroethene	.007

K017 nonwastewaters	Concentration (in mg/kg)
1,2-Dichloropropane	18
1,2,3-Trichloropropane	28
Bis(2-chloroethyl)ether	7.2

K017 wastewaters	Concentration (in mg/l)
1,2-Dichloropropane	0.85
1,2,3-Trichloropropane	0.85
Bis(2-chloroethyl)ether	0.033

K018 nonwastewaters	Concentration (in mg/kg)
Chloroethane	6.0
1,1-Dichloroethane	6.0
1,2-Dichloroethane	6.0
Hexachloroethane	28
Hexachlorobutadiene	5.6
Hexachloroethane	28
Pentachloroethane	5.6
1,1,1-Trichloroethane	6.0

K018 wastewaters	Concentration (in mg/l)
Chloroethane	0.007
1,1-Dichloroethane	.007
1,2-Dichloroethane	.007
Hexachloroethane	.007
Hexachlorobutadiene	.033
Pentachloroethane	.007
1,1,1-Trichloroethane	.007

K019 nonwastewaters	Concentration (in mg/kg)
Bis(2-chloroethyl)ether	5.6
Chlorobenzene	6.0
Chloroform	6.0
1,2-Dichloroethane	6.0
Hexachloroethane	28
Naphthalene	5.6
Phenanthrene	5.6
Tetrachloroethene	6.0
1,2,4-Trichlorobenzene	19
1,1,1-Trichloroethane	6.0

K019 wastewaters	Concentration (in mg/l)
Bis(2-chloroethyl)ether	0.007
Chlorobenzene	.006
Chloroform	.007
p-Dichlorobenzene	.008
1,2-Dichloroethane	.007
Fluorene	.007
Hexachloroethane	.033
Naphthalene	.007
Phenanthrene	.007
1,2,4,5-Tetrachlorobenzene	.017
Tetrachloroethene	.007
1,2,4-Trichlorobenzene	.023
1,1,1-Trichloroethane	.007

K020 nonwastewaters	Concentration (in mg/kg)
1,2-Dichloroethane	6.0
1,1,2,2-Tetrachloroethane	5.6
Tetrachloroethene	6.0

K020 wastewaters	Concentration (in mg/l)
1,2-Dichloroethane	0.007
1,1,2,2-Tetrachloroethane	.007
Tetrachloroethene	.007

K021 nonwastewaters	Concentration (in mg/kg)
Chloroform	6.2
Carbon tetrachloride	6.2

K021 wastewaters	Concentration (in mg/l)
Chloroform	0.007
Carbon tetrachloride	0.046
Antimony	0.057

K022 nonwastewaters (see also Table CCWE in § 268.41)	Concentration (in mg/kg)
Acetophenone	19
Sum of Diphenylamine and Diphenylnitrosamine	13
Phenol	12
Toluene	0.034

K022 wastewaters (see also Table CCWE in § 268.41)	Concentration (in mg/l)
Toluene	0.080
Acetophenone	0.010
Diphenylamine	0.52
Diphenylnitroamine	0.40
Phenol	0.039
Chromium (Total)	0.35
Nickel	0.47

K023 and K024 nonwastewaters	Concentration (in mg/kg)
Phthalic anhydride (measured as Phthalic acid)	28

K023 and K024 wastewaters	Concentration (in mg/l)
Phthalic anhydride (measured as Phthalic acid)	0.54

K028 nonwastewaters (see also Table CCWE in § 268.41)	Concentration (in mg/kg)
1,1-Dichloroethane	6.0
trans-1,2-Dichloroethane	6.0
Hexachlorobutadiene	5.6
Hexachloroethane	28
Pentachloroethane	5.6
1,1,1,2-Tetrachloroethane	5.6
1,1,2,2-Tetrachloroethane	5.6
1,1,1-Trichloroethane	6.0
1,1,2-Trichloroethane	6.0
Tetrachloroethylene	6.0

K028 wastewaters	Concentration (in mg/l)
1,1-Dichloroethane	0.007
trans-1,2-Dichloroethane	0.033
Hexachlorobutadiene	0.007
Hexachloroethane	0.033
Pentachloroethane	0.033
1,1,1,2-Tetrachloroethane	0.007
1,1,2,2-Tetrachloroethane	0.007
Tetrachloroethylene	0.007
1,1,1-Trichloroethane	0.007
1,1,2-Trichloroethane	0.007
Cadmium	6.4
Chromium (Total)	0.35
Lead	0.037
Nickel	0.47

K029 nonwastewaters	Concentration (in mg/kg)
Chloroform	6.0
1,2-Dichloroethane	6.0
1,1-Dichloroethylene	6.0
1,1,1-Trichloroethane	6.0
Vinyl chloride	6.0

K029 wastewaters	Concentration (in mg/l)
Chloroform	0.46
1,2-Dichloroethane	0.21
1,1-Dichloroethylene	0.025
1,1,1-Trichloroethane	0.054
Vinyl chloride	0.27

Appendix C: Pretreatment Standards

K030 nonwastewaters	Concentration (in mg/kg)
Hexachlorobutadiene	5.6
Hexachloroethane	28
Hexachloropropene	19
Pentachlorobenzene	28
Pentachloroethane	5.6
1,2,4,5-Tetrachlorobenzene	14
Tetrachloroethene	6.0
1,2,4-Trichlorobenzene	19

K030 wastewaters	Concentration (in mg/l)
o-Dichlorobenzene	0.008
p-Dichlorobenzene	.008
Hexachlorobutadiene	.007
Hexachloroethane	.033
Pentachloroethane	.007
1,2,4,5-Tetrachlorobenzene	.017
Tetrachloroethene	.007
1,2,4-Trichlorobenzene	.023

K031 wastewaters (see also Table CCWE in § 268.41)	Concentration (in mg/l)
Arsenic	0.79

K032 nonwastewaters	Concentration (in mg/kg)
Hexachloropentadiene	2.4
Chlordane	0.26
Heptachlor	0.066
Heptachlor epoxide	0.066

K032 wastewaters	Concentration (in mg/l)
Hexachloropentadiene	0.057
Chlordane	0.0033
Heptachlor	0.012
Heptachlor epoxide	0.016

K033 and K034 nonwastewaters	Concentration (in mg/kg)
Hexachlorocyclopentadiene	2.4

K033 and K034 wastewaters	Concentration (in mg/l)
Hexachlorocyclopentadiene	0.057

K035 nonwastewaters	Concentration (in mg/kg)
Acenaphthene	3.4
Anthracene	3.4
Benz(a)anthracene	3.4
Benzo(a)pyrene	3.4
Chrysene	3.4
Dibenz(a,h)anthracene	3.4
Fluoranthene	3.4
Fluorene	3.4
Indeno(1,2,3-cd)pyrene	3.4
Napthalene	3.4
Phenanthrene	3.4
Pyrene	8.2

K035 wastewaters	Concentration (in mg/l)
Benz(a)anthracene	0.059
Chrysene	0.059
Fluoranthene	0.068
Cresols (m- and p-isomers)	0.77
Napthalene	0.059
o-Cresol	0.11
Phenanthrene	0.059
Phenol	0.039
Pyrene	0.067

K036 nonwastewaters	Concentration (in mg/kg
Disulfoton	0.1

K036 wastewaters	Concentration (in mg/l)
Disulfoton	0.025

K037 nonwastewaters	Concentration (in mg/kg)
Disulfoton	0.1
Toluene	28

K037 wastewaters	Concentration (in mg/l)
Disulfoton	0.025
Toluene	.080

K038 and K040 nonwastewaters	Concentration (in mg/kg)
Phorate	0.1

K038 and K040 wastewaters	Concentration (in mg/l)
Phorate	0.025

K041 nonwastewaters	Concentration (in mg/kg)
Toxaphene	2.6

K041 wastewaters	Concentration (in mg/l)
Toxaphene	0.0095

K042 nonwastewaters	Concentration (in mg/kg)
1,2,4,5-Tetrachlorobenzene	4.4
o-Dichlorobenzene	4.4
p-Dichlorobenzene	4.4
Pentachlorobenzene	4.4
1,2,4-Trichlorobenzene	4.4

K042 wastewaters	Concentration (in mg/l)
1,2,4,5-Tetrachlorobenzene	0.055
o-Dichlorobenzene	0.088
p-Dichlorobenzene	0.090
Pentachlorobenzene	0.055
1,2,4-Trichlorobenzene	0.055

K043 nonwastewaters	Concentration (in mg/kg)
2,4-Dichlorophenol	0.38
2,6-Dichlorophenol	0.34
2,4,5-Trichlorophenol	8.2
2,4,6-Trichlorophenol	7.6
Tetrachlorophenols (Total)	0.68
Pentachlorophenol	1.9
Tetrachloroethene	1.7
Hexachlorodibenzo-p-dioxins	0.001
Hexachlorodibenzo-furans	0.001
Pentachlorodibenzo-p-dioxins	0.001
Pentachlorodibenzo-furans	0.001
Tetrachlorodibenzo-p-dioxins	0.001
Tetrachlorodibenzo-furans	0.001

K043 wastewaters	Concentration (in mg/l)
2,4-Dichlorophenol	0.049
2,6-Dichlorophenol	0.013

K043 wastewaters	Concentration (in mg/l)
2,4,5-Trichlorophenol	0.016
2,4,6-Trichlorophenol	0.039
Tetrachlorophenols (Total)	0.018
Pentachlorophenol	0.22
Tetrachloroethene	0.006
Hexachlorodibenzo-p-dioxins	0.001
Hexachlorodibenzo-furans	0.001
Pentachlorodibenzo-p-dioxins	0.001
Pentachlorodibenzo-furans	0.001
Tetrachlorodibenzo-p-dioxins	0.001
Tetrachlorodibenzo-furans	0.001

K046 wastewaters (see also Table CCWE in §268.41)	Concentration (in mg/l)
Lead	0.037

K048 nonwastewaters (see also Table CCWE in § 268.41)	Concentration (in mg/kg)
Benzene	14
Benzo(a)pyrene	12
Bis(2-ethylhexyl)phthalate	7.3
Chrysene	15
Di-n-butyl phthalate	3.6
Ethylbenzene	14
Naphthalene	42
Phenanthrene	34
Phenol	3.6
Pyrene	36
Toluene	14
Xylenes	22
Cyanides (Total)	1.8

K048 wastewaters	Concentration (in mg/l)
Benzene	0.011
Benzo(a)pyrene	0.047
Bis(2-ethylhexyl)phthalate	0.043
Chrysene	0.043
Di-n-butyl phthalate	0.060
Ethylbenzene	0.011
Fluorene	0.050
Naphthalene	0.033
Phenanthrene	0.039
Phenol	0.047
Pyrene	0.045
Toluene	0.011
Xylenes	0.011
Cyanides	0.028
Chromium (Total)	0.20
Lead	0.037

Appendix C: Pretreatment Standards

K049 nonwastewaters (see also Table CCWE in § 268.41)	Concentration (in mg/kg)
Anthracene	28
Benzene	14
Benzo(a)pyrene	12
Bis(2-ethylhexyl)phthalate	7.3
Chrysene	15
Ethylbenzene	14
Naphthalene	42
Phenanthrene	34
Phenol	3.6
Pyrene	36
Toluene	14
Xylenes	22
Cyanides (Total)	1.8

K049 wastewaters	Concentration (in mg/l)
Anthracene	0.039
Benzene	0.011
Benzo(a)pyrene	0.047
Bis(2-ethylhexyl)phthalate	0.043
Carbon disulfide	0.011
Chrysene	0.043
2,4-Dimethylphenol	0.033
Ethylbenzene	0.011
Naphthalene	0.033
Phenanthrene	0.039
Phenol	0.047
Pyrene	0.045
Toluene	0.011
Xylenes	0.011
Chromium (Total)	0.2
Lead	0.037

K050 nonwastewaters (see also Table CCWE in § 268.41)	Concentration (in mg/kg)
Benzo(a)pyrene	12
Phenol	3.6
Cyanides (Total)	1.8

K050 wastewaters	Concentration (in mg/l)
Benzo(a)pyrene	0.047
Phenol	0.047
Chromium (Total)	0.2
Lead	0.037

K051 nonwastewaters (see also Table CCWE in § 268.41)	Concentration (in mg/kg)
Anthracene	28
Benzene	14
Benzo(a)anthracene	20

K051 nonwastewaters (see also Table CCWE in § 268.41)	Concentration (in mg/kg)
Benzo(a)pyrene	12
Bis(2-ethylhexyl)phthalate	7.3
Chrysene	15
Di-n-butyl phthalate	3.6
Ethylbenzene	14
Naphthalene	42
Phenanthrene	34
Phenol	3.6
Pyrene	36
Toluene	14
Xylenes	22
Cyanides (Total)	1.8

K051 wastewaters	Concentration (in mg/l)
Acenaphthene	0.05
Anthracene	0.039
Benzene	0.011
Benzo(a)anthracene	0.043
Benzo(a)pyrene	0.047
Bis(2-ethylhexyl)phthalate	0.043
Chrysene	0.043
Di-n-butyl phthalate	0.060
Ethylbenzene	0.011
Fluorene	0.050
Naphthalene	0.033
Phenanthrene	0.039
Phenol	0.047
Pyrene	0.045
Toluene	0.011
Xylenes	0.011
Chromium (Total)	0.2
Lead	0.037

K052 nonwastewaters (see also Table CCWE in § 268.41)	Concentration (in mg/kg)
Benzene	14
Benzo(a)pyrene	12
o-Cresol	6.2
p-Cresol	6.2
Ethylbenzene	14
Naphthalene	42
Phenanthrene	34
Phenol	3.6
Toluene	14
Xylenes	22
Cyanides (Total)	1.8

K052 wastewaters	Concentration (in mg/l)
Benzene	0.011
Benzo(a)pyrene	0.047
o-Cresol	0.011
p-Cresol	0.011

K052 wastewaters	Concentration (in mg/l)
2,4-Dimethylphenol	0.033
Ethylbenzene	0.011
Naphthalene	0.033
Phenanthrene	0.039
Phenol	0.047
Toluene	0.011
Xylenes	0.011
Chromium (Total)	0.2
Lead	0.037

K060 nonwastewaters	Concentration (in mg/kg)
Benzene	0.071
Benzo(a)pyrene	3.6
Naphthalene	3.4
Phenol	3.4
Cyanides (Total)	1.2

K060 wastewaters	Concentration (in mg/l)
Benzene	0.17
Benzo(a)pyrene	0.035
Naphthalene	0.028
Phenol	0.042
Cyanides (Total)	1.9

K061 wastewaters (see also Table CCWE in § 268.41 and Table 2 in 268.42)	Concentration (in mg/l)
Cadmium	1.61
Chromium (Total)	0.32
Lead	0.51
Nickel	0.44

K062 wastewaters	Concentration (in mg/l)
Chromium (Total)	0.32
Lead	0.04
Nickel	0.44

K069 wastewaters (see also Table CCWE in § 268.41 and Table 2 in 268.42)	Concentration (in mg/l)
Cadmium	1.6
Lead	0.51

K071 wastewaters	Concentration (in mg/l)
Mercury	0.030

K073 nonwastewaters	Concentration (in mg/kg)
Carbon tetrachloride	6.2
Chloroform	6.2
Hexachloroethane	30
Tetrachloraethene	6.2
1,1,1-Trichloroethane	6.2

K073 wastewaters	Concentration (in mg/l)
Carbon tetrachloride	0.057
Chloroform	0.046
Hexachloroethane	0.055
Tetrachloraethene	0.056
1,1,1-Trichloroethane	0.054

K083 nonwastewaters	Concentration (in mg/kg)
Benzene	6.2
Aniline	14
Sum of Diphenylamine and Diphenylnitrosamine	14
Nitrobenzene	14
Phenol	5.6
Cyclohexanone	30

K083 wastewaters	Concentration (in mg/l)
Benzene	0.14
Aniline	0.81
Diphenylamine	0.52
Diphenylnitrosamine	0.40
Nitrobenzene	0.068
Phenol	0.039
Cyclohexanone	0.36
Nickel	0.47

K084 wastewaters	Concentration (in mg/l)
Arsenic	0.79

K085 nonwastewaters	Concentration (in mg/kg)
Benzene	4.4
Chlorobenzene	4.4

Appendix C: Pretreatment Standards

K085 nonwastewaters	Concentration (in mg/kg)
o-Dichlorobenzene	4.4
m-Dichlorobenzene	4.4
p-Dichlorobenzene	4.4
1,2,4-Trichlorobenze	4.4
1,2,4,5-Tetrachlorobenzene	4.4
Pentachlorobenzene	4.4
Hexachlorobenzene	4.4
Aroclor 1016	0.92
Aroclor 1221	0.92
Aroclor 1232	0.92
Aroclor 1242	0.92
Aroclor 1248	0.92
Aroclor 1254	1.8
Aroclor 1260	1.8

K085 wastewaters	Concentration (in mg/l)
Benzene	0.14
Chlorobenzene	0.057
o-Dichlorobenzene	0.088
m-Dichlorobenzene	0.036
p-Dichlorobenzene	0.090
1,2,4-Trichlorobenze	0.055
1,2,4,5-Tetrachlorobenzene	0.055
Pentachlorobenzene	0.055
Hexachlorobenzene	0.055
Aroclor 1016	0.013
Aroclor 1221	0.014
Aroclor 1232	0.013
Aroclor 1242	0.017
Aroclor 1248	0.013
Aroclor 1254	1.014
Aroclor 1260	1.014

K086 nonwastewaters (see also Table CCWE in § 268.41)	Concentration (in mg/kg)
Acetone	160
Acetopnenone	9.7
Bis(2-ethylhexyl)phthalate	28
n-Butyl alcohol	2.6
Butylbenzylphthalate	7.9
1,2-Dichlorobenzene	6.2
Diethyl phthalate	28
Dimethyl phthalate	28
Di-n-butyl phthalate	28
Di-n-octyl phthalate	28
Ethyl acetate	33
Ethylbenzene	6.0
Methyl isobutyl ketone	33
Methyl ethyl ketone	36
Methylene chloride	33
Naphthalene	3.1
Nitrobenzene	14
Toluene	28
1,1,1,-Trichloroethane	5.6
Trichloroethylene	5.6

K086 nonwastewaters (see also Table CCWE in § 268.41)	Concentration (in mg/kg)
Xylenes	28
Cyanides (Total)	1.5

K086 wastewaters (see also Table CCWE in § 268.41)	Concentration (in mg/l)
Acetone	0.28
Acetopnenone	0.010
Bis(2-ethylhexyl)phthalate	0.28
n-Butyl alcohol	5.6
Butylbenzylphthalate	0.017
Cyclohexanone	0.36
1,2-Dichlorobenzene	0.088
Diethyl phthalate	0.20
Dimethyl phthalate	0.047
Di-n-butyl phthalate	0.057
Di-n-octyl phthalate	0.017
Ethyl acetate	0.34
Ethylbenzene	0.0.057
Methanol	5.6
Methyl isobutyl ketone	0.14
Methyl ethyl ketone	0.28
Methylene chloride	0.089
Naphthalene	0.059
Nitrobenzene	0.068
Toluene	0.080
1,1,1,-Trichloroethane	0.054
Trichloroethylene	0.054
Xylenes	0.32
Cyanides (Total)	1.9
Chromium (Total)	0.32
Lead	0.037

K087 nonwastewaters (see also Table CCWE in § 268.41)	Concentration (in mg/kg)
Acenaphthalene	3.4
Benzene	0071
Chrysene	3.4
Fluoranthene	3.4
Indeno (1,2,3-cd) pyrene	3.4
Naphthalene	3.4
Phenanthrene	3.4
Toluene	0.65
Xylenes	0.070

K087 wastewaters	Concentration (in mg/l)
Acenaphthalene	0.028
Benzene	0.014
Chrysene	0.028
Fluoranthene	0.028
Indeno (1,2,3-cd) pyrene	0.028
Naphthalene	0.028
Phenanthrene	0.028
Toluene	0.008

K087 wastewaters	Concentration (in mg/l)
Xylenes	0.014
Lead	0.037

K093 and K094 nonwastewaters	Concentration (in mg/kg)
Phthalic anhydride (measured as Phthalic acid)	28

K093 and K094 wastewaters	Concentration (in mg/l)
Phthalic anhydride (measured as Phthalic acid)	0.54

K095 nonwastewaters	Concentration (in mg/kg)
1,1,1,2-Tetrachloroethane	5.6
1,1,2,2-Tetrachloroethane	5.6
Tetrachloroethene	6.0
1,1,2-Trichloroethane	6.0
Trichloroethylene	5.6
Hexachloroethane	28
Pentachloroethane	5.6

K095 wastewaters	Concentration (in mg/l)
1,1,1,2-Tetrachloroethane	0.057
1,1,2,2-Tetrachloroethane	0.057
Tetrachloroethene	0.056
1,1,2-Trichloroethane	0.054
Trichloroethylene	0.054
Hexachloroethane	0.055
Pentachloroethane	0.055

K096 nonwastewaters	Concentration (in mg/kg)
1,1,1,2-Tetrachloroethane	5.6
1,1,2,2-Tetrachloroethane	5.6
Tetrachloroethene	6.0
1,1,2-Trichloroethane	6.0
Trichloroethene	5.6
1,3-Dichlorobenzene	5.6
Pentachloroethane	5.6
1,2,4-Trichlorobenzene	19

K096 wastewaters	Concentration (in mg/l)
1,1,1,2-Tetrachloroethane	0.057
1,1,2,2-Tetrachloroethane	0.057
Tetrachloroethene	0.056
1,1,2-Trichloroethane	0.054
Trichloroethene	0.054
1,3-Dichlorobenzene	0.036
Pentachloroethane	0.055
1,2,4-Trichlorobenzene	0.055

K097 nonwastewaters	Concentration (in mg/kg)
Hexachlorocyclopentadiene	2.4
Chlordane	0.26
Heptachlor	0.066
Heptachlor epoxide	0.066

K097 wastewaters	Concentration (in mg/l)
Hexachlorocyclopentadiene	0.057
Chlordane	0.0033
Heptachlor	0.0012
Heptachlor epoxide	0.016

K098 nonwastewaters	Concentration (in mg/kg)
Toxaphene	2.6

K098 wastewaters	Concentration (in mg/l)
Toxaphene	0.005

K099 nonwastewaters	Concentration (in mg/kg)
2,4-Dichlorophenoxyacetic acid	1.0
Hexachlorodibenzo-p-dioxins	0.001
Hexachlorodibenzofurans	0.001
Pentachlorodibenzo-p-dioxins	0.001
Pentachlorodibenzofurans	0.001
Tetrachlorodibenzo-p-dioxins	0.001
Tetrachlorodibenzofurans	0.001

K099 wastewaters	Concentration (in mg/l)
2,4-Dichlorophenoxyacetic acid	1.0
Hexachlorodibenzo-p-dioxins	0.001
Hexachlorodibenzofurans	0.001
Pentachlorodibenzo-p-dioxins	0.001

Appendix C: Pretreatment Standards

K099 wastewaters	Concentration (in mg/l)
Pentachlorodibenzofurans	0.001
Tetrachlorodibenzo-p-dioxins	0.001
Tetrachlorodibenzofurans	0.001

K100 wastewaters (see also Table CCWE in § 268.410)	Concentration (in mg/l)
Cadmium	1.6
Chromium	0.32
Lead	0.51

K101 nonwastewaters	Concentration (in mg/kg)
Ortho-Nitroaniline	14

K101 wastewaters	Concentration (in mg/l)
Ortho-Nitroaniline	0.27
Arsenic	0.79
Cadmium	0.24
Lead	0.17
Mercury	0.082

K102 nonwastewaters (see also Table CCWE in § 268.41)	Concentration (in mg/kg)
Ortho-Nitroaniline	13

K102 wastewaters (see also Table CCWE in § 268.41)	Concentration (in mg/l)
Ortho-Nitroaniline	0.028
Arsenic	0.79
Cadmium	0.24
Lead	0.17
Mercury	0.082

K103 nonwastewaters	Concentration (in mg/kg)
Aniline	5.6
Benzene	6.0
2,4-Dinitrophenol	5.6
Nitrobenzene	5.6
Phenol	5.6

K103 wastewaters	Concentration (in mg/l)
Aniline	4.5
Benzene	0.15
2,4-Dinitrophenol	0.61
Nitrobenzene	0.073
Phenol	1.4

K104 nonwastewaters	Concentration (in mg/kg)
Aniline	5.6
Benzene	6.0
2,4-Dinitrophenol	5.6
Nitrobenzene	5.6
Phenol	5.6
Cyanides (Total)	1.8

K104 wastewaters	Concentration (in mg/l)
Aniline	4.5
Benzene	0.15
2,4-Dinitrophenol	0.61
Nitrobenzene	0.073
Phenol	1.4
Cyanides (Total)	2.7

K105 nonwastewaters	Concentration (in mg/kg)
Benzene	4.4
Chlorobenzene	4.4
o-Dichlorobenzene	4.4
p-Dichlorobenzene	4.4
2,4,5-Trichlorophenol	4.4
2,4,6-Trichlorophenol	4.4
2-Chlorophenol	4.4
Phenol	4.4

K105 wastewaters	Concentration (in mg/l)
Benzene	0.14
Chlorobenzene	0.057
o-Dichlorobenzene	0.088
p-Dichlorobenzene	0.090
2,4,5-Trichlorophenol	0.18
2,4,6-Trichlorophenol	0.035
2-Chlorophenol	0.044
Phenol	0.039

K106 wastewaters (see also Table CCWE in § 268.41 and Table 2 in 268.42)	Concentration (in mg/l)
Mercury	0.030

K115 wastewaters (see also Table CCWE in § 268.41)	Concentration (in mg/l)
Nickel	0.47

P004 nonwastewaters	Concentration (in mg/kg)
Aldrin	0.066

P004 wastewaters	Concentration (in mg/l)
Aldrin	0.21

P010, P011, and P012 nonwastewaters (see also Table CCWE in § 268.41)	Concentration (in mg/l)
Arsenic	0.79

P013, P021, P029, and P030 nonwastewaters	Concentration (in mg/kg)
Cyanides (Total)	110
Cyanides (Amenable)	9.1

P013, P021, P029, and P030 nonwastewaters	Concentration (in mg/kg)
Cyanides (Total)	1.9
Cyanides (Amenable)	0.10

P022 wastewaters (see also Table 2 in § 268.42)	Concentration (in mg/l)
Carbon disulfide	0.014

P024 nonwastewaters	Concentration (in mg/kg)
p-Chloroaniline	16

P024 wastewaters	Concentration (in mg/l)
p-Chloroaniline	0.46

P036 and P038 wastewaters (see also Table CCWE in § 268.42)	Concentration (in mg/l)
Arsenic	0.79

P037 nonwastewaters	Concentration (in mg/kg)
Dieldrin	0.13

P037 wastewaters	Concentration (in mg/l)
Dieldrin	0.017

P039 nonwastewaters	Concentration (in mg/kg)
Disulfoton	0.1

P039 wastewaters	Concentration (in mg/l)
Disulfoton	0.017

P047 nonwastewaters	Concentration (in mg/kg)
4,6-Dinitro-o-cresol	160

P047 wastewaters	Concentration (in mg/l)
4,6-Dinitro-o-cresol	0.28

P048 nonwastewaters	Concentration (in mg/kg)
2,4-Dinitrophenol	160

P048 wastewaters	Concentration (in mg/l)
2,4-Dinitrophenol	0.12

Appendix C: Pretreatment Standards

P050 nonwastewaters	Concentration (in mg/kg)
Endosulfan I	0.066
Endosulfan II	0.13
Endosulfan sulfate	0.13

P050 wastewaters	Concentration (in mg/l)
Endosulfan I	0.023
Endosulfan II	0.029
Endosulfan sulfate	0.029

P051 nonwastewaters	Concentration (in mg/kg)
Endrin	0.13
Endrin aldehyde	0.13

P051 wastewaters	Concentration (in mg/l)
Endrin	0.0028
Endrin aldehyde	0.025

P056 wastewaters (see also Table 2 in § 268.42)	Concentration (in mg/l)
Fluoride	35

P059 nonwastewaters	Concentration (in mg/kg)
Heptachlor	0.066
Heptachlor epoxide	0.066

P059 wastewaters	Concentration (in mg/l)
Heptachlor	0.0012
Heptachlor epoxide	0.016

P060 nonwastewaters	Concentration (in mg/kg)
Isodrin	0.066

P060 wastewaters	Concentration (in mg/l)
Isodrin	0.021

P063 nonwastewaters	Concentration (in mg/kg)
Cyanides (Total)	110
Cyanides (Amenable)	9.1

P063 wastewaters	Concentration (in mg/l)
Cyanides (Total)	1.9
Cyanides (Amenable)	0.10

P065 and P092 wastewaters (see also Table CCWE in § 268.41 and Table 2 in 268.42)	Concentration (in mg/l)
Mercury	0.030

P071 nonwastewaters	Concentration (in mg/kg)
Methyl parathion	0.1

P071 wastewaters	Concentration (in mg/l)
Methyl parathion	0.025

P073 wastewaters (see also Table CCWE in § 268.43)	Concentration (in mg/l)
Nickel	0.44

P074 nonwastewaters (see also Table CCWE in § 268.43)	Concentration (in mg/kg)
Cyanides (Total)	110
Cyanides (Amenable)	9.1

P074 wastewaters (see also Table CCWE in § 268.43)	Concentration (in mg/l)
Cyanides (Total)	1.9
Cyanides (Amenable)	0.10
Nickel	0.44

P077 nonwastewaters	Concentration (in mg/kg)
p-Nitroaniline	28

P077 wastewaters	Concentration (in mg/l)
p-Nitroaniline	0.028

P082 wastewaters (see also Table 2 in § 268.42)	Concentration (in mg/l)
N-Nitrosodimethylamine	0.40

P089 nonwastewaters	Concentration (in mg/kg)
Parathion	0.1

P089 wastewaters	Concentration (in mg/l)
Parathion	0.025

P094 nonwastewaters	Concentration (in mg/kg)
Phorate	0.1

P094 wastewaters	Concentration (in mg/l)
Phorate	0.025

P097 nonwastewaters	Concentration (in mg/kg)
Famphur	0.1

P097 wastewaters	Concentration (in mg/l)
Famphur	0.025

P098 nonwastewaters	Concentration (in mg/kg)
Cyanides (Total)	110
Cyanides (Amenable)	9.1

P098 wastewaters	Concentration (in mg/l)
Cyanides (Total)	1.9
Cyanides (Amenable)	0.10

P099 nonwastewaters (see also Table CCWE in § 268.43)	Concentration (in mg/kg)
Cyanides (Total)	110
Cyanides (Amenable)	9.1

P099 wastewaters (see also Table CCWE in § 268.43)	Concentration (in mg/l)
Cyanides (Total)	1.9
Cyanides (Amenable)	0.10
Silver	0.29

P101 nonwastewaters	Concentration (in mg/kg)
Ethyl cyanide (Propanenitrile)	360

P101 wastewaters	Concentration (in mg/l)
Ethyl cyanide (Propanenitrile)	0.24

P103 wastewaters (see also Table CCWE in § 268.43)	Concentration (in mg/l)
Selenium	1.0

P104 nonwastewaters (see also Table CCWE in § 268.42)	Concentration (in mg/kg)
Cyanides (Total)	110
Cyanides (Amenable)	9.1

P104 wastewaters (see also Table CCWE in § 268.42)	Concentration (in mg/l)
Cyanides (Total)	1.9
Cyanides (Amenable)	0.10
Silver	0.29

P106 nonwastewaters	Concentration (in mg/kg)
Cyanides (Total)	110
Cyanides (Amenable)	9.1

P106 wastewaters	Concentration (in mg/l)
Cyanides (Total)	1.9
Cyanides (Amenable)	0.10

Appendix C: Pretreatment Standards

P110 wastewaters (see also Table CCWE in § 268.41 and Table 2 in 268.42	Concentration (in mg/l)
Lead	0.040

P113 and P115 wastewaters (see also Table 2 in § 268.42)	Concentration (in mg/l)
Thallium	0.14

P114 wastewaters (see also Table CCWE in § 268.42)	Concentration (in mg/l)
Selenium	1.0

P119 and P120 wastewaters (see also Table 2 in § 268.42)	Concentration (in mg/l)
Vanadium	28

P121 and 123 nonwastewaters	Concentration (in mg/kg)
Cyanides (Total)	110
Cyanides (Amenable)	9.1

P121 and 123 wastewaters	Concentration (in mg/l)
Cyanides (Total)	1.9
Cyanides (Amenable)	0.10

U002 nonwastewaters	Concentration (in mg/kg)
Acetone	160

U002 wastewaters	Concentration (in mg/l)
Acetone	0.28

U003 nonwastewaters (see also Table 2 in § 268.42)	Concentration (in mg/l)
Acetonitrile	0.17

U004 nonwastewaters	Concentration (in mg/kg)
Acetophenone	9.7

U004 wastewaters	Concentration (in mg/l)
Acetophenone	0.010

U005 nonwastewaters	Concentration (in mg/kg)
2-Acetylaminofluorene	140

U005 wastewaters	Concentration (in mg/l)
2-Acetylaminofluorene	0.059

U009 nonwastewaters	Concentration (in mg/kg)
Acrylonitrile	84

U009 wastewaters	Concentration (in mg/l)
Acrylonitrile	0.24

U012 nonwastewaters	Concentration (in mg/kg)
Aniline	14

U012 wastewaters	Concentration (in mg/l)
Aniline	0.81

U018 nonwastewaters	Concentration (in mg/kg)
Benz(a)anthracene	8.2

U018 wastewaters	Concentration (in mg/l)
Benz(a)anthracene	0.059

U019 nonwastewaters	Concentration (in mg/kg)
Benzen	36

U019 wastewaters	Concentration (in mg/l)
Benzene	0.14

U022 nonwastewaters	Concentration (in mg/kg)
Benzo(a)pyrene	8.2

U022 wastewaters	Concentration (in mg/l)
Benzo(a)pyrene	0.061

U024 nonwastewaters	Concentration (in mg/kg)
Bis(2-chloroethoxy)methane	7.2

U024 wastewaters	Concentration (in mg/l)
Bis(2-chloroepoxy)methane	0.036

U025 nonwastewaters	Concentration (in mg/kg)
Bis(2-chloroethyl)ether	7.2

U025 wastewaters	Concentration (in mg/l)
Bis(2-chloroethyl)ether	0.036

U027 nonwastewaters	Concentration (in mg/kg)
Bis(2-chloroisopropyl) ether	7.2

U027 wastewaters	Concentration (in mg/l)
Bis(2-chloroisopropyl) ether	0.055

U028 nonwastewaters	Concentration (in mg/kg)
Bis-(2-ethylhexyl) phthalate	28

U028 wastewaters	Concentration (in mg/l)
Bis-(2-ethylhexyl) phthalate	0.54

U029 nonwastewaters	Concentration (in mg/kg)
Bromomethane (Methyl bromide)	15

U029 wastewaters	Concentration (in mg/l)
Bromomethane (Methyl bromide)	0.11

U030 nonwastewaters	Concentration (in mg/kg)
4-Bromophenyl phenyl ether	15

U030 wastewaters	Concentration (in mg/l)
4-Bromophenyl phenyl ether	0.055

U031 nonwastewaters	Concentration (in mg/kg)
N-Butyl alcohol	2.6

U031 wastewaters	Concentration (in mg/l)
n-Butyl alcohol	5.6

U032 wastewaters	Concentration (in mg/l)
Chromium	0.32

U036 nonwastewaters	Concentration (in mg/kg)
Chlordane (alpha and gamma)	0.13

Appendix C: Pretreatment Standards

U036 wastewaters	Concentration (in mg/l)
Chlordane (alpha and gamma)	0.0033

U037 nonwastewaters	Concentration (in mg/kg)
Chlorobenzene	5.7

U037 wastewaters	Concentration (in mg/l)
Chlorobenzene	0.057

U038 nonwastewaters (see also Table 2 in § 268.42)	Concentration (in mg/l)
Chlorobenzilate	0.10

U039 wastewaters	Concentration (in mg/l)
p-Chloro-m-cresol	0.018

U042 wastewaters (see also Table 2 in § 268.42)	Concentration (in mg/l)
2-Chloroethyl vinyl	0.057

U043 nonwastewaters	Concentration (in mg/kg)
Vinyl chloride	33

U043 wastewaters	Concentration (in mg/l)
Vinyl chloride	0.27

U044 nonwastewaters	Concentration (in mg/kg)
Chloroform	5.6

U044 wastewaters	Concentration (in mg/l)
Chloroform	0.046

U045 nonwastewaters	Concentration (in mg/kg)
Chloromethane (Methyl chloride)	33

U045 wastewaters	Concentration (in mg/l)
Chloromethane (Methyl chloride)	0.19

U047 nonwastewaters	Concentration (in mg/kg)
2-Chloronaphthalene	5.6

U047 wastewaters	Concentration (in mg/l)
2-Chloronaphthalene	0.055

U048 nonwastewaters	Concentration (in mg/kg)
2-Chlorophenol	5.7

U048 wastewaters	Concentration (in mg/l)
2-Chlorophenol	0.044

U050 nonwastewaters	Concentration (in mg/kg)
Chrysene	8.2

U050 wastewaters	Concentration (in mg/l)
Chrysene	0.059

U051 nonwastewaters	Concentration (in mg/l)
Naphthalene	1.5
Pentachlorophenol	7.4
Phenanthrene	1.5
Pyrene	28
Toluene	33

U051 wastewaters	Concentration (in mg/l)
Naphthalene	0.031
Pentachlorophenol	0.18
Phenanthrene	0.031
Pyrene	0.028
Toluene	0.028
Xylenes (Total)	0.032
Lead	0.037

U052 nonwastewaters	Concentration (in mg/kg)
o-Cresol	5.6
Cresols (m- and p-isomers)	3.2

U052 wastewaters	Concentration (in mg/l)
o-Cresol	0.11
Cresols (m- and p-isomers)	0.77

U057 wastewaters (see also Table 2 in § 268.42)	Concentration (in mg/l)
Cyclohexanone	0.36

U060 nonwastewaters	Concentration (in mg/kg)
o,p'-DDD	0.087
p,p'-DDD	0.087

U060 wastewaters	Concentration (in mg/l)
o,p'-DDD	0.023
p,p'-DDD	0.023

U061 nonwastewaters	Concentration (in mg/kg)
o,p'-DDT	0.087
p,p'-DDT	0.087
o,p'-DDD	0.087
p,p'-DDD	0.087
o,p'-DDE	0.087
p,p'-DDE	0.087

U061 wastewaters	Concentration (in mg/l)
o,p'-DDT	0.0039
p,p'-DDT	0.0039
o,p'-DDD	0.023
p,p'-DDD	0.023
o,p'-DDE	0.031
p,p'-DDE	0.031

U062 nonwastewaters	Concentration (in mg/kg)
Dibenzo(a,h)anthracene	8.2

U062 wastewaters	Concentration (in mg/kg)
Dibenzo(a,h)anthracene	0.055

U066 nonwastewaters	Concentration (in mg/kg)
1,2-Dibromo-3-chloropropane	15

U066 nonwastewaters	Concentration (in mg/l)
1,2-Dibromo-3-chloropropane	0.11

U067 nonwastewaters	Concentration (in mg/kg)
1,2-Dibromomethane (Ethylene dibromide)	15

U067 wastewaters	Concentration (in mg/l)
1,2-Dibromethane (Ethylene dibromide)	0.028

U068 nonwastewaters	Concentration (in mg/kg)
Dibromonethane	15

U068 wastewaters	Concentration (in mg/l)
Dibromonethane	0.11

Appendix C: Pretreatment Standards

U069 nonwastewaters	Concentration (in mg/kg)
Di-n-butyl phthalate	28

U069 wastewaters	Concentration (in mg/l)
Di-n-butyl phthalate	0.54

U070 nonwastewaters	Concentration (in mg/kg)
o-Dichlorobenzene	6.2

U070 wastewaters	Concentration (in mg/l)
o-Dichlorobenzene	0.088

U071 nonwastewaters	Concentration (in mg/kg)
m-Dichlorobenzene	6.2

U071 wastewaters	Concentration (in mg/l)
m-Dichlorobenze	0.036

U072 nonwastewaters	Concentration (in mg/kg)
p-Dichlorobenzene	6.2

U072 wastewaters	Concentration (in mg/l)
p-Dichlorobenzene	0.090

U075 nonwastewaters	Concentration (in mg/kg)
Dichlorodifluoromethane	7.2

U075 wastewaters	Concentration (in mg/l)
Dichlorodifluoromethane	0.23

U076 nonwastewaters	Concentration (in mg/kg)
1,1-Dichloroethane	7.2

U076 wastewaters	Concentration (in mg/l)
1,1-Dichloroethane	0.059

U077 nonwastewaters	Concentration (in mg/kg)
1,2-Dichloroethane	7.2

U077 wastewaters	Concentration (in mg/l)
1,2-Dichloroethane	0.21

U078 nonwastewaters	Concentration (in mg/kg)
1,1-Dichloroethylene	33

U078 wastewaters	Concentration (in mg/l)
1,1-Dichloroethylene	0.025

U079 nonwastewaters	Concentration (in mg/kg)
trans-1,2-Dichloroethylene	33

U079 wastewaters	Concentration (in mg/l)
trans-1,2-Dichloroethylene	0.054

U080 nonwastewaters	Concentration (in mg/kg)
Methylene chloride	33

U080 wastewaters	Concentration (in mg/l)
Methylene chloride	0.054

U081 nonwastewaters	Concentration (in mg/kg)
2,4-Dichlorophenol	14

U081 wastewaters	Concentration (in mg/l)
2,4-Dichlorophenol	0.044

U082 nonwastewaters	Concentration (in mg/kg)
2,6-Dichlorophenol	14

U082 wastewaters	Concentration (in mg/l)
2,6-Dichlorophenol	0.044

U083 nonwastewaters	Concentration (in mg/kg)
1,2-Dichloropropane	18

U083 wastewaters	Concentration (in mg/l)
1,2-Dichloropropane	0.85

U084 nonwastewaters	Concentration (in mg/kg)
cis-1,3-Dichloropropylene	18
trans-1,3-Dichloropropylene	18

U084 wastewaters	Concentration (in mg/l)
cis-1,3-Dichloropropylene	0.036
trans-1,3-Dichloropropylene	0.036

U088 nonwastewaters	Concentration (in mg/kg)
Diethyl phthalate	28

U088 wastewaters	Concentration (in mg/l)
Diethyl phthalate	0.54

U093 wastewaters (see also Table 2 in § 268.42)	Concentration (in mg/l)
p-Dimethylaminoazobenzene	0.13

U102 nonwastewaters	Concentration (in mg/kg)
2,4-Dimethylphenol	14

U102 wastewaters	Concentration (in mg/l)
2,4-Dimethylphenol	0.036

U102 nonwastewaters	Concentration (in mg/kg)
Dimethyl phthalate	28

U102 wastewaters	Concentration (in mg/l)
Dimethyl phthalate	0.54

U105 nonwastewaters	Concentration (in mg/kg)
2,4-Dinitrotoluene	140

U105 wastewaters	Concentration (in mg/l)
2,4-Dinitrotoluene	0.32

U106 nonwastewaters	Concentration (in mg/kg)
2,6-Dinitrotoluene	28

U106 wastewaters	Concentration (in mg/l)
2,6-Dinitrotoluene	0.55

U107 nonwastewaters	Concentration (in mg/kg)
Di-n-octyl phthalate	28

Appendix C: Pretreatment Standards

U107 wastewaters	Concentration (in mg/l)
Di-n-octyl phthalate	0.54

U108 nonwastewaters	Concentration (in mg/kg)
1,4-Dioxane	170

U108 wastewaters	Concentration (in mg/l)
1,4-Dioxane	0.12

U111 nonwastewaters	Concentration (in mg/kg)
Di-n-propylnitrosoamine	14

U111 wastewaters	Concentration (in mg/l)
Di-n-propylnitrosoamine	0.40

U112 nonwastewaters	Concentration (in mg/kg)
Ethyl acetate	33

U112 wastewaters	Concentration (in mg/l)
0.34	

U117 nonwastewaters	Concentration (in mg/kg)
Ethyl ether	160

U117 wastewaters	Concentration (in mg/l)
Ethyl ether	0.12

U118 nonwastewaters	Concentration (in mg/kg)
Ethyl methacrylate	160

U118 wastewaters	Concentration (in mg/l)
Ethyl methacrylate	0.14

U120 nonwastewaters	Concentration (in mg/kg)
Fluoranthene	8.2

U120 wastewaters	Concentration (in mg/l)
Fluoroanthene	0.068

U121 nonwastewaters	Concentration (in mg/kg)
Trichloromonofluoromethane	33

U121 wastewaters	Concentration (in mg/l)
Trichloromonofluoromethane	0.020

U127 nonwastewaters	Concentration (in mg/kg)
Hexachlorobenzen	37

U127 wastewaters	Concentration (in mg/l)
Hexachlorobenzene	0.055

U128 nonwastewaters	Concentration (in mg/kg)
Hexachlorobutadiene	28

U128 wastewaters	Concentration (in mg/l)
Hexachlorobutadiene	0.055

U129 nonwastewaters	Concentration (in mg/kg)
alpha-BHC	0.066
beta-BHC	0.066
Delta-BHC	0.066

Waste Management Guide

U129 nonwastewaters	Concentration (in mg/kg)
gamma-BHC (Lindane)	0.066

U129 wastewaters	Concentration (in mg/l)
alpha-BHC	0.00014
beta-BHC	0.00014
Delta-BHC	0.023
gamma-BHC	0.0017

U130 nonwastewaters	Concentration (in mg/kg)
Hexachlorocyclopentadiene	3.6

U130 wastewaters	Concentration (in mg/l)
Hexachlorocyclopentadiene	0.057

U131 nonwastewaters	Concentration (in mg/kg)
Hexachloroethane	28

U131 wastewaters	Concentration (in mg/l)
Hexachloroethane	0.055

U134 wastewaters (see also Table 2 in § 268.42)	Concentration (in mg/l)
Fluoride	35

U136 wastewaters (see also Table CCWE in § 268.41)	Concentration (in mg/l)
Arsenic	0.79

U137 nonwastewaters	Concentration (in mg/kg)
Indeno(1,2,3-c,d)pyrene	8.2

U137 wastewaters	Concentration (in mg/l)
Indeno(1,2,3-c,d)pyrene	0.0055

U138 nonwastewaters	Concentration (in mg/kg)
Iodomethane	65

U138 wastewaters	Concentration (in mg/l)
Iodomethane	0.19

U140 nonwastewaters	Concentration (in mg/kg)
Isobutyl alcohol	170

U140 wastewaters	Concentration (in mg/l)
Isobutyl alcohol	5.6

U141 nonwastewaters	Concentration (in mg/kg)
Isosafrole	2.6

U141 wastewaters	Concentration (in mg/l)
Isosafrole	0.081

U142 nonwastewaters	Concentration (in mg/kg)
Kepone	0.13

U142 wastewaters	Concentration (in mg/l)
Kepone	0.0011

U144, U145, and 146 wastewaters (see also Table CCWE in § 268.41)	Concentration (in mg/l)
Lead	0.040

U151 wastewaters (see also Table CCWE in § 268.41) and Table 2 in 268.42)	Concentration (in mg/l)
Mercury	0.030

Appendix C: Pretreatment Standards

U152 nonwastewaters	Concentration (in mg/kg)
Methacrylonitrile	84

U152 wastewaters	Concentration (in mg/l)
Methyacrylonitrile	0.24

U155 nonwastewaters	Concentration (in mg/kg)
Methapryrilene	1.5

U155 wastewaters	Concentration (in mg/l)
Methapyrilene	0.081

U157 nonwastewaters	Concentration (in mg/kg)
3-Methylcholantrene	15

U157 wastewaters	Concentration (in mg/l)
3-Methylcholanthrene	0.0055

U158 nonwastewaters	Concentration (in mg/kg)
4,4'-Methylenebis(2-chloroaniline)	35

U158 wastewaters	Concentration (in mg/l)
4,4'-Methylenebis(2-chloroaniline)	0.50

U159 nonwastewaters	Concentration (in mg/kg)
Methyl ethyl ketone	36

U159 wastewaters	Concentration (in mg/l)
Methyl ethyl ketone	0.28

U161 nonwastewaters	Concentration (in mg/kg)
Methyl isobutyl ketone	33

U161 wastewaters	Concentration (in mg/l)
Methyl isobutyl ketone	0.14

U162 nonwastewaters	Concentration (in mg/kg)
Methyl methacrylate	160

U162 wastewaters	Concentration (in mg/l)
Methyl methacrylate	0.14

U165 nonwastewaters	Concentration (in mg/kg)
Naphthalene	3.1

U165 wastewaters	Concentration (in mg/l)
Naphthalene	0.059

U168 wastewaters (see also Table 2 in § 268.420)	Concentration (in mg/l)
2-Naphthylamine	0.52

U169 nonwastewaters	Concentration (in mg/kg)
Nitrobenzene	14

U169 wastewaters	Concentration (in mg/l)
Nitrobenzene	0.068

U170 nonwastewaters	Concentration (in mg/kg)
4-Nitrophenol	29

U170 wastewaters	Concentration (in mg/l)
4-Nitrophenol	0.12

U172 nonwastewaters	Concentration (in mg/kg)
n-Nitrosodi-n-butylamine	17

U172 wastewaters	Concentration (in mg/l)
n-Nitrosodi-n-butylamine	0.40

U174 nonwastewaters	Concentration (in mg/kg)
N-Nitrosodiethylamine	28

U174 wastewaters	Concentration (in mg/l)
n-Nitrosodiethylamine	0.40

U179 nonwastewaters	Concentration (in mg/kg)
n-Nitrosopiperidine	35

U179 wastewaters	Concentration (in mg/l)
n-Nitrosopiperidine	0.013

U180 nonwastewaters	Concentration (in mg/kg)
N-Nitrosopyrrolidine	35

U180 wastewaters	Concentration (in mg/l)
n-Nitrosopyrrolidine	0.013

U181 nonwastewaters	Concentration (in mg/kg)
5-Nitro-o-toluidine	28

U181 wastewaters	Concentration (in mg/l)
5-Nitro-o-toluidine	0.32

U183 nonwastewaters	Concentration (in mg/kg)
Pentachlorobenzene	37

U183 wastewaters	Concentration (in mg/l)
Pentachlorobenzene	0.055

U185 nonwastewaters	Concentration (in mg/kg)
Pentachloronitrobenzene	4.8

U185 wastewaters	Concentration (in mg/l)
Pentachloronitrobenzene	0.055

U187 nonwastewaters	Concentration (in mg/kg)
Phenacetin	16

U187 wastewaters	Concentration (in mg/l)
Phenacetin	0.081

U188 nonwastewaters	Concentration (in mg/kg)
Phenol	6.2

U188 wastewaters	Concentration (in mg/l)
Phenol	0.039

U190 nonwastewaters	Concentration (in mg/kg)
Phthalic anhydride (measured as Phthalic acid)	28

Appendix C: Pretreatment Standards

U190 wastewaters	Concentration (in mg/l)
Phthalic anhydride (measured as Phthalic acid)	0.54

U192 nonwastewaters	Concentration (in mg/kg)
Pronomide	1.5

U192 wastewaters	Concentration (in mg/l)
0.093	

U196 nonwastewaters	Concentration (in mg/kg)
Pyridine	16

U196 wastewaters	Concentration (in mg/l)
Pyridine	0.014

U203 nonwastewaters	Concentration (in mg/kg)
Safrole	22

U203 wastewaters	Concentration (in mg/l)
Safrole	0.081

U204 and U205 wastewaters (see also Table CCWE in § 268.41)	Concentration (in mg/l)
Selenium	1.0

U207 nonwastewaters	Concentration (in mg/kg)
1,2,4,5-Tetrachlorobenzene	19

U207 wastewaters	Concentration (in mg/l)
1,2,4,5-Tetrachlorobenzene	0.055

U208 nonwastewaters	Concentration (in mg/kg)
1,1,1,2-Tetrachloroethane	42

U208 wastewaters	Concentration (in mg/l)
1,1,1,2-Tetrachloroethane	0.057

U209 nonwastewaters	Concentration (in mg/kg)
1,1,2,2-Tetrachloroethane	42

U209 wastewaters	Concentration (in mg/l)
1,1,2,2-Tetrachloroethane	0.057

U210 nonwastewaters	Concentration (in mg/kg)
Tetrachloroethylenen	5.6

U210 wastewaters	Concentration (in mg/l)
Tetrachloroethylenen	0.056

U211 nonwastewaters	Concentration (in mg/kg)
Carbon Tetrachloride	5.6

U211 wastewaters	Concentration (in mg/l)
Carbon tetrachloride	0.057

U214, U215, U216, and U217 wastewaters (see also Table 2 in § 268.42)	Concentration (in mg/l)
Thallium	0.14

U220 nonwastewaters	Concentration (in mg/kg)
Toluene	28

U220 wastewaters	Concentration (in mg/l)
Toluene	0.080

U225 nonwastewaters	Concentration (in mg/kg)
Tribromomethane (Bromoform)	15

U225 wastewaters	Concentration (in mg/l)
Tribromomethane (Bromoform)	0.63

U226 nonwastewaters	Concentration (in mg/kg)
1,1,1-Trichloroethane	15

U226 wastewaters	Concentration (in mg/l)
1,1,1-Trichloroethane	0.054

U227 nonwastewaters	Concentration (in mg/kg)
1,1,2-Trichloroethane	5.6

U227 wastewaters	Concentration (in mg/l)
1,1,2-Trichloroethane	0.054

U228 nonwastewaters	Concentration (in mg/kg)
Trichloroethylene	5.6

U228 wastewaters	Concentration (in mg/l)
Trichloroethylene	0.054

U235 nonwastewaters	Concentration (in mg/kg)
tris-(2,3-Dibromopropyl) phosphate	0.1

U235 wastewaters	Concentration (in mg/l)
tris-(2,3-Dibromopropyl) phosphate	0.025

U2239 nonwastewaters	Concentration (in mg/kg)
Xylenes	28

U239 wastewaters	Concentration (in mg/l)
Xylenes	0.32

U240 nonwastewaters	Concentration (in mg/kg)
2,4-Dichlorophenoxyacetic acid	10

U240 wastewaters	Concentration (in mg/l)
2,4-Dichlorophenoxyacetic acid	0.72

U243 nonwastewaters	Concentration (in mg/kg)
Hexachloropropene	28

U243 wastewaters	Concentration (in mg/l)
Hexachloropropene	0.035

U247 nonwastewaters	Concentration (in mg/kg)
Methoxychlor	0.18

U247 wastewaters	Concentration (in mg/l)
Methoxychlor	0.25

Land Disposal Prohibitions

Land disposal for the following is prohibited outright:

K004 nonwastewaters disposed of after Aug. 17, 1988, and not generated in the course of treating wastewater forms of these wastes (based on no generation).

K005 nonwastewaters generated by the process described in the waste listing description, disposed after June 8, 1989, and not generated in the course of treating wastewater forms of these wastes (based on no generation).

K007 nonwastewaters generated by the process described in the waste listing description, disposed after June 8, 1989, and not generated in the course of treating wastewater forms of these wastes (based on no generation).

K008 nonwastewaters disposed of after Aug. 17, 1988, and not generated in the course of treating wastewater forms of these wastes (based on no generation).

K021 nonwastewaters disposed of after Aug. 17, 1988, and not generated in the course of treating wastewater forms of these wastes (based on no generation).

K025 nonwastewaters disposed of after Aug. 17, 1988, and not generated in the course of treating wastewater forms of these wastes (based on no generation).

K036 nonwastewaters disposed of after Aug. 17, 1988, and not generated in the course of treating wastewater forms of these wastes (based on no generation).

K044 (based on reactivity)

LAND DISPOSAL RESTRICTION: TECHNOLOGY-BASED TREATMENT STANDARDS

POLICY GUIDE

In promulgating the land disposal regulations, the Environmental Protection Agency determined that for many "U" and "P" wastes, as well as some "F" and "K" wastes, complications arose over the reliability of quantifying the hazardous constituents in these wastes. As a result, the agency decided to establish technology-based best demonstrated available technology standards rather than concentration-based constituent specific standards for these wastes.

Table 1 provides a detailed description of the technology standard referred to by the five-letter technology code. See Table 2 for the appropriate technology-based standard for those wastes that EPA has decided are not easily quantified. Table 3 lists the standards for specific radioactive hazardous mixed wastes.

The full text of EPA's land disposal ban regulations (40 CFR 268) can be found in BNA's *Environment Reporter*, Federal Regulations 4, beginning at p. 161:2201.

TABLE 1. — TECHNOLOGY CODES AND DESCRIPTION OF TECHNOLOGY-BASED STANDARDS

Technology code	Description of technology-based standard
ADGAS	Venting of compressed gases into an absorbing or reacting media (i.e., solid or liquid) — venting can be accomplished through physical release utilizing valves/piping; physical penetration of the container; and/or penetration through detonation.
AMLGM	Amalgamation of liquid, elemental mercury contaminated with radioactive materials utilizing inorganic reagents such as copper, zinc, nickel, gold, and sulfur that result in a nonliquid, semi-solid amalgam and thereby reducing potential emissions of elemental mercury vapors to the air.
BIODG	Biodegradation of organics or non-metallic inorganics (i.e., degradable inorganics that contain the elements of phosphorus, nitrogen and sulfur) in units operated under either aerobic or anaerobic conditions such that a surrogate compound or indicator parameter has been substantially reduced in concentration in the residuals (e.g., Total Organic Carbon can often be used as an indicator parameter for the biodegradation of many organic constituents that cannot be directly analyzed in wastewater residues).
CARBN	Carbon adsorption (granulated or powdered) of non-metallic inorganics, organo-metallics, and/or organic constituents, operated such that a surrogate compound or indicator parameter has not undergone breakthrough (e.g., Total Organic Carbon can often be used as an indicator parameter for the adsorption of many organic constituents that cannot be directly analyzed in wastewater residues). Breakthrough occurs when the carbon has become saturated with the constituent (or indicator parameter) and substantial change in adsorption rate associated with that constitutent occurs.

Appendix C: Pretreatment Standards

TABLE 1. — TECHNOLOGY CODES AND DESCRIPTION OF TECHNOLOGY-BASED STANDARDS —Continued

Technology code	Description of technology-based standard
CHOXD	Chemical or electrolytic oxidation utilizing the following oxidation reagents (or waste reagents) or combinations or reagents: (1) Hypochlorite (e.g. bleach); (2) chlorine; (3) chlorine dioxide; (4) ozone or UV (ultraviolet light) assisted ozone; (5) peroxides; (6) persulfates; (7) perchlorates; (8) permanganates; and/or (9) other oxidizing reagents of equivalent efficiency, performed in units operated such that a surrogate compound or indicator parameter has been substantially reduced in concentration in the residuals (e.g., Total Organic Carbon can often be used as an indicator parameter for the oxidation of many organic constituents that cannot be directly analyzed in wastewater residues). Chemical oxidation specifically includes what is commonly referred to as alkaline chlorination.
CHRED	Chemical reduction utilizing the following reducing reagents (or waste reagents) or combinations of reagents: (1) Sulfur dioxide; (2) sodium, potassium, or alkali salts of sulfites, bisulfites, metabisulfites, and polyethylene glycols (e.g., NaPEG and KPEG); (3) sodium hydrosulfide; (4) ferrous salts; and/or (5) other reducing reagents of equivalent efficiency, performed in units operated such that a surrogate compound or indicator parameter has been substantially reduced in concentration in the residuals (e.g., Total Organic Halogens can often be used as an indicator parameter for the reduction of many halogenated organic constituents that cannot be directly analyzed in wastewater residues). Chemical reduction is commonly used for the reduction of hexavalent chromium to the trivalent state.
DEACT	Deactivation to remove the hazardous characteristics of a waste due to its ignitability, corrosivity, and/or reactivity.
FSUBS	Fuel substitution in units operated in accordance with applicable technical operating requirements.
HLVIT	Vitrification of high level mixed radioactive wastes in units in compliance with all applicable radioactive protection requirements under control of the Nuclear Regulatory Commission.
IMERC:	Incineration of wastes containing organics and mercury in units operated in accordance with the technical operating requirements of 40 CFR part 264, subpart O and 40 CFR part 265, subpart O. All wastewater and nonwastewater residues derived from this process must then comply with the corresponding treatment standards per waste code with consideration of any applicable subcategories (e.g., High or Low Mercury Subcategories).
INCIN	Incineration in units operated in accordance with the technical operating requirements of 40 CFR part 264, subpart O and 40 CFR part 265, subpart O.
LLEXT	Liquid-liquid extraction (often referred to as solvent extraction) of organics from liquid wastes into an immiscible solvent for which the hazardous constituents have a greater solvent affinity, resulting in an extract high in organics that must undergo either incineration, reuse as a fuel, or other recovery/reuse and a raffinate (extracted liquid waste) proportionately low in organics that must undergo further treatment as specified in the standard.
MACRO	Macroencapsulation with surface coating materials such as polymeric organics (e.g. resins and plastics) or with a jacket of inert inorganic materials to substantially reduce surface exposure to potential leaching media. Macroencapsulation specifically does not include any material that would be classified as a tank or container according to 40 CFR 260.10.
NEUTR	Neutralization with the following reagents (or waste reagents) or combinations of reagents: (1) Acids; (2) bases; or (3) water (including wastewaters) resulting in a pH greater than 2 but less than 12.5 as measured in the aqueous residuals.
NLDBR	No land disposal based on recycling.
PRECP	Chemical precipitation of metals and other inorganics as insoluble precipitates of oxides, hydroxides, carbonates, sulfides, sulfates, chlorides, flourides, or phosphates. The following reagents (or waste reagents) are typically used alone or in combination: (1) Lime (i.e., conaining oxides and/or hydroxides of calcium and/or magnesium; (2) caustic (i.e., sodium and/or potassium hydroxides; (3) soda ash (i.e., sodium carbonate); (4) sodium sulfide; (5) ferric sulfate or ferric chloride; (6) alum; or (7) sodium sulfate. Additional flocculating, coagulation, or similar reagents/processes that enhance sludge dewatering characteristics are not precluded from use.

TABLE 1. — TECHNOLOGY CODES AND DESCRIPTION OF TECHNOLOGY-BASED STANDARDS —Continued

Technology code	Description of technology-based standard
RBERY	Thermal recovery of Beryllium.
RCGAS	Recovery/reuse of compressed gases including techniques such as reprocessing of the gases for reuse/resale; filtering/adsorption of impurities; remixing for direct reuse of resale; and use of the gas as a fuel source.
RCORR	Recovery of acids or bases utilizing one or more of the following recovery technologies: (1) Distillation (i.e., thermal concentration); (2) ion exchange; (3) resin or solid adsorption; (4) reverse osmosis; and/or (5) incineration for the recovery of acid — Note: this does not preclude the use of other physical phase separation or concentration techniques such as decantation, filtration (including ultrafiltration), and centrifugation, when used in conjunction with the above listed recovery technologies.
RLEAD	Thermal recovery of lead in secondary lead smelters.
RMERC	Retorting or roasting in a thermal processing unit capable of volatilizing mercury and subsequently condensing the volatized mercury for recovery. The retorting or roasting unit (or facility) must be subject to one or more of the following: (a) A National Emissions Standard for Hazardous Air Pollutants (NESHAP) for mercury; (b) a Best Available Control Technology (BACT) or a Lowest Achievable Emission Rate (LAER) standard for mercury imposed pursuant to a Prevention of Significant Deterioration (PSD) permit; or (c) a state permit that establishes emission limitations (within meaning of Section 302 of the Clean Air Act) for mercury. All wastewater and nonwastewater residues derived from this process must then comply with the corresponding treatment standards per waste code with consideration of any applicable subcategories (e.g., High or Low Mercury Subcategories).
RMETL	Recovery of metals or inorganics utilizing one or more of the following direct physical/removal technologies: (1) Ion exchanges; (2) resin or solid (i.e., zeolites) adsorption; (3) reverse osmosis; (4) chelation/solvent extraction; (5) freeze crystallization; (6) ultrafiltration; and/or 6 simple precipitation (i.e., crystallization) — Note: this does not preclude the use of other physical phase separation or concentration techniques such as decantation, filtration (including ultrafiltration), and centrifugation, when used in conjunction with the above listed recovery technologies.
RORGS	Recovery of organics utilizing one or more of the following technologies: (1) Distillation; (2) thin film evaporation; (3) steam stripping; (4) carbon adsorption; (5) critical fluid extraction; (6) liquid-liquid extraction; (7) precipitation/crystallization (including freeze crystallization); or (8) chemical phase separation techniques (i.e. addition of acids, bases, demulsifiers, or similar chemicals); Note: This does not preclude the use of other physical phase separation techniques such as decantation, filtration (including ultrafiltration), and centrifugation, when used in conjunction with the above listed recovery technologies.
RTHRM	Thermal recovery of metals or inorganics from nonwastewaters in units defined in 40 CFR 260.10, paragraphs (1), (6), (7), (11), and (12), under the definition of "industrial furnaces".
RZINC	Resmelting in for the purpose of recovery of zinc high temperature metal recovery units.
STABI.	Stabilization with the following reagents (or waste reagents) or combinations of reagents: (1) Portland cement; or (2) lime/pozzolans (e.g., fly ash and cement kiln dust) — this does not preclude the addition of reagents (e.g., iron salts, silicates and clays) designed to enhance the set/cure time and/or compressive strength, or to overall the leachability of the metal or inorganic.
SSTRP	Steam stripping of organics from liquid wastes utilizing direct application of steam to the wastes operated such that liquid and vapor flow rates, as well as, temperature and pressure ranges have been optimized, monitored, and maintained. These operating parameters are dependent upon the design parameters of the unit such as, the number of separation stages and the internal column design. Thus, resulting in a condensed extract high in organics that must undergo either incineration, reuse as a fuel, or other revoery/reuse and an extracted wastewater that must undergo further treatment as specified in the standard.

TABLE 1. — TECHNOLOGY CODES AND DESCRIPTION OF TECHNOLOGY-BASED STANDARDS —Continued

Technology code	Description of technology-based standard
WETOX	Wet air oxidation performed in units operated such that a surrogate compound or indicator parameter has been substantially reduced in concentration in the residuals (e.g., Total Organic Carbon can often be used as an indicator parameter for the oxidation of many organic constituents that cannot be directly analyzed in wastewater residues).
WTRRX	Controlled reaction with water for highly reactive inorganic or organic chemicals with precautionary controls for protection of workers from potential violent reactions as well as precautionary controls for potential emissions of toxic/ignitable levels of gases released during the reaction.

NOTE 1: When a combination of these technologies (i.e., a treatment train) is specified as a single treatment standard, the order of application is specified in §268.42, Table 2 by indicating the five letter technology code that must be applied first, then the designation "fb." (an abbreviation for "followed by"), then the five letter technology code for the technology that must be applied next, and so on.

NOTE 2: When more than one technology (or treatment train) are specified as *alternative* treatment standards, the five letter technology codes (or the treatment trains) are separated by a semicolon (;) with the last technology preceded by the word "OR". This indicates that any one of these BDAT technologies or treatment trains can be used for compliance with the standard.

TABLE 2. — TECHNOLOGY-BASED STANDARDS BY RCRA WASTE CODE

Waste code	Waste descriptions and/or treatment subcategory	Wastewaters	Nonwastewaters
D001	Ignitable Liquids based on 261.21(a)(1) — Wastewasters.	DEACT	NA.
D001	Ignitable Liquids based on 261.21(a)(1) — Low TOC Ignitable Liquids Subcategory — Less than 10% total organic carbon.	NA	DEACT.
D001	Ignitable Liquids based on 261.21(a)(1) — High TOC Ignitable Liquids Subcategory — Greater than or equal to 10% total organic carbon.	NA	FSUBS; RORGS; or INCIN.
D001	Ignitable compressed gases based on 261.21(a)(3).	NA	DEACT**
D001	Ignitable reactives 261.21(a)(2)	NA	DEACT
D001	Oxidizers based on 261.21(a)(4)	DEACT	DEACT.
D002	Acid subcategory based on 261.22(a)(1)	DEACT	DEACT.
D002	Alkaline subcategory based on 261.22(a)(1)	DEACT	DEACT.
D002	Other corrosives based on 261.22(a)(2)	DEACT	DEACT.
D003	Reactive sulfides based on 261.23(a)(5)	DEACT	DEACT.
D003	Explosives based on 261.23(a)(6), (7), and (8)	DEACT	DEACT.
D003	Water reactives based on 261.23(a)(2), (3), and (4)	NA	DEACT.
D003	Other reactives based on 261.23(a)(1)	DEACT	DEACT.
D006	Cadmium containing batteries	NA	RTHRM.

TABLE 2. — TECHNOLOGY-BASED STANDARDS BY RCRA WASTE CODE —Continued

Waste code	Waste descriptions and/or treatment subcategory	Technology code Wastewaters	Technology code Nonwastewaters
D008	Lead acid batteries (Note: This standard only applies to lead acid batteries that are identified as RCRA hazardous wastes and that are not excluded elsewhere from regulation under the land disposal restrictions of 40 CFR 268 or exempted under other EPA regulations (see 40 CFR 266.80).).	NA	RLEAD.
D009	Mercury: (High Mercury Subcategory — greater than or equal to 260 mg/kg total Mercury — contains mercury and organics (and are not incinerator residues)).	NA	IMERC; or RMERC.
D009	Mercury: (High Mercury Subcategory — greater than or equal to 260 mg/kg total Mercury — inorganics (including incinerator residues and residues from RMERC)).	NA	RMERC.
D012	Endrin	BIODG; or INCIN	NA.
D013	Lindane	CARBN; or INCIN	NA.
D014	Methoxychlor	WETOX; or INCIN	NA.
D015	Toxaphene	BIODG; or INCIN	NA.
D016	2,4-D	CHOXD; BIODG; or INCIN	NA.
D017	2,4,5-TP	CHOXD; or INCIN	NA.
F005	2-Nitropropane	(WETOX or CHOXD) fb CARBN; or INCIN	INCIN.
F005	2-Ethoxyethanol	BIODG; or INCIN	INCN.
F024		INCIN	INCIN.
K025	Distillation bottoms from the production of nitrobenzene by the nitration of benzene.	LLEXT fb SSTRP fb CARBN; or INCIN	ICIN.
K026	Stripping still tails from the production of methyl ethyl pyridines.	INCIN	INCIN.
K027	Centrifuge and distillation residues from toluene disocyanate production.	CARBN; or INCIN	FSUBS; or INCIN.
K039	Filter cake from the filtration of diethylphosphorodithioc acid in the production of phorate.	CRBIN; or INCIN	FSUBS; or INCIN.
K044	Wastewater treatment sludges from the manufacturing and processing of explosives.	DEACT	DEACT.
K045	Spent carbon from the treatment of wastewater containing explosives.	DEACT	DEACT.
K047	Pink/red water from TNT operations	DEACT	DEACT.
K061	Emission control dust/sludge from the primary production of steel in electric furnaces (High Zinc Subcategory — greater than or equal to 15% total Zinc).	NA	NLDBR.
K069	Emission control dust/sludge from secondary lead smelting: Non-Calcium Sulfate Subcategory	NA	RLEAD.

Appendix C: Pretreatment Standards

TABLE 2. — TECHNOLOGY-BASED STANDARDS BY RCRA WASTE CODE —Continued

Waste code	Waste descriptions and/or treatment subcategory	Technology code Watewaters	Technology code Nonwastewaters
K106	Wastewater treatment sludge from the mercury cell process in chlorine production: (High Mercury Subcategory- greater than or equal to 260 mg/kg total mercury).	NA	RMERC.
K113	Condensed liquid light ends from the purification of toluenediamine in the production of touenediamine via hydrogenation of dintrololuene.	CARBN; or INCIN	FSUBS; or INCIN.
K114	Vicinals from the purification of toluenediame in the production of toluenediamine via hydrogenation of dinitrotoluena.	CARBN; or INCIN	FSUBS; or INCIN.
K115	Heavy ends from the purification of toluenediame in the production of toluenediamine via hydrogenation of dinitrotoluene.	CARBN; or INCIN	FSUBS; or INCIN.
K116	Organic condensate from the solvent recovery column in the production of toluene disocyanate via phosgenation of toluenediamine.	CARBN; or INCIN	FSUBS; or INCIN.
P001	Warfarin (0.3%)	(WETOX or CHOXD) fb CARBN; or INCIN	FSUBS; or INCIN.
P002	1-Acetyl-2-thoiurea	(WETOX or CHOXD) fb CARBN; or INCIN	INCIN.
P003	Acrolein	(WETOX or CHOXD) fb CARBN; or INCIN	FSUBS;or INCIN.
P005	Allyl alcohol	(WETOX or CHOXD) fb CARBN; or INCIN	FSUBS; or INCIN.
P006	Aluminum phosphide	CHOXD; CHRED; or INCIN	CHOXD CHRED; or INCIN.
P007	5-Aminoethyl 3-isoxazolol	(WETOX or CHOXD) fb CARBN; or INCIN	INCIN.
P008	4-Aninopyridine	(WETOX or CHOXD) fb CARBN; or INCIN	INCIN.
P009	Ammonium picrate	CHOXD; CHRED CARBN; BIODG or INCIN	FSUBS; CHOXD, CHRED; or INCIN.
P014	Thiophenol (Benzene thiol)	(WETOX or CHOXD) fb CARBN; or INCIN	INCIN.
P015	Beryllium dust	NA	RMETL; or RTHRM.
P016	Bis(chloromethyl)ether	(WETOX or CHOXD) fb CARBN; or INCIN	INCIN.
P017	Bromoacetone	(WETOX or CHOXD) fb CARBN; or INCIN	INCIN.
P018	Brucine	(WETOX or CHOXD) fb CARBN; or INCIN	INCIN.
P022	Carbon disulfide	NA	INCIN.
P023	Chloroacetaldehyde	(WETOX or CHOXD) fb CARBN; or INCIN	INCIN.
P026	1-(o-Chlorophenyl) thiourea.	(WETOX or CHOXD) fb CARBIN; or IN-CIN	INCIN.
P027	3-Chloropropionitrile	WETOX or CHOXD) fb CRBN; or INCIN	INCIN.

TABLE 2. — TECHNOLOGY-BASED STANDARDS BY RCRA WASTE CODE —Continued

Waste code	Waste descriptions and/or treatment subcategory	Technology code Wastewaters	Technology code Nonwastewaters
P028	Bensyl chloride	(WETOX or CHOXD) fb CARBN; or INCIN	INCIN.
P031	Cyanogen	CHOXD; WETOX; or INCIN	CHOXD; WETOX; or INCIN.
P033	Cyanogen chloride	CHOXD; WETOX; or INCIN	CHOXD; WETOX; or INCIN.
P034	2-Cyclohexyl-4,6-dinitrophenol	(WETOX or CHOXD) fb CARBN; or INCIN	INCIN.
P040	O,O-Diethyl O-pyrazinyl phosphorothioate	CARBN; or INCIN	FSUBS; or INCIN.
P041	Diethyl-p-nitrophenyl phosphate	CARBN; or INCIN	FSUBS; or INCIN.
P042	Epinephrine	(WETOX or CHOXD) fb CARBN; or INCIN	INCIN.
P043	Diisopropylfluorophosphate (DFP)	CARBN; or INCIN	FSUBS; or INCIN.
P044	Dimethoate	CARBIN; or INCIN	FSUBS; or INCIN.
P045	Thiofanox	(WETOX or CHOXD) fb CARBN; or INCIN	INCIN.
P046	alpha, alpha-Dimethylphenethylamine	(WETOX or CHOXD) fb CARBN or INCIN	INCIN.
P047	4,6-Dinitro-o-cresol salts	(WETOX or CHOXD) fb CARBN; or INCIN	INCIN.
P049	2,4-Dithiobiuret	(WETOX or CHOXD) fb CARBN; or INCIN	INCIN.
P054	Aziridine	(WETOX or CHOXD) fb CARBN; or INCIN	INCIN.
P056	Fluorine	NA	ADGAS fb NEUTR.
P057	Fluoroacetamide	(WETOX or CHOXD) fb CARBN; or INCIN	INCIN.
P058	Fluoroacetic acid, sodium salt	(WETOX or CHOXD) fb CARBN; or INCIN	INCIN.
P062	Hexaethyltetraphosphate	CARBN; or INCIN	FSUBS; or INCIN.
P064	Isocyanic acid, ethyl ester	(WETOX or CHOXD) fb CARBN; or INCIN	INCIN.
P065	Mercury fulminate: (High Mercury Subcategory — greater than or equal to 260 mg/kg total Mercury — either incinerator residues or residues from RMERC.	NA	RMERC.
P065	Mercury fulminate: (All nonwastewaters that are not incinerator residues from RMERC; regardless of Mercury Content).	NA	IMERC.
P066	Methomyl	(WETOX or CHOXD) fb CARBN; or INCIN	INCIN.
P067	2-Methylaziridine	(WETOX or CHOXD) fb CARBN; or INCIN	INCIN.
P068	Methyl hydrazine	CHOXD; CHRED; CARBN; BIODG; or INCIN	FSUBS; CHOXD; CHRED; or INCIN.
P069	Methyllactonitrile	(WETOX or CHOXD) fb CARBN; or INCIN	INCIN.
P070	Aldicarb	(WETOX or CHOXD) fb CARBN; or INCIN	INCIN.
P072	1-Naphththyl-2-thiourea	(WETOX or CHOXD) fb CARBN; or INCIN	INCIN.
P075	Nicotine and salts	(WETOX or CHOXD) fb CARBN; or INCIN	INCIN.
P076	Nitric oxide	ADGAS	ADGAS.

TABLE 2. — TECHNOLOGY-BASED STANDARDS BY RCRA WASTE CODE —Continued

Waste code	Waste descriptions and/or treatment subcategory	Technology code Watewaters	Technology code Nonwastewaters
P078	Nitrogen dioxide	ADGAS	ADGAS.
P081	Nitroglycerin	CHOXD; CHRED; CARBN; BIODG; or INCIN	FSUBS; CHOXD; CHRED; or INCIN.
P082	N-Nitrosodimethylamine	NA	INCIN.
P084	N-Nitrosomethylvinylamine	(WETOX or CHOXD) fb CARBN; or INCIN	INCIN.
P085	Octamethylpyrophosphoramide	CARBN; or INCIN	FSUBS; or INCIN.
P087	Osmium tetroxide	NA	RMETL; or RTHRM.
P088	Endothall	(WETOX or CHOXD) fb CARBN; or INCIN	FSUBS; or INCIN.
P092	Phenyl mercury acetate: (High Mercury Subcategory — greater than or equal to 260 mg/kg total Mercury — either incinerator residues or residues from RMERC).	NA	RMERC.
P092	Phenyl mercury acetate: (All nonwastewaters that are not incinerator residues and are not residues from RMERC: regardless of Mercury Content).	NA	IMERC, or RMERC.
P093	N-Phenylthiouea	(WETOX or CHOXD) fb CARBN; or INCIN	INCIN.
P095	Phosgene	(WETOX or CHOXD) fb CARBN; or IN-CIN/INCIN.	
P096	Phosphine	CHOXD; CHRED; or INCIN	CHOXD; CHRED; or INCIN.
P102	Propargyl alcohol	(WETOX or CHOXD) fb CARBN; or INCIN	FSUBS; or INCIN
P105	Sodium azide	CHOXD; CHRED: CARBN; BIODG: or INCIN	FUSBS; CHOXD; CHRED, or INCIN.
P108	Strychnine and salts	(WETOX or CHOXD) fb CARBN; or ICIN	INCIN.
P109	Tetraethyldithioprophosphate	CARBN, or INCIN	FSUBS; OR INCIN
P112	Tetranitromethane	CHOXD; CHRED; CARBN; BIODG; or INCIN	FSUBS; CHOXD; CHRED; or INCIN.
P113	Thalic oxide	NA	RTHRM; or STABL
P115	Thallium (1) sulfate	NA	RTHRM; or STABL
P116	Thiosemicarbazide	(WETOX or CHOXD) fb CARBN; or INCIN	INCIN.
P118	Trichloromethanethiol	(WETOX or CHOXD) fb CARBN; or INCIN	INCIN.
P119	Ammonium vanadate	NA	STABL
P120	Vanadium pentoxide	NA	STABL
P122	Zinc Phosphide (<10%)	CHOXD;, CHRED; or INCIN	CHOXD; CHRED; or INCIN.
U001	Acetaldehyde	(WETOX or CHOXD) fb CARBN; or INCIN	FSUBS; or INCIN.
U003	Acetonitrile	NA	INCIN.
U006	Acetyl Chloride	(WETOX or CHOXD) fb CARBN; or INCIN	INCIN.
U007	Acrylamide	(WETOX or CHOXD) fb CARBN; or INCIN	INCIN.

TABLE 2. — TECHNOLOGY-BASED STANDARDS BY RCRA WASTE CODE —Continued

Waste code	Waste descriptions and/or treatment subcategory	Technology code Wastewaters	Technology code Nonwastewaters
U008	Acrylic acid	(WETOX or CHOXD) fb CARBN; or INCIN	FSUBS; or INCIN.
U010	Mitomycin C	(WETOX or CHOXD) fb CARBN; or INCIN	INCIN.
U011	Amitrole	(WETOX or CHOXD) fb CARBN. or INCIN	INCIN.
U014	Auramine	(WETOX or CHOXD) fb CARBN; or INCIN	INCIN.
U015	Azaserine	WETOX or CHOXD) fb CARBN; or INCIN	INCIN.
U016	Benz(c)acridine	(WETOX or CHOXD) fb CARBN; or INCIN	FSUBS; or INCIN.
U017	Benzal chloride	(WETOX or CHOXD) fb CARBN; or INCIN	INCIN.
U020	Benzenesulfonyl chloride	(WETOX or CHOXD) fb CARBN; or INCN	INCIN.
U021	Benzidine	(WETOX or CHOXD) fb CARBN; or INCIN	INCIN.
U023	Benzotrichloride	CHOXD; CHERD; CARBN; BIODG; or INCIN	FSUBS; CHOXD; CHRED; or INCIN.
U026	Chlornaphazin	(WETOX or CHOXD) fb CARBN; or INCIN	INCIN.
U033	Cabonyl fluoride	(WETOX or CHOXD) fb CARBN; or INCIN	INCIN.
U034	Trichloroacetaldehyde (Chloral)	(WETOX or CHOXD) fb CARBN; or INCIN	INCIN.
U035	Chlorambucil	(WETOX or CHOXD) fb CARBN; or INCIN	INCIN.
U038	Chlorobenzilate	NA	INCIN.
U041	1-Chloro-2,3-epoxypropane (Epichlorohydrin)	(WETOX or CHOXD) fb CARBN; or INCIN	INCIN.
U042	2-Chloroethyl vinyl ether	NA	INCIN.
U046	Chloromethyl methyl ether	(WETOX or CHOXD) fb CARBN; or INCIN	INCIN.
U049	4-Chloro-o-toluidine hydrochloride	(WETOX or CHOX) fb CARBN; or INCIN	INCIN.
U053	Crotonaldehyde	(WETOX or CHOXD) fb CARBN; or INCIN	FSUBS; or INCIN.
U055	Cumene	(WETOX or CHOXD) fb CARBN; or INCIN	FSUBS; or INCIN.
U056	Cyclohexane	(WETOX or CHOXD) fb CARBN; or INCIN	FSUBS; or INCIN.
U057	Cyclohexanone	NA	FSUBS; or INCIN.
U058	Cyclophosphamide	CARBN; or INCIN	FSUBS; or INCIN.
U059	Daunomycin	(WETOX or CHOXD) fb CARBN; or INCIN	INCIN.
U062	Diallate	(WETOX or CHOXD) fb CARBN; or INCIN	INCIN.
U064	1,2,7,8-Dibenzopyrene	(WETOX or CHOXD) fb CARBN; or INCIN	FSUBS; or INCIN.
U073	3,3'-Dichlorobenzidine	(WETOX or CHOXD) fb CARBN; or INCIN	INCIN.
U074	cis-1,4-Dichloro-2-butene	(WETOX or CHOXD) fb CARBN; or INCIN	INCIN.

TABLE 2. — TECHNOLOGY-BASED STANDARDS BY RCRA WASTE CODE —Continued

Waste code	Waste descriptions and/or treatment subcategory	Technology code Wate-waters	Nonwaste-waters
	trans-1,4-Dichloro-2-butene	(WETOX or CHOXD) fb CARBN; or INCIN	INCIN.
U085	1,2:3,4-Diepoxybutane	(WETOX or CHOXD) fb CARBN; or INCIN	FSUBS; or INCIN.
U086	N,N-Diethylhydrazine	CHOXD; CHRED;CARBN; BIODG; orINCIN	FSUBS: CHOXD; CHRED; or INCIN.
U087	0,0-Diethyl S-methyldithiophosphate	CARBN; or INCIN	FSUBS; or INCIN.
U089	Diethyl stilbestrol	(WETOX or CHOXD) fb CARBN; or INCIN	FSUBS; or INCIN.
U090	Dihydrosafrole	(WETOX or CHOXD) fb CARBN; or INCIN	FSUBS; or INCIN.
U091	3,3'-Dimethoxybenzidine	(WETOX or CHOXD) fb CARBN; or INCIN	INCIN.
U092	Dimethylamine	(WETOX or CHOXD) fb CARBN; or INCIN	INCIN.
U093	p-Dimethylaminoazobenzene	NA	INCIN.
U094	7,12-Dimethyl benz(a)anthracene	(WETOX or CHOXD) fb CARBN; or INCIN	FSUBS; or INCIN.
U095	3,3'-Dimethylbenzidine	(WETOX or CHOXD) fb CARBN; or INCIN	INCIN.
U096	a,a-Dimethyl benzyl hydroperoxide	CHOXD; CHRED; CARBN; BIODG; or INCIN	FSUBS; CHOXD; CHRED; or INCIN.
U097	Dimethylcarbomyl chloride	(WETOX or CHOXD) fb CARBN; or INCIN	INCIN.
U098	1,1-Dimethylhydrazine	CHOXD; CHRED; CARBN; BIODG; or INCIN	FSUBS; CHOXD; CHRED; or INCIN.
U099	1,2-Dimethylhydrazine	CHOXD; CHRED; CARBN; BIODG; or INCIN	FSUBS; CHOXD; CHRED, or INCIN.
U103	Dimethyl sulfate	CHOXD; CHRED: CARBN; BIODG; or INCIN	FSUBS; CHOXD; CHRED; or INCIN.
U109	1,2-Diphenylhydrazine	CHOXD; CHRED; CARBN; BIODG; or INCIN	FSUBS; CHOXD; CHRED: or INCIN.
U110	Dipropylamine	(WETOX or CHOXD) fb CARBN; or INCIN	INCIN.
U113	Ethyl acrylate	(WETOX or CHOXD) fb CARBN; or INCIN	FSUBS; or INCIN.
U114	Ethylene bis-dithiocarbamic acid	(WETOX or CHOXD) fb CARBN; or INCIN	INCIN.
U115	Ethylene oxide	(WETOX or CHOXD) fb CARBN; or INCIN	CHOXD; or INCIN.
U116	Ethylene thiourea	(WETOX or CHOXD) fb CARBN; or INCIN	INCIN.
U119	Ethyl methane sulfonate	(WETOX or CHOXD) fb CARBN; or INCIN	INCIN.
U122	Formaldehyde	(WETOX or CHOXD) fb CARBN; or INCIN	FSUBS; or INCIN.
U123	Formic acid	(WETOX or CHOXD) fb CARBN; or INCIN	FSUBS; or INCIN.
U124	Furan	(WETOX or CHOXD) fb CARBN; or INCIN	FSUBS; or INCIN.

TABLE 2. — TECHNOLOGY-BASED STANDARDS BY RCRA WASTE CODE —Continued

		Technology code	
Waste code	Waste descriptions and/or treatment subcategory	Wastewaters	Nonwastewaters
U125	Furfural	(WETOX or CHOXD) fb CARBN; or INCIN	FSUBS; or INCIN.
U126	Glycidaldehyde	(WETOX or CHOXD) fb CARBN; or INCIN	FSUBS; or INCIN.
U132	Hexachlorophenene	(WETOX or CHOXD) fb CARBN; or INCIN	INCIN.
U133	Hydrazine	CHOXD; CHRED; CARBN; BIODG; or INCIN	FSUBS: CHOXD; CHRED; or; INCIN.
U134	Hydrogen Flouride	NA	ADGAS fb NEUTR; or NEUTR.
U135	Hydrogen Sulfide	CHOXD; CHRED, or INCIN	CHOXD; CHRED; or INCIN.
U143	Lasiocarpine	(WETOX or CHOXD) fb CARBN; or INCIN	INCIN.
U147	Maleic anhydride	(WETOX or CHOXD) fb CARBN; or INCIN	FSUBS; or INCIN.
U148	Maleic hydrazide	(WETOX or CHOXD) fb CARBN; or INCIN	INCIN.
U149	Malononitrile	(WETOX or CHOXD) fb CARBN; or INCIN	INCIN.
U150	Melphalan	(WETOX or CHOXD) fb CARBN; or INCIN	INCIN.
U151	Mercury: (High Mercury Subcategory — greater than or equal to 260 mg/kg total Mercury).	NA	RMERC.
U153	Methane thiol	(WETOX or CHOXD) fb CARBN; or INCIN	INCIN.
U154	Methanol	(WETOX or CHOXD) fb CARBN; or INCIN	FSUBS; or INCIN.
U156	Methyl chlorocarbonate	(WETOX or CHOXD) fb CARBN; or INCIN	INCIN.
U160	Methyl ethyl ketone peroxide	CHOXD; CHRED; CARBN; BIODG; or INCIN	FSUBS: CHOXD; CHRED;or INCIN.
U163	N-Methyl N'-nitro N-Nitrosoguanidine	(WETOX or CHOXD) fb CARBN; or INCIN	INCIN.
U164	Methythiouracil	(WETOX or CHOXD) fb CARBN; or INCIN	INCIN.
U166	1,4-Naphthoquinone	(WETOX or CHOXD) fb CARBN; or INCIN	FSUBS; or INCIN.
U167	1-Naphthlyamine	(WETOX or CHOXD) fb CARBN; or INCIN	INCIN.
U168	2-Naphthlyamine	NA	INCIN.
U171	2-Nitropropane	(WETOX or CHOXD) fb CARBN; or INCIN	INCIN.
U173	N-Nitroso-di-n-ethanolamine	(WETOX or CHOXD) fb CARBN; or INCIN	INCIN.
U176	N-Nitroso-N-ethylurea	(WETOX or CHOXD) fb CARBN; or INCIN	INCIN.
U177	N-Nitroso-N-methylurea	(WETOX or CHOXD) fb CARBN; or INCIN	INCIN.
U178	N-Nitroso-N-methylurethane	(WETOX or CHOXD) fb CARBN; or INCIN	INCIN.
U182	Paraldehyde	(WETOX or CHOXD) fb CARBN; or INCIN	FSUBS; or INCIN.

TABLE 2. — TECHNOLOGY-BASED STANDARDS BY RCRA WASTE CODE —Continued

Waste code	Waste descriptions and/or treatment subcategory	Technology code Wastewaters	Technology code Nonwastewaters
U184	Pentachloroethane	(WETOX or CHOXD) fb CARBN; or INCIN	INCIN.
U186	1,3-Pentadiene	(WETOX or CHOXD) fb CARBN; or INCIN	FSUBS; or INCIN.
U189	Phosphonus sulfide	CHOXD; CHRED; or INCIN	CHOXD; CHRED; or INCIN.
U191	Picoline	(WETOX or CHOXD) fb CARBN; or INCIN	INCIN.
U193	1,3-Propane sultone	(WETOX or CHOXD) fb CARBN; or INCIN	INCIN.
U194	n-Propylamine	(WETOX or CHOXD) fb CARBN; or INCIN	INCIN.
U197	p-Benzoquinone	(WETOX or CHOXD) fb CARBN; or INCIN	FSUBS; or INCIN.
U200	Reserpine	(WETOX or CHOXD) fb CARBN; or INCIN	INCIN.
U201	Resorcinol	(WETOX or CHOXD) fb CARBN; or INCIN	FSUBS; or INCIN.
U202	Saccharin and salts	(WETOX or CHOXD) fb CARBN; or INCIN	INCIN.
U206	Streptozatocin	(WETOX or CHOXD) fb CARBN; or INCIN	INCIN.
U213	Tetrahydrofuran	(WETOX or CHOXD) fb CARBN; or INCIN	FSUBS; or INCIN.
U214	Thallium (1) acetate	NA	RTHRM: or STABL.
U215	Thallium (1) carbonate	NA	RTHRM; or STABL.
U216	Thallium (1) chloride	NA	RTHRM; or STABL.
U217	Thallium (1) nitate	NA	RTHRM; or STABL.
U218	Thioacetamide	(WETOX or CHOXD) fb CARBN; or INCIN	INCIN.
U219	Thiourea	(WETOX or CHOXD) fb CARBN; or INCIN	INCIN.
U221	Toluenediamine	CARBN; or INCIN	FSUBS; or INCIN.
U222	o-Toluidine hydrochloride	(WETOX or CHOXD) fb CARBN; or INCIN	INCIN.
U223	Toluene diisocyanate	CARBN; or INCIN	FSUBS; or INCIN.
U234	sym-Trinitrobenzene	(WETOX or CHOXD) fb CARBN; or INCIN	INCIN.
U236	Trypan Blue	(WETOX or CHOXD) fb CARBN; or INCIN	INCIN.
U237	Uracil mustard	(WETOX or CHOXD) fb CARBN; or INCIN	INCIN.
U238	Ethyl carbamate	(WETOX or CHOXD) fb CARBN; or INCIN	INCIN.
U240	2,4-Dichlorophenoxyacetic (salts and esters)	(WETOX or CHOXD) fb CARBN; or INCIN	INCIN.
U244	Thiram	(WETOX or CHOXD) fb CARBN; or INCIN	INCIN.
U246	Cyanogen bromide	CHOXD: WETOX: or INCIN	CHOXD; WETOX; or INCIN.
U248	Warfarin (greater than or equal to 3%)	(WETOX or CHOXD) fb CARBN; or INCIN	FSUBS; or INCIN.
U249	Zinc Phosphide (<10%)	CHOXD; CHRED; or INCIN	CHOXD; CHRED; or INCIN.

CAS Number given for parent compound only.
This waste code exists in gaseous form and is not categorized as wastewater or nonwastewater forms.
NA — Not Applicable.

TABLE 3. — TECHNOLOGY-BASED STANDARDS FOR SPECIFIC RADIOACTIVE HAZARDOUS MIXED WASTE

Waste code	Waste descriptions and/or treatment subcategory	Technology code Wastewaters	Technology code Nonwastewaters
D002	Radioactive High Level Wastes Generated During the Reprocessing of Fuel Rods Subcategory.	NA	HLVIT
D004	Radioactive High Level Wastes Generated During the Reprocessing of Fuel Rods Subcategory.	NA	HLVIT
D005	Radioactive High Level Wastes Generated During the Reprocessing of Fuel Rods Subcategory.	NA	HLVIT
D006	Radioactive High Level Wastes Generated During the Reprocessing of Fuel Rods Subcategory.	NA	HLVIT
D007	Radioactive High Level Wastes Generated During the Reprocessing of Fuel Rods Subcategory.	NA	HLVIT
D008	Radioactive Lead Solids Subcategory (Note: these lead solids include, but are not limited to, all forms of lead shielding, and other elemental forms of lead. These lead solids do not include treatment residuals such as hydroxide sludges, other wastewater treatment residuals, or incinerator ashes that can undergo conventional pozzolanic stabilization, nor do they include organo-lead materials that can be incinerated and stabilized as ash.)	NA	MACRO

D008	Radioactive High Level Wastes Generated During the Reprocessing of Fuel Rods Subcategory.	NA	HLVIT
D009	Elemental mercury contaminated with radioactive materials.	NA	AMLGM
D009	Hydraulic oil contaminated with Mercury Radioactive Materials Subcategory	NA	INCIN
D009	Radioactive High Level Wastes Generated During the Reprocessing of Fuel Rods Subcategory.	NA	HLVIT
D010	Radioactive High Level Wastes Generated During the Reprocessing of Fuel Rods Subcategory.	NA	HLVIT
D011	Radioactive High Level Wastes Generated During the Reprocessing of Fuel Rods Subcategory.	NA	HLVIT
D151	Mercury: Elemental mercury contaminated with radioactive materials	NA	AMLGM

NA — Not Applicable.

Index

A

Acid gases 71, 96-97, 226, 230
Acids
   recycling of spent acids 159
   waste exchanges national classification system 167
Acute hazardous waste 25
Advertising, environmental claims in 196-197
AFCO Industries, case example of plastic recycling 191-192
Affirmative procurement programs 177
Agenda for Action, EPA solid waste program 60-62, 174
Agricultural waste 56, 102, 113
Air emissions from waste treatment, storage, and disposal facilities 95-106 (*see also* Incinerators)
   asbestos waste control 98
   benzene waste operations 98-99
   Clean Air Act rules 95-100
   containers, regulations 105
   covers on containers and units to control emissions 105
   hazardous waste incinerators 100-102
   hazardous waste landfills 102-103, 216
   industrial boilers and furnaces 236
   leakage from equipment as source 103-104
   municipal solid waste landfills 102-103
   municipal waste combustors 96-97, 229-232
   national emission standard for hazardous air pollutants (NESHAPS) 98-100
   President's Council on Competitiveness view on municipal waste combustors 96
   process vents as source 103-104
   radon emissions 99
   RCRA air pollution control rules 100-105
   storage tanks, regulations 105, 214-215
   surface impoundments, regulations 105, 216
   uranium mining waste 99-100
   volatile organic compounds (VOC) emissions, regulation 103, 105
Air pollution control (*see* Air emissions from waste treatment, storage, and disposal facilities; Clean Air Act; Resource Conservation and Recovery Act)
Alabama
   association of waste-importing states, role 82-83
   capacity assurance plans 86
   Emelle landfill 212, 242-247, 253, 269
   Fairhope recycling program 200-202
   hazardous waste fees 81
   Huntsville waste-to-energy incinerator 264-265
   Lee County landfill 264
   Salem waste disposal center 238-239
   siting of hazardous waste facility 269
   technical assistance programs 87
   Waste Reduction Resource Center for the Southeast 129
Alaska
   Health Project 153-154
   technical assistance programs 88
Alkalis 167
Aluminum recycling 183-184, 204-205
Aluminum Recycling Casebook 184
American Institute for Pollution Prevention 119
American Institute of Chemical Engineers 130
American Paper Institute 182, 185-186
American Petroleum Institute 215

American Society of Mechanical Engineers, paper on integrated solid waste management 55-56
Amoco Corp. pilot project with EPA 110
Analysis of hazardous waste by treatment, storage, and disposal facilities 41, 235
Antimony 70
Arizona
  Maricopa county landfill 261-262
  recycling program 75
  siting of hazardous waste facility, case study 279-283
Arkansas
  capacity assurance plans 86
  technical assistance programs 88
Arsenic 70-71, 247
Asbestos 98
Ash 31, 98, 231-232
Asphalt 196
Assessment of hazardous waste minimization program 142-145
Association for State and Territorial Solid Waste Management Officials 237
Atomic Energy Act 56
Audit of hazardous waste minimization 140
Automobile scrap 160

Birnesser, Donald J., author of paper on Mercer County, New Jersey integrated solid waste management plan 55-56
Blackstone Project 122
Boilers 162-164, 236 (*see also* Incinerators; Municipal waste combustors)
Browning-Ferris Industries 189, 249, 271
Budget (*see* Costs)
Building insulation, procurement guidelines for recycled materials 177, 181
Bureau of Indian Affairs 266-267
Burning (*see also* Municipal waste combustors)
  hazardous waste for energy recovery 162-164
  hazardous waste fuels, regulation by RCRA 8
  metals to recover precious metals 165-166
  open burning prohibited in sanitary landfills 57, 102
  toxic substances, prohibited by HSWA 4
Byproducts (*see also* Coke byproducts)
  recycling of hazardous materials involving 160
  waste exchanges 166-170

B

Baghouses 229-230
Ball-InCon Glass Packaging, case example of glass recycling 194
Barges for solid waste disposal 49
Batteries, lead acid 75, 159, 161, 166, 195
Benzene 98-99, 103, 113, 220
Beryllium 70-71
Best available technology (BAT) documents 218-219
Beverage containers
  aluminum, recycling 183-184
  automated container recycling 204-205
  plastics, recycling 189-190
Bioprocessing waste 219-220

C

CAA (*see* Clean Air Act)
Cadmium 70-71, 110, 113
Caithness King Co., case example of paper recycling 187
California
  association of waste-importing states, membership 83
  Indian reservations 267
  pollution prevention law 93
  Southern California Hazardous Waste Management Authority 250
  technical assistance programs 88
  Wste Reduction Innovative Technology Evaluations agreement 116

Index

California-list wastes 207
Capacity assurance plans (CAPs)
   hazardous waste, SARA requirements 84-87
   hazardous waste minimization, EPA seeking comments on applicability 138
   New York 85
   North Carolina 85
   regions 85-87
CAPs (see Capacity assurance plans)
Carbon dioxide 103
Carbon monoxide emissions 101, 226
Carbon tetrachloride 113
Carcinogens 70-71
Case studies (see Recycling)
Catalysts, recycling of spent catalysts 159
Center for Policy Alternatives 92-93
Center for Waste Reduction Technologies 130
CERCLA (see Comprehensive Environmental Response, Compensation, and Liability Act)
Cerrell Associates 250
Chemical analysis test methods 29
Chemical Manufacturers Association v. EPA 216
Chemical Waste Management, Inc. 242-247, 254, 269
Chloroform 113
Chlorotoluene 31
Chromium 70-71, 113
Citizen activist organizations (see Environmental activist groups)
Citizens Clearinghouse for Hazardous Waste 251-252
Citizen suits 121
Classification of hazardous waste 22-38
   characteristics of hazardous wastes 25-29
   delisting of waste 23-24
   hazardous waste defined 23
   recycling waste classification rules 158-161
   solid waste defined 23
   waste exchanges, national classification system 167
Clean Air Act (CAA)
   amendments under consideration 16
   applicability to waste management 2
   municipal waste combustor ash 231
   waste treatment, storage, and disposal facilities emissions 95-100
Cleanup of spills, CERCLA provisions 13
Cleanup prior to sale of industrial property 268
Clean Water Act (CWA)
   applicability to waste management 2, 138
   National Pollutant Discharge Elimination System 57
   spill cleanup 13
   underground injection well permits 39
Clearinghouses
   Citizens Clearinghouse for Hazardous Waste 251-252
   pollution prevention information 118-119
   waste exchange information 166-168
Closed-loop systems 159, 161, 219
Closure of hazardous waste treatment, storage, and disposal facilities 38-39, 45, 216, 234, 241
Coal, high sulfur 229
Coke byproducts 32, 99
Colorado
   hazardous waste facility 249, 259
   siting of hazardous waste facility, case study 271-279
Combustion (see Incinerators; Municipal waste combustors)
Commercial chemical products, recycling of hazardous materials 160
Commercial fertilizer 159, 161-162
Communication about risk 254-258
Community recycling programs 197-205
Composting 195-196 (see also *generally* Recycling)
Comprehensive Environmental Response, Compensation, and Liability Act (CERCLA) 269
   National Priorities List 69

purpose 12
spill cleanup 13
trust fund 13
Computers
  Florida Recycling Marketing System computer bulletin board 182
  importance of installing monitors 128
  model for OTA survey on solid waste management costs 63-67
Concerned Citizens of Eastern Colorado 272
Concord Resources, Inc. 277
Connecticut
  technical assistance programs 88
  Waste Reduction Innovative Technology Evaluations agreement 116
Consent decrees 110, 121, 138
Constituent Concentrations in Waste Extract tables 213
Constitutionality, state hazardous waste import limits 82
Containers (*see also* Beverage containers)
  air emissions from waste treatment, storage, and disposal facilities, to prevent 105
  landfill ban on containerized liquids 242
Contingency plans (*see* Emergency contingency plans)
Copper 165
Corrosion of storage tanks 215
Corrosive waste 25-26, 100, 234
Costs
  hazardous waste minimization program 147-151
  incinerator guidelines proposed by EPA 97
  OTA survey and computer model for solid waste management 63-67
  pollution prevention 128
  Pollution Prevention Branch, Risk Reduction Engineering Laboratory budget 114
  recycling programs 63, 66-67
  solid waste management 62-67

Council of State Governments model laws
  hazardous waste reduction 154-156
  solid waste management 58-59
CWA (*see* Clean Water Act)
Cyanide 113

D

Daily Telegraph-Nat/West Clean Technology Award 220
Deep wells (*see* Underground injection wells)
Definitions
  hazardous waste 23
  hazardous waste minimization 141
  "manner constituting disposal" 161-162
  pollution prevention 107-109
  precious metals 165
  recycling 158-159, 174
  solid waste 23
  waste 125
De minimis waste, exemptions to hazardous waste regulation 32
Demonstration programs (*see generally* Research)
Dichloromethane 113
Dikes 216
Dioxins 70, 101, 165, 207, 216, 217, 232
Disease control, sanitary landfill measures 57
Disposal of hazardous waste (*see* Treatment, storage, and disposal facilities for hazardous waste)
Distillation columns 127
Dow Chemical U.S.A. 124-129
Dredging permits 19
Drinking water, Safe Drinking Water Act 56, 240, 247
Dumps, open dumps for solid waste 56, 236-237

E

Earthquake protection for hazardous waste treatment, storage, and disposal facilities 46-47

Index

E.I. Du Pont de Nemours & Co., case example of pesticide bucket recycling 196
Electrostatic precipitators 230
Emelle, Alabama landfill 212, 242-247, 253, 269
Emergency contingency plans
   incinerators 226
   treatment, storage, and disposal facilities 6, 43-44
Emergency permits for hazardous waste facilities 40
Emergency Planning and Community Right-to-Know Act 16-17, 119-120, 133
Endangered species 57
Energy recovery
   burning hazardous waste for 162-164
   solid waste combustion plants 223-226
   used oil for 164-165
Enforcement of pollution prevention programs 109-112
ENSCO Corp. 281
Environmental activist groups 120, 250-252
Environmental Defense Fund 237
Environmental Protection Agency (EPA) (*see also* EPA manuals and publications)
   Agenda for Action, EPA solid waste program 60-62
   American Institute for Pollution Prevention 119
   Amoco Corp. pilot project with 110
   disapproval of hazardous waste programs by, criteria 80
   fines, reduction 110
   guidance on elements of waste minimization program 135
   hazardous waste generation reduction report 134-135
   hazardous waste guidance and papers 134
   hazardous waste minimization activities 134-138
   hazardous waste recycling regulations for industry 157-170
   incinerator guidelines 97-98
   initiatives toward multimedia, prevention-oriented regulatory program 111
   Municipal Solid Waste Task Force 60
   Office of Pollution Prevention 109, 118-119
   Office of Solid Waste 53-54, 134, 211
   Office of Solid Waste Minimization Branch 17, 108-109
   Office of Toxic Substances 109, 120, 142
   permits issued by (*see generally* Permits)
   Pollution Prevention Branch 114-119
   procurement hotline 181-182
   RCRA hazardous waste rules (*see* Hazardous waste rules)
   regional offices' promotion of pollution prevention 111-112
   research program for pollution prevention 111, 113-119
   Risk Reduction Engineering Research Laboratory 114-119
   state solid waste management plan guidelines 53-54
   strategy for pollution prevention 112-113
EPA manuals and publications
   Estimating Releases and Waste Treatment Efficiencies for the Toxic Chemicals Inventory Form 142
   Pollution Prevention News 119
   Pollution Prevention Training Opportunities 87
   Reusable News 183
   Sites for Our Solid Waste, A Guidebook for Effective Public Involvement 250
   Superfund LDS Guide 211
   Waste Minimization Opportunity Assessment Manual 140-153
Equipment leaks as air pollution source 103-104
Erie County, New York, Waste Reduction Innovative Technology Evaluations agreement 116

Estimating Releases and Waste Treatment Efficiencies for the Toxic Chemicals Inventory Form 142
Evaporation of hazardous waste 210, 220-221
Exchanges for waste (*see* Waste exchanges)
Exemptions to hazardous waste regulation 29-32
　generators of hazardous waste 36
　pending actions 31-32
Exemptions to solid waste regulation 56
Explosive gases, safety level 57

F

Fabric filter 229-230
Fairhope, Alabama recycling program 200-202
Farms (*see also* Agricultural waste)
　pesticide buckets, recycling 196
　pesticide residue, disposal restrictions 210
　sanitary landfills, proximity restrictions 57
　sewage sludge reuse programs 58
Feasibility analysis of hazardous waste minimization program 146-151
Federal legislation (*see also specific laws by name of act*)
　pollution prevention 107, 119-121
　solid waste management 51-53
Federal Register, announcement of approved state hazardous waste authorization 80
Federal Trade Commission (FTC), regulation of environmental advertising claims 196-197
Feedstocks 161
Fees, state hazardous waste programs 81
Fertilizer 159, 161-162
Fiberglass 181
Fines, reduction 110
Floodplains 57
Flood-proof design for hazardous waste treatment, storage, and disposal facilities 47
Florida
　capacity assurance plans 86
　Recycling Marketing System computer bulletin board 182
　siting of hazardous waste facility 269
　technical assistance programs 88
　Waste Reduction Resource Center for the Southeast 129
Fly ash 227
Follow-up evaluation of hazardous waste minimization project 152-153
Food and Drug Administration restrictions on recycled plastics 172
Foundries 216
Fuels (*see also* Petroleum)
　recycling activity to produce 159, 162-164
　waste-produced fuels 8-9
Furans 70, 101, 216, 217
Furnaces 236 (*see also* Incinerators; Municipal waste combustors) burning hazardous waste for energy recovery 162-164
　waste reduction opportunities 127

G

Garbage disposal (*see* Solid waste management)
Gases
　acid gases 71, 96-97, 226, 230
　explosive gases 57
　liquid tar and gas 229
　solid waste landfill owners converting into energy source 103
General Dynamics 123-124
Generators of hazardous waste 5, 34-38 (*see also* Small-quantity generators)
　accumulation restrictions 35-36, 162
　blended hazardous fuel, requirements 163-164
　burning hazardous waste for energy recovery 162-164
　exemptions from land disposal restrictions 210-212
　exemptions from regulation 36
　fertilizer produced by 161-162

pretreatment of hazardous waste 207-222
status of generators, determination 36-38
Georgia
  capacity assurance plans 86
  generation of hazardous waste, study figures on 84
  pollution prevention law 93
  recycling program 75
  technical assistance programs 88
  Waste Reduction Resource Center for the Southeast 129
Glass Packaging Institute 182, 193-194
Glass recycling 175, 193-194
"Green advertising" 196-197
Greenpeace 266, 286
Green Report 197
Grocery bags 193
Groundwater 57, 207, 215, 217, 237, 239
  monitoring 8, 45, 69, 240
Guide for Inspection of Refinery Equipment 215
Guidelines (*see specific subject of guidelines*)

H

Halogenated organic compounds 247
Hammer Plastics Recycling Corp., case example of plastic recycling 192
Hazardous and Solid Waste Amendments (HSWA) 3-9
  Ed. Note: These amendments to RCRA are covered more fully as part of Resource Conservation and Recovery Act.
  effective dates of provisions 3-4
  EPA report required on reduction of hazardous waste generation 134-135
Hazardous waste defined 23
Hazardous waste incinerators 100-102, 232-235
  analysis of waste 235
  closure of facilities 234
  development of facilities 232-234
  exempted waste 234-235

inspections 101
trial burns for new incinerators 235
Hazardous waste management (*see also* Hazardous waste rules; Pollution prevention laws; Resource Conservation and Recovery Act)
  burning (*see* Burning)
  disposal facilities (*see* Treatment, storage, and disposal facilities for hazardous waste)
  evaporation of hazardous waste 210
  exchanges for waste (*see* Waste exchanges)
  exemptions to hazardous waste regulation 29-31
  generators (*see* Generators of hazardous waste)
  identification and listing of hazardous waste 4-5, 25-29
  incinerators (*see* Hazardous waste incinerators; Incinerators; Municipal waste combustors)
  incompatible wastes 32-33, 42, 216, 217
  industrial property cleanup prior to sale 268
  landfills (*see* Landfills)
  minimization (*see* Hazardous waste minimization)
  national classification system for waste exchanges 167
  pretreatment requirements (*see* Pretreatment of hazardous waste)
  reclamation 146
  recycling 145-146, 157-170
  small-quantity generators of hazardous waste 5
  Southern California Hazardous Waste Management Authority 250
  state programs 73, 79-87, 134 (*see also* State hazardous waste programs)
  storage (*see* Treatment, storage, and disposal facilities for hazardous waste)
  transporters of hazardous waste (*see* Transportation of hazardous waste)

treatment (*see* Treatment, storage, and disposal facilities for hazardous waste)
Hazardous waste minimization 133-156
  Alaska Health Project 153-154
  assessment phase of program development 142-145
  audit 140
  Council of State Governments model law 154-156
  data gathering 135, 142
  definition 141
  economic evaluation 147-151
  EPA activities 134-138
  EPA 1986 report to Congress 133-156
  feasibility analysis 146-151
  final report of assessment 151-152
  follow-up evaluation of project 152-153
  incentive programs, EPA seeking comments 136-138
  long-term options to speed progress 136-138
  notice of proposed hazardous waste minimization regulations 134
  payback periods for projects 150-151
  program development 141-153
  promoting projects within companies 152-153
  quality circles to assist with waste assessment 143
  Rampart Industries, case study 138-140
  RCRA 133-156
  reclamation 146
  recycling 145-146
  screening options 144-145
  site inspection 143-144
  source reduction programs 144-145
  state programs 134
  task force to assist with 141
  technical evaluation 146-147
  transferable rights to generate waste, EPA seeking comments 136-138

Waste Minimization Opportunity Assessment Manual 140-153
Hazardous waste rules 2, 21-47
  applicability 24
  classification of hazardous waste 22-33
  exemptions 29-32, 36
  generators of hazardous waste 34-38
  scope 22
  test methods for determining hazardous waste 25-29
  treatment, storage, and disposal facilities standards 37-47
Hazardous Waste Treatment Council v. South Carolina 82
Heat exchangers, waste reduction opportunities 126-127
Heavy metals 247
Hempstead, New York resource recovery facility 262-263
Highway 36 Land Development Co. 271
Hospitals, medical waste management 13-14
Household waste 11 (*see also specific items* (e.g., Beverage containers))
HSWA (*see* Hazardous and Solid Waste Amendments)
Huntsville, Alabama waste-to-energy incinerator 264-265
Hydrocarbons 218, 226
Hydrochloric acid gases 71
Hydrogen chloride 101, 164, 236

I

Idaho, technical assistance programs 88
Ignitable waste 25-26, 216, 217, 234, 241
  exemption to RCRA air pollution control rules 100
  handling 42
Illinois
  association of waste-importing states, membership 83
  capacity assurance plans 86
  import of hazardous waste, study figures on 84

Index

technical assistance programs 89
Waste Reduction Innovative Technology Evaluations agreement 116
Impact statements, solid waste management programs 59
Import of hazardous waste (*see* State hazardous waste programs; *specific state*)
Incentive programs
  hazardous waste minimization programs, EPA seeking comments 136-138
  solid waste management programs, model law 59
Incinerators (*see also* Hazardous waste incinerators; Municipal waste combustors; Treatment, storage, and disposal facilities for hazardous waste)
  catalysts used to control air emissions 96-97
  EPA guidelines, costs 97
  equipment to control air emissions 96
  existing incinerator EPA guidelines 97-98
  Huntsville, Alabama waste-to-energy incinerator 264-265
  Kentucky solid waste management rules 77
  mass burn systems 228
  OTA survey and computer model on costs 65-66
  performance standards for hazardous waste incinerators 100-101
  permits 40
  RCRA provisions 6-7
  retort incinerators 229
  risk assessment 70-71
Incompatible wastes 32-33, 42, 216, 217, 241
Indiana
  association of waste-importing states, membership 83
  capacity assurance plans 86
  import of hazardous waste, study figures on 84
  pollution prevention law 93
  recycling program 75-76

technical assistance programs 89
Indian reservation lands used for waste disposal 266-267
Industrial activities for pollution prevention 123-129
Industrial property cleanup prior to sale 268
Industrial waste recycling 157-170
Infectious waste 73
Injection wells (*see* Underground injection wells)
Inorganic chemicals 167
Inspections
  consent decree provisions 121
  hazardous waste incinerators 101
  hazardous waste landfills 241
  hazardous waste minimization programs 143-144
  hazardous waste storage, treatment, and disposal facilities 41
  multimedia inspections, state programs 122
  solid waste management programs, model law 59
  storage tanks for hazardous wastes 215
Institute for Resource Recovery 224
Institutional aspects of pollution prevention 109-111
Insulated wires 165
Insulation, procurement guidelines for recycled materials 177, 181
Integrated waste management
  Agenda for Action, EPA report 60-61
  Mercer County, New Jersey integrated solid waste management plan 55
Interagency cooperation
  pollution prevention strategy for EPA targeted chemicals 113
  state solid waste management plans 54
Interim authorization for state hazardous waste management plans 79-80
Interim permits for hazardous waste facilities 40
International markets for waste exchanges 169-170

Interstate transport of waste (*see*
  Transportation of hazardous waste;
  Transportation of solid waste)
Iowa, capacity assurance plans 86
Irrigation return flows 56

J

James River Corp., case example of paper recycling 187-188
Jensen, Betty K., author of paper on risk analysis 252-253

K

Kansas
  capacity assurance plans 86
  technical assistance programs 89
Kentucky
  burning metals to recover precious metals 166
  capacity assurance plans 86
  hazardous waste reduction program 155
  recycling program 77
  solid waste management rules 77-78
  technical assistance programs 89
  Waste Reduction Resource Center for the Southeast 129

L

Land disposal restrictions (*see also* Landfills; Underground injection wells)
  pretreatment of hazardous waste 207-222 (*see also* Pretreatment of hazardous waste)
  RCRA provisions 7
Landfill Alternatives, Inc., case example of plastic recycling 193
Landfills
  containerized liquids, ban 242
  costs, OTA survey and computer model 64-65
  design proposal 241-242
  Emelle, Alabama landfill 212, 242-247, 253, 269
  groundwater protection 239-241
  hazardous waste 7-8, 102-103, 239-247
  household waste 11
  Kentucky solid waste management rules 77-78
  Lee County, Alabama landfill 264
  Maricopa, Arizona, county landfill 261-262
  minimum technological requirements 8
  OTA survey and computer model on costs 64-65
  permits for hazardous waste landfills 241
  prohibited wastes 213-214
  public/private partnerships to construct 264-265
  RCRA provisions 7-8, 11
  risk assessment 69
  Salem, Alabama waste disposal center 238-239
  sanitary landfills 56-58, 236-237
  siting requirements and studies 237-239, 258-263
  solid waste 11, 236-237
  state programs 74
Land treatment demonstration permits 40
Laser-printed paper 189
Last Chance, Colorado, case study of hazardous waste facility 271-279
Leachate collection systems 8, 215 (*see also* Toxicity Characteristic Leaching Procedure)
Lead 70, 113
Lead acid batteries (*see* Batteries)
Leather 167
Lee County, Alabama landfill 264
Liability, coverage for hazardous waste facilities 46
Liability, environmental; real estate transactions 267-268
Liquid waste 241
Litigation
  citizen suits 121
  environmental liability in property transactions 267-268
  surface impoundments 216-217
Louisiana

association of waste-importing states, membership 83
capacity assurance plans 86
hazardous waste disposal and transportation taxes 81
import of hazardous waste, study figures on 84
waste reduction programs 121-122
Love Canal, New York 2, 12, 21-22
Lubricating oils (*see* Recycled oil)

M

Manifests, RCRA provisions 5-6, 43-44
Maricopa, Arizona, county landfill 261-262
Marine Protection, Research, and Sanctuaries Act 18-19, 39
Marketers
blended hazardous fuel 163-164
used oil 164-165
Markets for recycled materials 175-183
Massachusetts
Blackstone Project 122
multimedia pollution prevention approach 122
siting of hazardous waste facility 269
technical assistance programs 89
Toxics Use Reduction Act 92
waste reduction programs 121-122
Mass burn systems 228
Medical waste management 13-15
Medical Waste Tracking Act 14
Mercer County, New Jersey, integrated solid waste management plan 55-56
Mercury 70, 113
Metal finishing industry 110
Metallic ore processing 31
Metals
carcinogenic 70-71
heavy metals 247
precious metal recovery 165-166
scrap 160
waste exchanges national classification system 167
Methane 103
Methylene chloride 103

Methyl ethyl ketone 113
Methyl isobutyl ketone 113
Michigan
association of waste-importing states, membership 83
capacity assurance plans 86
Rampart Industries, case study of hazardous waste minimization 138-140
technical assistance programs 89
Whitmore Lake recycling program 203
Milk containers, plastic recycling 189-190
Minimization of waste (*see* Hazardous waste minimization; Waste minimization)
Mining waste
hazardous waste regulation exemption 32
solid waste facility criteria exemption 56
uranium mining 99-100
Minnesota
Attorney General's Office, *Green Report* 197
capacity assurance plans 86
technical assistance programs 89
Waste Reduction Innovative Technology Evaluations agreement 116
Missile silos, deactivated %219
Mississippi
capacity assurance plans 86
hazardous waste incinerator requirements 231
pesticide buckets, recycling 196
technical assistance programs 89
Waste Reduction Resource Center for the Southeast 129
Missouri, capacity assurance plans 86
Mobile Paperboard Corp., case example of paper recycling 188
Model laws, Council of State Governments
hazardous waste reduction 154-156
solid waste management 58-59
Monitoring (*see* Computers; Groundwater)
Monsanto Company 123

Montana, technical assistance programs 90
Multimedia pollution prevention approach 110-112, 122, 129
Municipal landfills, air pollution control 102-103
Municipal solid waste management programs 49-71, 171-206
(*see also* Municipal waste recycling)
Municipal Solid Waste Task Force 60-62
Municipal Waste Combustion-Ash Leachate Characterization Monofill 232
Municipal waste combustors (*see also* Incinerators)
  acid gas control 230-231
  add-on technology for air pollution control 229-232
  aesthetics 227
  air emissions 96-97, 229-232
  ash 98, 231-232
  baghouses, use 230
  Clean Air Amendments, ash restrictions 231
  design 225-226
  efficiency 231
  electrostatic precipitators 230
  emergency operation 226
  fabric filter, use 230
  fluidized beds 229
  Hempstead, New York resource recovery facility 262-263
  high sulfur coal 229
  malfunctions 226
  mass burn systems 228
  modular systems 228-229
  nitrous oxide control 231
  odors 227
  pyrolysis 229
  RDF systems 228
  recordkeeping 227
  residue 227
  retrofit technology 230
  safety 227
  site selection 225
  solid waste 223-232
  temperature 231
  types 227-229
  vectors 227
  water quality of discharged water 226-227
Municipal waste recycling 171-206
  automated container recycling 204-205
  hybrid collection facilities 203
  technologies 203-205
  types of products recycled 183-194

N

National Agricultural Chemical Assn., case example of pesticide bucket recycling 196
National Association of Corrosion Engineers 215
National Association of Counties 172-173
National emission standard for hazardous air pollutants (NESHAPS) 98-100
  asbestos waste control 98
  benzene waste operations 98-99
  exemptions 99
  uranium mining 99-100
National Environmental Law Center 92-93
National Fertilizer and Environmental Research Center 220-221
National Governors' Association 78-79
National Pollutant Discharge Elimination System (NPDES) 39, 57, 239, 284
National Polystyrene Recycling Co., case example of plastic recycling 192
National Priorities List, Superfund 69
National Recycling Coalition, Inc. 175
National Solid Wastes Management Association (NSWMA)
  proposed criteria for solid waste landfills 237
  reports on state solid waste management plans 74, 78
  study on state hazardous waste management 83-84
  survey on recycling and other methods of waste management 171-172

Index

Waste Age's Recycling Times 182-183
Nebraska, capacity assurance plans 86
NESHAPS (*see* National emission standard for hazardous air pollutants)
Nevada
  association of waste-importing states, membership 83
  hazardous waste incinerator requirements 231
New England (*see also specific states that constitute New England*)
  Northeast Multimedia Pollution Prevention Program 129
New Jersey
  Environmental Cleanup Responsibility Act 268
  Northeast Multimedia Pollution Prevention Program 129
  technical assistance programs 90
  Waste Reduction Innovative Technology Evaluations agreement 116
New Mexico
  capacity assurance plans 86
  recycling program 76
Newsprint 178-179, 189
  recycling market 175
New York
  association of waste-importing states, membership 83
  capacity assurance plans 85
  Erie County, Waste Reduction Innovative Technology Evaluations agreement 116
  Hempstead resource recovery facility 262-263
  Northeast Multimedia Pollution Prevention Program 129
  technical assistance programs 90
  waste exchange programs 156
Nickel 70, 113
NIMBY (Not in my backyard) syndrome 49, 250-254, 283
Nitrous oxide emissions 96, 231
No-migration exemption for land disposal facilities 211-212, 247
Nonhazardous solid waste 49-71 (*see also* Solid waste management)

national classification system for waste exchanges 167
North Carolina
  capacity assurance plans 86
  hazardous waste problems and CAP 85
  siting of hazardous waste facility, case study 284-286
  technical assistance programs 90
  Waste Reduction Resource Center for the Southeast 129
Northeast Multimedia Pollution Prevention Program 129
No Smoking signs 42
Notification requirements for hazardous waste facilities 40-41
Not in my backyard (NIMBY) syndrome 49, 250-254, 283
NPDES (*see* National Pollutant Discharge Elimination System)
NSWMA (*see* National Solid Wastes Management Association)

O

Ocean dumping 18-19, 39, 233
Ocean Dumping Ban Act 18-19
Odors from incinerators 227
Office of Management and Budget (OMB) 237
Office of Pollution Prevention (*see* Environmental Protection Agency)
Office of Solid Waste (*see* Environmental Protection Agency) Office of Technical Assessment (OTA)
  computer model for costs of solid waste management 63-67
  survey of solid waste management costs 62-67
Office of Toxic Substances (*see* Environmental Protection Agency)
Off-site generators, regulation 34-35
Ogden Projects 264
Ohio
  association of waste-importing states, membership 83
  capacity assurance plans 86
  import of hazardous waste, study figures on 84
  technical assistance programs 90

Oil (*see* Recycled oil)
Oklahoma
    association of waste-importing states, membership 83
    capacity assurance plans 86
    recycling program 76
On-site generators, regulation 34
Open burning (*see* Burning)
Open dumps for solid waste 56
Oregon
    pollution prevention law 93
    recycling program 76
    technical assistance programs 90
    waste reduction programs 121
    Woodburn landfill 232
Organics 167
OTA (*see* Office of Technical Assessment)
An Ounce of Toxic Pollution Prevention: Rating States' Toxics Use Reduction Laws 92-93

P

Packaging
    recycled paper 178-179
    source reduction programs 173-174
Paper (*see also* Newsprint)
    American Paper Institute 182, 185-186
    case examples of recycling 187-188
    guidelines for recycled paper 178-179
    laser-printed paper 189
    market 189
    procurement of recycled paper 176-177
    recycling 184-189
    types and grades 186
    waste exchanges national classification system 167
PaperMatch 185
Particulates 101, 229-230
PCBs 6, 17-18, 165, 212, 233, 247
Penalties (*see also* Fines)
    solid waste management programs, model law 59
Pennsylvania
    import and export of hazardous waste, study figures on 84

technical assistance programs 91
Permits
    dredging permits 19
    hazardous waste incinerators 100-102, 233-234
    hazardous waste landfills 241
    hazardous waste treatment, storage, and disposal facilities 6-7, 37-47
    Marine Protection, Research, and Sanctuaries Act 19
    multimedia permitting 110
    solid waste management programs, model law 58-59
Pesticide buckets, recycling 196
Petroleum
    NESHAPS, applicability to refineries 99
    underground petroleum tanks 13
Piping, waste reduction opportunities 128
Plastics
    case examples of recycling 190-193
    Food and Drug Administration restrictions on recycling 172
    grocery bags 193
    high-density polyethylene 189-190
    lumber 191-192
    mixed plastic recycling 192
    polyethylene terephthalate (PET) 189-190
    polystyrene 192-193
    recycling 189-193
    waste exchanges national classification system 167
PLC Eastern, case example of plastic recycling 193
Pollutants (*see also specific types (e.g., Dioxins)*)
    risk assessment 67-71
    targeted chemicals in EPA pollution prevention strategy 112-113
Pollution Prevention Act 16-17, 107-108, 119-121
    history 133-134
    Resource Conservation and Recovery Act, relationship to 133-134
Pollution Prevention Branch 114-119

Index

Pollution Prevention Information Exchange System 118
Pollution prevention laws
  definition of pollution prevention 107-109
  enforcement 109-112
  federal act (*see* Pollution Prevention Act)
  state laws 92-93
  waste minimization vis-a-vis 107-109
Pollution Prevention News 119
Pollution Prevention Office (*see* Environmental Protection Agency)
Pollution prevention programs
  American Institute of Chemical Engineers 130
  Center for Waste Reduction Technologies 130
  costs 128
  Dow Chemical U.S.A. 124-129
  General Dynamics 123-124
  how-to guide by Dow Chemical U.S.A. 124-129
  industrial activities 123-129
  Monsanto Company 123
  Northeast Multimedia Pollution Prevention Program 129
  RecycleNet Bulletin Board 131
  regional and private pollution prevention assistance sources 129-131
  Risk Reduction Engineering Research Laboratory 114-119
  state programs 121-123
  vapor recovery 128-129
  Waste Reduction Resource Center for the Southeast 129
Pollution Prevention Training Opportunities 119
Polychlorinated biphenyls (*see* PCBs)
Polyethylene terephthalate (PET) 189-190
Polystyrene 192-193
Postclosure plans (*see* Closure of hazardous waste treatment, storage, and disposal facilities)
PPA (*see* Pollution Prevention Act)
Precious metal recovery 165-166

President's Council on Competitiveness 96
Pretreatment of hazardous waste 207-222
  best available technology (BAT) documents 218-219
  bioprocessing waste 219-220
  chemical, physical, or biological treatment units 218-219
  concentration-based standards 212-214
  Constituent Concentrations in Waste Extract tables 213
  deactivated missile silos 217
  exemptions 210-212
  facilities, standards 214-218
  implementation 208-212
  land treatment facilities 217
  methods 218-221
  miscellaneous facilities 217-218
  no-migration exemption petition for land disposal facilities 211-212
  open burning or open detonating explosive wastes units 217
  recycling, distinguished 221-222
  residue standards 212-214
  second-third wastes 208-209
  "soft-hammer wastes" 208-209
  solar evaporation 220-221
  standards 212-214
  storage tanks 214-215
  surface impoundments 210
  technology-based treatment standards 214, 218-219
  thermal treatment units 217
  third-third wastes 209
  Treatment Standards Expressed as Waste Concentrations tables 213
  underground injection wells 208, 212, 217
  waste piles 217
Printing industry (*see generally* Paper)
Private pollution prevention assistance sources 129-131
Process vents as air pollution source 103-104
Procurement of recycled materials
  EPA guidelines 175-181

EPA procurement hotline 181-182
Profiting from Waste Reduction in Your Small Business 154
Public Involvement: Moving Beyond Public Relations 253
Public/private partnerships for waste disposal facilities 263-265
Pumps, waste reduction opportunities 127
Pyrolysis 229

Q

Quality circles 143

R

Radioactive hazardous mixed waste 214
Radioactive Material Disposal Impact Assessment 19
Radon emissions 99
Rampart Industries, case study of hazardous waste minimization 138-140
Raw materials, waste reduction opportunities 125
RCRA (*see* Resource Conservation and Recovery Act)
RDF systems 228
Reactive waste 25, 27, 216, 217, 234, 241
    exemption to RCRA air pollution control rules 100
    handling 42
Reactors, waste reduction opportunities 125-126
Real estate transactions, liability for environmental problems 267-268
Reclamation
    definitions 158-159
    hazardous waste 146
    precious metal recovery 165-166
Recordkeeping requirements
    hazardous waste landfills 241
    hazardous waste treatment, storage, and disposal facilities 43-44
    municipal waste combustors 227
Recycled oil
    energy recovery, for 164-165

exemptions to hazardous waste regulation 9, 31
guidelines for recycling 179-180
procurement guidelines 177
RCRA provisions 9, 31
state programs 75
RecycleNet Bulletin Board 130
Recycle Seattle 198-199, 203-204
Recycling (*see also* Municipal waste recycling)
    abuses 158
    Advisory Council 174-175
    affirmative procurement programs 177
    aluminum 183-184
    asphalt 196
    automated container recycling 204-205
    automobile scrap 160
    batteries (*see* Batteries)
    burning hazardous waste for energy recovery 162-164
    businesses as target of state provisions 78
    byproducts 160
    case studies 187-189, 190-193
    closed-loop process 159, 161
    commercial chemical products 160
    community recycling programs 197-205
    costs of programs 63, 66-67
    curbside programs 183
    definitions 158-159, 174
    drop-off centers 183
    EPA guidelines 11-12
    Fairhope, Alabama recycling program 200-202
    feedstocks 161
    Florida Recycling Marketing System computer bulletin board 182
    Food and Drug Administration restrictions on recycling plastics 172
    glass 175, 193-194
    hazardous waste 145-146, 157-170
    industrial waste 157-170
    lubricating oils (*see* Recycled oil)
    "manner constituting disposal" defined 161-162

Index

markets for recycled materials 175-183
national and regional recycling councils, EPA recommendation 62
newsprint 175, 178-179
nonhazardous materials 160-161
OTA survey and computer model on costs of programs 66-67
paper (*see* Paper)
pesticide buckets 196
plastics 189-193
pretreatment of hazardous waste, distinguished 221-222
procurement of recycled materials, EPA guidelines 175
RCRA regulations for recycling activities 161-166
RecycleNet Bulletin Board 130
regulated activities 159
research 117
Reusable News, EPA publication 183
scrap metal 160
Seattle, Washington recycling program 198-200, 203-204
sorting of recyclables 78, 203-205
sources on recycled materials markets 181-183
spent materials 159
state programs 74-77
technologies 203-205
tires (*see* Tires)
Waste Age's Recycling Times, NSWMA publication 182-183
waste classification rules 158-161
waste-like materials 160
Recycling Advisory Council 174-175
Regional and private pollution prevention assistance sources 129-131
Regional capacity assurance plans (*see* Capacity assurance plans)
Reporting requirements
 hazardous waste minimization assessment project 151-152
 hazardous waste treatment, storage, and disposal facilities 44-45
 Massachusetts Toxics Use Reduction Act 92
 Pollution Prevention Act 119-120
 state hazardous waste laws 81
 Toxic Release Inventory Forms 16-17, 119-120
Representative sampling methods 29
Research
 American Institute for Pollution Prevention 119
 American Institute of Chemical Engineers 130
 anticipatory research 117-118
 Center for Waste Reduction Technologies 130
 clearinghouse for pollution prevention information 118-119
 EPA pollution prevention research program 111, 113-119
 hazardous waste treatment facilities permits 40-41
 Medical Waste Tracking Act, under 14
 Pollution Prevention Information Exchange System 118
 process research program 116
 product research program 115
 RCRA, under 11
 RecycleNet Bulletin Board 131
 recycling and reuse research 117
 Risk Reduction Engineering Research Laboratory 114-119
 socioeconomic and institutional research 117
 Superfund site cleanup costs 21
 technology transfer and technical assistance 118
 University City Science Center, Philadelphia 118
 Waste Minimization Opportunity Assessment Manual, demonstration of use 116
 Waste Reduction Innovative Technology Evaluations program 116
Residue in incinerators 227
Resource Conservation and Recovery Act (RCRA)
 air pollution control rules 95, 100-105
 burning of hazardous waste 8
 hazardous waste minimization (*see* Hazardous waste minimization)

hazardous waste provisions 2-9 (see also Hazardous waste management)
HSWA 3-9
identification and listing of hazardous waste 4-5
hazardous waste recycling regulations 157
hazardous waste rules (see Hazardous waste rules)
history 1-2
HSWA 3-9
incinerators for hazardous waste, standards 233-235
incinerators for solid waste, guidelines 224-227
interim authorization for state compliance 79-80
land disposal 7
landfills (see Landfills)
minimum technological requirements 8
PCB incinerators 233
permits for storage, treatment, and disposal facilities for hazardous wastes 6-7, 37-47
Pollution Prevention Act, relationship to 133-134
pretreatment (see Pretreatment of hazardous waste)
procurement of recycled materials guidelines 175-181
reauthorization by Congress 120
recycled oil (see Recycled oil)
recycling rules 161-166
siting requirements 46-47
solid waste management 9-12 (see also Solid waste management)
state hazardous waste programs to conform to 79
studies required 11
transportation of hazardous waste 5-6
treatment, storage, and disposal facilities for hazardous waste 6-7, 37-47 (see also Treatment, storage, and disposal facilities for hazardous waste)
underground injection wells 247
untreated wastes, prohibitions 207

variances from minimum technological requirements 8
Resource recovery facilities (see Incinerators; Municipal waste combustors)
Retread tires (see Tires)
Reusable News 183
Reused materials (see Recycling)
Rhode Island, technical assistance programs 91
Rice v. Rehner 267
Risk assessment 67-71
citizens' view of risk 252-254
incinerators 70-71
landfills 69
rules of risk communication 254-258
Risk Reduction Engineering Research Laboratory 114-119
Roy F. Weston, Inc. 253
Rubber 167
Rubbermaid Commercial Products, Inc., case example of plastic recycling 190-191

S

Safe Drinking Water Act 56, 240, 247
Safety measures
incinerators 227
sanitary landfill 57
Salem, Alabama, waste disposal center 238-239
Salt deposits 232
Salt domes 7
Sanders, Whitney A., author of paper on Mercer County, New Jersey integrated solid waste management plan 55-56
Sanitary landfills 56-58, 236-237
SARA (see Superfund Amendments and Reauthorization Act)
Scrap metal 160
Scrubbers 234
Seattle, Washington recycling program 198-200, 203-204
Second-third wastes, pretreatment 208-209
Security of hazardous waste facilities 41

Index

Septic tanks 56
Settlement decrees 110, 121, 138
Sewage sludge
    hazardous waste regulation 32, 160
    national management program 57-58
Ships, medical waste management 15
Sierra Club 266
Silos, pretreatment of hazardous waste 217
Siting requirements
    Arizona hazardous waste facility, case study 279-283
    Colorado hazardous waste facility, case study 271-279
    hazardous waste treatment, storage, and disposal facilities 46-47, 269-286
    Indian reservation lands 266-267
    landfills 237-239, 258-263
    municipal waste combustors 225
    North Carolina hazardous waste facility, case study 284-286
    public/private partnerships for waste disposal facilities 263-265
    waste facilities 249-268
Sludge (*see* Sewage sludge)
Small businesses
    Profiting from Waste Reduction in Your Small Business 154
Small-quantity generators
    hazardous waste 5, 210
    solid waste 11
"Soft-hammer wastes" 208-209
Solar evaporation 220-221
Solid waste combustors (*see* Incinerators; Municipal waste combustors)
Solid waste defined 23
Solid Waste Disposal Act 2
Solid waste management 49-71 (*see also* Recycling; Resource Conservation and Recovery Act)
    Agenda for Action, EPA report 60-62
    barges 49
    capacity planning and need 54
    comprehensive plans 9-10
    costs 62-67

    Council of State Governments model laws 58-59
    exemptions from facility criteria 56
    facility criteria 56-58
    federal legislation 51-53
    guidelines 53-54
    history 51-53
    integrated waste management (*see* Integrated waste management)
    landfill criteria 11
    municipal programs (*see* Municipal waste recycling)
    open dumps 56
    RCRA provisions 9-12
    risk assessment 67-71
    sanitary landfill 56-57
    scope of plans 53-54
    sludge management program 56-57
    small-quantity generators of solid waste 11
    state plans 53-54, 74-79 (*see also specific state*)
    statistics 49
Solid Waste Office (*see* Environmental Protection Agency)
Solvents
    pretreatment requirements 207
    recycling of spent solvents 159
    waste exchanges national classification system 167
Sorting of recyclables 78, 203-205
Source reduction programs
    hazardous waste 144-145
    manufacturers 173-174
    superiority to recycling or reclamation 141, 145, 157
    Toxic Release Inventory Forms, to report 16-17
South Carolina
    association of waste-importing states, role 82-83
    capacity assurance plans 86
    hazardous waste import limits 82
    Waste Reduction Resource Center for the Southeast 129
Southern California Hazardous Waste Management Authority 250
Spent materials, recycling 159, 221
Spill cleanup, CERCLA provisions 13

State hazardous waste programs 73, 79-87, 134
  announcements in *Federal Register* 80
  association of waste-importing states 82-83
  capacity assurance plans 84-87
  constitutionality of import limits 82
  disapproval by EPA, criteria 80
  fees 81
  import limits 82
  interim authorization for RCRA compliance 79-80
  National Solid Wastes Management Association study on state hazardous waste management 83-84
  RCRA conformance 79
  reporting requirements 81
  taxes for disposal and transportation 81
  technical assistance initiatives 87-92
  variations in state laws 81-87
  Waste Reduction Innovative Technology Evaluations agreements 116
State pollution prevention laws 92-93
State solid waste programs 53-54, 74-79
  batteries, waste management 75
  businesses as target of recycling provisions 78
  Council of State Governments model law for state solid waste management 58-59
  infectious waste 73
  landfills 74
  recycling 74-77
  technical assistance initiatives 87-92
  tires, waste management 75-77
  used oil 75
  Waste Reduction Innovative Technology Evaluations agreements 116
State technical assistance initiatives 87-92
State waste reduction programs 121-123
Storage facilities for hazardous waste (*see* Pretreatment of hazardous waste; Treatment, storage, and disposal facilities for hazardous waste)
Sulfur dioxide 229
Superfund (*see* Comprehensive Environmental Response, Compensation, and Liability Act)
Superfund Amendments and Reauthorization Act (SARA)
  capacity assurance plans for state hazardous waste 84-87
  Pollution Prevention Act, relationship 108
  Title III (*see* Emergency Planning and Community Right-to-Know Act)
Superfund LDS Guide 211
Surface impoundments
  litigation over 216
  pretreatment requirements 210, 215-216
Surface water 57

T

Tables
  Constituent Concentrations in Waste Extract 213
  Treatment Standards Expressed as Waste Concentrations 213
Talco Recycling Inc., case example of plastic recycling 192
Tanks (*see also* Pretreatment of hazardous waste)
  pretreatment of hazardous waste 214-215
Taxes
  Louisiana, hazardous waste disposal and transportation taxes 81
  state taxes to finance waste management programs 75
TCLP (*see* Toxicity Characteristic Leaching Procedure)
Technical assistance programs by states 87-92
Technology-based treatment standards 214
Telephone numbers
  American Paper Institute 185
  EPA procurement hotline 181-182

Index

Florida Recycling Marketing System computer bulletin board 182
Office of Pollution Prevention 109
Office of Toxic Substances 109
Pollution Prevention Information Exchange System, for computer connection 118
RecycleNet Bulletin Board 131
Recycling Advisory Council 175
Risk Reduction Engineering Research Laboratory 114
Viridian Bioprocessing Ltd. 219-220
Waste Minimization Branch, Office of Solid Waste 109
Temporary permits for hazardous waste facilities 39-40
Tennessee
  capacity assurance plans 86
  pollution prevention law 93
  technical assistance programs 91
  Waste Reduction Resource Center for the Southeast 129
Test methods for determining hazardous waste 25-29
Tetrachloroethylene 113
Texas
  association of waste-importing states, membership 83
  capacity assurance plans 86
  generation of hazardous waste, study figures on 84
  technical assistance programs 91
  waste exchange programs 156
Textiles, waste exchanges national classification system 167
ThermalKEM 285
Thermal treatment units, pretreatment of hazardous waste 217
Third-third wastes, pretreatment 209
Tires
  guidelines for recycling 180-181
  procurement guidelines for retreads 177
  state programs for waste management 75-77
Title III of SARA (*see* Emergency Planning and Community Right-to-Know Act)
Toluene 113, 219

TOSCA (*see* Toxic Substances Control Act)
Toxicity Characteristic Leaching Procedure (TCLP) 8, 25, 27-28
Toxic Release Inventory Forms 16-17, 112, 119-120
Toxic Substances Control Act (TOSCA)
  flexible application in EPA pollution prevention strategy 112
  incinerators burning PCBs 233
  PCB regulation 17-18
Toxic Substances Office (*see* Environmental Protection Agency)
Toxic waste 25 (*see also* Hazardous waste management)
  Massachusetts Toxics Use Reduction Act 92
Training
  hazardous waste treatment, storage, and disposal facilities 41-42
  Pollution Prevention Training Opportunities 119
Transformers 165
Transportation of hazardous waste, RCRA provisions 5-6
Transportation of solid waste 59, 78-79
Trash disposal (*see* Recycling; Solid waste management)
Treatment, storage, and disposal facilities for hazardous waste 6-7, 37-47
  air emissions 95-106 (*see also* Air emissions from waste treatment, storage, and disposal facilities)
  closure of facilities 38-39, 45, 216, 234, 241
  earthquake protection 46-47
  emergency permits 39
  existing facilities 38
  flood-proof design 47
  handling ignitable, reactive, or incompatible waste 42
  incinerator permits 39
  inspections 41
  interim permits 40
  land treatment demonstration permits 40

liability coverage 46
new facilities 38
notification requirements 40-41
permits, generally 37-47
permits by rule 39
precious metal recovery 165-166
pretreatment of hazardous waste (*see* Pretreatment of hazardous waste)
RCRA-exempt facilities, long-term incentives to minimize waste; EPA seeking comments 138
recordkeeping and reporting requirements 43-44
research, development, and demonstration permits 40
security 41
siting 46-47, 249-268, 269-286 (*see also* Siting requirements)
special permits 39-40
standards 40-47
training of employees 41-42
waste analysis 41
Treatment Standards Expressed as Waste Concentrations table 213
Trial burns for new incinerators 235
1,1,1-Trichloroethane 113
Trichloroethylene 103, 113
TSD facilities (*see* Air emissions from waste treatment, storage, and disposal facilities; Treatment, storage, and disposal facilities for hazardous waste)

U

UIC (Underground injection control) (*see* Underground injection wells)
Underground injection wells 7, 247-248
permits 39-40
pretreatment of hazardous waste 208, 212, 218-219
Underground petroleum tanks, cleanup 13
Underground storage tanks, HSWA regulation 4
University City Science Center, Philadelphia 118

University of Cincinnati, American Institute for Pollution Prevention 119
University of Louisville 118
University of Tennessee 118
Uranium mining 99-100
U.S. Conference of Mayors' Coalition on Resource Recovery and Environment 232
U.S. Corps of Engineers, dredging permits 19
U.S. Public Interest Research Group, report on state pollution prevention laws 92-93
Used materials (*see* Municipal waste recycling; Recycling)
Used oil (*see* Recycled oil)
Use of Solid Waste Quantification and Characterization Program to Implement an Integrated System in Mercer County, New Jersey 55-56
Utah, member of association of waste-importing states 83

V

Vapor recovery 128-129
Variances, RCRA landfill provisions 8
Vectors, cleaning 227
Vending machines, automated container recycling 204-205
Vermont, technical assistance programs 91
Vinyl chloride 103
Viridian Bioprocessing Ltd. 219-220
Volatile organic compounds (VOC) 103, 105

W

Washington
pollution prevention law 93
recycling program 76-77
Seattle recycling program 198-200, 203-204
technical assistance programs 91
Waste Reduction Innovative Technology Evaluations agreement 116
Waste Age's Recycling Times 182-183
Waste classification rules 158-161

Index

Waste exchanges 166-170
  constraints to use 168-169
  Florida Recycling Marketing System computer bulletin board 182
  future opportunities 169-170
  information clearinghouses 166-168
  international markets 169-170
  market determinations 167-168
  materials exchanges 166-167
  national classification system 167
  types 166
Waste-like materials, recycling 160
Waste Management, Inc. 212, 233
Waste minimization
  pollution prevention laws vis-a-vis 107-109
  RCRA hazardous waste minimization 133-156
Waste Minimization Branch of Office of Solid Waste 17, 108-109
Waste Minimization Opportunity Assessment Manual 116, 140-153
Waste piles 7, 217
Waste Reduction Innovative Technology Evaluations program 116
Waste Reduction Resource Center for the Southeast 129
Water quality *see also* Clean Water Act; Groundwater; Safe Drinking Water Act)
  incinerator-discharged water 226

Waxes, waste exchanges national classification system 167
Wells (*see* Underground injection wells)
West Virginia, technical assistance programs 92
Whitmore Lake, Michigan recycling program 203
Wires, insulated 165
Wisconsin
  capacity assurance plans 86
  recycling program 77
  technical assistance programs 92
Wood, waste exchanges national classification system 167
Woodburn, Oregon landfill 232
Wyoming, technical assistance programs 92

X

Xylene 113

Y

Yuma County, Arizona, case study of hazardous waste facility 279-283

Z

Zoning, combustion facilities 225

BIBLIOGRAPHY

Alaska Health Project. *Profiting from Waste Reduction in Your Small Business* (Anchorage, AK: 1988).

Allen, Russell. *Waste Reduction Assessment and Technology Transfer Training Manual* (Knoxville, TN: Tennessee Valley Authority, 1989).

American Paper Institute. *PaperMatcher, A Directory of Paper Recycling Sources* (Washington, DC: 1990).

Arkin, Elaine Bratic. *Evaluation for Risk Communication* (Washington, DC: Insitute for Health Policy Analysis, Georgetown University Medical Center, 1988).

The Bureau of National Affairs, Inc., *U.S. Environmental Laws* (Washington, DC: 1988).

Cearley, Jack E. and Youngblood, Phillip L. *PCB Compliance Guide for Electrical Equipment* (Washington, DC: The Bureau of National Affairs, Inc., 1988).

Center for Hazardous Materials Research, University of Pittsburgh Applied Research Center. *Hazardous Waste Minimization Manual for the Small Quantity Generator* (Pittsburgh, PA: 1988).

Chemical Manufacturers Association. *Waste Minimization Resource Manual* (Washington, DC: 1989).

The Complete Handbook of Hazardous Waste Regulation: A Comprehensive, Step-by-Step Guide to the Regulation of Hazardous

Wastes under RCRA, TSCA, and Superfund (Falls Church, VA: Perry-Wagner Publications, 1988).

Council of State Governments' Center for the Environment and Natural Resources. *State Actions for Reducing Hazardous Wastes* (Lexington, KY: 1989).

Covello, Vincent T., McCallum, David B., and Pavlova, Maria T. *Effective Risk Communication: The Role and Responsibility of Governmental and Nongovernmental Agencies* (New York: Plenum Press, 1989).

Covello, Vincent T., Sandman, Peter M., and Slovic, Paul. *Risk Communication, Risk Statistics, and Risk Comparisons: A Manual for Plant Managers* (Washington, DC: Chemical Manufacturers Association, 1989).

Energy Systems Research Group, et al. *Managing Municipal Solid Waste: A Comparative Risk Analysis of Landfill and Resource Recovery Facilities* (Boston, MA: CONEG Policy Research Center, 1988).

Environmental Information Limited. *Hazardous Waste Movement in the United States* (Washington, DC: National Solid Wastes Management Association, 1991).

Fortuna, C. Richard, et al. *Hazardous Waste Regulation—The New Era: An Analysis & Guide to RCRA and the 1984 Amendments* (New York: McGraw-Hill, 1987).

Frost & Sullivan. *Hazardous Waste Resource & Recovery Market* (New York: 1987).

Government Advisory Associates (GAA). *1986-1987 Resource Recovery Yearbook* (New York: 1987).

Government Institutes (GI). *EPA's Pretreatment Guidelines* (Washington, DC: 1990).

Jessup, Deborah H. *Guide to State Environmental Programs*, Second Edition. (Washington, DC: The Bureau of National Affairs, Inc., 1990).

Bibliography

Jessup, Deborah H. *Infectious Waste: The Complete Resource Guide,* A BNA Special Report (Washington, DC: The Bureau of National Affairs, Inc., 1988).

Kline, Mark, Chess, Caron, and Sandman, Peter M. *Evaluating Risk Communication Programs: A Catalogue of "Quick and Easy! Feedback Methods"* (New Brunswick, NJ: Rutgers University, 1989).

Krimsky, Sheldon, and Plough, Alonzo. *Environmental Hazards: Communicating Risks as a Social Process* (Dover, MA: Auburn House Publishing Co., 1988).

Lindgren, Gary F. *Managing Industrial Hazardous Waste: A Practical Handbook* (Chelsea, MI: Lewis Publications, 1989).

National Association of Manufacturers (NAM). *Waste Minimization: Manufacturers' Strategies for Success* (Washington, DC: 1989).

National Research Council. *Improving Risk Communication* (Washington, DC: National Academy Press, 1989).

Ontario Waste Management Corp (OWMC). *Industrial Waste Audit and Reduction Manual* (Toronto, Canada: 1990).

Phifer, Russell and McTigue Jr., William R. *Handbook of Hazardous Waste Management for Small Quantity Generators* (Chelsea, MI: Lewis Publications, 1988).

Rhode Island Department of Environmental Management *Guide for Preparing Commercial Solid Waste Reduction and Recycling Plans* (Providence, RI: 1990).

Rhode Island Department of Environmental Management (Ocean State Cleanup and Recycling Program; OSCAR). *Handbook for Reduction and Recycling of Commercial Solid Waste* (Providence, RI: 1990).

Streng. Disposal of Municipal, Industrial & Hazardous Wastes (New York: Wiley Publishing Co., 1987).

U.S. Conference of Mayors (USCM). *Municipal Waste Combustion—Ash Leachate Characterization Monofill—Third Year Study* (Washington, DC: 1990).

U.S. Congress, Office of Technology Assessment. *Facing America's Trash: What Next for Municipal Solid Waste?* OTA-0-424 (Washington, DC: U.S. Government Printing Office, 1989).

U.S. Environmental Protection Agency (EPA). *Characterization of Municipal Solid Waste in the United States: 1990 Update.* EPA/530-SW-90-042 (Washington, DC: 1990).

U.S. Environmental Protection Agency (EPA). *Decision-Makers Guide to Solid Waste Management* (Washington, DC: 1989).

U.S. Environmental Protection Agency (EPA). *Estimating Releases and Waste Treatment Efficiencies for the Toxic Chemicals Inventory Form.* EPA 560/4-88 02 (Washington, DC: 1988).

U.S. Environmental Protection Agency (EPA). *Office of Policy, Planning and Evaluation.* Pollution Prevention Benefits Manual (Washington, DC: EPA, 1990).

U.S. Environmental Protection Agency (EPA). *Pollution Prevention Training Opportunities* (Washington, DC: 1990).

U.S. Environmental Protection Agency (EPA). *Report to Congress: Solid Waste Disposal in the United States,* Vol. 11. EPA 530-SW-99-011B (Washington, DC: 1988).

U.S. Environmental Protection Agency (EPA). *Sites for Our Solid Waste: A Guidebook for Effective Public Involvement* (Washington, DC: 1990).

U.S. Environmental Protection Agency (EPA). *The Solid Waste Dilemma: An Agenda for Action* (Washington, DC: 1989).

U.S. Environmental Protection Agency (EPA). *Waste Minimization Opportunity Assessment Manual.* EPA/625/7-88/003 (Cincinnati, OH: 1988).

U.S. Environmental Protection Agency (EPA). *Petitions to Delist Hazardous Wastes: A Guidance Manual.* EPA/530-SW-85-003 (Washington, DC: 1985).

U.S. Environmental Protection Agency (EPA). *Guides to Pollution Prevention, The Pesticide Formulating Industry, The Paint Manufacturing Industry, The Fabricated Metal Industry, The Printed*

Circuit Board Manufacturing Industry, The Commercial Printing Industry, Selected Hospital Waste Streams, and Research and Educational Institutions. 625/7/90/004 through 625/7/90/010, respectively (Cincinnati, OH: 1990).

U.S. Environmental Protection Agency (EPA). *Locating Air Emissions from Sewage Sludge Incinerators.* EPA/450/2-90-009 (Washington DC: 1990).

U.S. Office of Technology Assessment. *Technologies & Management Strategies for Hazardous Waste Control* (Melbourne, FL: Krieger Publications, 1988).

BNA REFERENCE FILE SERVICES

Air Pollution Control (BNA Policy and Practice Series)

Chemical Regulation Reporter

Chemical Substances Control (BNA Policy and Practice Series)

Environment Reporter

Water Pollution Control (BNA Policy and Practice Series)